Terror at Beslan

A Russian Tragedy
with Lessons for America's Schools

By John Giduck

Published by Archangel Group Inc.

Published by Archangel Group Inc.

First Edition 2005

The Library of Congress has cataloged this edition as follows:
LCCN 2005902484

ISBN 0-9767753-0-1

For information about special discounts for bulk purchases or to purchase
additional copies send an email to info@terroratbeslan.com, fax
a request to 303 215 0780 including your name and contact information
or visit www.terroratbeslan.com

Designed by Michel Hogan
Manufactured in Canada

Warrior's Epitaph

When it comes my time to go,
I hope with fervent zeal,
That my merits have been proved
On life's battlefield.
Enough to earn for me
One small place of rest,
Just over on the other side,
Beyond the reach of death.

— *Ralf Grant Edens*

TABLE OF CONTENTS

This book is dedicated to the brave men
of Alpha and Vympel.
And to Special Operators the world over.
We need you.
Now, more than ever.

In Memoriam.

Eleven men from Russia's elite Alpha and Vympel
Counter Terror units lost their lives fighting to save
1,181 hostages – many of them children –
at the Beslan Middle School No. 1,
on September 3, 2004.
One has never been named.
The others are:

Warrant Officer Oleg Vyacheslavovich Loskov
Warrant Officer Denis Yevgeniyevich Pudovkin
Lieutenant Andrei Alekseyevich Turkin
Major Roman Yurievich Katasonov
Major Mikhail Borisovich Kuznetsov
Major Vyacheslav Vladimirovich Molyarov
Major Aleksandr Valentinovich Perov
Major Andrei Vitaliyevich Velko
Lieutenant Colonel Oleg Gennadiyevich Ilin
Lieutenant Colonel Dmitri Aleksandrovich Razumovskii

ACKNOWLEDGEMENTS

As with any writer, this work – my first – is the culmination of a lifetime of academic study, work, travel and personal interest. As such, I cannot possibly list all of the people who have been instrumental in the many aspects of my life that led me to this point, that led me to be in Beslan, Russia in September 2004. As Dave Grossman said to me one day, "Being asked to write the foreword to a book is like being asked to be the godfather of someone's child." And while I am grateful to him for his own wonderful contribution, in many ways all of those who have had a role in this work should feel much the same as he. For those I have not mentioned by name – and there are many – you have my sincere apologies, and my hope is that you recognize your contribution both to this work and my life, as well as my appreciation for all that you have given me.

In my early life I was given the incredible advantage of having had many great male role models, all of whom influenced me more than they could know; and I know they doubted mightily on many occasions. Men like my own father, Richard, Tony DiVito and Ed Skalamera, were of incomparable influence. As were my grandfathers and uncles, including the six men in my family who took up arms and served America in World War II. Thank you Harry and Nick Giduck, Everett Burns, Charles Reynolds, Frank and Eddie Piepszowski. The legacy of your lives means more than you could ever have known. I am especially grateful to men like Larry "Pops" Pascale and Don Mercadante, who gave years of their lives coaching young boys; teaching them to not only be football players and champions, but men. You gave hundreds of us discipline, and a commitment to victory, and we all owe you a debt of gratitude. It is, indeed, sad to know that what you did for us so many years ago would, today, earn you merely the disdain of a weakened America. All of these men I have mentioned epitomized honesty, hard work, toughness and courage. They always took care of their families and friends, and never turned their backs on trouble. They are among America's best. No boy could have benefited more.

A special thank you is owed to Professor Mary Conroy, Russian historian and teacher at the University of Colorado at Denver. Mary, you are a true scholar, with a peerless understanding of Russian culture, history and affairs. Thank you for indulging my interest in the part of the world my family hales from, and lending your incredible insight, knowledge and encouragement to my own meager efforts early on.

A special thank you to retired Green Beret Sergeant Major John A. Anderson. Andy, you've been a friend, colleague, teammate, and adviser. You are a true, living American hero and, sadly, there are few like you. How many years has it been now?

Also, thanks to Mike Rich, the first person to always believe I had a book in me somewhere and a story worth telling. Thank you, Simon Luciow and Michel Hogan, for all of your technical, publishing and marketing expertise, as well as your friendship and support. And to my friend Dan Junevicus, another Green Beret whose own voracious appetite for history and expansive personal library on all things military enabled me to ensure the accuracy of many facts. Along those same lines, thank you Yuri Ferdigalov. Not only did you journey happily into places others would not go, but your own military and historical knowledge and expertise is greatly responsible for much of what is included in the pages to follow. If anyone ever needs a bodyguard, he is among the best (yuriyxf@yahoo.com). Melissa Pascale, if it weren't for you I wouldn't have gotten there at all.

Emmy, you are beautiful lady, trusted friend, and colleague. There isn't much in my life that could get done without you. I am as well grateful to the entire Board of Directors of Archangel, past and present, for their support. To Dave Grossman, I have been honored by your willingness to guide me through this process and greatly improve the quality of my work by placing your own words in the opening pages.

Thanks to "The Peaceful Warrior," author Dan Millman for giving me a glimpse into the editing and publication process, and letting me think it was possible. And to Ed Ray, long time friend, without whose assistance and letters of introduction I would never have gotten so far in my investigative efforts in Russia.

And to the people who gave up countless hours proofreading and editing my original manuscript: If this book is of any worth at all, I have your effort and willingness to impart your expertise to thank for it. Thank you Mike Rich, Dr. Jean Will, Dr. Walt Copley, Andy and Jody Anderson, Carrie, and Ernie Briggs; and Glen Karst and Gabe Oser who were saddled with the job of inputting thousands of changes. Special appreciation to Elena and Les - I wish I could say more. And to Joe Bail, who gave up an otherwise enjoyable vacation to lock himself up with me in a small room in the Carribean during final edits. I would also like to express my appreciation to Chris Sauser and the men and women of the Russian Martial Arts Training Center in Golden, Colorado, for tolerating my many long absences. You are, bar none, the toughest hand-to-hand combat training group in the country.

I am likewise grateful for the help of Lt. Col. Kenneth Hurst, Command Sergeant Major Charles "Mitch" Conway and Master Sergeant Tom Flaherty, of the U.S. Army 10th Special Forces Group (Airborne). As well, my deepest gratitude to my many friends from the Russian Special Forces. Without you, I would not have had the experiences necessary to even attempt this project. During my months of focusing on writing this book, I often lacked the time necessary to keep up on events in Russia and the War on Terror critical to my understanding and ability to impart a worthwhile message. Thanks to everyone who continued to send me crucial and timely information. I am especially grateful to friends and colleagues in the Russian government and military, some of whom risked much to bring this story to light.

A great many people have contributed facts and perspective to this book, all in an effort to help me produce a work of value to the reader. While I have relied greatly on their expertise, any mistakes or errors are solely my own doing.

FOREWORD

The world must never forget what happened in Beslan, Russia. The tragedy, the horror, can never be fully communicated, but to the best of our ability it must be remembered. That is one of the major objectives of this book.

There has been much disinformation and confusion about what happened in September of 2004. John Giduck is one of the few men in the Western world who had the knowledge, connections and ability to find out what really happened. He is one of America's leading experts on Russian special operations, having worked and trained with them for years. They know him and trust him, and they have told him their stories.

John Giduck was there. When he heard what was happening, he bought a ticket and arrived at Beslan as the last mopping up operations were taking place. Then he visited again, a few months later to gather more information. And then again a few months after that. So, one purpose of this book is to record and remember. And for that reason alone this is a vital, historical treasure.

The other major reason for this book is to apply the lessons. *Never* forget, Beslan *could* happen here. John Giduck is one of our nation's leading experts on terrorism. I have been a co-presenter with him at several international terrorism conferences.

The possibility of a mass murder of school children by terrorists is very real. It has happened in many other nations. Turkey has had over 300 schools destroyed by terrorist attacks. Pakistan, Algeria, and many other nations, in addition to Russia, have experienced brutal school massacres committed by terrorist groups.

One of the most tragic and devastating terrorist acts in Israel was the Ma'alot school massacre in 1974, in which 21 Israeli children were murdered in a brutal terrorist act that set the stage for many subsequent terrorist attacks on schools. As a result of this incident, Israel has lived for thirty years with armed security in every school, armed guards on every field trip and at sporting events, armored buses and armed security on their buses. Do you have any conception how much that has cost? Can anyone comprehend what it would cost the United States to have that kind of security for every school, every field trip and every bus in America? It would cost trillions of dollars and would take millions of people. You think your school, city, state or nation has budget problems now?

For those who would like more information on these terrorist attacks on schools in many other nations, I recommend "Innocent Targets: When Terrorism Comes To School," by Michael and Chris Dorn. For those who would want to know more in depth information about this most recent and horrific school massacre, in Beslan, Russia, this is the definitive book.

The sky is NOT falling. This is only one of many things that terrorists could do to us. If we over react, if we change our way of life because of the threat of school massacres, then we give way to fear and the terrorists get the victory they desire without having to fire a shot. So we must strike a balance between preparing for an unthinkable horror without giving way to unreasoned fear.

First, we must be educated. And that is exactly what John Giduck has done in this book. Second, we need to apply the lessons of Beslan. It is vital that we respond to this potential threat in a measured, realistic, balanced fashion. Too much fear or any fear-mongering will play into the hands of those who want to do us harm. If we are not careful, those who wish us ill can make us change our way of life without firing a shot or killing a single child. It is vital that we respond with a balanced, reasoned, informed, "all hazards" approach to this threat.

The situation is very much like fire protection. The probability of a student being killed or seriously injured by violence is significantly greater than the probability of being killed or seriously injured by fire. No child has been killed by school fire in North America in over a quarter of a century. Compare this to the fact that, in any given year, in our schools, dozens of students and employees are killed by acts of violence in American schools. These are usually random acts of violence, or shootings by students as opposed to acts of terrorism, but the defense against terrorist attacks in our schools, as outlined in this book, is largely the same as the defense against schools shootings.

Thus, our children are dozens of times more likely to be killed by violence than fire, and thousands of times more likely to be seriously injured by violence as compared to fire. In any school you can look around and see fire sprinklers, smoke alarms, fire exits, and fire extinguishers. If we can spend all that money and time preparing for fire (and we should, since every life is precious) shouldn't we spend time and money and time preparing for the thing that is far more likely to kill or injure a child?

The most negligent, unprofessional, obscene words anyone can ever say are: "It will never happen here." Imagine the firefighter saying, "There will never be a fire in this building, and we don't need those fire extinguishers." When someone asks, "Do you really think there will be a terrorist act or a school shooting here?" I just point to the fire exit and say, "Do you really think there will be a fire here?" No, I don't think there will ever be a fire here. But we would be morally, criminally negligent if we did not prepare for the possibility. And the same is far, far truer of school violence.

In an article published in the *Harvard Journal of Law* and *Public Policy*, my co-author and I stated that if a series of active shooter terrorist attacks happened in the US, as they have in Israel, we *will* arm our selves and get on with life – just like Israel. *But, you can't* arm the kids! Even Israel can't arm its children, and if a major terrorist attack on a school is successful, the terrorists can impact every family and every school in America, disrupting our economy and way of life unlike any other conventional attack. It is our job to prevent that and to protect our kids, and this book is a key tool to make that possible.

It was about a month after the 9-11 terrorist attacks, and I was training a group of special operations troops who were headed off to Afghanistan. A Special Forces (Green Beret) sergeant came up to me during one of the breaks and said, "Colonel, we're going to Afghanistan, and we're gonna kick their tails. While we're over there, you tell all those folks you teach, don't let them come kill our kids."

Our servicemen are over there dying for us, every day, trying to close down the terrorist camps, to keep the terrorists on the run, to keep them on the defensive, or as one Marine put it, "To keep it ta hell over there!" They believe in what they are doing. And they only ask one thing: "Watch my back, do your job ... don't let them come kill my kids." THAT is what this book is about. This book is a KEY step in the process of keeping our kids and our nation safe.

Although I live in Jonesboro, Arkansas, my wife and I heard about the school shooting that happened in our own town from my aunt who called us from Florida. When she told me that she had just heard on CNN that there had been a mass murder in a middle school in Jonesboro, my first thought was of my son who was attending middle school there. I turned on CNN and there it was. My God! A mass murder in our middle school in our town. I was paralyzed; I didn't know what to do.

My wife told me that I needed to go there. "But what could I do?" I asked. She told me I could help. She was right. I was one of the Army's experts on PTSD and was preparing to travel to Canada that week to train their military. She gave me a nudge out the door. I rushed to my son's school, only to discover that the shooting had not happened there, but rather at another middle school. I sped over to that one, and spent the entire day and evening working with a group of magnificent people, and helping to train and prepare mental health professionals. In my own hometown I was applying the lessons of mass critical incident debriefings learned from the battlefield.

I cannot tell you the magnitude of the horror when it happens in your child's school. When you read about Beslan, remember deep in your soul: it could be my school, it could be my child. On the night of the Jonesboro school massacre, I was at the school helping to train the mental health professionals who would work with the teachers and students in the coming days. A counselor who had been working at the hospital came to the school that night, and she told us a story that brought us all to tears. Clergy and counselors were working in small groups in the hospital waiting room, comforting the groups of relatives and friends of more than a dozen shooting victims. They noticed one woman who had been sitting silently, alone, in the midst of the crowd. A counselor went up to the woman, took her hand, and said, "Can I help you?" Sitting there in absolute psychological and physiological shock she said, "I'm the mother of one of the girls who was killed today. They called me, and said my little girl is dead. I just came to find out how I can get my little girl back. How do I get her body back?"

She had no friends, no husband, no family with her as she sat in the hospital, alone and stunned by her loss. But the body had been taken to Little Rock, 100 miles away, for an autopsy and she was told that the authorities would contact her when they were finished with the body, then she could tell them what funeral home to send the body to. After being told this, in her dazed mind her very next comment was, "Funeral home? Funeral home? We can't afford a funeral. We can't even afford a funeral."

That little girl was truly all that woman had in the world. There were no friends, no family, no husband. There was just a mama, and her little girl. That morning she had hugged her little girl, alive and warm and vital, the most precious thing on the face of the Earth... for the last time. That night, all she wanted in all the world was to wrap her baby's cold body in a blanket and take her home.

Every day, millions of parents hug millions of kids, their most precious possessions, the most precious things on the face of the Earth, and they send those kids to school, trusting US to keep them alive. This is the most important thing any society can do: to protect our young. So don't just read this book, study it. Study it and apply it. Be like the firefighter: put the risk in perspective, pray that it will never happen, know that it COULD happen, and work with all your heart and soul to prevent it from happening. It could be YOUR child's life that you save.

LT. COL. DAVE GROSSMAN, U.S. Army (Ret.)
Director, Killology Research Group
www.killology.com

About Lt. Col Dave Grossman

Lt. Col. Dave Grossman is a former West Point psychology professor, Professor of Military Science, and an Army Ranger who is the author of On Combat (which was nominated for a Pulitzer Prize), On Killing (with Loren Christensen), and Stop Teaching Our Kids to Kill (with Gloria DeGaetano). Col. Grossman's work has been translated into many languages, and his books are required or recommended reading in colleges, military academies, and police academies around the world, to include the US Marine Corps Commandant's reading list and the FBI Academy reading list. His research was cited by the President of the United States in a national address after the Littleton, Colorado school shootings, and he has testified before the U.S. Senate, the U.S. Congress, and numerous state legislatures. He has served as an expert witness and consultant in state and Federal courts, to include UNITED STATES vs. TIMOTHY MCVEIGH. He helped train mental health professionals after the Jonesboro school shootings, and he was also involved in counseling or court cases in the aftermath of the Paducah, Springfield, and Littleton school shootings. He has been called upon to write the entry on "Aggression and Violence" in the Oxford Companion to American Military History, three entries in the Academic Press Encyclopedia of Violence, Peace and Conflict and has presented papers before the national conventions of the American Medical Association, the American Psychiatric Association, the American Psychological Association, and the American Academy of Pediatrics. Today he is the director of the Killology Research Group (www.killology.com), and in the wake of the 9/11 terrorist attacks he has been on the road almost 300 days a year, training elite military and law enforcement organizations worldwide about the reality of combat, and he has written extensively on the terrorist threat with articles published in the Harvard Journal of Law and Public Policy and many leading law enforcement journals.

To Steve

ISA 6:8

FROM THE AUTHOR

When I returned to southern Russia in November 2004 to do further research for this book, I found a Beslan not so different from the one I had left less than two months before. The people were still in shock and the entire region still on "high, red alert" as one official told me we would call it in America. The border to Ingushetia was closed again, or still; it really didn't matter. Some small effort had been made to begin clearing the rubble from the school, but it seemed fruitless in light of plans to tear it down. The townspeople, always suspicious of outsiders, were more than characteristically closemouthed.

But this was not due solely to their xenophobia. I learned quickly that the FSB, or *Federalnaya Sluzhba Bezopasnostii*, the current version of the KGB, had instituted a complete lockdown on information about the school siege. These intelligence agents of the federal government had gone through this small town, knocking on the doors of every hostage and his family, ordering them not to speak with anyone, not to tell a single thing about what had occurred: *Or else*. They had done the same thing to all of the families living in houses and apartments in proximity to the school: canvassing homes throughout the town, extolling the citizens to speak to no one about the incident, to answer no questions of anyone, especially foreigners and reporters. The word had spread quickly through Beslan and neighboring Vladikavkaz: *Keep your mouths shut*. It was as though the dark days of the Soviet Union and its ruthless domination of a nation of people had returned. As if they had not already suffered enough.

Every single government official, soldier and policeman had likewise been warned. The best thing everyone could do was forget Beslan, pretend it never happened. Once the commission President Vladimir Putin convened to investigate the incident issued its report, the world would know all it would ever need to know. Or at least, it would know all the Russian government wanted it to. This conspiracy within the Russian government to keep the full story from reaching anyone outside the country did pose problems for me. Government agents, soldiers and police had been threatened with their jobs, and worse in some cases. Talking to me would be dangerous for them. Despite the fact that I had returned to Russia with an armful of letters of introduction and verification that I was representing Mr. Ed Ray, Security Chief of the Denver Public School system, and the entire school district, their fear was real and gripping. Many people risked a great deal to arrange meetings with officials of all ranks to assist in my efforts to gain sufficient knowledge to be of benefit to American law enforcement and school security. In many instances meetings took place in remote locations, in the dark of night. I was often provided only first names, or no names at all. For those whose names I was provided, we reached agreements as to how they would be described and referred to. Even in those instances when men I met demonstrated a remarkable degree of courage, and brazenly authorized me to use both their names and titles, as well as the information they provided, I have been circumspect in my references to them.

Throughout this book aliases, or no names at all, are used for the vast majority of people who met with me, to protect those who shared crucial information so that American children would not suffer as the children of Beslan did. In many cases, physical descriptions are altered to protect identities, as are ranks and backgrounds. In some instances I may have changed the gender of those I met. Where actual rank is used, other identifying characteristics are altered. In this way, no one can know whether I have accurately described some, all, or none of the personal characteristics of any single individual. Only Yuri Ferdigalov and I know, and we will go to our graves with that information. At no time, however, have I been misleading as to the importance of the people with whom I met. Where such things as titles and rank are changed, I have substituted equivalent - or nearly so – credentials so that the credibility and veracity of the person can still be fairly judged.

Throughout this book the term "military" is used frequently to refer to not only the actual Russian Army and the various units that responded to the Beslan siege, but the innumerable tactical, combat capable units of the several force ministries of the Russian Federation. In so employing this term, I am including all units of the Russian intelligence agencies and Ministry of the Interior, as well as the regular Army. Though both Russian government officials and purists might disagree with the generalized grouping of all such units under a single rubric, to the American mind and understanding, they are all government forces, highly trained for military operations. They have all seen combat, the majority in both Afghanistan and Chechnya, in addition to other wars we in the U.S. know little about, or have never heard of at all. Where distinctions are important, I have attempted to explain crucial differences.

Just as pseudonyms have been used for some of the heroes who assisted me – both those who fought to return Beslan to safety and those from the government and military who provided me with much needed information – so have I used a variety of terms to refer to the terrorists who seized the school and the almost 1,200 people therein. Intermittently, they are referred to as *terrorists, rebels, guerillas, militants, hijackers and hostage-takers*. Some of these terms might allow a reader to infer that their conduct is not the most vile, disgusting, inhuman and unconscionable possible among the human race. Nothing could be further from the truth. Various terms have been interspersed for no other reason than to improve the ease with which the text can be read. I well recognize that few things could be more mind-numbing than the redundant use of a single word or descriptive phrase over hundreds of pages. Still, I have put much effort into the careful selection of the descriptive phrases I have used. I have been disturbed for years at news media depictions of these perpetrators of inhumanity as *freedom fighters, revolutionaries,* and *independence seekers*, attributing to them a legitimate effort at mere self-determination that is unwarranted. And to the extent that certain of these phrases ring closely to my own descriptions of them throughout this book, it is important to know that, no matter how they are referred to in the pages that follow, only the necessity of readability of this text compelled me to use a variety of terms. As I drafted and redrafted this book, I made a remarkable discovery: with the exception of the term *terrorist*, there are no words that adequately capture the psychopathic evil that motivates these men and women and their acts; all supposedly in the name of a loving god.

While it is true that some Russian troops have committed their own crimes while serving in Chechnya, no one has been the architect of a willful campaign to kidnap and burn entire schools of children to death. No one has blown passenger airliners full of innocent civilians out of the skies. If the Russians were to grant themselves the same license as the Chechens have, then they too would simply blame "all" Chechen civilians for what their "revolutionary leaders" were doing, and exact a terrible toll on the entire Chechen population. No matter how tempting this may be – and it certainly has been to some – this has not occurred.

Nor is the perspective of this book the product of some anti-Islamic rage. The United States has taken up the cause of Muslim people throughout the world in recent years; steps that were both just and necessary, often coming long after other nations should have acted. In Mogadishu, Somalia, the Balkans and Kuwait, to name but a few, Americans have gone into harm's way to save the lives of innocent Muslims against mass murder, no matter who the perpetrators.

Make no mistake, I find the Chechens who have taken and brutalized hostages, and blown other innocents to bits in Russia, as well as those who support them, to be the most reprehensible human beings on the planet today. This is true for all terrorists that have committed, or are planning, such atrocities. The very countries and cultures they label as the "enemy," as infidels and evil – not the least of which is the United States – have never engaged in so heinous an act as to willfully and intentionally, with full malice aforethought, take hundreds of children hostage, terrorize, beat, rape and even murder them. And then blow them up or shoot them down, as the opportunity presented itself at Beslan when their scheme began to unravel. It is only through ridiculous and pandering Western governments, and the Western news media, in their support for the broader "Chechen cause," that these terrorists have for so long been able to continue on with their own efforts at genocide and garner the international support they have. It is a situation that must change.

John Giduck
Cozumel, Mexico
February 2005

Prologue

Then I heard the voice of the Lord saying,
"Whom shall I send?"
And who will go for us? And I said,
"Here I am. Send me!"
— Isaiah 6:8

It was dark among the towering apartment buildings that formed the neighborhood in which the young Alpha officer lived. Night was already coming early this far north, the cold of the Russian winter scant weeks away. Though physically conditioned in every way, he stumbles uncertainly across the parking lot, moving slowly with short, unsteady steps. He had not been permitted to tell his wife much when his team was ordered to the Air Force transports that were being quickly assembled the morning of September 1. All he could say on the phone was that he didn't know when he would be home. She had been a Special Forces wife long enough. She already knew where he was headed. It was all over the news. In the seconds he had to talk to her, she had whispered, "I love you." It was faint, barely audible. She could not trust her own voice. She knew it would be terrible. If his team was going, she knew people would die. They always did.

"Was it only three days ago?" His brain, consumed by all that had happened, didn't seem to be working quite right. He wasn't sure whether he had said that, or merely thought it. As he walked from the shed in which he parked his new car, a car he could not afford but was so proud to have bought for his growing family, he faltered. For once he was thankful that in Moscow there was no such thing as close parking, at least not in the inexpensive development he could scarcely pay for on his government salary. He needed the time alone.

All at once it hit him: the awful inhumanity and suffering he had witnessed. All the people he had killed, and those many more he had wanted to. The intolerable waiting before that. Waiting, while listening to the sounds of children being brutalized in ways that were unspeakable. Waiting, while listening to people being executed for having committed no other offense than being at the school that beautiful autumn morning. For having been born Christian.

He stumbles and falls to his knees in the twilight, his mind reeling. Images intrude on his thoughts. Images of his friends, now dead, falling beside him. Those friends, dying while shielding children with their own unprotected bodies. Images of all the children he could not save; so many of them. His own babies' faces rising up in his mind as he fought wildly to get to the children in the school, to kill anyone in his way. He can scarcely remember the unbridled emotion that nearly drove him to do almost anything possible to be killed too, to lay with his comrades. Anything never to bear the intolerable guilt of being one of those few to walk out of that place. They called it survivor's guilt, he knew. Despite his own frenzied efforts to save everyone, he wonders if he was a coward. "If I'm alive, I must be," his tortured brain accuses.

As he kneels there, wet leaves soaking his pant legs, he is racked with sobs. His body, muscled and scarred from years of torturous training and combat operations, shakes with the release of tears that stream down his handsome face, a face now contorted with grief. "I have to get myself together," a distant thought. He hopes his own children are asleep. They shouldn't see their daddy cry.

But the images won't leave him. As his body shudders with the release of tension built over days, he asks himself, "How could this have happened? All the death, all the destruction." Years of discipline re-assert themselves as he tries to get himself under control, at least enough to walk into his home, to hold his wife… kiss his children. He tells himself, "I am the elite of my country's Special Forces. This is what I am here for. This is what they have trained me to do. If I cannot handle it, who can?" Unknowingly, his distorted thoughts have struck close to the unofficial motto of his own counter-terror unit, a motto that answers the question of who can be depended upon to confront the evil that threatens so much of civilization today: *Yesle nye ya, to kto? If not me, then who?*

But even in his wildest imaginings, he knows he could never have prepared himself for what he saw, for what he did, and what he was unable to do. He could never have been prepared for the evil of what he encountered there; as though the devil himself had possessed the school and the men who had taken it. For, indeed, how could Beslan have happened? And who could ever truly have been ready for the day when terror came to a small town school?

* * * * *

Looking back on it all, I suppose I knew the call had to come. It was inevitable. John A. "Andy" Anderson was the chairman of the Archangel board of directors, the company I work for and - for all intents and purposes – my boss. He is also a 25 year Green Beret Sergeant Major, a benchpress record holder, and world combat pistol champion. His voice is unmistakable, not unlike the cold rumble of a diesel engine as it coughs to life on a winter morning. Only the voice never seems to warm up, erupting from a 250 pound frame overstuffed with muscle that scarcely belongs on a man in his late 50s. It was never a voice to ignore. The siege at Beslan had just begun.

"I think you need to go," he growled. He didn't wait for me to agree. After years as a combat leader with the world's most elite military unit, he is not a man familiar with refusal. Besides, I was our group's resident Russian specialist. "Who you taking with you?" This would constitute the remainder of his contribution to our conversation. "Yuri," was my immediate reply, and a perfect choice. Though Andy had been with us through Sudan and the Chechen Theater the previous year, and had seen combat in places he could never talk about, this trip would require a small number of Russian speakers who could blend in quickly, and move even faster, in the peculiar culture of that country. It would be just the two of us.

"Yuri," was Yuri Ferdigalov, a 36 year old Ukrainian and Soviet GRU Special Forces veteran of the Nagorno-Karabakh War. Though scarcely known in the West, this war, which was fought from 1989 to 1994, saw more than 80,000 deaths, and those soldiers who survived it were no strangers to danger. Yuri had been a critical member of our team from the previous year's efforts in the Chechnya region, and had proven himself to be a steady operator in high stress situations, at one point single-handedly talking a KGB colonel out of arresting us as spies on the border. At Archangel we called it a Spur Team – for Special *Pur*pose - its size and composition changing, dependent on the circumstances we were called into and what services we were asked to provide.

With his dark, model good looks, Yuri strikes acquaintances as someone better suited for gracing the cover of *GQ* magazine than living out of a rucksack in a war zone. But he has a toughness that belies his aesthetic delicacy, and is an expert at most tactical skills demanded in such environments. Now a professional bodyguard, he is one of the best in the world at his chosen profession. I could not have been in better company.

I knew that the Russian government would already have started – or would shortly – sealing off the borders and the city, making ingress a challenge. I needed someone who knew his way around, spoke Russian fluently, possessed the sales skill of a haberdasher and the thought processes of an unconventional warfare expert. It had to be Yuri. When I called to tell him we needed to go, he did not disappoint. "When do we leave?" was his cryptic concern.

It had been early when I awoke on the morning of September 1, 2004. Though only 4:30 a.m. high up in the Rocky Mountains, it was already 2:30 in the afternoon in Moscow, the capital of a nation I am professionally and personally connected to on many levels. As much of my work requires regular trans-Atlantic telephone calls with people from Russia, and a need to know the goings-on there that put it regularly in the international news, this early morning awakening was routine. I groggily flipped the switch on the coffee maker, unprepared for the horror I was about to see on the twenty-four hour Fox News Channel I tuned in daily. A school in Beslan, a tiny town in the Republic of North Ossetia in the Causcasus Mountain region of remote southern Russia, had been seized by terrorists. I knew this town and this region. Just one year before I, and a team from the Archangel Group, had been bouncing back and forth across the borders of Ingushetia, Chechnya and North Ossetia for much of the summer.

Though the war there is one of the most horrible ever witnessed by a planet battle scarred from millennia of internecine human aggression, Chechnya had seemed almost a vacation. We had traveled to the combat zones of Russia straight from weeks in the southern Sudanese desert. Sudan's own war was more than twenty years old, leaving a legacy of incomparable devastation, mutilated tribespeople and women raped on a mass, institutionalized scale that made Saddam Hussein's worst efforts at torture and degradation pale in comparison. In Sudan our five man team included veterans from elite military units of the United States, Russia and Great Britain. While there we had provided much needed security services and participated in the redemption of more than 3,000 slaves. They had all been women and children. The adult male villagers were never taken: they were either killed on the spot in raids or dispossessed of limbs by machete wielding assailants and left to stumble along in the desert as best as they could.

The women were taken as sex and labor slaves by government troops and Usama bin Laden's own constructed National Islamic Front. The children were mostly the illegitimate offspring of the female African slaves and their Arab Muslim masters; products of the daily assaults they endured. We were there to help the people of south Sudan, and the humanitarian aid groups trying to provide much needed care. We were not – as the European edition of *Newsweek* would call us – mercenaries. Nor were we "burly military advisors" there to help the SPLA, - the Sudanese People's Liberation Army - the rebel force attempting to stop the government onslaught.[1] While there we did attempt to arrange and fund a peace conference between the SPLA and Arab tribal leaders from the north. The peace conference did not occur. Despite our own humanitarian purposes, it was all we could do not to kill the Arab slave traders who brought the women down from the north to have their freedom purchased for backpacks full of Kenyan pounds. The fact that these same northern Arab Muslims had harbored bin Laden in the capital city of Khartoum from 1992 until 1996 didn't seem to impact them at all. Business was business.

After the unbearable heat of the Sudan desert, thrice daily meals of boiled goat, over-sweetened tea made from filthy water and the inescapable ravages of that war, anything would have seemed an improvement. The Caucasus Mountains were spectacular. Towering up to 20,000 feet above the steppe of southern Russia, the air was comparably cool, the food good, and the few English speakers we encountered happy for the assistance we could provide and the company of anyone from their own culture. So what if there was a war there too. Staging out of Vladikavkaz, the capital of North Ossetia, just 18 miles (30 kilometers) to the south of Beslan, we had crossed the many borders, and crisscrossed the innumerable roads and byways throughout that

---

[1]Benjamin Skinner, "Fighting a Peace Plan," *Newsweek*, August 18, 2003, 21.

region. Yuri and I knew Vladikavkaz. We knew Nazran and Magaz, and the ways into Chechnya that avoided military posts and border crossings. Most important of all, we knew Beslan.

When the siege at Beslan began, it was immediately apparent that the Russian government was downplaying the number of terrorists involved, but more importantly the number of hostages taken. Initial news reports claimed the terrorists to be no more than seventeen in number, and the hostages a little over one hundred. Coming just days after the election of the Kremlin-backed replacement for the assassinated Chechen President Akhmed Kadyrov, the attack had all the elements of a major conflagration, a resounding curtain call to the two weeks of terror Russia had been suffering in the final throes of the Chechen election campaign. The fact that the government was under-reporting the numbers did not bode well for a peaceful resolution. Despite the cheery reactions of news commentators, and even U.S. officials, to the release of some 32 young mothers and infants early on, I recognized that it was merely the terrorists' way of staving off an assault by the Alpha Counter Terror Unit that was almost certainly there already. It was their way of holding the government forces off until they did what they had gone there to do. I had been working and training with Russian Special Forces units for more than ten years. More so, I had been traveling to that country, working and going to school, and living among the Russians, for half again that time. I knew what was coming, and that we would have to hurry.

I needed a day to get a Russian visa expedited from the consulate, arrange things at work, and book airline tickets. I knew well the Russian Special Forces' history and tactics in such situations. Called Spetsnaz, which is a linguistic contraction for *Voiska Spetsialnogo Naznacheniya*, or Special Purpose Forces, they had never allowed any hostage siege to last more than a few days, and most were not granted even that luxury. We had to hurry if we were going to arrive quickly enough to obtain the tactical information that would make this effort worthwhile. Also, I knew that we would have to either do some fast talking or simply sneak into Beslan once there. One of the great things about Russia is that with a little effort one can usually find the perfect person to help with both – always for a price. The terrorists had gotten across the border and into Beslan, fully armed, for a few dozen American dollars. We would have to be at least that good.

As it turned out, the siege ended quickly. Though not unexpected, the manner of that ending came as a complete surprise to all who were there: terrorists and Spetsnaz alike. We arrived, after avoiding police and military checkpoints around the town, at the conclusion of the major battle. We stumbled into a town in shock, with truckloads of troops racing in every direction as mop-up operations were completed. Terrorists that had escaped, together with those posted around the town to provide support to their comrades inside the school, were being tracked down and killed. The place was thick with uniforms, armed citizens, and – most obvious of all – reporters. Avoiding all three, we found a room in a condemned building in which to spend several nights. For the equivalent of five U.S. dollars a day, the room was about the size of a laundry closet, with a foul and reeking community toilet, no running water and all the rats and bed bugs you could fit into two narrow, sagging cots at night. Sudan was already looking better.

From the moment the troops left the school unattended, scores of stunned and weeping citizens, police and soldiers, began leaving bottles of water and food throughout the gym and outside in the main courtyard, symbolically offering the victims the essentials they had been denied during the long days of the siege, locked inside a gym whose tall windows had turned it into a stifling oven. Despite the world's fixation on the gym, we needed to examine the rest of the school as well, to understand every aspect of the terrorists' operation and the tactical riddle presented to the Spetsnaz.

The agency I work for, Archangel, is an organization that exists to provide training, consulting and related services to U.S. military, law enforcement and government agencies in the anti-terrorism realm.

We train everything and everyone from Green Berets to SWAT teams and school security guards across the country. We cover the spectrum from academic courses and presentations, to security audits for those entering areas rife with terrorist activity.

For American law enforcement, school security officials and even the military to benefit from the Russians' experience at Beslan, we needed to understand all that had taken place. In anticipation of the possibility of a similar assault occurring in the United States, we recognized that this would likely serve as the blueprint for an attack on one of our own schools. Accordingly, we needed to know what the terrorists' plan had been for this operation and how the Russian government's forces had responded. We had to understand what had worked and what had not. We needed answers to everything.

We crawled around the school, strangely tolerated by grim-faced men in military uniforms. Other than the soldiers and police, we were the only ones in areas of the school outside of the gym, which was quickly becoming a public shrine. After days of taking photos and measurements, drawing diagrams of the building and surrounding areas, it was time to return to Moscow to begin the second part of our trip. Drawing on years of relationships with government and military officials, I met with everyone I could to ascertain exactly how this had happened. I have friends in all of the Spetsnaz units that had been sent to Beslan, including Alpha, the most famous and, conversely, one of the most highly secretive counter-terror units of the FSB, the new name for the KGB. Having deployed to Beslan, many of these contacts were not yet reachable. No one knew where they were by the time I returned to the Russian capital, or how to get a phone message to them. As my friends belong to some of the most classified units Russia has, their friendship with an American is always a delicate thing, and I was not about to jeopardize their status. In Russia, "jeopardized status" can sometimes carry severe consequences.

I ran into one friend completely by accident. It was a week after the siege ended, and Yuri and I were leaving Izmailova, an enormous and sprawling outdoor market in northeast Moscow. Lurching through a tightly packed crowd, with everyone seemingly headed in the opposite direction, I felt a tug at my arm and looked up to see the shocked and smiling face of one of my comrades from Alpha. Neither of us could believe it. In a city of fifteen million people it is not expected to run into someone you know. When we told him we had just come from Beslan, his eyes quickly shrouded. He managed to whisper that he had been there too. The day of our chance encounter happened to be September 11, the three year anniversary of the assault on America. He mentioned this, tearfully telling me how sorry he was for our own loss on that date. I hadn't even realized what day it was. It was obvious that he was still emotionally ravaged by what he had been through. It was equally obvious that no one came away from that place unscathed. Ironically, he would be the only person unable to meet with me to shed light on the mystery that surrounded Beslan.

By November of 2004, I had been working on a report about the Beslan siege and the tactics of the al Qaeda related and trained terrorists for two months. By then it was also clear that there were many questions yet unanswered. News media accounts differed from most of what I had learned, and their unwavering certainty about events on which I had reached different conclusions demanded a return. I had to face returning to the one place I promised myself I would never go back to. I wasn't worried about Yuri. He was a professional, and his Slavic stoicism never faltered. But I had to keep my own emotions in check. Beslan had been bad; the worst I had ever experienced. Not that anyone with Archangel was unfamiliar with blood and the effects of war, but at Beslan there had been the children. Their tiny, broken bodies, their blood, and their fear, had made it almost unbearable. It seemed as though that fear had soaked into the very walls of the school itself. You breathed it in the air; felt it deep in your lungs. At the same time, the children of Beslan - as well as those in America who might someday pray to be delivered from their own terrorist purgatory - cried out for answers. The dead of Beslan had haunted my dreams every night since returning home, seemingly demanding some effort be made to bring purpose to their horror, to make certain other short lives were not snuffed out as theirs had been. Someone had to do it. *If not me, then who?* I couldn't get the thought out of my own head. And so we went back.

The world can never be allowed to forget the terrifying siege of the Beslan School and the more than one thousand hostages held there. Nor can it afford to forget the brave men who risked - and in many cases gave - their lives to save them. It is a message the world needs to hear, and a story that demands to be told.

This is that story.

Introduction

The purpose of terrorism is to terrorize.

— *Vladimir Ilyich Lenin*

Though they cannot say it openly, or to the public or news media, for most American law enforcement officers and school security officials, the likelihood of an incident similar to the terrorist siege of hundreds of children in Beslan, Russia in September 2004, happening in America is more a question of *when*, than *if*.

Whether it be in the next year or two, or five or ten, it is possible – even likely – that another group of more than a dozen terrorists will take over an American school, or schools, and hold hundreds of children, teachers, and even parents, hostage. This group will be comprised of Arab terrorists, as well as non-Arabs, including born-and-raised Americans. They will be white, black and brown. There may be Asians from such places as the Philippines, Indonesia, Korea and Thailand. The group will include men and women; maybe even some teenagers. Some may even be from the very town in which the siege occurs. They will promise to kill groups of hostages in the most gruesome of ways every time a deadline passes and their demands are not met. They will execute some early on to make sure we realize they are serious. At the start, they will line up the adult males and biggest of the teenage children – if there are teenagers – and shoot them dead, taking away any possibility of resistance from inside. They will take advantage of all the great American technology that we so proudly place in our schools. They will utilize the in-school security camera systems throughout the campus for surveillance of police activity outside, giving them the ability to fend off any effort to storm the school. They will use the internet, cell and satellite phones to communicate with their leaders and the news media. They will demand the U.S. withdraw from Iraq at once. They will demand U.S. troops leave Afghanistan, and Saudi Arabia. And in light of recent geo-political events, they may even demand the new U.S. policy in support of Russia in its battle for control of Chechnya be abandoned.

How do we know this will happen? Renowned terrorism expert, and the preeminent authority on the psychology of killing, Lt. Col. David Grossman, maintains that it is a psychological fact that the greatest predictor of future behavior is past performance. In short, it has already happened. To an America that sleeps safely and securely in its beds, giving no thought to the world in which we exist or the horrors that other nations face - confident in the belief that *it can't happen here* - much has occurred which should be setting off alarm bells for all of us. Indeed those bells have been sounding for some time; we just haven't heard them. Yet.

Israel has faced this reality for years. Her schools are virtual fortresses, bristling with commandos, arms, and checkpoints. Russia's may soon be. We know this will happen because it already has. And where it has occurred, the terrorists have been successful in their efforts. And those efforts have been and will be simple: to sow terror through the deaths of innocents. To an America that wishes merely to remain immersed in a culture of celebrity divorces, money and retirement plans, shopping, the latest fashions and what kind of car to drive, it is far beyond the time when every one of us must realize that era in our history and culture is over. And it is over for good. We, as the rest of the world, now live in a time in which we must fight to defend the very society that was built on the blood and lives of those who sacrificed all, generations ago. For a very long time, we have been living on the interest of the sacrificial payments that were made by those who came before us. It is now our time to heed the call to arms that gave birth to this nation more than two and a quarter centuries ago, and which saw it protected and defended for those many years thereafter.

Stop and look at the development of terrorism in those nations that aligned themselves to any significant degree with the United States in World War II. The birth of the Jewish State immediately after that war – our ally in the war in terms of people, if not national status - was a natural outgrowth of the centuries-long Jewish plight and our efforts to save them from German genocide. Britain was America's staunchest ally. It, too, has been plagued by terrorism, and now with a teeming Muslim population and continued support of the U.S., is being threatened yet again. The United States has seen many assaults on its citizens, embassies and military overseas, and now within our borders as well. Russia, our ally in the Eastern Front of World War II, can scarcely count the number of people lost to terrorist attacks in recent years. Only France, and to a degree Canada, have so far been successful in avoiding direct assault. Though Canada has a great many people who believe deeply in preventing Islamist extremists from entering North America, it is only now becoming known that militant Muslims have been using it as a springboard to illegally enter the U.S. for years. With France's pandering attitude to the Islamic world and nascent anti-Americanism, it has willingly allowed its Muslim population to dictate its opposition to U.S. efforts.

But that is not all. Nations like Spain and Turkey that, since World War II, have aligned themselves with the U.S., and the victors' enjoyment of the spoils of that war, have suffered consequences at the hands of their own Muslim populations for their support of U.S. international policy. Certainly Australia, America's courageous ally in the Pacific Theater fighting under the British mantle, has not been left untouched by radical Islam. And Saudi Arabia, the jewel of the Muslim faith and home of the holiest muslim sites of Mecca and Medina, has been under constant assault for its coziness with America and its tolerances of the influences of a perceived decadent Western culture. And what of the destruction of Lebanon?

Perhaps this should have been foreseeable. The nations that were the victors in that last *war to end all wars,* comprised the Christian power base of that first post-colonial period. Even the officially atheist Soviet Union rallied its people to defend the *Rodina* – the Motherland - by resurrecting their Orthodox Christian chauvinism. And when the dust had settled, it was these victors who divvied up the spoils of a resource rich world, establishing – sometimes all too recklessly – new nations for our own indulgence. We entered a new age of colonialism, unable to see in ourselves the failed policies of mercantilism in centuries past. Britain, America, France, the Netherlands, Belgium, all allies of the U.S., enjoyed the fruits of our labor and sacrifice in World War II. Yet in re-constructing the world, we allowed our colonial subjects - serfs in almost every other way - the benefit of our own smug tolerance for religious freedom. We gave them our skills at infrastructure development. We gave them our technology, our genius for organization, and our proven, superior military expertise. They took all these and applied them to a burgeoning outrage at being treated as lessers among equals. It was our willingness to allow them the religion of their choice that cleaved all of these factors together in a single, malevolent, threatening force: Islamist extremism. From Africa, the Philippines, Burma, Indonesia, and Malaysia, to Iran, Lebanon, Syria, Jordan, Yemen, India and Pakistan, all felt the inertia of a wildly violent rejection of the West. For years the people of these regions had toiled at the demand of their Western, Christian masters. These same people already had a long history of blaming the West for all of their own failures. They blamed the West for their own inability to keep up with the forward march of the world, with its technology, with its developing value systems of individual human rights, of rights for women, and for its own indulgence in a world of conspicuous consumption and demonstrative wealth; a wealth they perceived as having been achieved on their backs.

By the 1960s and 70s, the West, in furtherance of its own evolving sense of freedom, minority rights and self-determination, had loosed the reins of control on these countries. Those with a well-entrenched Christian religiosity, like the Bahamas and other South Seas island nations, would become fast partners in the future of trade and tourism with their former masters. In later years, those with the same Christian underpinnings, though held firmly under the Soviet yoke – nations like Poland, the Baltics and Ukraine - would peacefully turn to the former allies of the nation that dominated them for so long. Yet, those from regions in proximity to the Middle East, the birthplace of Islam, would quickly foment disaster for their Western colonizers.[2] This would be seen throughout the Middle East, countries to the north, Southeast Asia and Africa. There would be no expression of appreciation for the decades of assistance in social and infrastructure development, education, medicine and technology. For these very assets of the West would be joined with their now improved military skills and weaponry, and turned on their former benefactors.

What we are now seeing is the culmination of decades of resentment, built on previous centuries of societies left behind in the rapid march of technology and cultural evolution. To them, the West is to blame. The West represents all that is bad in the world and that has caused their failures. And the West will pay.

The terrorists who have now linked up, organized and exported their brand of grisly Islam across the world are fueled, among other things, by psychological as well as social despair. They represent a culture that could not keep up with world modernity, and so rejects it. In so doing they face, once again, their inability to compete with the very

---

[2] With the conspicuous exception of India, though clearly not a Muslim nation.

culture and nations they revile; this time in military terms. And so, they have turned to a type of violence deplorable to the West. They have chosen to attack the rest of the world, the infidels, in ways that are designed to make the West's presence in the regions of Islam intolerable to it.[3]

Many Russian government officials and military officers agree. "All terrorists in the world were created by either the U.S. or Russia," says Colonel – soon to be General – Mikhail Ryabko. A twenty year Special Forces veteran, with many tours in both Afghanistan and Chechnya, Col. Ryabko is now the chief advisor to the Russian Minister of Justice, charged with the responsibility of developing solutions to the Chechen problem facing the country. At merely 5 feet 7 inches and 250 pounds, he is massive and round in the way truly powerful men are. His forearms and wrists are thicker than most men's legs, and his feet are slabs. His gentle smile and urbane manner belie the fact that he has been wounded in combat close to a dozen times, and is one of the Russian Spetsnaz' premier hand-to-hand combat experts. It is only when you look into the impossibly cold, gray eyes as they stare steadily back at you, that you realize you are in the presence of a man for whom death is a way of life. Despite these experiences, Colonel Ryabko's world view shows an insight few military men possess. Referring to Russia and the Soviet Union before it, in conjunction with America, he says, "We organized, then trained them and equipped them; every single person or group we now confront as terrorists. Just as Russians did with the Chechens before they rebelled in 1994, and the Americans did with the Taliban between 1980 and 1989. Now we are being revisited by our very own creations."

But in providing training and equipment, neither country inspired the militant Islamists to go on a worldwide terror spree. Our support was merely the catalyst. The motivation came from a sect within the Muslim faith unknown to most in the West until after 9-11: Wahhabism. Founded by Muhammad ibn Abdul Wahhab in the early

---

3 Lee Harris, in his treatise *Civilization and its Enemies: The Next Stage of History*, convincingly argues that these Islamist extremists are motivated not so much by despair as by a "fantasy ideology."

to mid-1700s, it was a fundamentalist belief system which was itself based on the extremist teachings and writings of Ibn Taymiyya in the early 14th century; writings still quoted by Islamist extremists today. Though initially rejected by the religious leaders of the time, by 1744 Wahhab had joined with local tribal leader Muhammed ibn Saud to create the first Saudi state, with Saud as the leader and Wahhab as the ultimate authority on morality and behavior of the people. Wahhab destroyed many tombs and places of worship under his belief that the people were following the Christian practice of saint veneration, of worshipping idols, something other than God himself. In addition to the Christians, he rejected the Shiite Muslims for believing that Muhammed's son-in-law Ali should have been his successor, worshipping him as they had Muhammed. He even reintroduced the 7th century Muhammedian practice of stoning women for adultery.

Eventually Wahhab's daughter married Saud's son, beginning a dynasty of rulers of a nation steeped in ancient, extremist practices that the rest of the world continues to deal with today.[4] This is the foundation of the modern Islamist extremist movement, and its assault on its hated masters, the victors of World War II who gave it the freedom to do so. This hate-based movement has marched unstoppably from one nation to the other. The believers in the erroneously developed *Domino Theory* of Communist expansion from the Cold War can now take some small consolation in its complete applicability and accuracy in predicting the expansion of radical Islam throughout the world. Communism could not succeed against the West during that period because it lacked an ideological strength that the masses would adopt. Here Lenin was proved right: Religion is truly the opiate of the masses. At least these masses. In so declaring, he well recognized that the single greatest threat to the way of life that the Bolsheviks were seeking to develop was a faith based ideology which saw everything in terms of right and wrong, good and evil, and called upon its followers to tolerate no compromise on those beliefs.

---

4 For a detailed account, see Todd M. Rassa, "A History of Usama bin Laden and Al-Qaeda," *Police Marksman*, November/December 2004, 23.

Extremist, militant Islamist fundamentalism has so far succeeded in this endeavor where Communism failed. It has been exported from the Middle East to, first, the Soviet war in Afghanistan; once again with U.S. assistance in military training, weaponry, organization and logistics. After that victory, it redeployed quickly to the first war in Chechnya. Though primarily, at that time, a war of the Chechen people for independence – much as the war in Afghanistan started – it has, since 1999, been completely perverted and conscripted into the greater jihad against infidels, against all non-Muslim oppressors. In the midst of this, the war in the Balkans saw another clash of religions. Though Serb atrocities against Croat and Bosnian Muslims were real, often these were provoked – and nearly always retaliated against - by Mujahideen Muslim fanatics intent on instigating another jihad in places like Kosovo and Bosnia. Russia, long time ally of Serbia, which saw the Afghan War fought strictly on Afghan soil, has now experienced the horror of its battles against Islam brought to its inner cities and other regions within the country. The war is no longer being fought by the Islamists solely on the soil of Islam.

Assault by Islamist terrorists, working in concert through an elaborate and growing worldwide network, has now appeared in Indonesia, Australia, Malaysia, the Philippines, Japan, Spain, Turkey, Iraq, Lebanon, Saudi Arabia, Mexico, Central and South America, and the U.S., among others. The end of the Cold War, and the release of the Soviet Union's control over many cultures and countries, saw an exponential rise in organized crime (OC) throughout the world, and the development of new relationships between OC groups that had previously been sequestered from each other. In much the same way, this new era in world history has seen the many disenfranchised, downtrodden Muslims and lower socio-economic masses around the world connect with each other for the first time. And they have connected with a commonality of ideology and hatred perhaps never before seen in history. Now the United States, which has engaged these same combatants in Afghanistan and Iraq, must prepare for more assaults on its own soil. For, if past performance is predictive of future conduct, it is indeed on its way.

PART ONE

THE LONG ROAD TO BESLAN

UKRAINE
KAZAKHSTAN
RUSSIAN FEDERATION
CHECHNYA
BLACK SEA
CASPIAN SEA
GEORGIA
AZERBAIDJAN
ARMENIA

STAVROPOL REGION
CHECHNYA
DAGESTAN
GROZNY
INGUSHETIA
BESLAN
VLADIKAVKAZ
NORTH OSSETIA
GEORGIA

Chapter One

Roots of Terrorism in Russia

If you would understand Russia, and interpret and forecast aright the march of great events, never forget that, for her, eastward the march of empire takes its way; that as the sap rises, as the sparks fly upward, as the tides follow the moon, so Russia goes to the sunrise.

— *Henry Norman, All the Russias*

In order to fully understand and appreciate what happened at Beslan on September 1, 2004 – and what may very well happen in America – we must educate ourselves about the history of Russia's conflict in Chechnya, and the circumstances and events leading up to that fateful day. For if recent Chechen terrorist threats are to be taken seriously, they just may be coming to the U.S.

The history of the Chechen people relative to that of their Russian masters is both long and cruel. The current struggle for independence first arose out of an ages-old conflict between the Slavic Russians and the Caucasian tribes. Ancient chronicles are replete with stories of battles fought by the Cossacks against the Chechens along the Terek River. These battles were fought even as recently as the latter 19th century. The Muslim Chechens, always disdainful of the Russian government and clinging to a culture, value system and way of life disparate from that of Russia proper and its Orthodox Christianity, were independence-minded and therefore were viewed as a threat. Though the Chechens and the Ingush, their neighbors to the west, are really different groups with distinct languages, they are so closely related as to be described together by many experts, and to be seen as a common group – and in many cases as a common problem – by the Russian government.

The Chechens come from a sub-group of the Vainach, which descended from the Benos people; the other sub-group being the Ingushians or *Ingush*. The earliest written references to the Chechens as a people are found in 7th century Armenian texts, though scholars believe they have existed in the Caucasus for 7,000 years. The term "Chechen" is an ethnonym, derived by the Russians in the 18th century from the nearest village to their fort at Grozny, called Chechen Aula or Chechen *aul*. The people refer to themselves not as Chechen but "Nokhchi." The same is true for the Ingush, a name derived from the geographic designation of Angushta. Those people refer to themselves as Ghalghay or Galgalians. The Chechens, however, are the largest North Caucasian group, of all Caucasian groups, second only to the more numerous Georgians. The lands of Chechnya and Ingushetia lie immediately east of the main road traversing the central Caucasus Mountains, through the Darial Pass, and extend from mountains and foothills to plains and lowland forest. The lowland regions are fertile, and the combination of abundant rainfall, a decent growing season - relative to much of Russia - and even the presence of oil, make it an asset worth fighting for. Ingushetia lies to the west, a thin strip of land separating Chechnya from North Ossetia. Though the Ossetians look upon themselves as a distinct group, many Slavic Russians also inhabit the region, and speak a dialect of the Iranian branch of Indo-European languages.

Tensions have historically run high between the Orthodox Christian people of North Ossetia, and both the Ingushetis and Chechens.

The North Ossetians tend to view the Ingushetians and Chechens as a single enemy, of common ancestry and religion as well as geo-political orientation. The Ossetians, themselves, are a unique group, suspicious of Russians from more populated and urban regions, historically refusing to acknowledge their Slavic roots, and practicing a sometimes unusual brand of Christianity.

Within Chechnya there are two major cities: Grozny, the capital, and Gudermes. Both Grozny and Vladikavkaz, in North Ossetia, were originally founded as forts during 18th Century's Tsarist Russian efforts to conquer the region and control the Darial Pass. In those early years Cossacks moved into the area at the government's behest and have maintained a significant presence ever since. Until 1995 the population of Grozny was about 400,000, with Vladikavkaz being somewhat smaller, with 300,000 people. Though Vladikavkaz's population has since grown slightly, the decimation wrought by wars and the resulting exodus of people have virtually eradicated Grozny's population base. It is important to keep in mind, however, that of the 400,000 originally in Grozny fully three-quarters of them were ethnically Slavic Russians. It is they who have largely been affected by the war and driven from their homes by Chechen attacks, not the rebel Chechens themselves.

The Chechen people are not Slavic, and in fact their entire group is believed to be indigenous to the Caucasus Mountains. Many Turks even claim a common or related ancestry to the Chechens, a major reason for Turkey's solidarity with the Chechen cause against the Russians. The Chechen social structure is based on family and clan. Called *tieps*, each clan is an independent social unit, comprised of related or united families. There are 165 to 170 tieps in Chechnya today, the majority of which have traditionally inhabited the mountain areas. Among the Chechens, two distinct groups have thus emerged from the geographical orientation of the various tieps: mountain dwellers and flatlanders. And as with many evolving cultures throughout history, there are distinct differences between the two groups in terms of lifestyle, values and desires. The lowland people, or flatlanders, have always led a more sedate, peaceful, agricultural existence. The mountain tieps are more pugnacious and nationalistic, clinging to ancient notions of honor and warriorship. In recent years, the lowlanders have been largely supportive of the Russian government, not objecting to Chechnya's inclusion in the Federation, while the war has been fought by the 100 or so mountain clans. This division has been exacerbated by the mountain tieps who consider themselves "pure" and ethnically unadulterated, conflicting with the lowland clans who are partially intermixed with Terek Cossacks, Cherkassians and Georgians. A fact the ethnically bigoted mountain people find intolerable. This has caused a significant split between the people of Chechnya themselves.

The Chechens share a common religion with both the Turks and Ingush, as they are all Sunni Muslims of the Hanafi sect. Islam originally came to Chechnya at the end of the 8th century, with conversion of the peoples of the region occurring between then and the 9th century. The first contact – and conflict – between the Chechens and Russians did not take place until 1663, when Russia began its efforts to conquer the Caucasus. The effort was drawn out over decades, but eventually Russia established its power throughout the region early in the 18th century. Though anti-government sentiment has always existed among the Muslim groups, the Christian Ossetians populating the same broad region voluntarily accepted the Russian Empire centuries ago. Only after the bloody Caucasus Wars of the 1700s were the Chechens conquered and assimilated into the Tsar's Russia. For years the Tsar's armies remained to ensure the region's pacification.

The Chechens never quite accepted their conscription into Russia, and rose up many times over the years. Renewed efforts for independence became particularly intense when Chechen Shayk Mansur rose to power in 1785, leading an insurrection that the Russsians did not quash until 1791. He was followed by insurgent Muslim leaders,

Imam Gazi Muchamed and Imam Shamil, who attempted to create a united Islamic nation through the unification of Chechnya and Dagestan to the east. By 1859 these resistance efforts had failed. The battles of this period were extremely bloody, and the Chechens proved themselves to be more than capable defenders, a trait not unexpected in a culture where murder and fighting to the death over slights to honor were commonplace, and the blood feud was law. At the end of these wars, the Russians prevailed, and in 1865 700,000 people - much of the Chechen population - was deported. Others were slaughtered. Many were forced to migrate to Middle Eastern countries like Jordan and Syria, forever linking these people with the very regions fomenting terrorism today.[5]

The Russians struggled for more than half a century to reconquer Chechnya. But the Chechens were not through. It is part of the Chechen culture that children are raised to fight all who are perceived as enemies, Russians and all non-Muslims alike. They are indoctrinated early on in the techniques of terror, and Chechens insist that there will always be enough fighters to carry on the battle against Russia. From an early age, boys are taught the fundamental code of Chechen warriorship: "Do not fear the enemy because he may not have a weapon. If he does, it may not be cocked. If cocked, it may not fire. If fired, it may miss. And if the bullet strikes you, you may not die. If you die, you will then gain Allah's grace."[6]

The exile of the Chechen population gave the Tsar a new advantage when oil was discovered there in 1893. By 1914 oil taken from beneath Chechnya comprised 14 percent of all petroleum produced in Russia. Of course, rulers had long struggled for control over Chechnya for its

---

5 Interestingly, Leonid Tolstoy's service in the Tsar's Army featured him fighting Chechens in the Caucasus Mountains, which became the setting for a number of his stories, and make for interesting reading. Also, for a short overview of Chechen history from their perspective, see www.chechen8m.com

6 See generally, Stasys Knezys and Romanas Sedlickas, *The War in Chechnya*, (Texas A&M University Press, Texas Station, Texas, 1999), and also at 14

strategic location, and it now proved beneficial as a route and hub for transportation lines into other regions.[7]

The October Revolution, and the Civil War it spawned, finally gave the Chechens their chance for freedom from 1918 until 1921. The Bolsheviks had promised them independence in exchange for their support in the battle against Tsarist forces. However, Lenin and his cronies soon proved to be worse even than the Tsar. In 1920 the Red Army occupied Chechnya, and the following year forcibly annexed it into the new Soviet structure as the Mountain Autonomous Region of the USSR. In 1922 Chechnya became an autonomous region of its own, and then in 1934 it was combined with Ingushetia to create the Chechen-Ingush Autonomous Republic. Throughout this period of Communist restructuring of former Russian lands, the Chechens rose up in rebellion twice more. The first revolt took place from September 1920 until May 1921. The second lasted only two weeks in 1932 before being quashed in a bloody attack by the Red Army.

Chechnya was to suffer its worst punishment during World War II. On the evening of February 23, 1944, Stalin had the Red Army deport the region's entire population to the frigid and barren steppes of Kazakhstan and other parts of Siberia. Though the official reason for this action was his suspicion that the Chechens and Ingush – as well as other groups - had aided the Nazis, this seems farfetched. The Germans had never penetrated the Chechen-Ingush Republic at any time during the war. While anti-Soviet resistance among the Chechens had continued and the Chechens likely had killed hundreds if not thousands of Red Army soldiers, it is far more likely the government merely saw this as an opportunity to rid itself of a long-time thorn in its side, and gain control of land desirable not only for its resources, but its strategic position. Though no accurate records appear to have been kept – or at least acknowledged – it is estimated that between one-quarter and one-half of the Chechen population was killed in this movement. At this time Stalin "encouraged"

---

7 Ibid.

the remaining Ossetians and area Cossacks to occupy much of the land left by those forced out.

Though officially "rehabilitated" by Krushchev during the 20th Party Congress in 1956, and permitted to return the following year when the autonomy of the Chechen-Ingush Autonomous Soviet Socialist Republic (ASSR) was re-established, it took decades before the return migration was complete. With the disbanding of the Soviet Union and the new Russian government's combined lack of concern and inability to control the movement of its people, the Chechens and Ingush completed the return pilgrimage to their homes in the region in 1992. When they arrived, they found that both rights and land had been lost to them for good.[8]

In 1992, subsequent to the Soviet Union's dissolution on December 25, 1991, North Ossetia and Ingushetia fought a short but violent war over the disputed district of Prigorodny in North Ossetia. Close to 1,000 people died and between 40,000 and 60,000 Ingush were forced out of the area, in addition to the displacement of more than 5,000 Ossetian refugees from the common border area, before Russian troops were deployed to end the fighting. The conflict between the two provinces has been seething ever since.

This tension was something I had experienced first hand. In the summer of 2003, along with a team from Archangel, I spent weeks in this region studying the war in Chechnya, and providing security consulting and anti-kidnap training to several of the humanitarian aid groups working with refugees. The IDP (Internally Displaced Persons) camps that were strung along the Chechen-Ingusheti border teemed with people seeking refuge from the fighting. The FSB was everywhere, as were various Interior Ministry – or MVD - military units. Each day we crossed the border from North Ossetia into Ingushetia, and then on toward Chechnya. The very first day, as we lined up at the first checkpoint, we were passed by more than

---

[8] For an exhaustive history of the Chechen people, see Knezys and Sedlickas', *The War in Chechnya*

a hundred Russian armored personnel carriers, tanks and troop carriers. Piled atop all these vehicles sat dirty and vacant-eyed young men, many in their teens, as they sped back to the war they had left all too short a time ago. As we came abreast of this seemingly endless convoy of military might, bristling with weapons of every kind, four Hind-D attack helicopters roared overhead, barely clearing the treetops. The noise from the convoy joined with the unmistakable *whomp-whomp* of the chopper blades to form a deafening crescendo. We knew we were back at war.

To Americans, the thought of crossing the border from one region of Russia into another brings to mind the unnoticeable borders between our own states. To us, aside from the occasional Department of Transportation truck-weighing station, and a brief glimpse of a sign along the road welcoming everyone to the new state and reminding us to "Buckle Up – It's The Law!", there is nothing to acknowledge in crossing from one U.S. territory to another. Not so in Russia. Though the war was officially in Chechnya, the hostility between North Ossetia and Ingushetia was palpable. To go from North Ossetia into Ingushetia at a border crossing a short drive from Beslan, one first had to cross a North Ossetian checkpoint. Local military and police, fully armed with assault rifles, stood about en mass. Soldiers inspected passports and visas, and questioned identities and purpose for travel at length. Approximately a kilometer further stood the Russian Federation's FSB checkpoint. The inspection process was repeated, with the intensity of the interrogation increasing. This was the middle of no-man's land: a strip of turf in which both the Ingush and Ossetians eked out a living in uneasy peace with each other. Old women and farm animals seemed to be the only living things that could wander freely, unnoticed by stern men in uniforms who seemed to be always in search of a reason to use the weapons that hung ominously from their shoulders.

And yet another kilometer further on, stood another military checkpoint, manned by representatives of the Ingusheti government. To enter their region required an even more thorough question and answer session, and a physical search. The Ingush would not allow entry to anyone whom they perceived as a potential problem, either for themselves or their friends to the east, the Chechens. That they merely tolerated the Russian military racing through on their way to the war, as well as the presence of federal military bases throughout their territory, was apparent. Here, it seemed, no one liked anyone else. And we were outsiders, strangers resented by everyone. It was made painfully clear to our small, five man team that everyone in this region had been fighting – in one form or another – for a very long time, and interlopers were not welcome.

The Chechens, many of whom had been displaced from this region for almost half a century, had made their presence known in a big way upon their complete return in 1992. They quickly began a fight for independence, led by then-Chechen President Dzhokhar Dudayev. Even before this, however, they had sent signals to Moscow of their intentions: declaring independence from the Soviet Union as early as November 1, 1991, less than two months before that nation crumbled. This resulted in the First Chechen War in Russia, which began when the Kremlin sent troops into that region on December 11, 1994 to bring the republic to heel. Officially called Ichkerija, the territory of present-day Chechnya covers approximately 16,000 square kilometers (10,000 sq. miles) and is about the size of Connecticut. This war was fought to a virtual stalemate, continuing until April 1996, at which time the Chechens were successful in forcing a weary Russia to withdraw its forces, providing it some of the sought-after provisional autonomy. Much of this was accomplished by the Chechens through their incorporation of terrorist tactics, including taking and executing many hostages in various terror-type sieges. The success of this approach to their campaign against their Russian masters, would see a return in subsequent years.

On August 30, 1996, Russian and Chechen representatives signed a formal cease-fire at Khasaviurt, with decisions on the republic's ultimate political status postponed. Russian troops pulled out the next day. More than 100,000 Chechens were killed in this first war, mostly civilians. But the war was not fought by the Chechens alone, as they had been aided in this effort by thousands of Taliban and al Qaeda combat veterans, who emerged from the Afghanistan War looking for the next chapter in their worldwide jihad. In an interesting turnabout, Chechens would later be seen back in Afghanistan, helping the Taliban against American and Northern Alliance forces during Operation Enduring Freedom in 2001 and 2002.

Subsequent to the Russian rapprochement with the Chechens in the mid 1990s, a far more radical and fundamentalist Islamist element – Wahhabism - began to develop in Chechnya, influencing the rebel leaders. Though Islam had remained an important aspect of Chechen culture and life since their conversion centuries before, much of this new influence was imported from other regions already seething with extremist Islamist designs. An influx of Arab extremists incited increasing Islamic radicalism, terrorism and militarism. Aslan Maskhadov had become president of Chechnya after the Russian withdrawal in 1996. Though Muslim, he was generally perceived by the Russian government as tolerably secular, or at least only moderately religious. As time went on, however, he too fell under the sway of radical Islamists, including the influential rebel leader, Shamil Basayev. Under this pressure, Maskhadov declared the region subject to the Shari'a, or Islamic law, a move the general Chechen population did not wholly support.

After the end of the First Chechen War, Chechnya slipped into a horrible criminal situation with rampant organized crime and Muslim terrorism. Kidnap for ransom became a regular occurrence, with the all-too-often lack of success seen in the form of hostages' severed heads left along Chechen roads. Almost simultaneously with a wave of terrorist attacks, including the bombing of three apartment buildings in Moscow that killed 304 people in September 1999, Shamil Basayev, together with the Saudi-connected terrorist warlord, Habib Abdul Rachman, better known as Emir Ibn Khattab, invaded the neighboring Russian region of Dagestan, looking to create and expand a pan-Islamic nation. According to the Russian Government, a deal had been struck between Basayev and the Turkish Secret Service, which provided financial support for the Dagestan invasion. It was also reported by Russian government officials that fugitive oligarch Boris Berezovsky had, as well, provided substantial funding for this invasion.

According to a report declassified by the U.S. Defense Intelligence Agency on November 19, 2004, Usama bin Laden sent Khattab, aka "The Black Arab and One Hand Akhmed," a Jordanian born terrorist whose moniker derived from the fact that he was missing fingers from one hand due to a grenade incident, to Chechnya as early as 1995. Released on November 19, 2004, the report established that bin Laden had been actively involved in the terrorist insurgency in Chechnya since before the end of the First Chechen War. According to the six-page document, at that time, in addition to Khattab, bin Laden sent nine instructors whose mission was to set up terrorist training camps. Though the report indicates that the information has not been definitively established as accurate, it goes far to support the long-held contention of the Russians that a link to al Qaeda has always existed. Russian Special Forces killed Khattab several years ago.

Well before the start of the Second Chechen War, other radical Arab fighters entered Chechnya to assist in its renewed efforts against the Russians. In 1999, Basayev even made an offer to the Kosovo Albanians to bring his brigade into that war to support them against the Serbs. The Kosovars refused this offer. Perhaps they were fearful such an audacious move would erode U.S. support.

Then-Prime Minister Vladimir Vladimirovich Putin, in launching a second war with the Chechen militants, declared before the Russian parliament on Tuesday, September 14, 1999, that Chechnya had become "a vast terrorist camp." He immediately ordered a "temporary tough quarantine regime" around Chechnya's borders in addition to economic sanctions. Responding to the last of the apartment bombings on Monday, September 13, which killed 118 innocents, he reasserted Russia's long held belief that the Chechen movement was one of international terrorism, and not mere ethnic independence, declaring that the recent attacks had been carried out by "well trained international subversives." The Russian authorities publicly stated that the bombings had been carried out with Hexagon, commonly known as RDX, a military explosive that the Chechen rebels were known to have taken from various Russian military depots in the region. A fourth apartment building in Moscow had been rigged to blow that same day, though the device failed to detonate.

On September 30, 1999, Russian troops were again on the march into Chechnya. By February 1, 2000, the rebels had abandoned Grozny and fled into the nearby Caucasus Mountains due to continuous bombing of the capital. From their bases in the mountains, they organized and launched their own military campaign against the Russian oppressors. Putin's move was well received by the Russian people – despite the overall lack of popularity of the First Chechen War – and he was elected president later in 2000. More than two years after, the Chechens managed to strike back at the Russians in the heart of their own capital. In late October 2002, Chechen rebels seized the Nord-Ost Theater in Moscow, taking more than 800 people hostage. No longer would the war be waged only in the Chechens' capital of Grozny. In an effort by the Kremlin to show some control of the region, a Moscow-framed constitution was adopted by the voting citizens of Chechnya on March 23, 2003, affirming that republic's status as part of the Russian Federation.

Russia continued to press its advantage in establishing a formal – that is, pro-Kremlin – government in Chechnya. On October 5, 2003, Moscow-backed candidate Akhmad Kadyrov was elected president of the republic. Following the lead of the Chechen rebels, the Russian government sought to attack the Chechen insurgents wherever they could be found, even if outside Chechnya. On February 13, 2004, three Russian intelligence officers killed former Chechen president

Zelimkhan Yandarbiyev near his home in Qatar - where he lived in exile - by wiring his Toyota Land Cruiser to explode. The FSB operatives were quickly arrested by Qatar authorities and charged with the murder. One managed to evade prosecution and return to Russia due to diplomatic immunity. The other two were convicted of murder and are now serving prison terms there.

Though terrorist attacks have continued, Putin was re-elected by an enormous margin in March 2004, helped by increased governmental control over various institutions in Russia, not the least of which was the media. In seeming retaliation, on May 9, 2004, by way of explosives, Chechens assassinated the Moscow-backed Chechen President Kadyrov and six others in Grozny. Since that time, many of the conflicts in this region have taken on a decidedly more terror-oriented form.

Since the commencement of the Second Chechen War, Putin has not appeared willing to seek a political solution. His recent policy of *Chechenization* – similar to the efforts of the U.S. in Vietnam in the early 1970s – has resulted in little more than a Kremlin picked leader being putatively elected to the position of president of the Chechen Republic. After Kadyrov's death, and upon the run-up to the election of a new president, the weekend of August 28, 2004 saw much-protested and reportedly flawed Chechen elections put Alu Alkhanov, a second Kremlin-backed leader, in place.

Despite going through the motions of democratically electing an administration to govern, Moscow's policies in Chechnya have not looked to any type of valid diplomatically negotiated solution, and its own military efforts have in many instances made an already bad situation worse. Clearly, the Chechens are guilty of their own acts of unspeakable horror on both enemy soldiers and civilians; however, the broad license given to Russian forces has seen them abduct, torture and kill young Chechens as well. It is claimed that the deaths of Chechen fighters and civilians at the hands of Russian troops has spawned the "Black Widow" cult. This is a group of Muslim Chechen women who have survived the deaths of their own husbands and male family members, and have been recruited to serve as human bombs in terrorist attacks, as in the Nord-Orst Theater siege in late October 2002. These female human bombs are classified as either "Black Widows," for those 25 years of age or older, or "Fiancées of Allah" for those under 25. The first use of female suicide bombers by Chechens was in 2000, when a woman named Barayeva, a cousin and second wife to Chechen terror leader Arbe Barayev, attacked an OMON (*Otryad Militsiy Osobogo Naznacheniya* or Special Operations State Militia) *blockpost*, or garrison, in Alkhan-Yurt, killing two and wounding five. Clearly, such activities were no longer to be confined merely to Chechnya. Ingushetia, despite being supportive of the Chechens' efforts, has been suddenly and unprecedentedly the host of many murders as well as kidnappings. Few have seen the return of the hostages.

One of the most important factors, and one that cannot be discounted at this time, is the internationalization of the Chechen conflict. When the Soviet Union withdrew from Afghanistan in 1989 it left thousands of well trained, battle hardened *jihadists* looking for a new cause. The Soviet-Afghanistan War produced – with the help of the United States and the CIA – at least 5,000 Saudis, 3,000 Yemenis, 2,800 Algerians, 2,000 Egyptians, plus other non-Afghans, all of whom were combat experienced, well trained and religiously committed to the furtherance of Muslim interests and jihad. Many of these jihadists went on to create new terror groups. All of them – in conjunction with al Qaeda and the Taliban – had stores of both U.S. supplied and Soviet captured weapons, and had benefited greatly from their U.S. para-military training. Since then, these men have all greatly expanded their numbers through recruitment within their own countries and cultures. Not only is a significant number of bin Laden's personal bodyguards purportedly Chechen but Chechnya is part of his "national caliphate." Just as disturbing, is that through their common history and combined efforts in Chechnya, these terror groups have also come to develop close relationships with Chechen and other "Russian" organized crime groups.[9] The various groups have continued to work well together in new enterprises. Starting several years ago they even began engaging in commercial fraud and identity theft through the establishment of anonymous automated teller machines. Al Qaeda has already made substantial amounts of money by becoming involved in this one new crime alone.

When Russian troops were sent into Chechnya in 1994 at the start of the First Chechen War, bin Laden, al Qaeda and other groups saw in this conflict the continuation of their holy war against the Russian infidels. Though predominantly a war for separatism at first, the Muslim Chechens still accepted assistance from these holy brethren. Since 1999, the Second Chechen War has seen a completely different picture in terms of combatants, tactics and purpose. Aided by many radical Islamists from Saudi Arabia, Jordan, Syria, Afghanistan and Iran, this new war has taken on a decidedly pan-Islamic purpose. For example, the recent metro bombing and aircraft attacks in Moscow - within a week of one another at the end of August 2004 - were claimed by a group which, under the title Islambouli Brigades of al Qaeda, was also behind the attempted assassination of Pakistan's newly designated prime minister, Shaukat Aziz, the previous month.

If, indeed, this new group of al Qaeda related extremists is controlling any faction of the Chechen militants, including the Black Widows, it foretells a war which will see many similar incidents taking the lives of more and more innocent civilians. As well, there has been a demonstrative shift in tactics by the Chechen fighters and their allies. Not seen to such a degree in the First Chechen War, suicide bombings have taken center stage as the most effective tactic in the campaign against anyone associated with their Russian enemies. The Chechen extremists, like their Arab counterparts, make little distinction

---

9 Throughout the book, "Russian" Organized Crime groups or OC groups, will be used to include all organized crime organizations from the former Soviet Union, including Central and Eastern Europe, Asia, and the Caucasus.

between combatants and non-combatants, old and young, men and women, and even children. The Chechens in the Nord-Ost siege rationalized their refusal to let the countless child-hostages go free: "Under Chechen law a child that is twelve years old is an adult." In response to pleas from the hostages that they were just everyday citizens and not the ones who had ever killed anyone in Chechnya, the terrorists argued that they had elected their president and were thus responsible for his acts. The Chechens did not seem to acknowledge the fact that they, too, were Russian citizens and part of the voting public for both the Russian Federation presidency, and Chechnya.

For all this – including more recent atrocities committed by the Chechens – the Russian perspective is that terrorism inside that country is more economically based than ideological. In the North Caucasus, the Russians do not see ideology as the real underpinning of the terrorist acts committed by the Chechens. Though the Russians are viewed internationally as harboring an horrendous ethnic bigotry against the Chechens, the facts prove that these people are in many ways guilty of exactly what the Russians accuse them of.

Sitting in a nondescript wing of a building on an already dark evening in November, deep in the bowels of Moscow and with no sign to indicate the entity or its inhabitants therein, I am surrounded by a number of Russia's top analysts for military and political threats to the country. Refusing to provide the name of the operation, other than to simply refer to it as an analytic center, these former career GRU Spetsnaz, military intel and FSB counter-intelligence officers have agreed to answer my questions about Beslan on condition of anonymity. This group is united in its belief that the Chechens themselves lack the ideological commitment or discipline to commit terrorist acts for purely religious reasons. Though committed Muslims, the people of that region are viewed as little more than "fertile soil" for other organizations such as al Qaeda to take advantage of. It is clear in the grim visages of these men that they have lived much of what they contend, having survived the horrors of at least one, and in some cases both, Chechen Wars. "Chechnya and its various tieps have connected with al Qaeda and other groups all around the world," says Volodya, a veteran of the wars in both Afghanistan and Chechnya. "Even the Secret Service of Turkey is supporting Chechnya, in addition to Jordan, Yemen, Qatar, Syria and Saudi Arabia." Mikhail, a former GRU military counter-intelligence officer and now FSB officer, adds, "The Chechens are not that ideologically motivated as a people, but these other countries are, and pay the Chechens to commit these types of acts."

That the Chechens would be "fertile soil" for international terrorism is in large part due to their own history, value system and culture. One Russian police psychologist, dispatched to Beslan to assist with the psychological suffering of the hostages' families and the many that were called to duty at the school, believes that it is difficult for anyone not familiar with this ethnic group to truly appreciate them. "Marina" is red haired and pretty, chatty and engaging, with soulful eyes. Her work has given her insights into much of what was experienced by both police and government forces. A noted hostage negotiator with half a dozen successful criminal-hostage negotiations to her credit, in addition to time in Chechnya, she draws heavily on her psychological expertise in attempting to put all of this in context for someone not living this Russian nightmare. She patiently explains that most people from other regions cannot possibly understand the minds of terrorists in the first place, and that those from the North Caucasus are far more inscrutable. She says that normal people have normal limitations on their thinking and most cannot go past these very "human" limits. But, people from the North Caucasus region, especially Chechens, "have a long history of working to overcome those human limits for things like torture, and dismembering infants and breastfeeding babies." I have personally seen captured video tape from the war proving that Chechen children are exposed to the torture and beheading of captives from a very early age, and are compelled to take part in celebrations of this horror such as dancing with the severed heads of their victims.

In this, the Chechens seem to validate the belief of one Spetsnaz general who told me that they were not human at all, but animals, vermin who – like rats – had to be completely wiped off the face of the earth. He explained that they were not a culture, as we understand the word to apply to groups of humans living according to human value systems, lifestyles or religious beliefs. Rather, they are a collection of vicious terrorists, committed merely to the torture and murder of every single human being not belonging to their group, like an al Qaeda organization whose members mate to have children for the sole purpose of rearing successive generations of the most vicious terrorists.

At first this talk appears to be the product of all wars' efforts to dehumanize the enemy throughout history. Necessary for any nation to ask its young men to go out and kill complete strangers with impunity, such efforts were even seen in America's own propaganda in World War II that dehumanized the Japanese and Germans both, depicting them variously as monkeys, bats and vampires. But after many years in Russia, and numerous trips to the North Caucasus spanning both Chechen Wars, I have come to recognize that for the Russians this is not merely the creation of a government as part of its war effort, as part of its drive to motivate its young people to serve in the military. The fear they feel for the Chechens is real, it is ages-old, and it is not without its reasons.

Yuri Rodin, a full colonel in an elite Spetsnaz unit, is a tall, hulking man with a friendly demeanor. Despite his ready smile, with his near 7-foot frame and chiseled face, he reminds one of the actor Richard Kiel, most known as the evil character "Jaws" in the old *Roger Moore* James Bond movies. Though he was part of the opening assault in the First Chechen War, the first assault in the Second Chechen War, and was with the assault teams at both the Nord-Ost Theater and Mineralniy Vodi hostage sieges, Col. Rodin himself lived for a number of years in Grozny. He speaks the Chechen dialect, and counts among his many friends a number of Chechens. Yet for all his compassion and objectivity, he, too, recognizes the inherent danger of these people, especially the mountain tribes. “Chechens are a people who don’t work and won’t work, even if given the opportunity,” he explains. “For them, the very best thing to do is to commit fraud and hurt people of other religions. They live for this *game*, as they see it.” He articulates their refusal to work as being a cultural behavior that goes back centuries: “Historically, they would rob, steal, kidnap and sell slaves for money rather than ever develop an economy. They can betray anyone at any time, no matter the friendship.” On the issue of friendship, Col. Rodin understands that even his Chechen “friends,” would turn on him in a moment if it brought them some advantage or financial reward. “The only answer to Chechnya is to drop bombs on the entire region. They are like a cancer. There is no dealing with them. As soon as countries like the U.S. and Great Britain accept that Chechnya is a cancer, President Putin will have the freedom he needs to deal with them like a cancer,” he laments. There is no anger in his voice, merely an exhausted resignation from too many years fighting there. This would not be the only time I would encounter this attitude from both military and government officials.

When asked if the general population of Russian civilians sees the solution to Chechnya the same way, in light of the unpopularity of the First Chechen War, Col. Rodin responded: “The Russian people want to see the war in Chechnya won, they want a final solution to this problem and realize there won’t be such a solution unless they are all killed. The problem with the first war under Yeltsin was that they weren’t seeing any result other than soldiers dying.” It is a sad and regrettable conclusion, but he reminds me that the American people have yet to acknowledge the true threat under which they, themselves, are living. And that it will be some time before Americans accept that their threat is the same as what the Russians have been facing for years. “It is all international Islamist based terrorism, “ he says. “And they are coming for both of our countries.”

Chapter Two

Chechen Terrorist Ascension

He, who comes to Russia with a sword,
shall die by the sword.
— Aleksandr Nevskiy (12th Century)

When Chechen acts of terrorism first began, the Russian government – like most others who have suffered its onslaught - was unprepared and looked merely toward peaceful resolutions. They had not yet developed an irreconcilable policy of non-negotiation. Hardly did they know at the time what acts of tolerance would yield for them later. In 1992 in Mineralniy Vodi, a Dagestani resort town and what would become a hospital center for Russia's troops during both Chechen wars, two armed hijackers seized a bus and held the passengers hostage. They demanded the release of two jailed associates, also Chechens. Ultimately this situation was resolved when the hijackers were allowed to flee to Chechnya. There, they were welcomed by the rebel leadership.

In May 1994, six terrorists armed with guns and grenades again took a bus, this time with 29 hostages including children, teachers and parents on board. Ultimately, they released all of the hostages and escaped into Chechnya in a helicopter, in exchange for an eight million dollar ransom paid by the Russian government. Once the hostages were freed, however, Russia's Alpha commandos went immediately to work. Within weeks, five of the six were captured and imprisoned, and the last killed in a shootout. Sultan-Said Idiyev, born in 1967, received a six-year prison sentence, the shortest of all of the hijackers.

Just two months later, in July 1994, four Chechens took a bus with 42 passengers, including children, teachers and parents, and demanded US$15 million in ransom. Having reached the limit of their tolerance for hijackings and escaped terrorists, the Russian government sent in the Alpha and Vympel counter-terror troops, who assaulted the vehicle. In the ensuing fight five hostages and one terrorist were killed. Fifteen people were wounded and the remaining hostage-takers imprisoned. The First Chechen War began two months later.

On June 14, 1995, half way into the First Chechen War, one of the worst terrorist-hostage situations Russia would ever face began. Two hundred fifty Chechen militants, led by Chechen commander Shamil Basayev, crossed the border and attacked a hospital in southern Russia. Buddenovsk was a city in the Stavropol region of Russia, with a community of approximately 10,000 Chechens. Three months earlier a commercial company called Irbis had rented the basement of the hospital. There they prepared heavy weapons including RPGs, .50 caliber (12.7 mm) DShK machine guns, explosives and ammunition. Terrorists reached the city in two KAMAZ trucks, an ambulance, and a police cruiser. While driving through the city, local police stopped and questioned them as to their purpose and destination. Dressed in military camouflage, the terrorists told the authorities that they were transporting the dead bodies of fallen soldiers from Chechnya. The police said to follow them, providing the terrorists exactly what they wanted. The officers led them to the police headquarters, where two hundred employees worked. At that time, on the day in question, the majority of the law enforcement officers were away, undergoing firearms qualifications training. The terrorists had been well aware of this. Their intel gathering effort in advance of the raid had paid off.

At some point during the trip to the police department the ambulance managed to sneak away. When the convoy arrived at police headquarters, the terrorists immediately attacked. Their purpose was to demoralize the town and its government officials, as well as secure additional weapons. Between 10 and 15 police officers died. Some managed to lock themselves in rooms inside the building. After helping themselves to weapons from the storage locker of the headquarters, the terrorists proceeded to the city's central hospital. On the way they shot citizens they passed, fomenting panic throughout the town. It was the terrorists' purpose to wound as many as possible, knowing they would all be delivered to the hospital.

The main building of the hospital had three floors. Once inside, the terrorists took approximately 2,500 hostages. Basayev demanded reporters be brought in, and when they arrived he told them he had 3,000 hostages. Though many of the raiders were from the local Chechen community, the terrorists also brought, as part of their raiding party, a professional and well-trained demolition squad comprised of Arab naval commandos. They also had a skilled sniper team which assumed advantageous positions around the hospital. Every other terrorist was equipped with a GP-25 grenade launcher affixed to his assault rifle. Armed with upwards of five .50 caliber machine guns, twenty 7.62 mm PKM machine guns, and RPG 7s and 18s (known as the "Fly") they were a formidable occupying force.

Brimming with confidence, the terrorists believed no one could attack them, fortified as they were in the hospital with thousands of hostages and hundreds of armed men. The Moscow division of Alpha was sent in with Alpha units from its other main base in Krasnodar. Vega - formerly Vympel, meaning "Banner" or "Pennant" – also arrived and joined the inner cordon of assault teams. Behind them was Vityaz, SOBR and other special units from MVD, such as *Vnnutreye Voiska,* known simply as VV. As a foreshadowing of Beslan, the terrorists had back-up teams spread throughout the city. Patrols of Special Forces tracked and located some of these teams outside the city limits in rural areas. Each was engaged and destroyed.

After three days of failed negotiations, assault operations started early on the morning of June 17. Up to that point, the terrorists had executed those males they deemed to constitute the greatest threat. Approximately ten men, who were firefighters, helicopter pilots and police, were summarily shot to death early in the siege. This, too, would be repeated years later at Beslan. When the order to assault came, even the brave men of Alpha and Vympel thought the notion of storming the building was ridiculous. To the commandos, assaulting an enormous building across open campus grounds with only 200 men against entrenched and fortified superior numbers of terrorists holding close to 3,000 hostages, seemed a suicide mission, and a homicide mission for the innocent victims. Still, they were up to the task and threw themselves into the fray with a courage rarely seen. It took half of a day for the assault teams just to reach the building across open ground, fighting their way inch by inch through withering fire from the barricaded terrorists. Once at the building they secured the first floor, all the while under heavy machine gun and RPG fire. Until then, the terrorists had been extremely confident in going up against Alpha and Vympel in the long and medium range battle their plan had envisioned. However, the terrorists' confidence faded quickly when confronted with the prospect of having to engage these elite commandos in close quarters battle, where Spetsnaz excelled. It was the trademark of Alpha and Vympel to close and kill, and this is just what they sought to do.

As night came on, the assault teams were inexplicably ordered to pull back, abandoning the hospital to the terrorists. Before this assault, Basayev had summarily rejected any government efforts at negotiations. When the troops were pulled back, the terrorists' will and confidence had been broken and Basayev was then ready to enter meaningful negotiations. During the assault three men from the assault teams were killed, and 24 wounded. The Russian Army unit providing outer security and support lost two men, a mechanic and driver of a supply truck, and his superior. The terrorists had previously suffered 10 killed in the battle at the police department alone.

During the assault on the hospital another 58 had been killed. In addition, by this time they had also lost their support teams throughout the city. Recognizing the use of such teams to be standard for the Chechens, government forces had tracked and killed them all.

Government officials – many of whom were coming up for re-election shortly – insisted that no further efforts be made to take the hospital by force. A negotiated agreement was reached with Basayev for safe passage back to Chechnya, along with buses equipped with refrigerators for the bodies of the dead terrorists. Certain of the invested government officials agreed to accompany them into Chechnya, conscious of the boost such behavior would give them at the polls. With so many dignitaries among the terrorists, Alpha and Vympel were refused permission to attack them en route to Chechnya. When the siege was over, 33 hostages had been killed with another 145 wounded. The government had waited three days before attacking, after repeated assurances that it would not do so. This would be one of the last incidents in which Chechen rebels would be successful in exporting their battle into neighboring areas and then escaping.

No more than six months later, on January 9, 1996 at 4:00 o'clock in the morning, a terrorist team of between 300 and 350 Chechens and Ingush, led by Salman Raduyev, attacked the Kizlyar Air Force Base in Dagestan, destroying four helicopters. As part of the assault they seized the weapons depot, taking many automatic rifles, sniper rifles, handguns and explosives. From there they proceeded to the Kizlyar city hospital. Following the same blueprint used in Buddenovsk the previous year, they shot civilians along the way. Once at the hospital they seized it, taking many hostages and barricading themselves inside. Raduyev did negotiate with a member of the local government, ultimately entering an agreement to be provided safe passage into Chechnya, along with buses for both the terrorists and hostages. However, Alpha and members of the GRU's elite 22nd Spetsnaz Brigade were ordered to attack the convoy before it reached Chechnya. The government was not going to allow a repeat of Buddenovsk.

Unexpectedly, however, the buses changed route and entered the village of Pervomaiskoye. There the terrorists seized a military garrison, capturing the entire Novosibirsk division of OMON, some 30 supposedly elite Special Forces soldiers. While there, other terrorist teams already inside the town joined them. Refusing to go quietly on to Chechnya, the terrorists began preparing breastworks in anticipation of a major battle with government troops. They did allow the citizens of the village to leave; however, they retained the hostages they had taken from Kizlyar and the OMON troopers. Using them as laborers, they continued to fortify their position and prepare for the battle that was sure to come.

Large numbers of Alpha, SOBR, Vityaz, the Spetsnaz from the GRU 22nd Brigade, even the Russian Airborne and army mountain infantry companies, were called in and surrounded the village. On January 15, the government troops began to attack the village, for hours simply shelling it with artillery. Under cover of this barrage, the 22nd Spetsnaz Brigade conducted a successful feint, seeming to launch a major assault on one side of the village, while Alpha and the others hit the far side. At the end of the day all forces were ordered to withdraw. This included those teams that had successfully entered the village and secured positions. By this time, most of the terrorists had been killed. Late at night on the 17th of January, Raduyev and a small group of the remaining terrorists managed to break through the 22nd Brigade's sector of the security cordon ringing the town, and escaped into Chechnya. Raduyev had lost 250 of his men. During the same period only 29 government troops died: 11 from the mountain infantry group, 7 from the 22nd Spetsnaz Brigade, 2 from Alpha, and 9 from the other units. Much of the town had been destroyed, and Russia had served notice on the Chechens and their allies that terrorism would be met with cold resolve. The First Chechen War would come to a close just three months later, and despite the government's victory, the sieges at Buddenovsk, Pervomaikskoye and Kizlyar served as significant factors in Russia's decision to end the war.

Between the two conflicts - officially from August 1996 to September 1999 - Chechnya deteriorated into a criminal and terrorist haven. Despite almost daily instances of kidnapping, torture, rape and murder within the Chechan borders, the Russian government did its best to ignore the disintegration of the region. Then on March 27, 1999 – while Chechnya was supposedly still at peace with the rest of Russia – a passenger bus traveling from Rostov to Temryuk in the North Caucasus was taken when it entered a police checkpoint in Krasnodar. A passenger, Konstantin Romanov, took the bus and the other passengers hostage, using a cut down rifle and a grenade. Romanov was a career criminal with a history as a contract murderer. In short order the Krasnodar division of Alpha attacked the bus, killing Romanov. No passengers were injured.

Shortly thereafter, between August and September of 1999, three apartment buildings were blown up in Moscow by the increasingly Islamist-extremist Chechens, killing more than 300 people. Not satisfied with the deaths of hundreds of innocent civilians, the Chechens invaded neighboring Dagestan that same month. Even in the face of such bold aggression and terrorism, it still took three months for Russian troops to re-invade Chechnya, which marked the start of the Second Chechen War.

The re-commencement of military action did little to put an end to the terrorism; it merely provided the Chechens with a rationalization to continue the rampage. Three months into this second conflict, on March 12, 2000, Vympel received information that Raduyev and his personal bodyguard of 80 men would be in Novogroznyenskoye village. Still on the loose since his failed raid on Kizlyar and Pervomaiskoye, Raduyev had passed through numerous military cordons dressed as a woman, and managed to enter the village. At 5:00 a.m. one assault team, having determined his location in a house, attacked and captured him, taking advantage of his own team's lapse of security during prayer time. The surrounding houses contained many of Raduyev's heavily armed bodyguards. With no shots fired at all, the Vympel team managed to execute this daring capture in merely 20 seconds.

After a year of armed conflict with Russian forces inside Chechnya, the rebel leaders began making every effort to expand this new war outside their borders through acts of terrorism. In March 2001, 21 people were killed when a bomb was detonated in the central market of the city of Mineralniy Vodi, Dagestan. The Chechen leaders had clearly learned from their experiences in the First Chechen War.

July 2001 saw one of the most involved and successful Special Forces counter-terror operations since the first war. At 6:45 a.m. on July 31, 2001, a Chechen gunman seized a bus full of civilians traveling from Nevinomysk to Stavropol in Dagestan, approximately 900 miles south of Moscow. The hijacker, Sultan Said Idiyev, by then 34 years old and a convicted felon, took 36 passengers hostage near the Chechen border with one and a half kilograms of TNT in a bomb strapped to his body, one F1 heavy hand grenade and one AK assault rifle. He had been involved in the May 1994 hijacking in the same area. After serving his six-year prison term for that crime, he had been freed in April 2000. On July 29, 2001, two days before taking the bus that would gain him notoriety, he and his brother, Said-Hussein Idiyev, had killed the driver of a commercial truck and attacked a roadside police post when they were flagged down by officers. Though the 34-year-old Sultan Idiyev escaped, his brother was captured.

Two days later, on the 31st, under the alias "Aslan," Sultan Idiyev commandeered another bus early in the morning and forced the driver to proceed, once again, to Mineralniy Vodi, about 60 miles away. At 8:30 a.m., as the bus approached the Mineralniy Vodi police station on the outer boundary of the city, the police stopped it. The hijacker sent one hostage out to deliver his demands. He said that he had three dozen hostages and the police were not to stop him, or he would blow the bus up. The hostage who was sent out, 26-year-old Viktor Zhukov, apparently spent too much time talking with police and the terrorist became suspicious that he was conspiring with police to attack him. When Zhukov returned to the bus, he was summarily shot.

From there police allowed the bus to proceed, and at 9:30 that morning it stopped within 600 meters of the Mineralniy Vodi airport. Aslan, really Idiyev, had positioned the bus atop an overpass in the middle of a cloverleaf highway intersection, which allowed him a panoramic view of all approaches. At this point he communicated his first substantive demands to government negotiators: the release of the five Chechens who had been held in prison since they all hijacked the bus together back in May 1994. As he had received the lightest prison sentence, the rest were all still languishing behind bars. He also wanted a police radio and the release of his brother, who was arrested two days earlier. He agreed to release five hostages in exchange for the radio. But when he turned the radio on, he learned through news media reports that Alpha had been dispatched to the scene of his barricade. At this point, the head of FSB for the Stavropol region, General Lieutenant P. Kondratov, arrived and took over negotiations with Idiyev.

At 5:00 in the afternoon, the FSB brought two of the demanded interned men to the scene: his brother and one of his comrades from the 1994 hijacking. Three others were held in Yakutia, in the far eastern part of Russia, and could not possibly have been delivered in the time allotted. The last hijacker had previously died of tuberculosis, a common plight in Russian prisons. One of the imprisoned hijackers made an unsuccessful attempt to persuade Idiyev to give himself up and not harm any more hostages. Kondratov offered to substitute a group of the hostages in the bus for Idiyev's brother and the other hijacker. Idiyev refused, saying a trade would be made after all of the Chechens had arrived. At this point he made his second significant demand: a helicopter, radios, a large sum of money, six machine guns, ammunition, and camouflage uniforms.

Though Kondratov had initiated negotiations remotely, he persuaded Idiyev to let him onto the bus for further discussions. This gave the

FSB leader the ability to determine if reports of a second hijacker were true, and assess the tactical situation and the condition of the hostages. While meeting the negotiator on the bus, Idiyev engaged in a ruse, holding a grenade in a water glass, indicating that if he were shot the glass would be broken, detonating the grenade. When Kondratov brought this information out with him, Alpha quickly obtained an identical glass and determined that there was no way the terrorist had a live grenade inside the glass. Just as significant, Kondratov had been able to establish that there were no other terrorists. Early reports had indicated the possible presence of a second hijacker; however, due to the season and unbearable heat inside, all other passengers had been stripped down to essential clothing only, rendering it impossible for anyone else to be hiding a weapon. With all of this information at their disposal, the members of Alpha believed they could launch a successful assault. The number of potential victims was now smaller, as seven other hostages, including all the children on board, had also been released.

The entire airport was sealed off, and fire trucks and ambulances were brought on scene. In the hours of the standoff, the temperature inside the bus had passed 100 degrees Fahrenheit, and passengers were seen peering around the curtains, which had been pulled shut against the sun's glare. Many of the windows had been broken to allow ventilation. The passengers' suffering compelled the hijacker to allow a female doctor, Margarita Karishnina, to be brought onto the bus to treat them.

Then at approximately 7:30 p.m. Idiyev refused to negotiate any further, and said no more hostages would be released. Throughout the day he had fired his weapon numerous times into the air – or the bus ceiling – to demonstrate his resolve and growing impatience. Toward the end of the day his demands began to change, signaling to the Russian commandos an increasing instability in the hijacker. Then in the early evening, at 7:45, more than 12 hours into the hostage siege, Alpha stormed the bus in what was described by many as a lightning raid. Using concussion grenades to distract him, two snipers positioned under KAMAZ trucks 200 meters to the front of the bus shot the terrorist in the left leg as he went down the steps with a grenade in one hand and an assault rifle in the other to investigate the noise. Simultaneously, four teams of commandos – positioned forward of the bus - assaulted from the front, surrounding it and entering through the door and windows on both sides. Idiyev fell, wounded and in shock. At this point two other snipers, some 500 meters to the bus's 2:00 o'clock position, each shot him one time in the chest, killing him. Contrary to news media reports, the grenade never detonated, no hostages were killed, and only a few were injured by flying glass. The entire assault had taken a mere 15 seconds. The Alpha commandos chalked up another success; though, it would not be the last time they would fall victim to an unsympathetic news media that reported that Idiyev had been shot in the thigh only, detonating his own grenade when he fell.

The Chechens wasted no time in exacting revenge for not only the death of Idiyev, but the return to prison of the two other hijackers. On Friday evening, August 24, 2001, they attacked a Russian military base, burning down the commandant's headquarters, killing 20 and wounding another 40. Just hours after the base assault, the Chechens attacked a Russian troop column in the Vedeno region, killing another 15. When Russian commanders sent a reserve column to Vedeno for support, they, too, were attacked, at the mountain village of Tsa-Vedeno, resulting in another 18 Russian soldiers dead and 20 more wounded. On Saturday, August 25, 2001, within 24 hours of these attacks, and with the Chechens bragging they had killed more than 50 Russian soldiers while losing only four of their own, a bomb exploded in the marketplace of the Chechen city of Gudermes, the second largest town in the republic. Three more people were killed and 11 injured. This time the victims were Chechen civilians. As would be the case at Beslan, the target for this explosion was close to the city's main police barracks; leaving experts to conclude a clear point was being made with the selection of the terror sites.

Though the Chechens have proven themselves capable and tenacious fighters, their insistence on attacking innocents has begun to erode their international support. One of the most notorious and tragic events, which would have a direct connection to both the tactics of the terrorists in the Beslan siege, and their decision to attack a school, was the Nord-Ost Theater incident. I had been engaged in a training program with the MVD's Vityaz Spetsnaz Anti-Terror Unit on the Balashikha Army Base approximately 50 km east of Moscow the week prior. Vityaz, known as *Krapovoi Bereti,* or the Blood Red Berets, was one of the units tasked with responding to this crisis, and through Archangel Director Igor Livits, himself a Spetsnaz veteran, our group was in regular contact with them throughout.

The spectacular musical, and first ever all-Russian theater production of Nord-Ost had opened at the theater of the same name on October 13, 2002. A tall, modern building, it sits on Dubrovka Street, a wide and open tree lined boulevard in north Moscow. Playing to a packed house, and enjoying overwhelming critical acclaim, its fame continued in the days following its debut. Then at 9:05 p.m. on Wednesday, October 23, 2002, at the beginning of the second act, a masked man dressed in camouflage stormed onto the stage, firing an AK 47 assault rifle into the air. More Chechen terrorists, with bombs and automatic weapons, quickly appeared and took more than 800 theatergoers, dancers, actors and production personnel, including many children, hostage. The performers were made to sit with the audience. At first, many in the audience thought it was part of the show. Symbolically, they had waited until the scene in which actors, dressed in World War I Russian Air Force uniforms, were dancing. Female terrorists, seated in the audience throughout the performance, quickly donned black Muslim robes and veils, and strapped suicide belts about their waists.

The terrorists had arrived in three SUV type vehicles which were left running outside, perhaps as a fallback in the event their initial takeover proved unsuccessful. Strangely, no one who saw the driverless vehicles, idling just outside the front doors, seemed to think this suspicious. The use of several large vehicles for delivery would be repeated at Beslan.

The entire theater was quickly rigged with explosives, including one major device in the center of the main seating area of the auditorium, and another in the balcony. An additional 20 smaller bombs were spread throughout the theater, in addition to 25 suicide bombs strapped to the females. The Chechens had brought with them an additional 100 hand grenades. The women, part of the Black Widows and Fiancées of Allah, wore bomb belts, each containing 3 to 5 kilograms (6.6 to 11 pounds) of explosives, wrapped with metal nuts, bolts and ball bearings. The women were constantly in the theater with the hostages, working in shifts, a schedule of terrorist control they also used at Beslan. The women held the detonators, literally their own lives and those of the hostages around them, in their hands.

The Chechen leader was 25-year-old Mozar Barayev, though Russian intelligence determined his original name to have been Barsayev. It was speculated that he had dropped the single "s" from his surname in order to create the impression there was some connection between him and the famed Chechen rebel leader Arbe Barayev. He demanded that Russia completely withdraw from Chechnya or all the hostages would die. He addressed the captives, telling them that Russia had just three days to pull out of Chechnya, and that if troops tried to storm the building it would be blown up. He also encouraged the hostages to use their cell phones to call police and loved ones, informing them of their dire situation and the steps necessary for the government to take in order for them to live.

Throughout the 58-hour ordeal the Chechens would periodically shoot their weapons into the theater ceiling, and scream across the auditorium to each other rather than utilize any type of radio, fearing Spetsnaz might tap into a communications system. This only had the effect of further terrifying the already inconsolable and panic stricken hostages. Prior to taking the theater, the terrorist group had prepared a videotaped explanation. "Every nation has the right to decide their own fate. Russia has taken this right away from Chechnya. We have long waited for the world to notice that the innocent are dying in Chechnya. That women, children and the weak are being killed."

Barayev was the last to speak. Eyes downcast throughout his speech, he said: "Each of us is ready to give over life for Allah, and the freedom of Chechnya. I swear by Allah we desire death more than you desire life." The hostages were told: "We have come here to die, and you are going to die with us." This haunting refrain would be repeated to the children of Beslan.

Winter comes early in Russia. By 10:00 o'clock that black, wet and frigid October night police and the Moscow contingents of several Special Forces units surrounded the theater. Alpha, Vympel, SOBR and the famed Vityaz Anti-Terror group of the Interior Ministry had all responded to the call. Historically, Alpha and Vityaz had worked together, trained together, and had launched several successful joint operations. Vympel, with its focus on its own terrorist assault operations, was the newcomer to Russia's battle against terror in its own capital. The hostages could not have been in better hands. Within an hour after their arrival at 11:00 p.m., the elite Spetsnaz forces had sealed off the entire area, leaving outer perimeter security to Vityaz and SOBR, in addition to the lesser trained police and other government units. Russian Spetsnaz career officer, Major Konstantin Komarov, was an eight year veteran of the GRU's 12th Spetsnaz Brigade and a seven year commander with the MVD's SOBR Special Forces Rapid Reaction Team. Possessing a Ph.D. in psychology, he had been called in to develop psychological profiles of all of the terrorists, particularly the women, to aid in the assault groups' plans.

The Spetsnaz were able to learn that the women were wearing black *djellabas*, face veils and headscarves. This was certainly not the cultural dress of Chechen women. All of the terrorists were wearing cravats with Arabic sayings scrawled across their foreheads. The terrorists had also hung a large Arabic flag in the theater. Notably, Chechens do not even speak Arabic, and it was unlikely that any single one of them could have read the Arabic expressions of hatred with which they had adorned themselves and the theater. This did not bode well for a peaceful resolution. All of this, together with the Palestinian style suicide belts, demonstrated the Arabization of the Chechen cause, and that this group of terrorists was well under the influence of Arab terrorist doctrine.

But, as would be seen at Beslan, appearances could not be allowed to incite fear. According to one SOBR colonel, the women were ultimately found to have dyed their hair blonde and were wearing blue jeans under their dresses, signs they hoped to escape the holocaust that would eventually take their lives. While this was one expert's opinion, and must be accorded commensurate consideration, it is just as likely that they had dyed their hair blonde and wore jeans in order to enter the theater with the other members of the audience, taking their seats without arousing suspicion. Police harassment of Chechens, or anyone who appears to hail from the North Caucasus, is a constant occurrence in Moscow.

Later that morning, Barayev, in communication with outside forces, threatened to begin killing groups of hostages within 48 hours if his earlier demands were not met. At this point, the negotiators attempted to persuade Barayev to release the children. He refused. Rather, he distributed cell phones to the child hostages, ordering them to call their parents and tell them not to let the government troops storm the building. They were told to say that if the parents organized televised, public demonstrations against the war in Chechnya, the kids would be released. The family members of the children quickly did so, but none of the government controlled TV stations would air them. Accordingly, Barayev reneged on his agreement and the children remained.

For all this, it is surprising that the male terrorists raped no women, and up to the time of the assault no hostage executions were carried out. Still, one colonel with MChS, the Russian federal emergency services department, in full uniform and attending the play, was killed outright. Another girl was reported to have taken some kind of drug due to the stress of the situation. It caused her to behave uncontrollably and she, too, was shot. On the second day two girls jumped from a second story window. One broke her leg on landing. A soldier came to help and he was shot and wounded, as was the other girl who had not been injured in the fall.

As dawn came on that Thursday – the first morning of the siege – Alpha, Vympel and Vityaz commandos were already practicing storming the Nord-Ost Theater at an identical building nearby. No one expected a peaceful outcome to this drama. The terrorists were constantly fearful they would be attacked through the roof of the theater and focused much of their attention in that direction. Conditions inside continued to deteriorate and the hostages were forced to use the orchestra pit as a communal toilet.

At 11:45 p.m., on Friday, October 25, only seven hours remained until Barayev was to begin executing hostages. He had been promised that Russian Army General Kazantsev, the highest profile commander in the Chechen War, was coming to negotiate with him. Barayev said that if Kazantsev did not appear, he would begin "cutting the heads off" the hostages and "throwing them outside." In reality, the officials in charge of the situation had never even contacted Kazantsev. At 5:00 in the morning, Saturday, October 26, the tasked Special Forces units flooded the theater with what Western analysts have surmised to have been a fentanyl-enhanced gas. The Russians have never said what it was.

The male terrorists, including the leaders, had positioned themselves in the corridors leading to the auditorium, rendering it impossible for them to give the order to the women to detonate their belt bombs;

an act they were trained not to undertake absent an express order. As the gas poured in, pandemonium broke out in the theater. Hostages began screaming. The male terrorists put on gas masks and took up position for the battle that was to ensue in the hallways outside. The females had not been given masks, and they quickly succumbed to the gas. Alpha and Vympel waited 30 full minutes from the delivery of the gas to assault the building. Vityaz and SOBR were held in reserve. The assault began at 5:30 a.m. Thirty minutes later the battle was over and all of the terrorists were dead. The females, seemingly unconscious in their seats, each received a bullet to the head.

The Russian Special Forces would, ridiculously, come under fire from an unrealistic and Chechen-sympathizing international press for their shooting of the female terrorists. In reality, this was a tactic to be criticized only for its reliance on a single round, rather than putting two bullets in the head of each of the terrorists, ensuring their immediate deaths. Not everyone had succumbed to the gas, and many of the hostages were found stumbling about. The female terrorists were found lying back in their seats, gripping the handles of their belt bombs and the detonators of the larger devices. They could just as easily have been feigning sleep, awaiting the moment when government forces entered the theater before detonating all of the bombs, substantially increasing the body count. In such circumstances, there can be no other solution than immediately ensuring the terrorists are denied the ability to throw the switches on their detonators.

That the storming of this building and the saving of these hostages would not go down in history as the single greatest hostage rescue in the world was not the fault of the Russian Special Forces. The government officials calling the shots had failed entirely to alert area hospitals that an assault of the building was to take place, or to inform doctors that gas was to be used. Once confronted with scores of affected gas victims, the government still refused to tell physicians what substance had been used, or that gas had been used at all. Moreover, no ambulances were in place and the entire area had been surrounded by enormous dump trucks, filled with sand, to absorb the blast in the event the terrorists had blown the entire building up. The drivers of the trucks were long since gone, and no one had the keys. When word finally reached emergency services, the sand trucks and crowds prevented the ambulances from approaching the building. Many hostages, suffering the effects of the gas, died in city buses, driving for hours while ignorant bus drivers sought hospitals they were unfamiliar with. Still, others died when soldiers attempted to drag them outside to fresh air, pulling them along by their arms, allowing their heads to tilt back and suffocating them.

Problems aside, the soldiers of Russia's Special Forces still managed to save more than 600 of the 800-plus hostages, losing only 129, including many children. In the process they dispatched every single one of the 42 terrorists. It is a reminder of the grim reality of such situations to think that not a single one of those 129 victims would have died, if only the government had cared enough to prepare for the aftermath of the assault. Sadder still is the recognition that Nord-Ost was a show with numerous child performers. The terrorists knew this, planned the assault, and refused to release the children. Who could not have seen this as a harbinger of things to come at Beslan?

But these would prove not to be the only mistakes repeated at Beslan. One MVD Spetsnaz officer on scene at Nord-Ost contends that a main mistake in Russia's recent experiences in dealing with terrorist-hostage situations is a division between government units. He explains that he and his team had been deployed to the theater. At that siege the FSB, through its "arms" Alpha and Vympel, had unilaterally planned the assault and the use of gas. Being in the loop, the Alpha and Vympel commandos entered the theater with gas masks. The other units, to which the overall plan had not been fully disclosed, entered behind them – with no gas masks. Upon entering the building to neutralize terrorists and begin assisting the hostages, twelve MVD operators were stricken. This very failure to coordinate between government units was a factor in the chaos that would ultimately engulf Beslan.

In December 2003, a little more than one year later, a female suicide bomber killed five people near Red Square. Two months after that, in February 2004, a bomb was detonated inside a Moscow subway car during morning *chas peak*, or rush hour, taking the lives of at least 39 people. On May 9, 2004, Chechen President Akhmad-hadji Kadyrov, along with a number of other top Chechen and Russian officials, was killed when a bomb exploded under their box at Grozny's *Dinamo* Stadium, while they were viewing World War II Victory Day celebrations. Also in this assault, Russia's top commander in Chechnya, General Valeriy Baranov, was severely wounded. The bomb had been planted some nine months before during construction. The election of a new Kremlin-backed leader to take Kadyrov's place in Chechnya, the weekend prior to the Beslan siege, is believed by Russian officials to have been a major motivation for that attack.

Chechen leader Shamil Basayev claimed credit for the killing, which took place just two months after Putin was reaffirmed for another term as president. He posted a message on the Chechen website *Kavkaz Tsentr*, or Kavkaz Center, in which he called the murders "Operation *Bekham*" or "Retribution," and warned that Putin and his Prime Minister Mikhail Fradkov would soon meet a similar end. From there the intervals between terrorist attacks in Russia began to shorten.

On the 21st and 22nd of June 2004, some 950 Chechen militants and Ingush Wahhabis, led by a bodyguard of Chechen leader Shamil Basayev and an Ingusheti turncoat police officer, expanded the Chechen field of operations. They simultaneously attacked four towns in Ingushetia, killing 98 people, including 60 law enforcement agents and other government and military officials. Among these were the acting Interior Minister Abukar Kostoyev; acting police chief of Ingushetia, Abubakar Kostoev; the deputy police chief, Ziaudin Kotiev; as well as prosecutors of the Nazran District and the capital Nazran. Many of the targeted officials were regional heads of the FSB, MVD, and other Russian agencies. Working from well-developed intelligence, the terrorists even ambushed a number of them in their homes, killing them and their families. As part of these attacks on the towns of Nazran, Magaz, Karaboula and Malgobek, three large government and military facilities were assaulted. One was an FSB base for Border Guards units. The Chechens looted military arms depots, rearming themselves for future operations, including those against children. In these attacks, the Chechen assailants had bribed their way past the myriad military checkpoints. Inexplicably, by some accounts, federal security forces took 10 hours to come to the aid of local forces that were under siege. Only six Chechens were killed in the raids, though 30 were ultimately arrested. It is a sad irony that terrorists would later cross military checkpoints into North Ossetia utilizing identical tactics of bribing border guards, on their way to Beslan. The leaders of the raids in Ingushetia turned out to be some of the same leaders who took the Beslan School.

Then, during a single week in July 2004, two bus stops were bombed in the city of Voronezh, 600 km south of Moscow, killing three people. In the website *chechenpress.com*, on July 27, Chechen guerilla commander Aslan Maskhadov praised all of the assaults - a continuation of Operation Retribution - as proof of the commitment and resolve of his troops. Maskhadov had been the elected leader of the Chechen Republic after Russian troops withdrew in 1996. However, he and his entire administration had been forced to flee into the mountains around Grozny, the capital, in 1999 when Russian troops re-entered that city. Despite repeated requests to meet and negotiate with Maskhadov to end the Chechen conflict, Putin has consistently refused, labeling Maskhadov a terrorist and asserting that he lost the legitimacy of his position when he launched terrorist attacks around Russia in 1999. The United States put him on its international terrorist blacklist in August of 2003. Maskhadov ultimately took a major role in the operation to kill children in Beslan.[10]

---

[10] The 53 year-old Maskhadov would ultimately be killed by Russian forces on March 8, 2005 when cornered in a bunker in the town of Tolstoy-Yurt.

It is generally believed that the Beslan School attack was in part incited by, and in part the progression of, the series of attacks that began with the bombing death of Kadyrov. Moreover, the Beslan School assault was also the culmination of eight days of terror, which saw a total of six separate assaults. Two weeks before the Beslan assault, some 150 Chechen guerillas took over two districts of the Chechen capital, Grozny. At least 120 people were killed. Then on August 24, 2004, just days before the presidential election in Chechnya for Kadyrov's replacement, a bomb was detonated at a Moscow bus stop killing four. Less than three hours later, two female suicide bombers detonated bombs on two separate passenger jets within three minutes of each other after taking off from Moscow's Domodedovo Airport, downing the planes and killing 90. At both crash sites, hundreds of kilometers from each other, traces of the explosive Hexogen, also known as RDX, were found. Then on August 31 a woman blew herself and nine others up, injuring an additional 37, outside Moscow's Rizhskaya Metro station near the Ostankino Television tower in north-central Moscow. The al Qaeda related group, the Islambouli Brigades, took credit for these attacks, the first five coming in the run-up to the presidential election in Chechnya and the last just two days after the 29 August victory of the Moscow supported candidate, Alu Alkanov.

As cited by the intrepid Roman Kupchinsky in the September 16, 2004 edition of the internet *Radio Free Europe/Radio Liberty*[11], "The attacks and the Islambouli Brigades' messages immediately led many to conclude that if the authenticity of the group's claimed connections and deeds panned out, it could only serve as evidence to prove an argument that Russia has been making for years. 'If one of the terrorist organizations has claimed responsibility for this and it is linked to al-Qaeda, that is a fact that confirms the link between certain forces operating on the territory of Chechnya and international terrorism,'" according to President Putin.

---

[11] Vol. 4, No. 17

What cannot be discounted in recognizing the likelihood of al Qaeda involvement with and support of the Chechens is the fact that on September 24, 2001, less than two weeks after the U.S. was attacked, a resident of the city of Argun, Chechnya was captured during a special operations raid. At the time he was found to possess written plans for airplane strikes on the World Trade Center towers in New York. The plan called for the seizing of the very commercial aircraft that had been used. The word *jihad* had been written on the cover of the plans.

By only the 3rd day of September more than 500 people had been killed by terrorist assaults in 2004, compared to 369 in 2002 and 2003 combined. However, in 2003 more than 600 had been wounded in such attacks. According to the Rosbalt News Agency, the Russian Interior Ministry's Yuri Demidov stated, "This is due to the ongoing subversive and terrorist activity of rebel groups, who gave up the struggle for an independent Chechnya a long time ago. Now they are just carrying out the plans of international terrorists." Indeed, it appears that in addition to the invasion of Dagestan in 1999 and increasing forays into neighboring Ingushetia, the purpose of Beslan was to spread the Islamist war and influence across the Caucasus, and to take advantage of already existing tension between Georgia and Russia, over the former's South Ossetian breakaway region, which are now in an uneasy peace, but with military forces on both sides.

Chapter Three

Special Forces Counter-Terror Units of Russia

We sleep safe in our beds because rough men
stand ready in the night to visit violence
on those who would do us harm.

George Orwell

Just who were these men that Russia called on time and again to protect her citizens from the rabid viciousness of Chechen terrorism? Before one can understand the chess match that took place between these elite Russian forces and their terrorist enemies at the Beslan Middle School, some background on their creation, history, training, experience, mental and physical preparation, and combat capabilities is essential.

Special operations theory in the Russian military goes all the way back to Denis Davidov, hero of Russia's war with Napoleon in 1812, who in 1822 wrote a thesis entitled, *Theory of Guerilla Warfare in Practice*. From there, special operations theory and practice continued to develop, seeing significant inroads in both army and navy units in World War II, or the Great Patriotic War, as it is known to Russians. Today, and throughout the Soviet era, the composition and infrastructure of Russia's special units are unique. Unlike in the U.S. and most other Western countries, Russia's Special Forces, or literally its "Special Purpose Forces" (*Voiska Spetsialnogo Naznacheniya*, or *Spetsnaz* as earlier provided) are not found exclusively in the Army or Navy, but throughout all of that country's "force" ministries. In the actual military – Army and Navy – many of these units fall under the command and control of the General Staff's Main Intelligence Directorate. The GRU, or *Glavnoye Rasvedivatelnoe Upravleniye*, is a military version of the KGB, and exists and operates outside the command structure of the Air Force, Navy and Army. In the Army these take the form of such units as: the GRU's 2nd Spetsnaz Brigade in Pskov, the former Leningrad Military Region; the 14th Brigade in Ussurisk in the Far East Military Region; the 16th out of the Moscow military region of Chuchkova; the 22nd Brigade based in the Rostov region of the North Caucasus; the 24th in the small village of Kyahta near Ulan Ude in Siberia; and the 67th Spetsnaz Brigade, based in Berdsk in the Siberia Military Region. Recently, the 45th VDV, or Airborne Division, has been redesignated a Spetsnaz Brigade. Standing for *Vozduzhniy Desantniy Voiska*, or "troops of the airborne," they are the descendants of the world's first and most sophisticated air delivery forces ever seen. On the Navy side, the extremely selective *Delfin* (Dolphin) and *Kasatka* (Orca in Russian) units, some based on the Kolskiy Peninsula, are under FSB control. The Navy also maintains counter-SEAL type units called PDSS. Among these various units are the heretofore unknown naval commandos of the *Sputnik* and *Saturn* groups.

But this is not all. Being a nation which has traditionally been unable to depend completely on the trustworthiness of any branch of the government, and one in which the military cannot be expected to follow the orders of the civilian leadership, counter-force Spetsnaz units abound. These are under the jurisdiction of the KGB (now FSB), MVD, even the Federal Agency for Government Communications and Information, as well as the Ministry of Emergency Situations (MChS).

While the MVD has the greatest number of Spetsnaz units – now more than 120 – the FSB remains the most powerful arm of the government, particularly since the ascension of former KGB career officer, Vladimir Putin. Now called the Federal Security Service, it is divided into a number of directorates, exactly as the KGB was structured before it. Of those, the Investigations Directorate is viewed as the most important, with jurisdiction over the investigation and prosecution of all criminal cases. Under the FSB's imprimatur for protecting the country from both external and internal threats, these include all terrorist cases. This places the investigation of such terrorist assaults as the two downed passenger jets, bus bombing and subway bombing that took place in the two weeks prior to Beslan, and even the Moscow apartment bombings of 1999, squarely under its authority. The structure of this one directorate is virtually identical to that of the entire Federal Security Service as a whole, each constituted of counterintelligence, counterterrorism, and military intelligence sub-divisions, in addition to others.

This is not to say that the former KGB has been without its travails, nor did it simply affect a name change after the collapse of the Soviet Union in late 1991, in the faint hope of leaving behind its bloodthirsty reputation. For a period of years after the dissolution of the Soviet Union, it went through a succession of evolutionary changes. During former Russian President Yeltsin's term, for instance, he disbanded the Investigations Directorate entirely, including its use of the infamous Lefortovo Prison, and placed it all under the umbrella of the more civilized Interior Ministry. Throughout these years the KGB also underwent a series of name changes. In the 1990s it was known as the FSK, for *Federalnaya Sluzhba Konterrazvedkii*, or Federal Counter-intelligence Service. It would not land on the current FSB moniker until April 12, 1995. At another point, it was split into two groups, along the lines of United States' FBI and CIA. Today, the FSB performs the function of the FBI, and is responsible for investigating federal crime and handling counter-intelligence domestically. Of late, the FSB has even been referred to in Russia as their "FBI." The foreign intelligence branch is called the SVR, for *Sluzhba Vneshney Razvedkiy* or External Intelligence Service. So named on December 18, 1991, it is akin to the CIA, and is responsible for running Russia's intelligence operations around the world.

In 1996 I led a group of U.S. law enforcement officers and criminal justice students on a trip to study at the police academies of Moscow and St. Petersburg. A friend and colleague, Anatoli Kurkov – former head of the KGB for the entire St. Petersburg *oblast* or region – arranged a tour of the intelligence service's headquarters, the famed Lubyanka located right next to Russia's largest toy store, *Detskii Mir* or Children's World. While inside the notorious headquarters, we were chaperoned by a full colonel, who patiently explained the new name of the service, concluding with the statement: "But you can just call us the KGB, because that's still how we think of ourselves." As of today, this has never changed.

The final and most recent restructuring of the intelligence service occurred in the summer of 2004, prior to the Beslan incident, when Putin ordered yet another series of reforms to move the agencies forward. Whatever the specifcs of these reforms were, it is clear they were not sufficient to render the service capable of successfully handling either Beslan, or the series of terror attacks that have plagued Russia since.

Whether any unit is considered elite, or allowed to adopt the proud title of "Spetsnaz," is a function of two factors: (1) whether it exists to fulfill "special" operations outside the scope of the traditional military or other government units; and (2) whether it receives specialized training and equipment to fulfill these missions. Since the collapse of the Soviet Union, the Russian Federation has undergone a movement to expand the numbers of Spetsnaz units. There are now more than 130 different units that are considered to be "special," with some obviously far better suited to that name than others. Though outside the conventional military, many of these groups stay fully staffed through the draft process that all Russian males are subject to upon reaching the age of 18. The mandatory two year military conscription can be served directly with units such as the MVD's SOBR, Rus, Rossich, or Vityaz, as well as FSB's Alpha or Vympel. Many longer term or career officers will seek service with these units, or even with the Alpha counter terror unit, after fulfilling a first term of service with a lesser unit, or even one of the GRU Spetsnaz brigades. Naval service carries with it a minimum three-year obligation.

The fact that many of these highly trained units fall under the auspices of civilian governmental ministries and agencies provides an all-too-easy rationalization for the Russian government when deploying them for politically sensitive operations. In many cases this amounts to little more than unleashing military pitbulls on civilians for suspected criminal offenses, to appease international and news media scrutiny. This was seen through the 1990s when units like OMON and SOBR were used to raid the offices of the MOST financial group on May 12, 1996, and then again four years later in May 2000, only four days after President Putin's first inauguration. This sent a signal to all those opposing the government that Special Forces in Russia could and would be used to achieve not only political and military goals, but also financial ones. Or they might be used simply to bring governmental challengers to heel. During and since that time, Spetsnaz units have deployed against organized crime elements, to seize offices of large corporations for alleged tax evasion, and even to respond to pedestrian level bank robberies and quell prison discontent.

The most obvious utilization of these units under the auspices of "civilian law enforcement" has been in Chechnya. Bowing to international pressure to cease the deployment of the army and its Special Forces against Chechen separatists, who are Russian citizens, President Putin officially turned the conflict over from the military to "federal police" in early 2001. Chechnya was then flooded with units not technically part of the military, including Special Forces from such groups as Vityaz, SOBR, Rus, Rossich, Don, Alpha and Vympel, that were used as civilian "police" forces. This is a step akin to using commandos from the U. S. Navy's Reserve SEAL Teams, or 19th and 20th Special Forces (Green Beret) Groups of the Army National Guard against white supremacists or separatists in Idaho, and calling them "police officers merely keeping the peace." In substance, nothing had changed: the Chechens were still up against elite commandos.

Of the many Russian Special Forces units bandied about in the Western news media, it is important to understand that at the federal level there were merely five units that were deployed to Beslan Middle School No. 1 on the 1st of September 2004. They were the SOBR Rapid Reaction Force; MVD's Rus unit; the Alpha Counter Terror Group; the Vympel Division; OMON and MChS. Of these, Alpha and Vympel were the most critical, the best trained, and the units designated to lead any assault that might become necessary.

Alpha

Although today it enjoys unprecedented fame and notoriety throughout the world, the FSB's Alpha Counter-Terror Detachment - or Group - was at one time the most secretive of all. Alpha was first created on July 28, 1974, when the KGB determined that an epidemic of terrorist assaults was sweeping the world, including Europe. As has been the practice of Russia throughout history, before creating the unit it first launched an in-depth study of all the elite counter-terror special operations units existing in other nations at the time. In particular, they analyzed the American Special Forces and SEALs, the British SAS, West German GSG-9, the Israeli Mossad, and other elite units of the Israeli Defense Forces (IDF).

The composition of Alpha included already well-trained commandos from other units in and around Moscow, as well as other regions of the country. Priority was given to those who excelled in competitive athletics, a preference that continues to this day. As with America's own Special Forces, certain teams were tasked with different specialties, including demolitions and underwater operations. Everyone in Alpha is a warrant officer or officer, from lieutenant to colonel. They are all trained in explosives, mountain climbing and rappelling, skydiving, hand-to-hand combat, negotiations, intelligence and psychology. Most are sniper trained.

Originally designated as "Group A," the unit won quick notoriety as a capable counter-terror force, successfully completing many missions without the loss of a single soldier, earning it full membership in the opaque world of elite Special Forces. Its first exposure to international notoriety came on December 27, 1979 when – along with the diversionary unit Vympel – Alpha teams stormed the palace of the Afghan President, beginning the Soviet occupation of Afghanistan and the Soviet - Afghan War.

Concerned by the lack of stability and trustworthiness of the President, Hafizullah Amin, and ever sensitive to its own vulnerabilities through its "near abroad," the Soviets decided that Afghanistan – well within its perceived sphere of influence – had to be secured. The assault teams were ordered to invade the country and assassinate Amin. Additionally, they were to conduct reconnaissance on various critical aspects of the country's infrastructure, determine the location and intention of the mujahideen, and capture and liquidate its leaders. Furthermore, they were to locate and destroy weapons and ammunition depots, as well as the army headquarters and signal centers, rescue friendly soldiers from captivity, and form the Afghan Army into recon and sabotage units.

To accomplish all of this, Alpha assaulted with two other groups – *Grom* (Thunder) and *Zenit* (Zenith). Grom was comprised of 25 men, two ADV vehicles equipped with the ZSU 23-4 "Shilka" cannon, six BTR-60s (wheeled armored personnel carriers) and six BMP-1s (tracked APCs). Zenith had 24 commandos in all. Attached to them were two other units. The first was a Muslim battalion consisting of draftee soldiers. It was there to provide cover and assist in dealing with the locals. The second, and more useful, was a smaller team comprised of soldiers detached from Grom, Zenith, and one of the Soviet airborne divisions. As Alpha and Vympel together advanced on the palace in the middle of the night, they were engaged by heavy automatic weapons and anti-tank fire. They quickly dismounted their armored vehicles, and suffered 13 Alpha commandos wounded in the opening minutes of the battle.

Amin's palace was three stories tall, and built on elevated ground with a 360 degree panoramic view of the surrounding area. There was only one road leading in, which was under the constant surveillance of the 2,000 guards based inside the compound. But the KGB had done its intelligence gathering before launching the assault, and knew that on the night of the 27th, only 200 guards would be present. Still, reinforced by 11 tanks, two of which were dug into bunker emplacements outside the palace, the Afghans were a formidable force.

As the Soviet units assaulted, the Afghan guards lobbed grenades at them from the windows above, and put them under heavy machine gun fire from their superior, elevated positions. Alpha fired its big Shilka guns upward as cover, while the assault teams advanced on the palace. Once inside, they made their way quickly upstairs, taking the Afghan guards out with grenades and automatic weapons fire. Once on the second floor, they proceed down the hall, tossing grenades into each room. Accounts differ as to whether Amin was killed in his study during the assault by gunfire or a nearby exploding grenade. Either way, he was dead.

Unlike previous operations, every single member of Alpha had been wounded, and five were killed. By morning the Vitebsk Airborne Division landed at the Bagram City Airport, signifying the next step in an almost decade long Soviet investment of men, machinery, and blood in Afghanistan.

Alpha's next major operation did not come for two years. On December 17, 1981, in the city of Sarapul, two Soviet draftee soldiers took 25 boys hostage at a school. Threatening their captives with AK 47 assault rifles and 120 rounds of ammunition, they demanded foreign passports, visas and airline transportation out of the country. Through the course of negotiations, 15 of the boys were released. As this process was being carried out, Alpha penetrated the building. Once in position outside the doors of the room in which the remainder of the hostages were being held, Alpha prepared to assault. Before that could happen, the hostage-takers released the rest of the boys and surrendered. The men of Alpha were confident in their ability to eliminate the two kidnappers while saving the remainder of the students.

While the U.S. struggled in governmental paralysis over the taking of hostages in Beirut, Lebanon, and Tehran, Iran in the late 1970s, and early to mid-1980s, the Soviet Union found that it, too, was not immune to the problem, despite its cultivation of relations with many of the terrorist groups. Contrary to the hand-wringing over terrorist behavior that the U.S. was guilty of, the Soviet government – backed by its elite counter-terror units – had its own approach.

On September 30, 1985, several officials from the Soviet Embassy in Beirut were traveling through the city in an official car with diplomatic license plates. The car was stopped by gunmen and the Soviets dragged from it. The diplomats were forced into a waiting van and driven off. Of the four hostages, two were KGB intelligence officers. The terrorists quickly delivered their demands: the Soviet Union was to force Syria to cease its offensive in north Lebanon, or all four hostages would be killed.

The Soviet governmental and intelligence machines went quickly to work. They soon determined that Yassir Arafat, a Soviet ally, had betrayed them and had planned and authorized the kidnapping. Because their counterterrorist capability was still in its infancy, the Soviet Government attempted to resolve the situation peacefully. The Russians had yet to learn a lesson America would wait until 2001 to realize: assistance to or friendship with Islamist extremists means nothing to them. If you are not one of them, you are nothing more than an infidel whom they will exploit until such time as it becomes expedient for you to die.

USSR President Mikhail Gorbachev even went to such lengths as to attempt to persuade the Syrians to stop the offensive. The hostages still were not released. At this point the terrorists killed one of the Soviet diplomats, dumping his body in the street with a message that another would be killed within 24 hours. When this occurred, Alpha sprang into action. Brought into Beirut immediately after the kidnapping, Alpha's commandos had been developing intelligence on the identities of the members of the terrorist group that had taken the government officials, and had also located the offices and staging areas of the terrorists. Upon the killing of the first hostage, Alpha delivered a message to the terrorists that they had 48 hours to release the remaining three hostages.

When the 48-hour deadline passed, Alpha kidnapped four pre-targeted Lebanese members of the terrorist group. The following day, the terrorist leaders received the heads and other body parts of their colleagues in a box left on the front steps of their headquarters. This was coupled with a threat from Alpha to the Hizballah leadership that they would destroy all of its terror bases throughout Lebanon if the hostages were not freed. Forty-eight hours after receiving the heads of their friends, the Hizballah terrorists released the remaining Soviet diplomats. They were home in time for Christmas.

Then on May 10, 1989, in a criminal detention facility in the city of Saratov, four inmates took two female employees of the facility hostage, along with two minors who themselves were under investigation. Armed only with self-made knives, the inmates demanded four handguns, 10,000 rubles in currency, a car and a safe corridor through which to escape. The managers of the facility – unprepared for a situation of this nature – immediately gave the hostage takers a mini-bus with a full gas tank, and a loaded PM pistol with 24 rounds of ammunition. The criminals released one of the women and a teenager before making their escape. The other woman, severely beaten, was thrown from the moving vehicle while the kidnappers drove through the city. They proceeded to locate and kidnap one of the witnesses against them in their pending criminal case, and then burst into an apartment, taking an entire family of three – father, mother and two-year old daughter – hostage as well.

After the authorities located them, the hostage takers demanded a plane, vodka, drugs and a substantial amount of money. By then Alpha had arrived on the scene. As negotiations came to a standstill, Alpha located an apartment building identical to the one where the hostages were being held, and had been practicing its assault on an apartment with the same layout. With an assault plan in place, Alpha snipers took the kidnappers under surveillance. On their signal, assault teams with climbing equipment threw flash bang grenades through the windows. As soon as the devices exploded, Alpha commandos burst through the windows themselves, in a simultaneous entry with another team that came through the apartment door. The criminals were killed, with no injuries sustained to any of the hostages or Alpha members. The hostage takers shot two commandos, but both rounds lodged in their protective body armor. The identification and use of identical buildings in preparing an assault in hostage situations became a trademark of Alpha, and would ultimately cause problems for them at Beslan.

Alpha remained busy, being deployed to more terrorist-hostage situations than most commandos experience in a lifetime. On August 11, 1989, seven convicted felons took three employees of their temporary detention facility hostage in the city of Sukhumi. They attempted to free another 68 criminals being held in the jail. Unfortunately for the authorities, this building also served as a storage facility for weapons, and contained 3,000 rifles, handguns and shotguns, along with 24,000 rounds of ammunition. It was a formidable task for anyone ordered to deal with the kidnappers.

The convicts demanded a mini-van, which the authorities provided. Ten criminals and two hostages – all with masks over their faces to prevent identification – got in the van and drove away. The van had been rigged with flashbang grenades set to detonate once it began moving, but these failed to work immediately. The bus traveled ten meters before the devices went off. Alpha assaulted immediately, neutralizing all of the kidnappers. Neither of the hostages was injured, and only one Alpha member was wounded.

The speedy return of the three Soviet Embassy officials in Beirut, and the rescue of these and other hostages, only cemented Alpha's growing reputation for efficiency and ruthlessness. Alpha's honeymoon period ended, however, in early 1991, when news cameras filmed it storming the television center in Vilnius, the capital of the independence minded Baltic republic of Lithuania.

As part of their efforts to secede from the Soviet Union, the people of Lithuania had taken over the central television and broadcasting center of the capital. Tens of thousands of protesters were packed into the streets outside the TV tower, all in support of those seeking independence. Only a 67 man contingent of Alpha was present in the city at the time. Ordered by Gorbachev and the KGB director to retake the communications center, Alpha evaluated the situation. The protestors – both inside and outside the building – were armed with Molotov cocktails, rocks, sharpened metal rods and clubs. The independence seekers were making broadcasts from the tower throughout the country for the people to rise up against their Soviet oppressors. Alpha was promised the arrival of an Army division for support, but it failed to show. With 5,000 to 6,000 protestors in front of the TV center alone, a grossly outnumbered Alpha approached the building in trucks. Tossing flashbang grenades into the crowd, the Alpha commandos leapt out, only to be attacked by the mob. Fighting back with the butts of their rifles, they advanced on the building. None of the Alpha members had live ammunition in their weapons, using instead non-lethal rounds. Shots were fired from the crowd, and one of the Alpha members was hit. He later died inside the building. The group secured the main floor, and was followed by a team of eight who advanced to the second floor and neutralized the transmissions.

What the world saw was a large group of commandos, armed with the Spetsnaz's deadly weapon-of-choice combat shovels and AK assault rifles, burst into the TV station decimating everything and everyone in its path. Many Americans, mesmerized with the rapidly changing situation of their Cold War enemy, the Soviet Union, can recall the horror of that assault captured on film and shown round the world.

In the face of both domestic and international outrage at this incident, then Soviet President Mikhail Gorbachev and KGB Chairman Vladimir Kryuchkov both denied having ordered Alpha to assault the building. Until this point, Alpha had enjoyed the distinction of having never been given written orders for any of its operations, being always at the ready to deploy upon a single telephone call from the director of the KGB. This betrayal resulted in Alpha's leadership questioning the propriety of its use by the government for political – as opposed to military or terrorist – purposes. Its concerns were found to be prescient several months later during the August 19, 1991, *putsch* against Gorbachev, which saw the unilaterally created National State of Emergency Committee (GKChP) seize power. This ad hoc group of mutineers ordered Alpha to assault the White House, which was home to the government of the Russian Republic, the largest of the Soviet Autonomous Republics. Alpha, upon receiving this oral order, demanded it be put into writing, something no member of the overthrow group was willing to do. Alpha's refusal to storm that building literally saved the lives of Boris Yeltsin – the recently elected president of the Russian Republic – and his supporters, ensuring the release and return to power of Gorbachev, and subsequently catapulted Yeltsin to full control of the Russian Federation upon the dissolution of the Soviet Union some four months later.

But Alpha's political luck did not last. In October 1993 the Soviet Union was long since gone and its heir apparent, the Russian Federation, was in crisis. The new constitution of Russia, adopted by national referendum on December 12, 1993, granted to the president the power to dissolve parliament upon a succession of voting deadlocks. Russian President Boris Yeltsin ordered the Duma – the lower house of parliament – to disband. The legislators refused, holing up in the Russian White House and attempting to wrest control of the country from Yeltsin. These "rebels" – as they are known in Russian Special Forces circles – also took over the Ostankino Television tower in north Moscow, effectively seizing control of the main source of media and communications. It was Vilnius all over again.

This time it was Yeltsin who ordered Alpha to storm the White House. They refused. The president confronted Alpha's commanders, delivering to them the ultimatum of either siding with the president of Russia, or opposing him. Alpha opted to support the president, with "all the consequences which flowed from that" in his "settling of accounts" with the rebellious legislators. Alpha launched a jointly-coordinated attack with Vityaz, during which Alpha assaulted and took the White House. Simultaneously, Vityaz assaulted the Ostankino tower, defeating all of the opposition forces and their supporters. Many of the bystanders were injured and some killed in the fighting. Matching the long-standing reputation and success of its associate-unit, Alpha, Vityaz lost only one man in this battle. It was here that Vityaz commander, Colonel Sergei Ivanovich Lisyuk, was awarded the Gold Star – Hero of the Russian Federation, that nation's highest award for valor. Vityaz had not hesitated to follow the president's orders.

Though Alpha's operation in favor of the president was an enormous and speedy success, it still suffered political alienation from the man holding the highest office; one whose power base in that country they had just secured. For their hesitation in following the president's orders they received only his wrath. As well, the losses of hundreds of lives at both the White House and Ostankino resulted in the Russian people turning away from their much-celebrated heroes. Fearing retribution from Alpha, and in order to punish the unit, Yeltsin moved the counter-terrorist force far away from Moscow, and ordered it transferred out of the Federal Security Service to the Internal Affairs Ministry (MVD). Through this disgrace, Alpha quickly went from a full strength detachment of 3,000 commandos to a demoralized unit of as few as 200. During this period Alpha was thrown into numerous conflicts throughout the huge republic, without the benefit of its historically large budget for training and weapons, or personnel resources and expertise. Its performance in these operations fell far short of the stellar successes for which it had been known.

One such humiliation had been the Budennovsk siege in the summer of 1995 when, after an attack on the city police headquarters and subsequent days-long siege of the central hospital, Chechen rebel leader Basayev's unit was able to disappear into the Caucasus mountains, leaving Alpha behind to lick the wounds of its numerous losses in the battle. But by this time, it was no longer the same Alpha that had scored glorious success after glorious success for almost two decades.

Though Alpha was later transferred back to the Main Protection Directorate of the FSB, this occurred long after the luster was gone from its military experience, skill, and its pride in its own elite status. Alpha suffered another loss in January 1996, in the village of Pervomaiskoye, when terror leader Salman Raduyev seized a military garrison and took control of an entire town. After Alpha shelled the village mercilessly, losing more than two dozen troops in the process, the Chechen leader and his remaining band were able to slip away into Chechnya. When the dust settled on this battle the number of dead in Raduyev's group was far less than those innocent civilians and hostages killed. Alpha lost two men killed, with two more wounded due to an accidental discharge of an APC's Grom (Thunder) cannon by a regular Russian soldier.

Following this period of political doldrums, and with Putin's emergence, the KGB's favored unit has risen from its ashes. Today, the operators of Alpha are, once again, some of the best-trained counter-terror professionals in the Russian arsenal, as well as throughout the world. Each is a career military officer, with many applying for selection into Alpha after years of decorated service with other top units. The men of Alpha are skilled at all forms of weapons. They are each sniper trained, scuba certified, and are mountain climbers, as well as being schooled in such academic studies as psychology and hostage negotiations. To this day, Alpha maintains sister divisions under the same name at main bases and training schools in places like Belarus, Ukraine and Kazakhstan.

Alpha's last great coup prior to Beslan would come in October 2002, when 42 Chechen terrorists seized the Nord-Ost Theater in north Moscow and took more than 800 people hostage. There, in joint operations with its old and trusted partners Vityaz and Vympel, and in a new tandem operational relationship with SOBR, it successfully assaulted the theater after deploying a nerve gas, and killed all the terrorists. Had the government notified area hospitals, informing doctors and emergency response personnel of what the hostages would be suffering from, and had it called up ambulances for emergency transport of those suffering from the effects of the gas, most, if not all, of the 129 dead hostages would have lived, scoring Alpha the hostage rescue victory of all time.

Vympel

Unlike Alpha, or even America's Delta Force (1st Special Forces Operational Detachment – Delta, or CAG as it is now known), or the U.S. Navy's elite counter-terror SEAL Team Six, Vympel is not a *counter*-terror unit, but a *terror* unit. In Russia it is called a *diversionary* unit. It exists for insertion into foreign countries in times of war or political hostility, to foment fear and uncertainty through the sabotage of critical infrastructure and the neutralization of government via kidnappings and assassinations of important political leaders, judges and even businessmen.

Vympel was originally created by a joint mandate of the USSR Council of Ministers and the Central Committee of the Communist Party of the Soviet Union on August 19, 1981, prior to the death of Leonid Brezhnev. Originally, it was created as an independent sub-unit of Directorate "S" of the KGB's 1st Chief Directorate, which meant that it handled the work of illegal operatives and operations abroad. At the time, operational orders to Vympel could only come personally from the chairman of the KGB – then Yuri Andropov - who would later become president of the Soviet Union and general secretary of the Communist Party (CPSU). Unlike Alpha, the KGB director's orders to Vympel had to be in writing.

At first Vympel was staffed with veterans from the Soviet-Afghanistan War's elite Special Forces units Zenit and Kaskad, in addition to other officers of the KGB, the Soviet Army, Navy, and the KGB's Border Guards. The minimum requirements for entry into Vympel were exacting in such areas as education, physical conditioning and ability, and expert tactical skills in disciplines like mountain climbing, parachuting, and scuba diving. Applicants were even expected to possess such unique abilities as being glider pilots, geography experts, marksmen, improvised weapons experts, demolitions experts, tactical drivers, radio operators, cryptographers, medics, hand-to-hand combat experts, prisoner interrogators, wilderness survivalists and linguists. Many Vympel operators could speak up to three foreign languages, including local dialects, and it was rumored that each one had memorized the maps of up to thirty nations' capitals throughout the world. The ability to adapt, improvise and overcome; to make calm, professionally detached decisions in critical situations, far from home and with little to no support, were absolutely essential to the functioning and success of every Vympel soldier. The slogan of the sub-unit became, "Anywhere, any time, any mission."

Early on, Vympel recruited officers between the ages of 25 and 27. Much like our own Army SF and Delta, rather than young, inexperienced

– though perhaps highly trained – recruits, Vympel was looking for men with greater maturity and experience. It sought those young enough to undergo the three to five years of additional training planned for them, and still allow for up to ten years of military service before retirement. Vympel cut its teeth in covert operations during the Afghanistan War, where it was best known for its reconnaissance and intelligence gathering, its training of special units of the Afghan army, and leading that army in special operations against the Mujahideen. Applying its diversionary expertise, Vympel took its greatest pride in its ability to manipulate the leaders of individual tribes fighting the government into armed conflict against each other.

After Afghanistan, Vympel continued to apply its special abilities and hone its skills in such countries as Cuba, Nicaragua, Mozambique, Angola and Yugoslavia. In these foreign postings, its officers often functioned as instructors to foreign militaries in much the way our own Green Berets do, in addition to leading covert operations. As is the case with the Russian military in general, however, Vympel, like other Spetsnaz units, suffered from a shooting disability. As a result of both cultural dimensions, which precluded comfort with firearms, and a budget insufficient to ensure regular firearms training and development, Vympel fell far below the tactical shooting ability of its counterpart Special Forces units in countries like the U.S. It wasn't until Vympel operated in Nicaragua for a lengthy time that its members even developed the ability to shoot tactically while maneuvering, rather than standing still in front of an exposed target.

In 1988, with the changing atmosphere within the Soviet Union, Vympel's operational mandate began to change as well. With "hot spots" occurring inside its own country, Vympel went quickly from a foreign soil-only diversionary unit under the control of the international arm of the KGB, to one which operated at home, in such places as Baku, Karabakh, Yerevan, Nakhichevan and Abkhazia.

With the restructuring of many former Soviet ministries as the USSR's end drew near, Vympel found itself in search of a home. In

1991 Vympel was removed from under the control of the Foreign Intelligence Service of the KGB, and assigned to the newly formed Russian Federation Federal Security Service. Soon thereafter, the Federal Security Service was reorganized into the Russian Ministry of Security. Vympel's darkest time came during the revolt of October 1993. Most Americans remember tanks shelling the Russian White House - its parliament building's windows darkened by shells while smoke billowed out into the overcast Moscow autumn day. Then-President Boris Yeltsin ordered the attack when the parliament refused to disband, as it was obliged to do under the newly minted constitution of Russia. In the West, little is known of the intense fighting that went on in that city for a several day period. Afterward, in addition to fuming at Alpha, Yeltsin accused certain "sub-units" of Vympel of refusing to assault the members of parliament holed up in the White House. Accordingly, on December 23, 1993, President Yeltsin signed an order disbanding the Russian Ministry of Security. Vympel, along with Alpha, was transferred to the Ministry of Internal Affairs (MVD).

By the time of this changeover, Vympel comprised merely 400 soldiers, and when this occurred fully 112 of them took retirement, with another 150 opting to transfer to other sub-units of the KGB and lateral units of Russia's security administration. Vympel itself was redesignated "Vega" and offered only different missions than those for which it was originally formed and trained. Much of its new focus was on defending against nuclear terrorism, and it lost tremendous momentum and credibility when, due to the its own lack of professionalism, its efforts to neutralize terrorists in the Dagestan city of Mineralniy Vodi resulted in the deaths of five hostages on July 29, 1994, immediately prior to the beginning of the first Chechen War. Some time later it was again transferred, this time to the anti-terrorism department of the Russian Federal Security Service, or FSB, the newly constituted domestic arm of the former KGB.

Though many experts have cited Vympel's resultant embarrassing lack of service in the first Chechen conflict (1994 to 1996), it has served proudly and effectively in the second war in Chechnya (1999 to present), with its operators often working in combined force reconnaissance units. The composition of these recon teams has often included counterparts from such Spetsnaz groups as Alpha, Vityaz, Rus, Don, Rossich and SOBR.

Subsequent to the first war in Chechnya, however, Vympel's operational mandate became almost exclusively domestic, including the application of its exhaustive training in terrorist-type activities to the new emphasis on anti-terrorism. Fulfilling a Red Cell[12] type mandate, Vympel went to work uncovering the weaknesses at high security installations throughout Russia. Perhaps its greatest accomplishment in this effort was its capture of the nuclear naval vessel *Sibir*, at the time docked at Murmansk in the middle of the Russian Navy's nuclear icebreaker fleet. Whether assaulting military bases or myriad nuclear weapons and energy facilities, Vympel amassed an impressive record of success, having never failed in its training objectives. This, despite the fact that in every instance the opposing security forces were alerted to the upcoming attack.

Today, as part of its continued training and "diversionary operations," which necessarily include its expertise at finding and attacking vulnerable points in security, Vympel works steadily in the area of strategic defense of high security installations. Also, the job of freeing hostages held in foreign and enemy states falls squarely on its soldiers. This is why its expertise was called upon in the major hostage sieges and rescue efforts at both the Nord-Ost Theater in Moscow in October 2002 and the Beslan School.

---

[12] Red Cell, or the Naval Security Coordination Team (OP-O6D), as it was officially known, was a special unit of the United States Navy. Created in 1984 under the order of Deputy Chief of Naval Operations Vice Admiral James A. "Ace" Lyons, Jr., and commanded initially by Captain Richard Marcinko, its purpose was to probe security at high-level governmental installations. It was disbanded in 1992.

PART TWO

ATTACK ON THE SCHOOL

Chapter Four

Attack on Beslan Middle School – Day One

All that is necessary for the triumph
of evil is that good men do nothing.

— Edmund Burke

In Russia, the first day of September is the traditional beginning of the school year. Unlike in America, this is a special day of festivities, similar to what Americans would recognize as something akin to a springtime school fair. Called the Day of Knowledge, it is not unusual for entire extended families to go celebrate their children's first day at school, bearing gifts for the teachers. For Russians, the very first time a child trundles off to school, leaving forever the protective blanket of the family, is a special and highly emotional event. On the first day of September 2004, no parent in Beslan knew just how far, and in some cases eternal, that trip would be.

Beslan is an agricultural and industrial community of 40,000, some 900 miles south of Moscow. Surrounded by undeveloped agricultural land, it sits as if in a picture frame, at the foot of the majestic and spiraling Caucasus Mountains. It is only 30 km, about 18 miles, north of the larger metropolis of Vladikavkaz, the capital of North

Ossetia, with its more than 300,000 residents. Despite this pastoral setting, Beslan is a small, very poor community seemingly in the middle of nowhere. With its odd mix of industry and agriculture, sitting against a dramatic mountain backdrop, it brings to mind what Greeley, Colorado might have been like more than 100 years ago. But Greeley never had a war a short drive away. Beslan itself is strategically located between many towns and military bases. It has the largest vodka factory in the region, and so many people travel a long way to buy alcohol. Much goes out the back door. Other than the meager existence eked out of the soil by old men and women driving their small herds of cattle and goats along the roadways, many of the people of Beslan are forced to exist on vodka production and smuggling.

Roads and dirt tracks crisscrossing the area lend aid to the smuggling of vodka, cigarettes, guns, and almost anything that will bring money. But the market is not limited to these things. An active slave trade threatens any outsider venturing into this region, which is not untouched by the nearby war. From Chechnya to Ingushetia, and even North Ossetia, many kidnap victims are quickly sold into slavery, never to be heard from again. For those taken in Ingushetia and Chechnya, the rule of thumb is that if one is not ransomed back, or his head not found on the side of the road, he has been sold as a slave. Many end up in the Middle East and even Asia, passing through a highly evolved international network of Islamist extremists. Despite having made this journey several times in the past, I have been implored by colleagues in Russia to not return, being warned that even the police and some justices of the top courts in the region have their own stables of slaves, a fate which could be the best among the possible outcomes of my insistence on going back. I am told that returning to Beslan is like going to the war in Iraq right now.

One Spetsnaz general stares intently into my eyes. Despite the fact we are sitting among a group of friends – all decorated veterans of Russia's Special Forces – in the comfort of his well appointed kitchen in south Moscow, I feel the cold fire in his eyes as he argues the dangers associated with my returning to Beslan, and attempting to make the border crossing into Ingushetia, as was my plan. "Just *tell* everyone you went," he commands. When I reply that we have already bought our plane tickets, he advises me to just use the tickets as false evidence I went, while remaining in Moscow. "I'll tell you everything you want to know about Beslan," he assures. "There is no reason to go back down there." Despite his protestations and genuine concern for my safety, Yuri and I, needing only a quick glance between us – his black eyes conveying more than words - turn down the general's offer of arranging security for us when we arrive. We had been through too many difficult places together to start relying on others.

Our plan, as always, was to not let anyone know where we would be or when, typically arriving unannounced at shabby hotels and boarding houses, moving around constantly with no one knowing our plans. Besides, with the government's complete crackdown on information being disseminated to outsiders, it seemed even less likely that anyone would talk to us if we were surrounded by a team of Special Forces commandos from that region. Interestingly, we would end up at one point staying at the Hotel Vladikavkaz, a foreboding, Stalinist-era structure that sits above the wide Terek River. In the hotel with us were a number of the top appointees to Putin's commission investigating the Beslan massacre. Frequently we found ourselves in the company of General Lieutenant Valeriy Dyatlenko, former Chief of the FSB for the entire Rostov region, and commission member. His polite demeanor each time we encountered one another belied his intelligence agent's inquisitiveness as to who we were. He must have wondered just who these men were who conversed in smatterings of Russian, Ukrainian and English, one of whom sported the hat of the Chester, Pennsylvania SWAT team affixed with a gold and silver Alpha team pin.

As for the terrorists we were all there to investigate, they had obviously been well aware of the highly evolved black market in the area.

This was evident in their use of military uniforms and troop carriers to cross the border and enter Beslan. Everyone there does, and two more being driven by men in the ubiquitous camouflage uniforms favored by males in that part of the world would hardly have been noticed as they paid the pre-arranged bribes at the border crossings and drove through town on the morning of September 1. At 8:00 a.m. in the wide plaza on the north side of the Beslan Middle School No. 1, a combined facility for grades 1 through 11 at which time Russians graduate high school, with just under 1,000 students from ages 6 to 17, there were at least several thousand teachers, students, siblings, parents, grandparents, and onlookers. For many families, every single member was present, all enjoying the festiveness and mixed emotionalism of seeing their children face a new chapter in their futures. The main police headquarters for the town was approximately 200 meters immediately to the east of the school, up an alleyway. This would do the hostages little good when the assault came.

The Russian government had developed some intelligence that an assault might take place. The Russians received information as early as eight to ten days before the attack that a school somewhere in the regions around Chechnya was going to be hit. The problem was, no one knew where. Despite this warning, no one seemed to have noticed that three days prior to the first of September, many of the Ingush families living in Beslan had simply packed up and traveled back across the border to their homeland. Still, the information was enough to take some precautions. That is the only reason one guard was on hand at the Beslan School early that morning. Moreover, the families and friends of some of the Alpha commandos would note the soldiers' sudden disappearances one week prior. In many such instances, the families of these soldiers were told merely that they were being deployed to the North Caucasus. At their greatest numbers, however, there were too few to place teams of commandos at every school in Southern Russia. All they could do was prepare. And wait.

At approximately 8:45 a.m., as the outdoor activities were winding down, two vehicles sped along Comintern Street, little more than a dirt path paralleling railroad tracks to the west of the school. One Russian made GAZ 66 troop carrier, with a canvas tarp hiding what was in the back, pulled up sharply inside the fence next to the main entrance to the school on the west side. Along with it was a Russian made SUV, and possibly two other large sedans. Even today no one is exactly sure how many of the vehicles found parked at the west gate had been used by the terrorists. They had crossed the border, bribing guards at the three check points between Ingushetia and North Ossetia. More than three dozen terrorists leapt out. They came prepared, carrying automatic weapons, grenades, sniper rifles, night vision goggles, gas masks, explosives and silenced weapons. Other terrorists, believed to be 49 in total, were already in the crowd at the school. Having been deposited in the town earlier, they simply walked to the school on that beautiful fall morning. The terrorists quickly surrounded the crowd, predominantly comprised of older women and children, who found themselves pressed against the north wall of the school. One group of terrorists immediately entered the school through the main entrance, moving quickly through the warren of corridors, driving anyone they found inside ahead of them and into the gym.

The second group started to force the crowd of revelers into the adjacent courtyard to the east. Shooting into the ground and above the crowd they began herding everyone into the gym, through the door at its northeast corner on the far side of the courtyard. In addition to the lone security guard, one police officer happened to be in the crowd with a sidearm only. The two attempted to engage the terrorists. One managed to kill a terrorist, but outnumbered and outgunned, both died on the spot in the first seconds of what would become a 62-hour ordeal. The terrorists were successful only in herding approximately 60 percent of the crowd into the school. Of the remaining 40 percent, most managed to escape, fleeing across the pavement to the east side gate and the relative safety of the residential neighborhood bordering the school. Many of the older students – fleeter of foot and reaction – managed to avoid capture this way. One woman and a dozen students took advantage of the chaos and ducked into the boiler room in the far wing of the school, hiding behind the heating boilers in the dark recesses of the maintenance section.

Numerous commandos who ultimately fought the battle at the school two days later claim media reports that fathers attempted to fight off the terrorists are untrue. "There was nothing anyone could have done," they all tell me. Likewise, reports that 12 people were killed in the initial attack and left to rot in the north courtyard throughout the siege are denied by the soldiers. Two commanders who were among the first on scene say no one was killed there and no bodies left in that area outside the gym. Despite this, even North Ossetian Interior Minister Kazbek Dzantiyev claimed that many fathers attempted to protect children and died for their efforts. The Special Forces believe this is wishful thinking on the part of the North Ossetians, attempting to create some heroes out of such a tragedy. The terrorists did, however, kill two fathers early on. Immediately after the crowd was forced into the gym one father walked up to the school and approached the door. He said he wanted to know the status of his children inside. They shot him on the spot and then dragged his body into the gym by his legs, an example they said, to the rest of the hostages. Within the first hour another father, sensing the tension and explosiveness of the terrorists, tried to calm the children and families inside the gym. A terrorist walked over, put the barrel of an assault rifle to his head, and pulled the trigger. He was killed in front of his two young sons, and an entire panic-stricken gym full of hostages. Terrified girls were ordered to clean up the blood.

When the assault first started, people were in shock and refused to believe it was real. "Most thought it was a military training exercise," explains Dr. Alexei Savaliev, an MVD officer and psychologist who was there. Even though people were being shot down, most just stood there in shock, unable to move or react in any way. "Even after the siege had begun, for quite a while the people of Beslan, and even the police, did not accept that the school had really been taken over," another MVD colonel based in Vladikavkaz, who had responded to the school siege, tells me one dark night after a clandestine meeting on the bridge over the Terek River. "Everyone believed that at any moment it would be disclosed that the whole thing had been a Spetsnaz field exercise," he says.

The terrorists' first objective was to drive all of the hostages into the gym. This took no more than 15 minutes from the moment they leapt from their trucks. By approximately 9:05 a.m., officially 1,181 hostages, most of whom were children, were in the gym, completely at the mercy of a group of men and women who had long since lost the capacity to feel any human compassion. At one point a local committee set up by teachers compiled a list of 1,220 hostages, whose names were posted on a website at www.beslan.ru. Some reported that when they first entered the gym, other terrorists were already there, having deployed immediately to that collection point, while their associates herded the crowd in from outside. Reports that terrorists even booby-trapped some of the bodies left in the courtyard are, as well, false. A number of students managed to flee to other areas of the school and hide. Some were found. Of those, some were killed. Others managed to escape.

From the beginning the hostages were shocked at the feral, animalistic behavior of the terrorists. "Once inside they just went crazy, beating people, raping girls, killing some hostages, all the while shooting and screaming threats," one military officer told me. "The girls were raped in the most brutal ways imaginable," several government and military representatives who were on scene reported. Some were raped right on the floor of the gym in front of all the hostages and small children. Among those, a number of the girls were raped with the barrels of the terrorists' guns, and any other objects that were at hand. Those who lived later required emergency surgery to repair the internal damage done by the sadistic assaults. Many of the girls were dragged upstairs to the auditorium where they were held and raped repeatedly throughout the ordeal. In all, the behavior of the terrorists, as a group, was very abnormal, both Marina the police psychologist and another military psychologist explained. "The Ingush and Chechens, in particular, would constantly beat the child hostages, laughing at the sport of it all," said one young man who had been a student at the school and who had friends inside. Both mental health professionals concluded that the terrorists were brainwashed to carry out their assignments, "like programmed robots, to cause all the terror they possibly could." They believe that it was for this reason that the terrorists told the hostages, "We came here to die with you."

After the siege was over, the government first reported that there were 32 terrorists, though more recent evidence indicates there were as many as 50. Numerous government officials explained to me that the number 32 was released to the news media, as 31 had been killed and 1 captured. Several officials admitted to me that the others managed to escape, some during the siege and the rest in the chaos of the assault on the third day. Rumors that the government has several secretly hidden and alive continue to this day. Just days before this book went to print a two hour Russian television special reported that they had confirmed the government had four terrorists secretly in captivity.[13] If that is the case, none of the soldiers I met with, and who had been at Beslan throughout the siege and the battle, knew where the other three prisoners came from. Two Spetsnaz team leaders assured me, over a long day of discussions, that they personally saw the remains of 30 terrorists including three who were killed in the town.

Reports that the head of the terrorists was Ruslan Khuchbarov, nicknamed "The Colonel," are also denied by those who were there. No one disputes that a leader with that nickname was in the school

---

[13] This special indicated that of 49 total terrorists 31 were killed, 13 escaped, 4 were captured and one killed by the crowds outside the school.

with the terrorists. But several different Spetsnaz officers believe that this moniker belonged to Chechen leader Magomet Yevloyev, a former MVD major and the security chief for Ingushetia's President Ruslan Aushev during his term in office. Khuchbarov – reported in the news media as "Khusbarov" – was a lower echelon Chechen leader, they all say. The Russians are doubtful that Khuchbarov would have been capable of leading such a raid or group. Completely independent of each other, numerous Spetsnaz officers told me that, "There were three leaders inside the school." One was Vladimir Hodov, initially believed to be an Ossetian, he was a Ukrainian who had lived in Ossetia for years before joining the Chechen rebels. The two Special Forces team leaders told me that they had "clearly identified his body," and that it "was in good condition." Another leader has never been identified by Russian security services by name, though I was told he was a brigade general in the Chechen rebel forces, far above the rank of Khuchbarov. The last was Yevloyev. Though he used the name "Colonel" or "Polkolvnik" while inside the school, he was monitored in telephone transmissions using the codename "Magaz," which Russian intelligence had long before determined to be Yevloyev. His body was also officially identified among the terrorist dead at the school.

On a couple of occasions Yuri Ferdigalov was told that a number of the terrorists, including the Arabs in the group, had traveled from Georgia – a former Soviet republic – further fueling the current tensions between Russia and that country. The terrorist group was reportedly comprised of ten different nationalities, with as many as ten being ethnic Arabs. Ultimately, Chechen leader Shamil Basayev would admit that at least two were from Arab countries. The composition of the group, as best as can be determined even at this late date, included up to 20 Ingush, 10 Chechens, 10 Arabs (including at least one North African, most likely from Sudan or Libya), 5 ethnic Russians, in addition to Uzbekis, Tatarians, and Kazakis. There were also one or two Ossetians, which only inflamed the outrage of the people of Beslan. Finally, there were two female Shaheeds, or suicide bombers. One whole group of the terrorists had arrived from the town of Malgobek in Ingushetia. With this international and interethnic composition the Chechens and their Arab sponsors had taken a big political step in their terrorist message to the world. Many of the terrorists were reported by the hostages to have had young faces, with some as young as 17, and many in their 20s. When the fight was over on the last day, only 17 of the 31 bodies of the terrorists were identified; the rest had been blown or shot to ribbons, making positive identifications impossible.

Early reports in the news media claimed there were three women among the terrorists, though two is the correct number. Later review of videotape taken by the terrorists showed both women wearing all black dresses and face veils, encumbered with belted pistols and suicide bombs strapped to their waists. Both were Chechen. Reports that one of the women had refused to follow the orders of the Colonel, Khuchbarov, and he shot her or blew her up are contradicted by the Special Forces who entered the school. They claim to know where, when and how each of them died, and it was not by someone else's hand. They point out how difficult and unnecessary it would have been for any of the leaders to walk around with remote detonators for the women's belt bombs when they had an entire school packed with larger explosives. The fact that both women had dyed their hair blonde, however, may have been evidence of their hopes ultimately to escape the school rather than be martyred there, according to Col. Rodin and others.

Once inside the school all of the hostages' cell phones were taken from them. Having prevented outside communication, the terrorists quickly set explosives throughout the gym and in other areas, particularly in most of the six main entrances or access ways. Bombs in the areas in which hostages were held were concentrated to kill as many of them as possible. Some hostages reported that most of the terrorists who had the duty of guarding them in the gym appeared to be largely Chechen and Ingush. The Arab terrorists were reportedly charged with the responsibility of securing and guarding the building and entrances against an assault by government troops, and did not come into much contact with the hostages. The tops of the gym walls and basketball backboards were draped with explosives, twisted black wires connecting the bombs to each other, and many to the two foot pedal, pressure-release detonation devices that sat menacingly on the gym floor. Three explosive devices were tied into the basketball net at the far east end of the gym, with another wired to the bottom of the backboard. Wires from it ran to two other bombs, and to one of the pedal detonators. Some bombs hung so low that the adults and taller children had to stoop to walk under them or risk banging their heads as they were led to the bathroom. Early on in the siege, the hostages were permitted water and bathroom trips. This quickly changed, however.

Congeries of wires snaked right through the children seated on the floor. The fear of the hideous network of bombs and wires was overcome only by the horror of the hostages as they watched the two men with their feet on the pedal detonators. Even those who knew nothing about bombs instinctively realized the threat these devices posed. The terrorists made it clear that they were prepared to die, and that any movement would result in everyone's death. "Bear this in mind, they are planning a storm. We will defend you to the last bullet and then blow ourselves up. We have nothing to lose, we came here to die," one of the leaders told the group of cowering hostages, referring to the counter-terror commandos who had surrounded the building. Another terrorist said that a Russian plane had killed his entire family, and now he wanted to kill, too. He did not care if his victims included women and children.

The terrorist group had also brought IEDs (Improvised Explosive Devices), which were mostly plastic bottles filled with nails, bolts and screws as shrapnel and a homemade version of dynamite. It would later be revealed that, in all, they had about 30 kg (66 lbs.) of explosives, in addition to the many hand and rocket propelled grenades. In an After Action Report, the head of the 58th Army's Sapper (Demolitions/Combat Engineer) unit, Bakhtiyar Nabiyev, would say

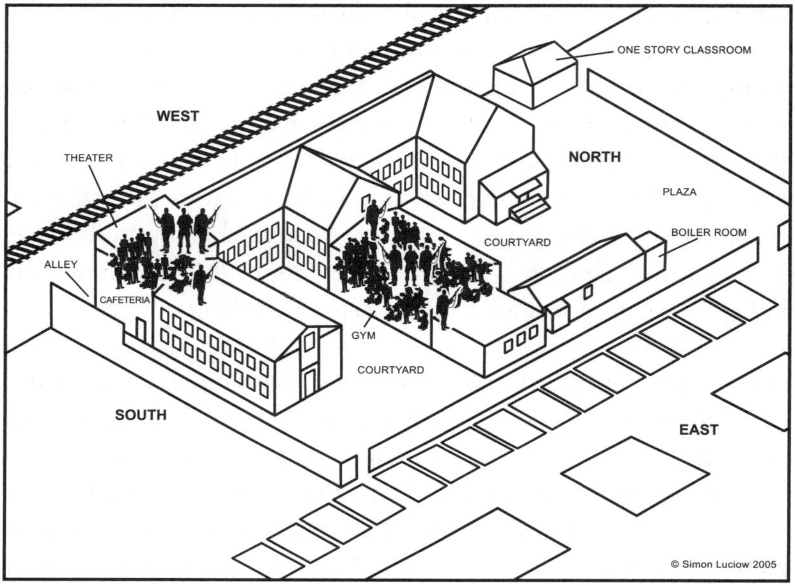

Majority of hostages grouped together in gym, first floor cafeteria and second floor theater.

that many of the bombs could be detonated from various locations within the school. At the end of the siege, government troops disarmed more than 100 booby traps the terrorists had set throughout the school.

At the same time the gym was wired, most of the main entrances to the school were rigged with booby trap explosives as well, protecting the most important access ways against a possible assault. Those not booby-trapped were either barricaded or defended with heavily armed terrorists round the clock. The windows, however, were not rigged with explosives, which would have been impossible because they numbered in the hundreds throughout the school. In all areas of the school other than the gym, the terrorists broke the windows to diminish the effects of an attack utilizing gas, demonstrating that they had learned from Nord-Ost. Some of the children were initially stood up in the windows as human shields to ward off any notions of a quick rescue by police and military. Some of them escaped by leaping through these windows, as they were made to pile desks, books and furniture in front of them. Reports, even in the Russian government, that the terrorists brought their own security camera system with them have proven untrue. By 9:45 a.m. the call had gone out from the Ministry for Emergencies (MChS) in North Ossetia that the school had been taken. At 10:00 a.m. the Special Forces of the FSB and MVD were alerted and ordered to get ready to travel.

Reports that almost two dozen older teenage boys and men were herded into the adjacent room to the east of the gymnasium, lined up against the wall and killed, would prove to be – unprecedentedly - underrated. In the morning of the first day 16 adult men and older boys were taken onto the second floor and executed. These would not be the only ones so brutally dispatched. The Chechens and Ingush are not large people physically, and are generally intimidated by the bigger Ossetians who hale from a wrestling culture. They feared organized resistance and so prevented any such efforts by killing outright the largest of the hostages. Still, some Spetsnaz told me that among those executed there were some shockingly small teenage boys. With this demonstration of the terrorists' power, others were conscripted into the labor efforts of the terrorists to fortify the school. Furniture was moved and stacked at the windows and other crucial choke points in the school's corridors. In the industrial arts shop in the far southern arm of the "W" that formed the building's basic shape and enclosed the south courtyard, wood and metal working machinery was moved about as fortifications for the Arab terrorists who used the large room as a base of operations. Throughout the first day and morning of the second, as the usefulness of these older, larger males ended, they were executed. At least 21 men and boys would ultimately be killed in this manner.

Once fortifications were well underway on the first day, gunmen separated different groups of hostages. With the exception of the girls, the hostages reported that there was no particular scheme or design to the groupings. Many were held in the cafeteria on the first floor in the southwest corner of the building. Others were taken to the school's second floor theater and primary school classrooms. Many were held in various other rooms on the second floor.

As hours dragged by on Day One, the eight high cathedral windows of the gym turned the interior into an oven. The temperature soared, and the hostages, with no fresh air or water, fell ill with heat and nausea. Some children fainted, others vomited and everyone began stripping their clothes off. As the siege wore on, there was no consistency in the treatment of hostages. Some were allowed to go to the bathroom, and some of those were given water. Others were forced to relieve themselves where they sat, many by necessity urinating into plastic bottles to later consume against dehydration. One teacher, popular and pretty Elena Kosomova, would drink her young son's urine, saving the last for him. Adults poured urine over the children to keep them cool. The terrorists put bottles of water in front of the dehydrated children, telling them they would be killed if they reached for them.

Thirst was not the only problem. Denied any type of food, children began eating the flowers they had brought to the festivities as gifts for the teachers. Many shared with those who did not have even that. One 82 year old World War II veteran was made to reverse his jacket and put it back on to hide his medals. They were told, "No one cares about you. Not your president. Not your government. You are not needed."

The quickest on the scene after the initial assault were the citizens. The government would later be shocked at the number of assault rifles, hunting rifles, handguns and shotguns in the possession of the common citizenry, never having quite realized that with the war and the dreaded Ingush so close, Beslan was a virtual armed fortress. Even rocket-propelled grenades (RPGs) and SVD machine guns were in abundance. To the citizens, it appeared the government was doing nothing at first. Angry, scared, completely untrained and unorganized, and in many cases completely drunk, they arrived first by the dozens, and then by the hundreds. Spetsnaz officers would say these men were unorganized and leaderless, and lacking any military or even para-military training. Massing in every position around the school that offered a view, this crowd of vigilantes would surge inward, shouting at the terrorists and firing rounds at the school. For their part, the terrorists seemed to take delight in the crowd's behavior; doing everything they could to incite them further: from screaming their own threats and dares, to shooting down into the crowd whenever a target presented itself. Throughout the siege eruptions of gunfire in other parts of the town would send troops, reporters and "volunteers" scurrying to the sounds of battle, only to learn it was other civilians catharsizing pent up emotions.

The only uninvited volunteers to show up with any semblance of military training and experience came from South Ossetia. South Ossetia is a region of Georgia that has been attempting to secede from that country, in order to realign itself with Russia. Sent by the president of South Ossetia, they arrived in full camouflage uniform, organized into military squads. Identifiable at the siege by the white bands they wore on their upper arms, these were part of the military of that breakaway republic, having recently fought battles against the official army of Georgia. Desirous of rejoining Russia, it appeared they were willing to do anything they could to help their cousins to the north.

By approximately 10:30 a.m. local police from Beslan and neighboring Vladikavkaz had attempted to establish a cordon around the school and adjacent neighborhood. However, they were too few, poorly armed and completely untrained for this sort of thing. These men would forever lament the fact that they simply waited for government troops to take over, and did not seize the opportunity to do what they could early on. They were soon joined by members of Russia's 58th

Army, which could provide little more than regular, conscript troops to stand posts around the area. The police, facing superior arms and numbers among their own citizens, were powerless to do anything.

Notwithstanding Putin's immediate pledge not to assault the school, by 10:30 a.m. government forces began pouring into the area. Many of the first to arrive were not Special Forces and were not up to the task. The *Rus* Spetsnaz group, another Red Beret unit of the Dzherzhinskiy Division, had been 200 kilometers across the border in Chechnya. At 10:00 a.m. it was mobilized and redeployed to Beslan. Though not a counter-terror unit, it was the first to deliver teams of battle-hardened young Special Forces commandos to the scene. Even then, it took them three hours to arrive, not appearing until after 1:00 o'clock that day. In addition, local units of OMON and the SOBR Rapid Reaction Force answered the call, as well as the VV interior army, from Mazdok in Ingushetia. All were charged with establishing outer and inner perimeter security and stabilizing the scene. Rus was ordered to place snipers in the buildings around the school. This largely meant the three apartment buildings to the east, the residential homes to the east of the broad plaza that had clear line of sight to the school, and the enormous, new sports complex on the other side of the railroad tracks to the west, a minimum 300 meter shot. They were also ordered to establish three concentric security perimeters around the school, but between the – by then – thousands of onlookers and the difficulty of posting men throughout the neighborhoods and fences surrounding the school, this proved impossible.

The regional units of Alpha and Vympel, both of the FSB, arrived from their base in Khankala, near Grozny, between 1:00 and 3:00 p.m. After coordinating with their Moscow counterparts, these local units delivered 100 men each, taking over putative command from Rus, the MVD group. Everyone told me that these units arrived in bits and pieces, sending men as soon as they were assembled. A command post was established at the Beslan Culture Center, some two hundred meters to the northeast of the school. This was the only location in any proximity to the school that had a large expanse of open area. It would also become the staging area for news media and journalists from all over the world, with hundreds of enormous satellite antennae reaching for the autumn sky as the siege dragged on.

Shortly after the siege began, the news media reported government estimates that there were only about 120 hostages. Later this was increased to 354 hostages, with 17 terrorists, including 2 women. With the knowledge of many eyewitnesses, the citizens recognized at once that these numbers were grossly understated, in terms of both the hostages as well as the number of terrorists. As word spread, even more citizens began racing to the school. Under reporting by the government would later be cited as a major cause for the collapse in negotiations with the terrorists, who were closely monitoring the news on televisions inside the school. They were outraged at the numbers being released by the government. When the government increased the estimated number of victims to 354, the terrorists told them: "They say there are only 354 of you, so we will reduce you to that number." It was at this point that they ceased allowing any of the hostages to use the bathrooms. No one was given so much as another sip of water.

At 11:30 that morning the border with Ingushetia, and all schools and stores in Beslan and Vladikavkaz, were closed by order of the Interior Ministry. Police and government forces were put on the streets everywhere, in large part due to reports that the terrorists had other groups hiding in Beslan to provide support.

At 12:30 p.m. twelve children and one woman, having hidden in the boiler room at the far northeastern end of the school for three and one-half hours, emerged and raced to safety. At about the same time the terrorists delivered a video they had shot of the interior of the gym. They did this by simply throwing it out toward the troops and yelling that someone should come pick it up and they wouldn't shoot. Later, the government told journalists and the public the tape had been blank. Though the tape of the terrorists and their captives would eventually make it onto television worldwide, by March 2005 the government was again claiming that the original had disappeared.

The terrorists later used their cell phones to call someone to whom they gave one of their phone numbers, with instructions that it was to be passed on to the government officials on scene. Up until this point they had refused any efforts at negotiations. Once contacted by government negotiators they refused to make any demands, baffling the FSB officials in charge. Not until hours later, after repeated requests by Russian negotiators, did they finally offer any reasons for the taking of the hostages at all. They demanded the release of the 30 Chechens and Ingush held by Russian authorities, who had attacked four towns in Ingushetia on June 21 and 22. The Russian authorities, however, refused to publicly confirm the demand was made. The terrorists also demanded that a negotiation team be put together for them, comprised of North Ossetian President Aleksandr Dzasokhov, Ingusheti President Murat Zyazikov and former Ingush President Ruslan Aushev.

News media reports that the terrorists had also demanded the intervention of the famed pediatrician, Leonid Raschal were false, according to the Special Forces. Raschal was noted for his supposed involvement as a negotiator in the Nord-Ost Theater siege in October 2002. Alpha, Vityaz and SOBR officials all claimed that, despite his notoriety, he had merely received permission to go into the theater as a volunteer to aid those stricken by gas. At Beslan, all of the officials I spoke with insisted that no one there asked for him; not the terrorists and certainly not the government. That he had arrived at Beslan late in the night of Day One was, according to them, completely on his own. One intelligence officer said that it was his belief Raschal had come of his own volition, and "some government official thought it might be a good idea to let him stay." However, I was warned by several Spetsnaz leaders that the "official" government version is that Raschal had been requested and they delivered him there, proving they had done everything they could to work with the terrorists to save the children.

At the time of the assault, Ingushetia's current president, Zyazikov, was reported to be in Spain on vacation and unreachable. Though North Ossetian President Dzasokhov would later be reported as having taken a lead role in the negotiations, those on scene for the government and military units would insist he never appeared. *Time* magazine later reported that he claimed he had been detained by the Russian military for his own safety to prevent him from being taken hostage; a general reportedly told him that orders had been issued to arrest him for his own protection if necessary.[14] After the crisis, it became apparent that Dzasokhov had never appeared at Beslan at all.

Despite Zyazikov's inability to return from his vacation, Russian President Vladimir Putin managed to race back from his own at the seaside resort town of Sochi. He was not again going to suffer the political fallout of enjoying his own recreation while a national crisis was at hand, as had happened on August 12, 2001, with the sinking of the submarine *Kursk*. At Beslan Putin did all he could to demonstrate that he was in full command, while at the same time refusing to compromise his own policy against dealing with terrorists. According to reports, he immediately dispatched Russian FSB Director Nikolai Patrushev and Interior Minister Rashid Nurgalieyev to Beslan to assume operational command and control of the siege. However, no one remembers ever seeing either of them in Beslan at any time during the crisis, nor were they present with Putin upon his arrival there shortly after it ended.

Earlier in the day, Putin's special envoy to Russia's Southern Federal District, Vladimir Yakovlev, had told reporters that one Mikhail Pankov, head of the Ministry of the Interior (MVD) for that district was in command. Later that same day, President of North Ossetia, Aleksandr Dzasokhov, was said to have taken over. Since then, official

---

[14] "The Talks That Failed," *Time*, Sept. 20, 2004, p. 15.

statements from North Ossetian President Dzasokhov's press secretary, Lev Dzugayev, indicated that the FSB had assumed command through Director Patrushev's first deputy, Vladimir Pronichev. Even more confusing is the fact that throughout the ordeal, regional head of the FSB Valeriy Andreyev was put before the cameras on numerous occasions, with reporters being told that as head of the FSB in North Ossetia, he was in command. To a person, everyone I spoke with from the MVD, FSB and other government agencies and military units insisted that "Andreyev was never in charge of anything," and that his only role was that of spokesman to the media. Nevertheless, shortly after the crisis was over, Putin fired him. What became of Pronichev is unknown, though certainly no harm has come to FSB Director Patrushev, one of the two who never appeared at Beslan as ordered.

By 5:00 p.m. on Day One news reporters were saying that the terror leader sent out a note with a single released hostage. Supposedly, this note provided a cell phone number at which negotiators could reach him. The note was further reported to have said that 50 hostages would be executed for every single one of them killed, and 20 for each one of them wounded. No note was sent, and certainly no hostage released. These threats were communicated during the terrorists' first cell phone call with government officials after having their number forwarded to them. Throughout the rest of the day, negotiators attempted to persuade the gunmen to accept food, water and medicine for those held in captivity. Fearing poisoning, or a trick of some kind, they repeatedly refused. The terrorists, having studied Russian tactics in such situations, proactively threatened to begin executing hostages if the school's electricity was shut off, or if telephone communications were shut down or intercepted by government forces. In anticipation of another known government tactic, the terrorists told negotiators that if any of their own relatives were brought to the school as prisoners, they would not hesitate to shoot their own loved ones down, too. One reporter indicated that he was told the government had already identified at least one of the terrorists, and was then considering bringing that man's wife to the school. The negotiators quickly abandoned this plan.

By the time government forces had a critical mass of men on scene, the citizen "volunteers" had already been there for many hours. They attempted to incite a confrontation with the troops, yelling that they were already there, knew what they were doing, and they were "not going to let you kill our children."

As for the "elite of the elite" - the Moscow divisions of Alpha and Vympel - they had received the call to deploy late in the morning of September first. Those on duty quickly began packing their equipment, and others, on leave, were called in. Lacking their own dedicated aircraft, some time passed before Air Force cargo planes were arranged. After the almost three hour flight from Moscow to Vladikavkaz Airport, they arrived at Beslan over a span of 12 to 14 hours after the siege had begun. Thus, it was 11:00 o'clock at night before all forces to be deployed to the siege were in place. In the interim, no one was still quite sure who was in charge.

Throughout the ordeal, the teeming crowds would prove to be the single greatest obstacle to the elite counter-terror teams establishing positions, developing an assault plan, and attempting to stabilize the situation sufficiently to even attempt a surprise attack. The crowds provoked the terrorists at every opportunity and made a mess for the commandos. As the siege wore on, the level of drunkenness increased. Fights broke out between the "volunteers" over whose turn it was to hold the guns.

As the terrorists were fortifying the school and establishing defensive positions, they began checking floors and walls against possible invasive action by government forces. This involved the use of grenades to create holes, allowing them to see beneath the floorboards. Countless news media reports that the terrorists had stored weapons, ammunition and explosives in the school during remodeling throughout the summer are said to be incorrect by the Spetsnaz. "Only because of the large number of guns and bombs does it seem that this was possible," one Red Beret major told me. It is true that some cosmetic remodeling had been done on the school during the summer. However, everything the terrorists had, they brought with them in their vehicles, with the GAZ 66 troop carrier capable of carrying at least 20 men with full equipment and weapon loads itself.

In the wake of the attack, the FSB contacted and interrogated all workers who had access to the school over the summer. With only one exception, all were local workers and teachers at the school, and everyone staunchly insisted that hiding weapons and bombs in the school without detection was impossible. The sole exception to the use of exclusively local, Beslan residents and school employees, was the brother of one Beslan teacher who traveled from Dagestan to assist in the construction.

The section of the library floor, which was shown on Russian television as having been torn up – purported proof that weapons had been stored there – was still completely barricaded amidst the rubble of furniture and bookshelves when I first arrived. No one could access it at the time, and the door into the very small room in which the floor had been torn up was never breached by the Special Forces at any time during the battle. The holes themselves were small, little different from the numerous other holes that had been made by the terrorists as a preventive measure against Alpha tunneling under the ground floor, or using the wide, manhole size sewer system to attack from below. The terrorists had also been concerned about government troops accessing the school's communication system or air ventilation ducts, as they had at Nord-Ost, and probed many areas of the school to prevent a similar gas attack. When we returned two months later to examine the school further, it was clear that the library still sported the same, decades-old floor it had for most of its life. This eliminated any possibility that weapons had been stored during its replacement.

The question of whether the terrorist siege at Beslan was dependent on previously stored armaments seemed to pervade even the U.S. government and news media. In an effort to disseminate important information regarding the siege to American police and schools, only 40 days after the Beslan siege ended a joint FBI/DHS report was distributed to federal government agencies, state and local school officials and law enforcement, relating a number of supposed facts, including information that the weapons at Beslan might have been cached in advance. Unfortunately, some of this information was inaccurate. With regard to the storage of the weapons, many U.S. officials inferred that not only was this an established fact, but that the Beslan School siege could not have happened at all but for the secreting of weapons in the school months ahead of time. From this, many school officials concluded that so long as they remained vigilant and watchful of suspicious persons trying to hide things in their schools, such an event could not possibly happen in America.

In an effort to prevent just such a dangerous approach in our own preparation, immediately upon returning from Beslan in September I attempted to send an email to Homeland Security Secretary Tom Ridge through one of his top officials, offering to travel immediately to brief him on the actual events of that tragedy. In part this was motivated by a syndicated report I had read in a newspaper on my return flight from Russia, in which Secretary Ridge was quoted as saying that DHS was attempting to learn all it could about the incident, but up to that point they had been forced to rely solely on media accounts. My offer went unanswered and a trusting American public allowed itself to believe it had little cause for concern.

As night came on, one young man was told to begin throwing more of the bodies of the many that had been killed throughout the day out the window into the west side yard. Recognizing that it was too dark for anyone to see him, he leapt from the window while the terrorists were busily loading spare magazines for their assault rifles. When dawn's early light touched that distant yard, 16 twisted, mostly naked bodies – school employees, teachers, fathers and students – were heaped in a pile under that window.

Chapter Five

The Siege – Day Two

The life of your friend is always
more important than your own.
You can die yourself,
but rescue your friend.

Cossack Code

It was not until almost 2:00 o'clock in the morning of September second, that Dr. Leonid Raschal arrived. Though not requested by either side, it appeared he was allowed to contact the Chechen terror leaders by phone. During that call he was assured that all the hostages were fine. His offer of food, water and medicine was refused, as were the others before it.

At 3:00 a.m., as Alpha and Vympel continued to get set up, the terrorists demanded that Aslanbek Aslakhanov, Putin's special adviser on Chechnya, be added to the negotiation mix. Aslakhanov, who had been one of the negotiators at the Nord-Ost Theater crisis, arrived later that afternoon.

By dawn the terrorists were high on drugs, distributed to keep them alert after a long and tense night. No one knows exactly what they were given, though Russian military officers confirm their belief that it was some new type of amphetamine. They were already beginning to crack under the strain, and arguments were breaking out amongst them. They spent the day constantly shooting at any person who showed himself outside, and firing wildly into the ceiling of the school. The killing continued. At one point, in the course of these cold-blooded murders, one of the terrorists taunted the hostages, asking if they thought 22 bodies were enough. Later in the morning of that second day the final group of five men and boys were lined up and shot in the upstairs hallway overlooking the northern courtyard, thereby completely eliminating any threat of resistance from the hostages. The second floor had become the terrorists' favored killing field.

The siege dragged on throughout the day. By then twenty thousand people were crowded around both the school and the Culture Center 200 meters to the northeast, adding to the circus-like atmosphere. The command post was surrounded by hundreds of reporters with their hi-tech vans, space age communication systems, and snakelike wires running in every direction. The crowds at the Center implored the military command not to assault the school. They were assured by all of the government officials on scene that no assault would take place. The terrorists were not the only ones feeling the strain. Several people in the crowds outside, older citizens of Beslan, suffered heart attacks.

Alpha and Vympel, by then firmly in place, had established tactical positions around the school with the aid of the Rus' snipers who were still in position. A poor contingency assault plan, to be used reactively should the terrorists begin killing all the hostages, was hastily thrown together, though soldiers were not maintained in the positions necessary to launch such an assault. Plans for an offensive assault began to be discussed. Though some within these units were in favor of a rapid assault, it was ultimately determined that with the bombs in the gym, it would be too dangerous to attempt. The men were told to wait. With no real official leadership, no one wanted to be responsible for making a decision.

Later accounts suggested that when the two anti-terror assault units were told there would be no storming of the building, they simply packed their gear and stood down. They are also false. No one wanted to see a grisly end to the siege. Rather, they apportioned perimeter sectors and shifts on duty around the school between them, and waited, ever vigilant. Neither the lack of actual leadership or command, nor the fact that they had no decent contingency assault plan in place, in any way detracted from the courage of these men or their commitment – should it become necessary - to race headlong into harm's way to save the innocent children inside.

Earlier in the day, when the last group of teenage boys and men had been executed on the second floor of the building the commandos had not reacted. The crowd, however, continued to provoke the terrorists by shouting insults and threats, as well as firing their weapons at the very school containing their loved ones. Undaunted by the deteriorating situation and almost an entire day of failed negotiation efforts, former Ingusheti President Ruslan Auschev arrived on the scene in the afternoon. The terror leader quickly agreed to meet with Aushev, a respected politician and leader throughout the region, who persuaded him at once to release three women with breastfeeding babies. Some time later he got them to release another 26 hostages, mainly women with the youngest children, for a total of 32 hostages. After the constant killing, this move by the terrorists baffled negotiators.

Despite the delight of the townspeople, Russian government officials, and the commandos at this seeming demonstration of compassion, the terrorists could not achieve even this single act of kindness without proof of their barbarism. They selected those women with infants who had been steadily getting on their nerves. As the women and babies were lined up in the hallway just inside the main entrance – the same entrance they had pulled up to in their trucks endless hours ago - one of the terrorists pulled 27 year old Zalina Dzandarova aside. The young mother of a six-year-old daughter, Alana, and two-year-old toddler, Alan, they laughed as they forced her to choose between leaving with her infant son, or remaining with both children. Zalina, and every single one of the mothers permitted to depart, were made to leave behind at least one school age child. In the end, she was forced to abandon her daughter in order to save her little boy. One mother, scant feet from the threshold of the doorway that would bring her safety – and life – thrust her baby into the arms of a nearby terrorist, imploring Aushev to take it away, and raced back into the gym to be with her son. The cruel irony of the terrorists' ultimatum would come when, at the end of the siege, Alana Dzandrova would be found alive. Zalina and Alana Dzandarova will need a lifetime to attempt to repair the damage done to their small family in that one instant. The same is true for all of the mothers forced to abandon their children; at least it is true for those who lived.

Many of the terrorists were Ingush, including Aushev's former bodyguard, as well as several others who were reportedly close to his family. These connections boded well for him in affecting the quick release of the women and children. As negotiations continued, Aushev even offered himself and numerous other important political and law enforcement figures as substitute hostages, in exchange for more of the terrified women and children inside. The terrorists were promised a "corridor to Chechnya" and safe passage, with these high-ranking figures as collateral against attack. The terrorists refused. They were outraged that Russian President Vladimir Putin would not negotiate with them personally or send any direct messages. One Chechen hostage-taker reportedly told the crowd of victims that no one would receive so much as a mouthful of water until Putin talked to them.

After the release of almost three dozen hostages, the terrorists went no further, and continued to refuse any food, water, or medicine deliveries into the school. A number of the hostages, including children, suffered from diabetes as well as other medical conditions that made the regular administration of medication crucial to their survival. They received nothing. In between negotiation sessions, the terrorists detonated small bombs and grenades and fired their weapons, often toward the teeming crowd outside to keep them back. Periodically, they became unnerved when troops appeared to have closed in some small distance, and they would shoot directly at them, forcing them back. An ambulance was destroyed by an RPG.

Despite Putin's long-standing refusal to negotiate with terrorists, in this one instance he did agree both to refrain from assaulting the building, and to grant the hostage-takers safe conduct into Chechnya; an unexpected – if not unprecedented - concession due to the many children inside the school. Moreover, it was reported that he even attempted to enlist the aid of Aslan Maskhadov, the former Chechen president and one of the top rebel leaders. *Time* magazine reported that North Ossetian President Dzasokhov said that he had personally contacted Maskhadov's London representative, Akhmed Zakayev. Zakayev himself, is an accused terrorist in Russia, and has been living under political asylum in Britain since his indictment. In response to this supposed overture from Dzasokhov, he claims to have conveyed Maskhadov's horror "at this atrocity," and pledged his cooperation.

According to news reports it took some time to iron out the details of Maskhadov's guaranteed safe passage into Beslan and back with the Russian authorities. *Time* reported that on Day Three, the Russians and Maskhadov needed just two more hours to reach an agreement for Maskhadov's entry into North Ossetia. Forty minutes later "a bomb went off in the school and the slaughter began," according to *Time*. Maskhadov would later be implicated in the planning of the siege, despite his protestations against the savagery of his own people's attack on the school. Several highly placed Spetsnaz officers who were at Beslan during the siege said that Maskhadov had, in fact, attempted to contact Putin through the prime minister of the Netherlands. They reported that his proffer to assist in the negotiations was designed to accomplish two things: (1) place him in a position to gain information on government forces' plans for dealing with the siege; and (2) to change his reputation in Russia's – and the world's – eyes as a terrorist, to his own benefit. As the Russians were certain that Maskhadov himself was in on the planning of the siege, along with Basayev, and that the Chechen leaders at the school were in regular contact with him throughout, the Putin government would have nothing to do with him. Despite these protestations against any altruistic efforts on Maskhadov's part, The *Moscow Times* would later report Zakayev, his representative, as insisting that Putin had attempted to reach him through the president of North Ossetia: "Knowing what a functionary Dzasokhov is and given what kind of responsibility was on his shoulders at the time, I don't think he would have done that without the Kremlin's sanction, even if it was his own initiative," according to Zakayev. At one point later Maskhadov, would be quoted by others as confirming that his forces were involved.

As Day Two wore on, North Ossetia's Speaker of the Parliament, Taimuraz Mamsurov, whose own son and daughter were in the school, began drafting an agreement for an end to the siege along with Dmitri Rogozin, head of the Russian Parliamentary Committee on International Affairs. Though they had reached no agreement with the terrorists, they hoped that if seen in writing, an offer of a substantial amount of money and a helicopter would have some positive effect. All they wanted was the children freed. By evening the terrorists sent out a note, purportedly handwritten at the direction of rebel leader, Shamil Basayev, during a telephone call. After a day and a half of government negotiators pleading for any type of substantive demands from the hostage takers, this note finally provided them with a starting point. It ordered the withdrawal of all Russian forces from Chechnya and independence for the Chechen Republic. After all this time, the government negotiators were shocked. Such an unrealistic demand did not bode well for a peaceful resolution to the situation. The Chechens had levied the same demand at Nord-Ost.

And just as at Nord-Ost, Alpha and Vympel were busy training for a potential assault. Dividing their units up – with some on perimeter duty at the school – they were transported to a building similar to the Beslan Middle School No. 1. Contrary to hundreds of news reports this was not at the large and sprawling BMK Vodka Factory in Beslan, only three kilometers away from the school. The only building they had been able to find that came close to the school's complex design was in Vladikavkaz, 30 kilometers (18 miles) away. There they began practicing to storm the building. At one point, being alerted that gunfire was erupting elsewhere in Beslan, many of the citizen volunteers and soldiers alike broke from the crowd at the school and went racing to the vodka factory, guns at the ready, believing a different faction of terrorists had seized another building. This was likely the cause of the many reports of the factory being used for assault training. Beslan was incendiary, and it was quickly reaching uncontrollable proportions.

They could not prepare fast enough. Additional hostages were still being periodically executed in the second floor auditorium, where many of the girls were held, and elsewhere in the school. Beatings were rampant. There appeared to be no reason to any of it. The terrorists were now fighting among themselves. From the beginning, one faction of them seemed to know exactly what the plan was. These were the committed *jihadists*, ready to die for their cause. The fact that they had not attempted to cover their faces was not a good sign. The others, mercenaries in addition to being committed Muslims, appeared angry that they had taken a school full of children. It seemed that was not what had been expected. The two groups argued, and the stress of the situation outside increased the tension and hostility between them. Media reports were as well rampant that at one point one of the women, strapped with a suicide bomb, had argued with the leader, Khuchbarov, who then shot her in the head. Other reports claimed he detonated her belt bomb. Alpha and Vympel soldiers who were inside the school during the fighting on Day Three say neither story is accurate. Those who took part in the bloody battle to control the first floor of the school maintain both women blew themselves up at different points in that corridor as the troops closed on them, attempting to take as many commandos with them as they could.

Three cars in the area around the school were fired on with RPGs, Russian rocket propelled grenades. One of them was parked more than 100 meters away on Soslan Botagov Street, to the east of the school. The people in it managed to escape. Still other reports that from the start of the siege the terrorists held a tiny two-room classroom building just 15 meters outside the main entrance where the terrorists rolled up in their troop carriers are incorrect. The terrorists never split their forces this way, and anyone in the small one story building would have been quickly eliminated by assault troops early in any attempt to storm the building, if not earlier during the standoff.

Late at night on the second day, a number of the terrorists slipped out of the school, attempting to find some breach in the cordon of troops through which they might escape. But the crowd was everywhere and saw them. Minor skirmishes erupted, and the would-be escapees were forced back into the school. The siege continued.

Top commanders told me that a decision had been made at the highest levels of the government. Due to the physical and psychological condition of the hostages, their extreme dehydration, hunger, and lack of necessary medication, the Special Forces were going to launch an assault on Day Four if there had been no peaceful resolution to the standoff. Government officials were concerned that the hostages, in such a dire state, might begin acting in unpredictable and uncontrollable ways, endangering all of them. No plan was yet ready, and no final decisions had been made on how it would be managed. The troops knew only that they would assault early on September 4. The use of gas was part of that plan. Despite public and international media protestations, it had proven shockingly effective at Nord-Ost. If they could achieve the same kind of results, the men would feel that they had done the impossible. However, no one knew what to do with the crowds of armed civilians. Though the men of the assault units were professionals, among the best in the world, up to this point the crowds alone had prevented any opportunity to launch a surprise attack. Even if a good plan were devised, any chances for success would likely have been eradicated by the sudden inquisitiveness of the citizens once they realized something was happening. Alpha and Vympel, alone and frustrated, continued to train through the night.

Chapter Six

The Assault – Day Three

Dear God, where do we get such men?
What loving God has provided,
that each generation, afresh,
there should arise new giants in the land.
Were we to go but a single generation
without such men, we should surely
be both damned and doomed.

— Anonymous military officer
As quoted by
Lt. Col. Dave Grossman, On Combat

Morning dawned on the third day with little change in the situation. Bright sunshine basked the members of the Special Forces in a gentle glow. The air was cool, the sun warm. "It does not seem right," they thought, "that such ugliness could be unraveling on so glorious a morning." It was a morning that would have served as a reaffirmation of the existence of God, but for the evil inside the building before them.

As was becoming commonplace, the terrorists – under the influence of their morning doses of narcotics - began shooting out of the school windows at the surrounding soldiers. No one was immune. Even local police and citizens were shot at anytime one of them showed his head round a corner or over a vehicle. The government forces extended their outer perimeter, attempting to move everyone back another hundred yards in some places. By this point the townspeople were demanding something be done, to save the people inside. No one – it seemed – could take much more. The terrorists, despite the failing physical state of the children, continued to refuse food, water and medicine. The sun, so gentle to those outside, would shortly return the gym to its greenhouse-like state. The heat was unbearable; and intolerable humidity rose off the bodies of those packed inside. The stench was unbearable.

At approximately 12:50 that afternoon the terrorists agreed to allow the command post to send four representatives of MChS, the federal emergency services department, to remove some of the bodies inside the school, as well as those that had been lying in a twisted heap in the west yard, below the second story window from which they were flung more than a day before. These were the rotting corpses of the many men and boys they had murdered, some of which were still stacked inside the school on the second floor. The deal was that the terrorists would drop the remainder of the bodies into the western yard, from which MChS personnel would remove them. Despite the courage necessary to walk out into the open, into the crosshairs of the killers, the MChS high command was inundated with volunteers. Still, they had to be careful; the terrorists had unobstructed views of the yard and could shoot all who entered beneath them. There was no door along that entire side of the building.

One van carrying the MChS members - all from its "Leader" special response group - entered the fenced yard on the west side of the school along the railroad tracks. As agreed, they were unarmed and wearing the clearly identifiable blue and orange uniforms of their agency. None of them wore body armor. They exited the vehicle and prepared to remove the bodies thrown from the second story windows. News accounts that the terrorists sent an observer into the yard during this body recovery effort are incorrect. The school's western side was almost a football field long, and there was no way in or out of the building from there. All of the first floor windows were heavily barricaded. To place an observer in the fenced yard with the MChS men, one of the terrorists would have had to walk out the heavily barricaded main entrance on the north side and proceed another thirty feet to the opening in the fence. A long way under the guns of hundreds of troops and berserk citizens. Unlike the men of the MChS special unit, the terrorists were not that brave. This barricade was never removed, however. Not even during the assault. On September 4, long after the dust had settled and the smell of gunpowder cleared from the air, the door remained completely fortified. The next closest exit point by which the terrorists could have sent an observer was more than a dozen yards away. The terrorists, guns trained downward, simply watched the MChS men from the upstairs windows.

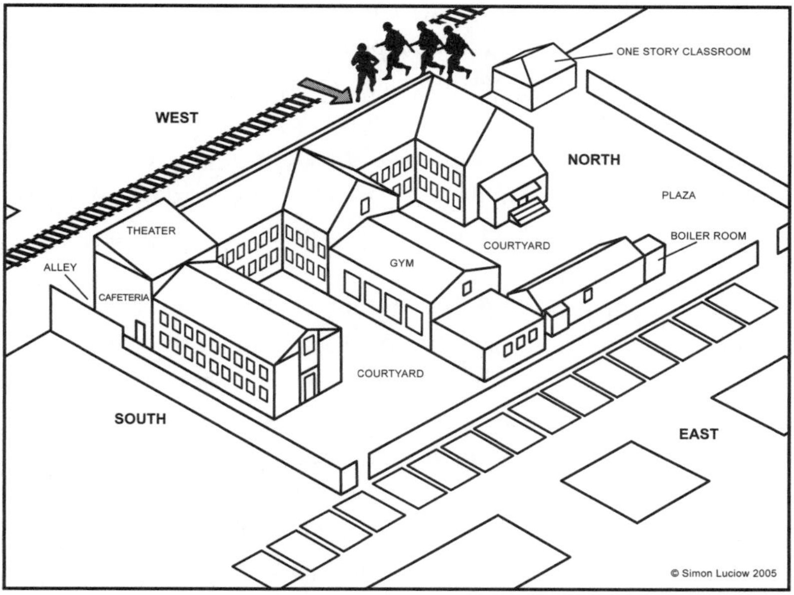

MChS Leader Group enters west yard to retrieve bodies.

At 1:05 p.m. witnesses said the terrorists began pushing more bodies out of the windows to the men below. According to one of the MChS men, just as the first body was loaded into the truck, there was an explosion. Seven seconds later it was followed by another. Everyone in the yard froze. The terrorists at the windows even seemed startled. They didn't know what had caused the bombs to go off, but appeared to believe that they had been duped. It was clear that they quickly concluded the government had used the retrieval of the bodies as a diversion to begin its assault. From their vantage point in the upstairs western windows, the terrorists were a long way from the gym - at least 45 yards - and on the wrong floor. They could not possibly know what was happening there. Some raced out of the classroom they were in and across the eight foot wide upstairs hallway to look out the windows down at the gym. Later reports from hostages in the gym would conflict as to the cause of the explosions. Those who seemed to be looking in one direction, say one of the bombs simply fell from the basketball backboard and detonated, an accident. Others insist one of the terrorist's feet slipped from the pedal detonator he was standing on. It is most probable that the falling bomb caused the other terrorist's foot to slip off of his device, resulting in the two explosions in rapid succession heard by a crowd of people that had feared this moment – feared it every minute – for two days. Whatever the cause, it started a chain reaction of events.

Hostages began panicking, leaping out of the windows decimated by the blast. Some had been blown clean through the windows on both sides of the gym. They streamed out into both the southern and northern courtyards, as terrorists began to shoot them. The terrorists who had been watching the MChS men, and who had then moved to the windows on the other side of the building overlooking the courtyard and the gym, started shooting into the mass of hostages racing for freedom, and life. They had what, in military terms, are called clear fields of fire and open kill zones. Everything below them was a target; they could shoot indiscriminately. Some of the fleeing children stopped once they were a few meters from the gym, confused and believing that once outside they were safe. They were mowed down with ease. Others, escaping out of west side windows, ran toward the small emerald-painted single story classroom to the north. Haggard from thirst, they stopped at an outdoor faucet to quench the thirst that had tortured them for two days. They, too, made easy targets and died gulping life sustaining water. Some of the terrorists on that west side of the second floor also began shooting down at the MChS men. Of the four, one was killed and another wounded before they could be withdrawn. At one point one of the terrorists leapt from the west side second story window, landing in the fenced yard. He is believed to have escaped in the melee.

When the explosions occurred that incited panic among the hostages and the assault by government troops, the terrorists' reaction was exacerbated by the conflict that had already been ongoing among them. The mercenary group used this opportunity – and the resulting chaos – to attempt to escape, while the rest sought the honor of dying for Allah, taking as many of the hated infidels with them as they could. The fact that the hostages who were left – after the heinous executions of the men – were mostly horror stricken children whose lives would be forever destroyed, and sobbing women, made wretched by the days of torture and abuse, did not matter. They should all die.

The Russian Spetsnaz units were reported to have opened fire immediately. Certainly, the Rus and Alpha snipers began taking out any terrorist who showed his head in a window. But assaulting the building was another matter. One of the great axioms of war is that no plan survives first contact with the enemy. But with no one in command, and government officials paralyzed by the unexpected turn of events, the commandos were left with no orders. The civilians in the crowd, however, suffered from no such affliction. Hundreds of angst-ridden fathers, uncles, grandfathers, brothers and friends, as well as many local police and security, engaged in panic fire, fueled by three days of sleepless, gut wrenching fear over the plight of their loved ones and neighbors. One general on scene was reported as having fretted that all these people merely "got in the way."

Within 30 minutes the four Mi 8/MT "Hip" helicopters, split between the distant vodka factory near the Terek River and the Vladikavkaz airport some eight miles away, were in the air. But with no teams in them to be inserted into the school or onto other areas of the roof, their pilots could only watch, impotent to use their mighty cannons or the rockets that hung ominously from their sides. The most they could do was attempt to direct fire at the school building, but in the roiling mass of people below, even this was fruitless. BTR 80s, Russian armored personnel carriers, maneuvered toward the north courtyard. The southern courtyard, too narrow for the bulky tank-like vehicles to negotiate, was left to the men of Alpha and Vympel to move through on foot, with no cover. Valeriy Andreyev, the FSB spokesman, was quoted as saying, "To save their lives, we retaliated." This statement would attach a level of organization and purpose to the government's plan that was scarcely justified.

In ten short minutes the interior of the gym ceiling fell in, a burning kaleidoscope raining timber, metal, glass and fire down on the helpless victims. It took but a few more minutes for the fire to burn in earnest, and the rest of the roof – the outside structural part – to collapse. Many were struck and killed, others trapped or buried alive, burning to death amid the heart wrenching screams of almost a thousand other souls. Outside, the Spetsnaz units of Alpha and Vympel held off entering the building, continuing to wait for orders. When all of this happened it was mostly Vympel that was on duty at the school. The rest of Alpha – those not on stand-down – were 18 miles away training at the building in Vladikavkaz. It took them until 1:50 p.m. to receive word of the events, leap into transports and arrive back at the school. Men from both of those units not on the perimeter when the fighting began grabbed the nearest weapon and raced to the school. With the sounds of combat erupting all about them, and the screams of dying children in their ears, most did not take time to retrieve body armor or helmets.

It was 1:40 p.m. before Vympel began to assault the school, but seemingly not according to any real plan. They merely reacted to events as best they could, drawing on every bit of training and experience they possessed. Those already on station attempted to move quickly to their previously assigned assault positions. Once joined by their backup, the forward Vympel teams began working feverishly to untangle the intricate and delicate web of wires set to detonate the explosives at the doors to the school. They had no success at the far eastern door of the south wing. Eventually Vympel had a tank that had been on station to the west move up. This monstrous clanking vehicle had been brought in under the order of FSB General Sobolev, the same man who authorized the two BTR 80 armored personnel carriers that had been standing by. Vympel team leaders had it approach the entrance to the narrow alleyway from the west. Taking the best position it could for an angled shot, it fired a non-exploding shell into the doorway just inside the alley, blowing a hole more than sufficient for the teams to enter. The shell, however, did not stop there but took out several interior brick walls separating classrooms on the south side of that wing. It was a risk for any hostages inside that section of the building, but the commandos had no choice. Those inside were going to die anyway if they didn't get inside the building quickly.

Under a hailstorm of bullets from the south side second story windows, Vympel raced along the south wall and through the newly opened door on the main floor, just inside of which was a stairway leading to both the second floor and basement. The gaping hole that resulted was proof that they were prepared to bring to bear maximum violence against anyone and anything in their way. Though Vympel troops succeeded in entering from the south, the courtyard to the north remained awash in a hailstorm of bullets, from both the volunteers and terrorists. Nothing could move, and many escaping hostages were shot down in the few yards they had left to cross, many dying within scant feet of loved ones and safety. Many of the Special Forces men I met with said that everyone realized this was no longer a military operation; they were just trying to rescue children.

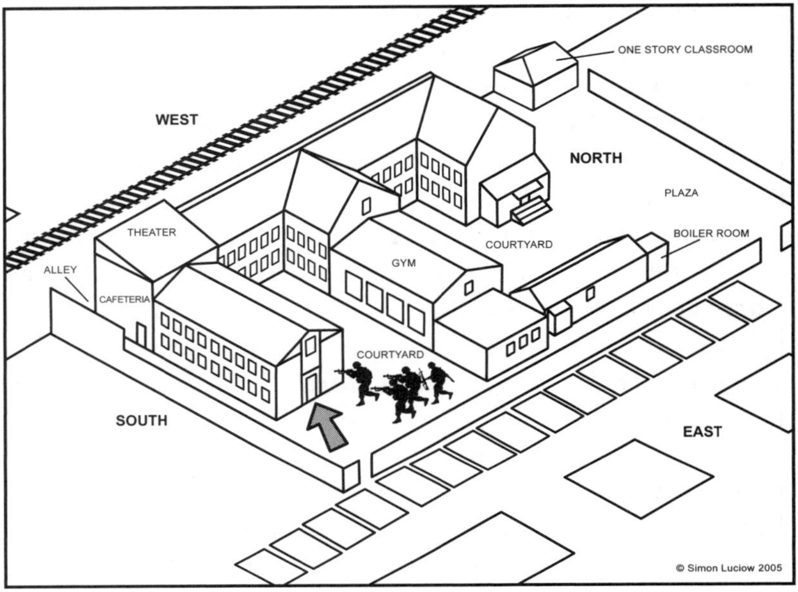

Vympel fails to breach south wing eastern entrance due to booby traps.

When the first bomb went off, Aida Sidikova, a tiny waif of a seven-year-old girl, clad only in a pair of white panties, had been blown through one of the large gym windows into the south courtyard. She laid there, a miniature figure surrounded by the tangled bodies of adults who had also been thrown through the windows by the blast. The woman right next to her quickly regained consciousness and fled. The Rus snipers, from their vantage high up in the adjacent apartment buildings, believed the rest all dead. After several minutes Aida's small form began to stir. Picking herself out from among the corpses, she stood there by the wall, small, frail, scraped, burned and bleeding, her blanched face evidence of the shock she suffered. She stood for mere moments, looking about, wrapped in the horror of the screams of those still inside.

Soldiers began yelling at her to lie down against the wall, the only place that offered sanctuary. To move in any direction meant sure death from the deluge of bullets. One young Rus sniper in a nearby building screamed into his radio, begging for permission to shoot her in a leg in the hope of dropping her miniature form to the ground, saving her life. That permission came too late. After looking about one final time, tears streaking white trails down her smoke covered face, the child turned back to the window ledge, pulled her little torso over it, and disappeared into the smoke, flame and screams of the gym, the only place her shattered mind could think would bring her the refuge of her mother and fellow hostages.

Amidst this conflagration of bullets and exploding bombs, innocent victims fell to the ground, eyes glazed over. Each would stare for eternity toward the point they had been running towards, for safety and refuge from the horror. Through it all – racing in the other direction - came the men of Alpha and Vympel. The Vympel teams crossed the open ground first, seconds ahead of their comrades in Alpha who had not been in Vladikavkaz. Some never attempted to find cover from which to engage an enemy gone mad with blood lust. An enemy who saw in this one terrible moment the chance to complete the defeat of the Crusaders, begun a millennia ago. In their ears, Allah shrieked for vengeance.

On the north side of the school, just 15 yards across from the main entrance, sat the small, one story building. Painted a beautiful emerald, its two rooms had been used as primary classrooms for the youngest children. The space between it and the main entrance of the school was open pavement where thousands of revelers celebrating the start of school stood just two days before. The school grounds, which opened for more than fifty yards to the east, formed an open killing field, and the hostages streaming out of the gym across the north courtyard had to pass through the deadly gunfire of the terrorists in the north arm of the school just across from the small structure to reach safety among the neighborhood buildings and houses. This would be one of the bloodiest episodes of all. In the tightly packed herd of fleeing victims, the terrorists could not miss. Shooting into the crowd, they killed people with ease. Vympel Major Andrei Velko had been positioned with his team across that open killing field. Velko, like many of the men who comprise these commando units, was young. They are shockingly young when you meet them. Despite their rank, in many cases they seem to be scarcely beyond childhood themselves.

Realizing there was no other way, Andrei Velko raced to the one point that placed him directly at the apex of the arc of fire from the terrorists in the school. Cutting off the angle of the terrorists' fire at the fleeing children, there he stood before his men, fighting back with everything he had. He knew there would be no returning. He and his men could not move away from the fire, could not use corners or other cover. All they could do was stand in the open – human shields - hoping the seconds they bought might save children's lives. Andrei Velko was killed by gunfire from the terrorists in the school building he never turned away from. He was barely thirty years old.

Fighting outside the gym raged, as desperate teams sought the means to gain entry into the school. Small groups of commandos raced up to the school, then back again across open ground as they attempted to cover the withdrawal of hostages from the gym. Lt. Col. Dima Razumovski led one such group. In the open, using his body to shield his fleeing charges, he was shot above his body armor and killed.

As was seen by people the world over in televised images, sections of the school's roof collapsed in other places as well. As explosives planted by the terrorists throughout the second floor detonated, the concussions collapsed the aged and weakened roof of the 115-year-old building in a number of spots. Meanwhile, the two BTR 80s finally rolled into the north courtyard, behind which citizens and troops took cover while firing on terrorists who dared show their heads in the windows. Large, wheeled armored personnel carriers, they looked like ancient monolithic creatures come to rescue all in need. Despite their seemingly gigantic size, they provided scant cover to the dozens of men trying to drag injured hostages from the horror.

Major Misha Kuznetsov of Vympel had approached the building from the west, the yard in which one man from MChS now lay. The terrorists were maintaining a steady fire at everyone on that side of the structure. The government forces held fast; they had to keep the hostage-takers from escaping across the railroad tracks. As the battle raged, Major Kuznetsov saw children huddling behind the barricade of one of the ground floor windows. Racing to the school, he found a table and placed it outside the window, clearing the glass and debris as best he could to help the children come through unhindered. As they leapt through the window and ran for safety he covered them, firing up at the terrorist snipers in the second floor windows. One of those sniper rounds found the main artery in his neck. Knocked to the ground, he continued to fire on the murderers above him, his own blood spraying across the manicured lawn – dotting the children red - as they raced past. It would be some time before his teammates could reach him. He died later that day in a Vladikavkaz hospital.

When Vympel managed to enter the main door on the south side, the team quickly split. One group remained at the base of the stairs leading to the second floor to prevent an ambush from above. Just past the stairwell to the right was a hallway running east. It led to the shop class where the terrorists had readied their most heavily fortified position. Many of them had already fled there, preparing for a final battle. But the cafeteria to the left, immediately past the stairwell entrance, had to be dealt with at the same time. While one fire team engaged the terrorists down the hall leading to the shop, the rest prepared to assault the cafeteria. The Vympel insertion teams were all alone, with several battles to wage at once. There had been fewer than 150 commandos on station at the school when the killing and explosions had erupted. With those on stand-down having joined them, there were still fewer than 300 men to save over 1,000 hostages, and attempt to secure and enter an enormous building with

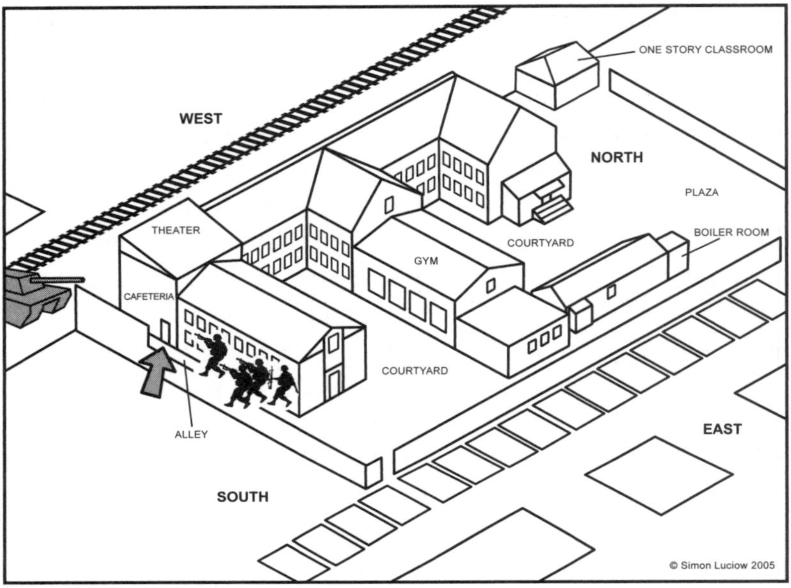

Vympel has tank maneuver to west side alley entrance to blow door.

dozens of terrorists and hundreds of grenades and IEDs inside. They positioned themselves outside the room that, until two days ago, had known only the happy cacophony of children at lunch.

The cafeteria had been the second largest holding area for hostages, and a bloody firefight erupted between the Vympel soldiers and the entrenched terrorists, with the innocents between them. The cafeteria was small, 8 yards by 15 yards, slightly over 1,000 square feet, not including the tiny kitchen which jutted off the main eating area. Toward the end the terrorists took refuge in a narrow hallway running behind the stoves. It was pitch dark inside, with numerous small side closets and places to hide. The battle to secure this area took a long time, and the fight in this one room would continue through most of the day. It was ugly close quarters fighting. Combat at its worst. Grenades were thrown at will by the terrorists; eager to create as big a body count as possible. Many of their intended victims would never leave the room alive. Hours later, there they lay: heroes and hostages alike on the floor. Their bodies touching in seeming reassurance that the victims' horror was finally over. One way or the other, the commandos had been true to their word; they had delivered the innocent from their suffering.

Though the commandos battling in the dining hall needed all the help they could get, the teams could not afford to let the terrorists approach up the main hallway in numbers. Nor could they allow the terrorists to kill hostages held elsewhere without interruption. With the cafeteria battle raging, other Vympel teams proceeded northward up the main first floor hall of the building. Unlike American tactical doctrine of never moving past an area until it is completely secured – a painstaking and slow process – Russia's elite recognized

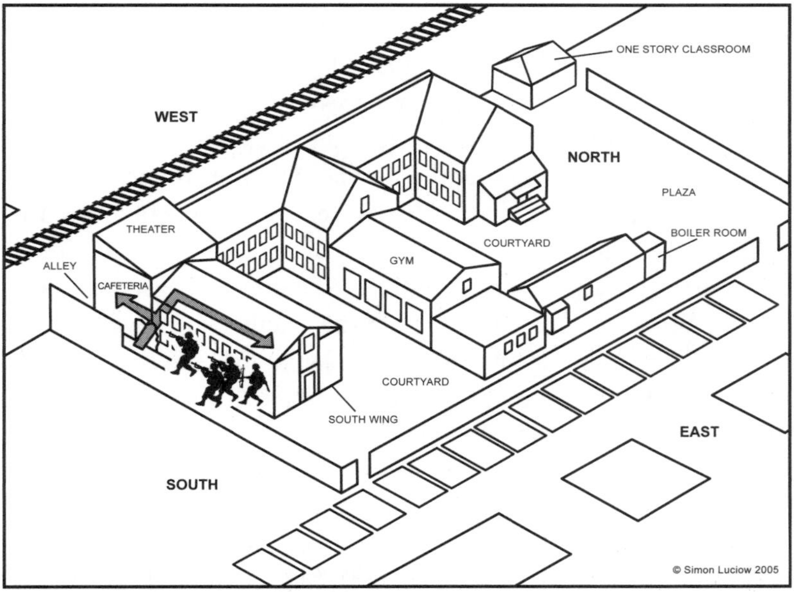

Vympel engages terrorists in south wing shop and simultaneously assaults cafeteria

that children's lives were at stake.[15] They moved quickly from room to room. Firefights erupted in a number of places throughout the hall. One heavy machine gun nest had been erected by the terrorists, a short distance up the hall. As soon as they entered the 90 degree right turn into the main corridor that took them around the cafeteria, one of the women blew herself up in front of them. Her shattered remains stuck to their visors and uniforms, ran down the walls and made footing slick and difficult. The horror of this did not even cause them to hesitate, however. These were not men to trifle with. Tough and well trained, they were there to kill.

Tactics in the first floor classrooms were simple. At the classrooms on the left, each assault leader stepped quickly in with his right foot, sweeping his AK 74 assault rifle from right to left, spraying high up on the walls. On full automatic this had the effect of putting the heads down of anyone inside. The terrorists crouching there were then killed, as teams leapfrogged from room to room as quickly as possible. The same tactics were repeated in reverse order in the classrooms on the other side of the hall. The Spetsnaz had chosen the AK 74 over its more famous predecessor the AK 47, for one main reason: its smaller 5.45 mm round did not cause over penetration of the school's walls the way the heavier 7.62 mm round might. It is smaller even than the much criticized 5.56 mm bullet fired by America's M16 and its more modern variant, the M 4. That hundreds of enraged and drunken fools in the crowd outside began peppering the school with 7.62 rounds was not their fault. There was nothing they could do about it, and they were as vulnerable to the withering fire coming from that mob as the terrorists and hostages. Tight faced, they moved on through the school. Though their teammates and

---

[15] While the Columbine massacre has caused law enforcement agencies across the U.S. to develop policies for moving in the direction of gunfire in active shooter scenarios, few if any have contemplated a situation in which officers would find themselves in the midst of numerous, well trained terrorists, in fortified positions, with hostages held in various locations. This reality necessitates the development of new protocols to deal with moving quickly toward the sound of gunfire, while still ensuring that responding tactical teams are not attacked from areas they have already moved through or past.

friends were engaged in heavy combat in several places behind them – in the shop class hall and cafeteria, at the stairs leading up – they could not go back.

Halfway down, they moved past a narrow hallway on the right, which led into the gym. It was only five feet wide, containing a gymnastics balance beam, whose base spanned the entire width of the hall. With that apparatus, and other debris piled inside, the hall was barely negotiable. Some of the assault team broke off to clear the bathrooms and girls' dressing room branching off to the left of this hall, before proceeding to the gym and engaging whatever terrorists remained inside. Other Alpha assault teams were already in the gym, having approached from the opposite end. The girls' locker room was full of discarded clothes and underwear. Bras and panties were thrown everywhere, a grim reminder that many had been raped repeatedly over the past days. After the battle would be completely over,

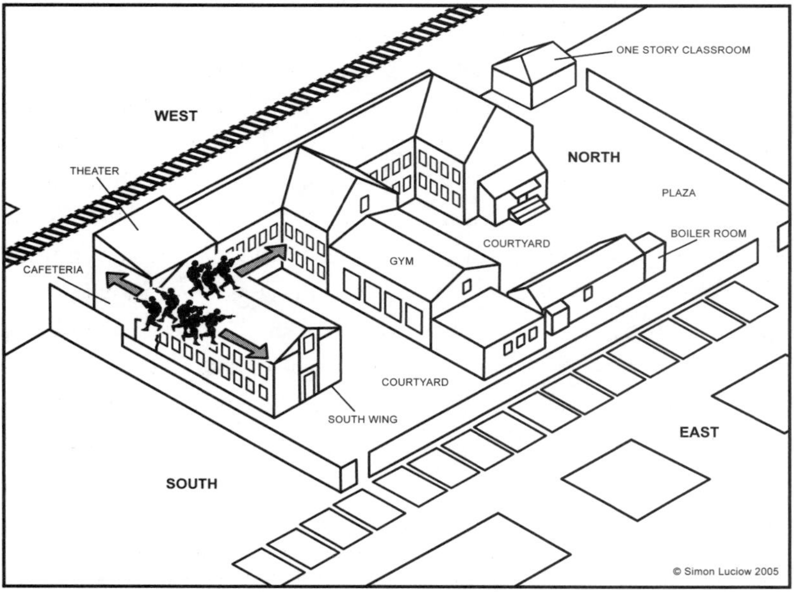

Commandos proceed north along first floor main hallway. Other teams continue to battle terrorists in south wing shop and cafeteria

someone would come into that dressing room and delicately hang all of the girls' clothing on hangers and hooks on the wall, a final act of decency for those who had been so brutalized. There they remained months later, even as the building was prepared for demolition.

As members of the assault team moved through the claustrophobic hall into the gym, the terrorists were caught between them and an Alpha team positioned on the far side of the gymnasium. At the beginning of the assault, this Alpha group had scaled the six-foot high wall behind the long white wing of the school that connected to the gym at its eastern end. Coming in through the back windows, they had quickly moved through a small, adjacent gymnastics room and to the door leading into the gym. Other teams raced up to the enormous gaping holes that were once the gymnasium windows, now framed with jagged teeth of glass and wood. They needed to coordinate their entry with the team that was only then preparing

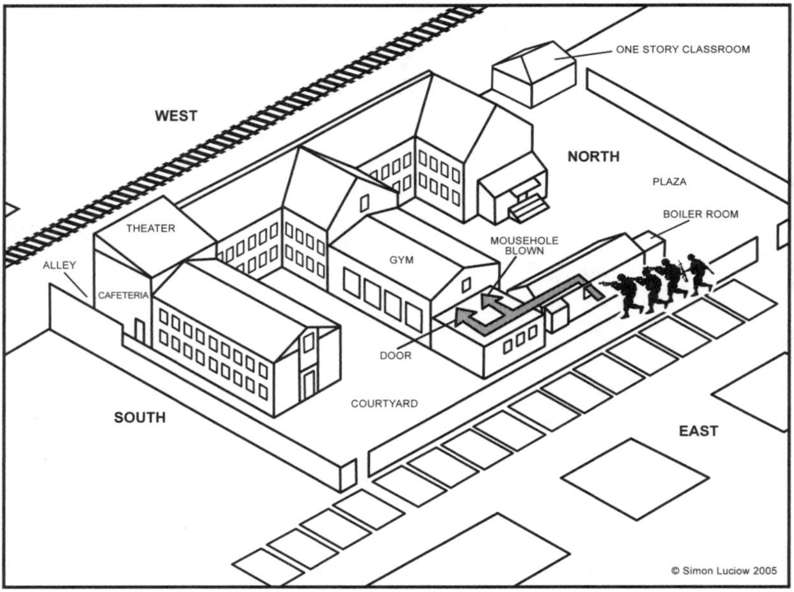

Alpha crossed fence and entered east side white wing. From there they entered gym at door on left and through mouse hole.

its Mouse Hole charge to blow a hole in the east wall under the backboard. Though only seconds passed, it was taking too long. They were out in the open, exposed to fire from above. Hostages were dying; they could not wait. The explosion, when it came, sent bricks and mortar hurtling into the gym. Though the hole was only two feet high and three feet wide, the sound, concussion and debris flying into the gym gave them all the opportunity they needed for one team to come pouring through it, while the other groups assaulted through the doorway and fired through the windows. Those standing at the windows shooting inside were completely exposed to terrorist gunfire from second story windows. They had only the cover of their comrades standing beside them, exposed as well, firing upward. Hostages were rushed back through the tiny hole and door to the sanctuary of the gymnastics room. For a time the fighting inside the gym was intense.

Vympel Lieutenant Andrei Turkin – himself barely out of his teens – massed children behind his back in the gym. His teammates tried to help him get them out. Suddenly, a terrorist leapt out of a side storage room and into the gym with a hand grenade. As he brought the grenade to his chest in an effort pull the pin, arming it, the young lieutenant grabbed him in a mighty bear hug that would last for the rest of his life. With the bomb pressed tightly between their bodies, they fell to the floor. The grenade exploded, killing Turkin and the terrorist; the children were saved.

Much later, when all the terrorists in the gym were dead, the commandos moved back through the hallway, past the balance beam and into the main hall. Terrorists in the hall back at the southern end leading to the shop were still being engaged by the Vympel team assigned that sector. The main entrance door to that hallway at the far eastern end, forming the right leg of the "W", had not been breached. Completely booby-trapped, it had proven too difficult for Vympel to access from the outside. Now it prevented the terrorists from escaping out the same way. They were trapped in the shop class at the end of that hall.

As Vympel moved toward the end of the corridor to the north, Alpha teams – having finally arrived in force from Vladikavkaz – entered the same hall from the north. With the main entrance heavily barricaded, and not knowing if it was booby-trapped, they had come through the windows to the left of it. With the two groups of commandos moving toward each other fire control was critical. The second and last female shaheed blew herself up in the hall between the advancing soldiers. The terrorists not killed in this ambush had already fled up the north end stairs to the second floor. With firefights still ongoing in the cafeteria and elsewhere on the first floor, the assault teams quickly put together a plan to move to the second floor. There were three stairways total in the school, and they had to all be dealt with at once. The Vympel team that remained at the stairway just inside the demolished southern entrance was still in place. This stairway was also the only one that led down into the basement. When the

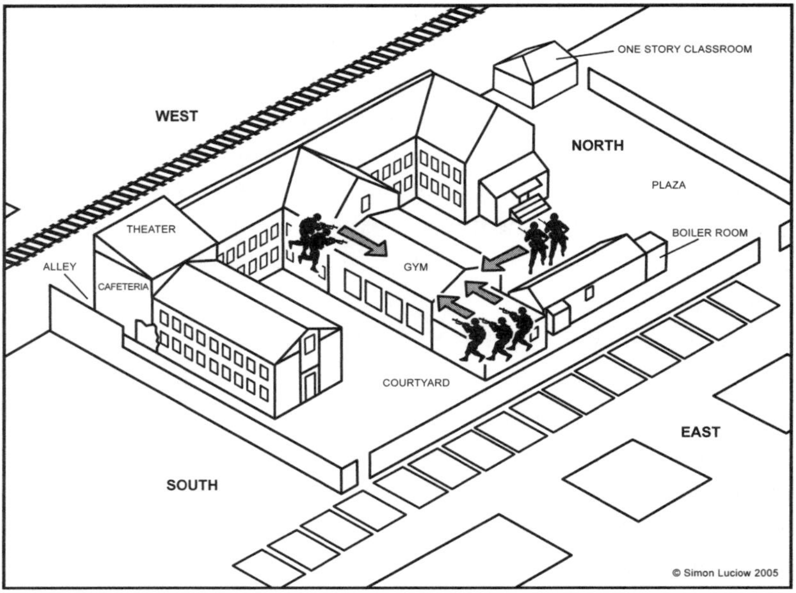

Vympel assaulted the gym through the narrow corridor from the west. Alpha entered gym from east and took positions at north side windows.

doorway was blown, debris and rubble clogged the stairs leading down. It would be some time before anyone would have the chance to move through the twisted metal and large chunks of concrete and other debris to finally secure the environs below the school. The next set of stairs was in the middle of the school, just to the left of the entrance into the small hallway containing the balance beam. The last one was at the far north end of the building, just inside the main entrance that had not been breached.

The men of Alpha and Vympel who fought their way into and through the first floor of the school quickly divided it into sectors of responsibility. Each sector had to be held secure, allowing the second floor advance teams to move ahead without fear of being ambushed from behind, from the valley of death they had already walked through. Each stairway was comprised of a first set of thirteen steps, at the top of which was a landing with a 180-degree turn and a second set of thirteen steps. The stairways were tight, only about four feet wide. The assault teams would be vulnerable to anyone at the top. At the beginning of the assault, in order to enter the building, brave men from Alpha had subjected themselves to open fire as they ran across the north courtyard to its interior corner just opposite the unopened main door. With no protection beyond suppression fire they had rigged another Mouse Hole demolition charge, seeking to access the building from a third point. The resulting hole initially was just enough to peer through. They were under the north side stairway, the one just inside the main entrance, as they had hoped. What they did not know - and could not have known - was that the school used this space as a storage area. The entire area under the stairs was crammed with furniture and an assortment of seasonal treasures used by the children throughout the school year. There was no getting through. They had to go back through the hail of gunfire and look for another way.

Though Alpha and Vympel teams would ultimately enter through the north side windows, next to the barricaded main entrance, the teams would not assault through the classroom windows on the west side, the same side where the MChS men had attempted to retrieve the bodies of the slain men and older boys. Though barricaded with bookshelves, tables and desks, the windows had no bars and were low enough to allow entry. However, team leaders were concerned about friendly fire casualties as the assault teams entered each room from the hallway inside. Hunkering outside to engage any terrorists who attempted to escape, the commandos were easy targets for the murderous snipers in the upstairs windows. The assault teams could not secure the second floor fast enough.

Back at the stairways, the decision was made for the teams assigned to the middle and south end stairways to hold on the first floor, ensuring no terrorists escaped downward at those points. They had to position themselves carefully, so that they could prevent any terrorists from moving down the stairs, while at the same time remaining protected

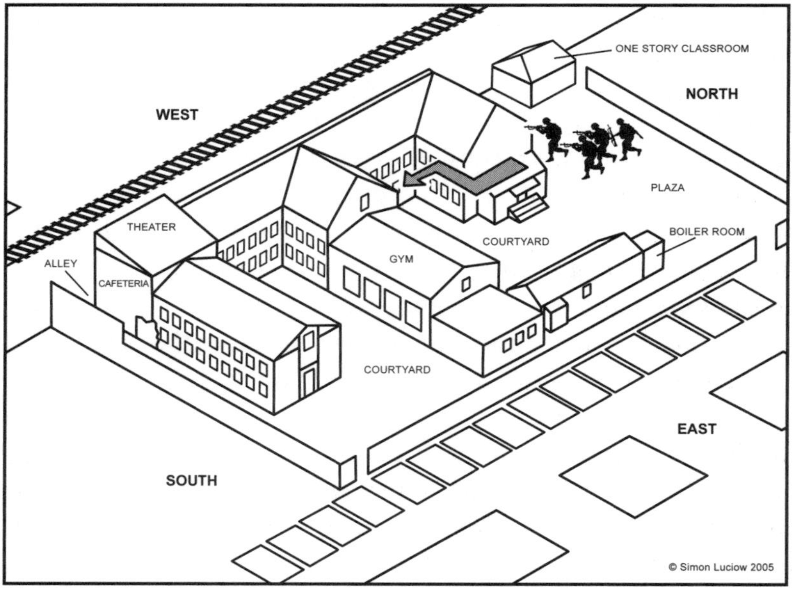

Alpha enters through north window near main entrance; and proceed south down main first floor corridor.

from grenades dropped from above. Only the teams at the stairs at the far north end, just inside the school's main entrance, would advance upward, driving the terrorists toward the other end and – hopefully – into the vengeful fire of their comrades at the base of the other two stairways. It was a classic hammer and anvil military plan. Vympel team leader Major Roman Katasonov launched a lightning assault up the steps. There was no other way to do it. Young, fit and strong, he and his men raced headlong up the steps, leaping over tripwires, shooting as they went.

On the top floor, hell broke loose. It was the battle in the cafeteria all over again. Terrorists, many with hostages as human shields, were holed up in different classrooms and behind barricades erected at various points in the hall. The floor of the hall itself was a mass of rubble, bodies and chunks of concrete strewn about from the many explosions that had collapsed walls and whole sections of the roof. The floors and walls were a collage of shrapnel and blood spray, pieces of human flesh and brain sliding down to pool amidst the ruin. The one advantage to being on the second floor was the lack of classrooms on the east side of the hall; there were merely windows overlooking the courtyards. All the classrooms were on the west, facing the fenced-in yard and sparse trees where the body of the slain man from MChS remained, his blue and orange jumpsuit stained crimson. Bodies of teachers, executed and abandoned, were found in the classrooms. Long after those bodies were removed, drying blood would create silhouettes of those who had been sacrificed. Makeshift altars of bottles, candles and burnt cigarettes, stacked upright in rows around them, would mark the final places they had laid.

The Spetsnaz drove the terrorists back down the hall to the south, hampered not only by incessant gunfire, but by the many anti-personnel bombs and booby traps the terrorists had planted along the way. Upon finally reaching the end, they encountered the same situation in the auditorium that they had in the cafeteria, immediately beneath it. The auditorium, too, was packed with hostages and terrorists. They wondered, "Would it never end?"

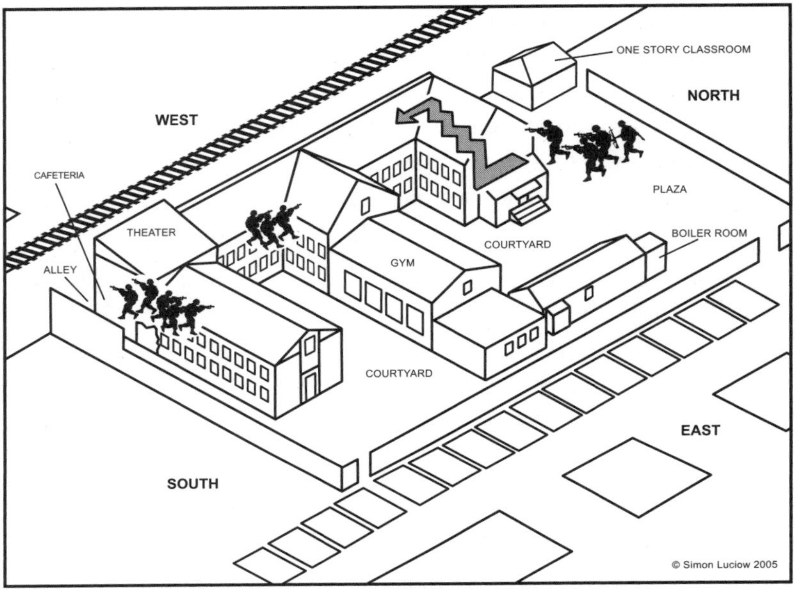

Commandos assault up north stairs while teams guard south and central stairways against attack from above.

The hall leading east across from the small auditorium, directly above the passageway leading to the industrial arts shop, contained three rooms on the right and access to the attic of the building. Terrorists had positioned themselves there as well. Alpha and Vympel still had their work cut out for them. Up to now, none of this had been easy. Most of the terrorists were well trained and battle tested from Chechnya and other conflicts. The Chechens have long had a reputation for being vicious – if not courageous - fighters, and they upheld that tradition in the school. A number of the men from the assault teams had already been killed and they still had many hours of fighting ahead of them. Plus, the terrorists had had more than two days to prepare for this, building barricades and developing their own plans. Individual teams of commandos had already paid a heavy price and in some cases were hobbling along under junior leadership.

Podpolkovnik is the Russian word for lieutenant colonel. Oleg Ilin held this rank, and was the leader of one of the first Vympel teams to reach the school after the initial explosions. Rather than wait for orders from above, he ordered his men to begin engaging the enemy immediately upon the appearance of hostages fleeing the gym. To protect them, he and his team had stepped out into the open, seeking to draw the fire of the terrorists away from the fleeing women and children. By the time they managed to get through the enormous and gaping hole they had blown at the south side main door, Ilin had suffered terribly, half of his face shattered by a grenade. With shrapnel burning in the flesh of his face, one eye and ear were completely gone. His blood-filled nose and throat made breathing difficult, talking worse. He was ordered to turn his team over to his second-in-command, and evacuate the building to receive medical care. Ignoring this order, he led his men first into the fight at the cafeteria.

Much of the combat with the terrorists inside the school was close, no more than five or six feet, hand-to-hand combat range. Ilin's team had been one of the first to sweep the entire ground floor. They had then proceeded upstairs. At the second floor landing, Ilin entered ahead of the rest. He was the leader, and no one in Spetnaz leads from the rear. Courage is not only a pre-requisite but a time honored tradition. As he turned a corner, a terrorist opened up with his AK 47 on full automatic. Refusing to turn back, to seek shelter, Ilin held his men back from moving around the corner behind him and into the line of fire. At the age of 36, he was dead. He would later be awarded the Gold Star – Hero of the Russian Federation, the country's highest medal for valor. Before the day ended, he would not be the only one so decorated; many posthumously.

Praporschik, or Warrant Officer, Denis Pudovkin, was also a member of Lt. Col. Ilin's team. Hit in the body with shrapnel from the same grenade that had shredded Ilin's face, he survived his commander's death and, seriously wounded himself, proceeded with the team as it took the classrooms on the second floor. As the terrorists in each room were neutralized, freed children massed behind the troops for cover. As the rest of the team entered one classroom, a terrorist jumped out from another. With his young charges behind him, Pudovkin stood tall and wide, a human wall, as he fired on the terrorist at the same moment bullets from the murderer's gun struck him. They both died instantly in the exchange.

Major Katasonov and his team continued to sweep the top floor. They quickly encountered a fortified machine gun nest the terrorists had erected in the hall for their PKM 7.62 mm weapon. In leading his team, Katasanov was engaged by the big gun. Covering his men and the hostages behind them with his own body, he died on that bloody floor. His men did not hesitate; they could not take the time to grieve, to lament the death of their leader. They moved quickly past his torn body to neutralize the weapon. In the tradition of the Spetsnaz there

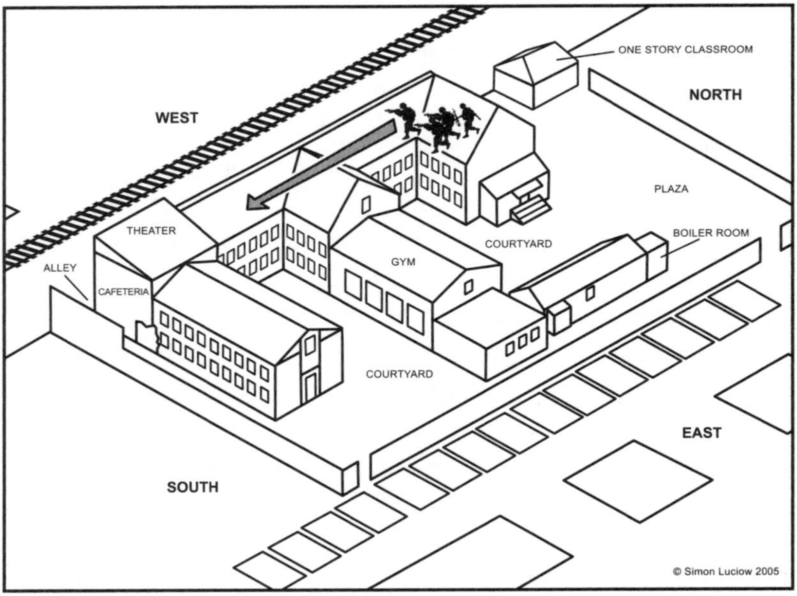

Alpha and Vympel proceed south on second floor battling terrorists in barricades and classrooms, freeing hostages.

would be time for toasts, and for tears, later. If they lived. There was fighting yet to be done.

What would make this all the worse, were the citizen "volunteers." Having raced up to the building in the chaos of the initial explosions, some had managed to get inside. Many more had followed Alpha and Vympel, spreading out behind their forward march. Now they seemed to be everywhere, in the way, in danger, and endangering the teams with their unpredictability and lack of discipline or training. They were crazy with fear, exhaustion and adrenaline. Catastrophically, their mere presence in the building allowed a number of terrorists to escape. Having changed into the tracksuits favored by people all over Russia for everyday wear, a number of the terrorists used the presence of the civilians to mingle and then slip out, becoming lost in the crowds. Some simply began acting like rescuers, there to help the assault squads or carry out the wounded. The commandos had to watch every direction. They couldn't know who was behind them.

At 2:30 p.m., less than an hour and a half after the explosions that started the battle, one group of terrorists tried to reach the railroad tracks 62 yards west of the school. In the confusion, as many as thirteen terrorists escaped with hostages to a nearby house. There, government troops ultimately tracked and killed some of them. Reports were rampant from hostages that terrorists had taken their clothes and changed into them, attempting to blend with the crowd of escaping hostages and disappearing into the streets around the school. One girl looked up from the stretcher she was being borne to safety on, to see that one of the men carrying her was among the terrorists who had brutalized her. Terrified, she told the first official she saw after being deposited at a waiting ambulance; the terrorist had already vanished into the crowd. Norpasha Kulaev, the only known terrorist to be captured alive, did not fight back at all. He was found hiding under a large truck far from the school.

By 3:00 p.m., additional Spetsnaz teams began searching throughout Beslan for other terrorists. They were rumored to have captured one person who was reported to have assisted the terrorists. The government never acknowledged having this individual in custody, and he was never heard from again. These sweeps of the town continued for days after the end of the siege. The atmosphere of martial law was relieved only by the countless reporters running about with their harried Russian interpreters, poking cameras into the faces of every soldier and citizen they encountered.

By 3:40 p.m., the battle at the school was reported to be almost over. This would prove premature. Firefights continued in some nearby buildings as troops ferreted out those terrorists who had escaped with hostages, as well as those who had been providing support to them from the outside. Alpha Major Vyacheslav Molyarov and Warrant Officer Oleg Loskov encountered four terrorists who had made it out of the school among a crowd of children. Suddenly lacking the religious commitment to meet Allah, they tried to get to some of the children to use as human shields. The soldiers did not hesitate; they had only a second to keep this situation from turning into yet another horror of close quarter fighting with innocents caught in the middle. The two men from Alpha leapt between the terrorists and the children. Everyone fired at once. All of the terrorists were killed in the hail of gunfire that lasted but a moment. Both Alpha men were dead.

At 4:10 p.m. the school was still burning from numerous explosions and thousands of tracer rounds. It was difficult, if not impossible, for firefighters to attack the fire due to the unexploded IEDs spread throughout the school. Spetsnaz units continued looking for booby traps. Hospitals and clinics began to accept the wounded and injured.

At 4:20 p.m., the fight at the school appeared to be winding down, but it was not over. Several more hours elapsed before the last shot was fired. Alpha Major Alex Perov saw a terrorist throw a grenade. He flung himself onto three children standing nearby. He died saving their lives. More fighting would occur when Vympel found terrorists and hostages hidden in the school's basement, and other terrorists were located squirreled away in the ceiling of the hallway above the shop class. Emergency teams and doctors entered the school at this time to treat the remaining wounded and begin removing bodies. Soldiers from Russia's 58th Army arrived on scene to assist in this effort. It would be more than eleven hours from the time the first bomb detonated before the school was deemed secure.

At 5:00 p.m., more than one hundred bodies were counted inside the gym, including hostages who died under the fallen roof. Spetsnaz continued to search for terrorists. On the south side of Beslan troops blockaded two small groups of terrorists with hostages in distant buildings. Elsewhere in the city civilians captured two terrorists who managed to escape from the school. They were literally torn apart by the enraged people.

With fighting still going on at the school and elsewhere, local fire-fighters moved into the school and attempted to put out the fire in the gym, in the south side wing, and in several spots on the roof. The

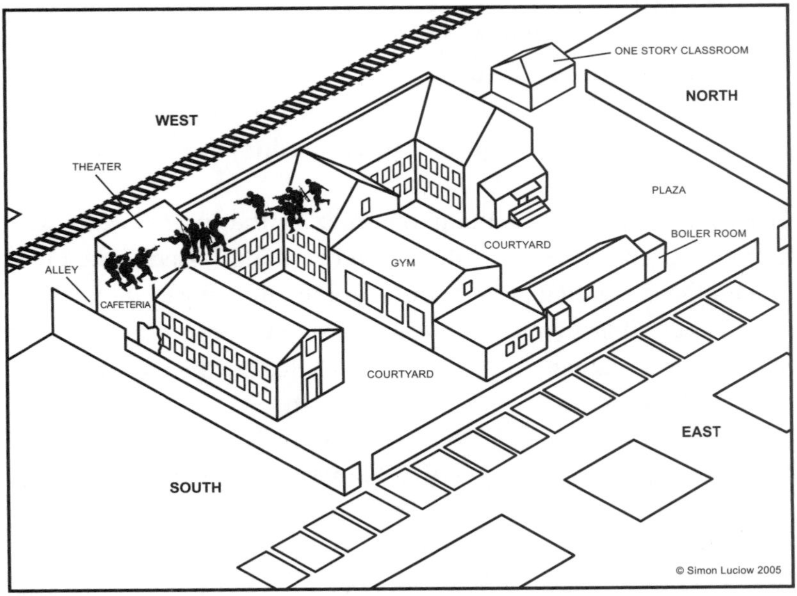

Commandos battle terrorists in second floor theater.

first of these units had arrived quickly, only ninety minutes after the initial bomb exploded. Unfortunately, that fire truck arrived with no water in its tank.

With bullets still pouring into the northern courtyard, firemen were forced to drag hoses up the alley along the south side, or through a narrow gap in the fence separating the school from the apartment buildings, in an attempt to reach the gym from that side. The alley was too narrow, and the turn into the south courtyard too tight, for any type of vehicle to enter. The MChS firemen were exposed the entire time. All were sickened by the charred remains of those trapped in the gym, burning under the remnants of the ceiling. Neither the firemen nor members of the 58th Army's Sapper group were able to approach the building before this point. Demolitions and engineering experts, the 58th's Sappers were too few in number to provide substantial tactical assistance. Combat Engineer Andrei Galagayev had been driving past the school with two other officers when they saw freed hostages running everywhere. They had no orders from any of their superiors as to what to do. Commandos just stopped them and asked if they were demo men. They immediately joined the assault teams and were some of the first to enter the school.[16]

At 8:00 o'clock in the evening, Spetsnaz of the FSB's Vympel and Alpha units conducted a final "special operation" assault when they located the last hiding place of the terrorists and "engaged to destroy them," according to one of the soldiers. A number of terrorists, including one known 17 year old, had fled to the fortified shop class in the south side wing, and in the attic above that. Whatever limitations the commandos had imposed on themselves up to this point were gone. Deploying their own RPGs and RPO "fire throwers" - recoilless rifles that deliver a high yield missile - they simply blasted that entire wing of the school into rubble. Nothing was left of either floor but a large gaping hole, lending to the overall appearance of the

---

[16] Nabi Abduallaev, "Beslan, Russia … Terror!", *Homeland Defense Journal*, September 2004, 28.

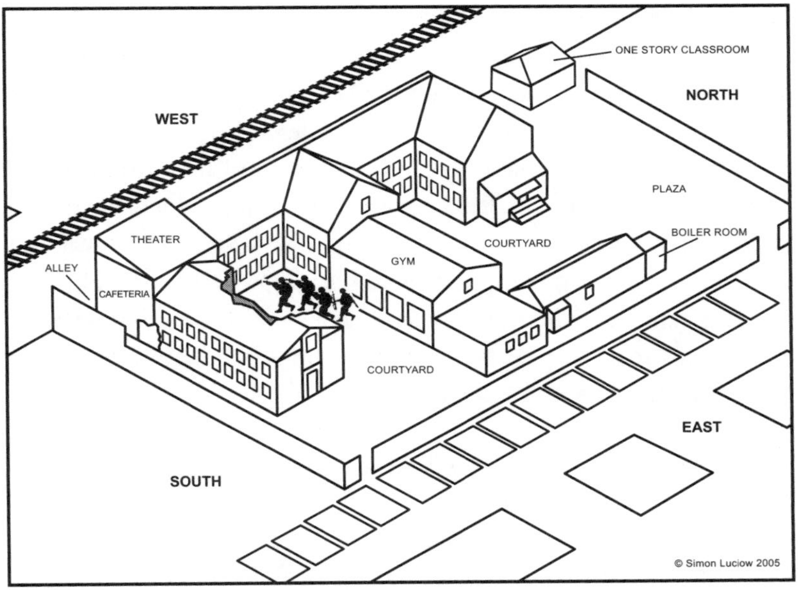

Government forces blow up entire section of south wing containing shop, final refuge of terrorists.

Beirut-type destruction the town suffered in this clash of religious intolerance and hatred.

This would be the last major battle of what became a war to recover the Beslan School. It would be several more hours before this destroyed section was searched for remaining terrorists, and the attic cleared, in addition to other remaining parts of the school. Another gunfight erupted in the school with terrorists hiding in the basement with hostages. A dark labyrinth with only one way in – down rubble choked stairs at the south entrance - the fight in the basement continued until after 10:00 p.m. The last terrorist was killed at 11:20 p.m.

At 9:00 that night, initial reports indicated that Beslan had suffered 150 dead, and 646 wounded. The numbers of the dead rose quickly, as did the number of wounded, to 767. Final numbers reported by

Vice Speaker of the League of the Russian Federation Aleksandr Torshin, the head of Putin's commission to investigate the Beslan catastrophe, were 330 dead, including 172 children, and 700 wounded. Prior to Torshin speaking, the number of dead had stayed at 338. No one knows what became of the other eight, and other government agencies continue to cite the larger number. Several weeks later 90 children remained unidentified; that number was lowered from 226 as parents recovered from their wounds and, in some cases, distant relatives came to claim the orphaned. Four months passed before all of the dead hostages were reported as having been identified, according to Deputy Prosecutor General Nikolai Shepel.

Eleven men from Vympel and Alpha gave their lives to save the terrified and suffering children at the Beslan School. Vympel suffered the greatest losses. Another ten from other units such as SOBR, Rus, OMON and MChS also died during the fight. Some of them were shot from behind by well-intentioned civilians as the commandos raced to the school to save the town's children. The number of the elite of Russia's military complex who died at Beslan is historically unprecedented.

In all, after piecing together various body parts, it was determined that 31 of the original 49 terrorists were killed in the battle for the school. Only 17 of those were ever identified. Of the ten Arabs the government first reported were part of the terror group, only two sets of remains have ever been sent to Interpol for identification. No conclusions can be drawn from these sparse numbers. There was little left of many of the terrorists' bodies to even identify them as ever having been human beings. But it was not only the terrorists who suffered this. In the gym the fire was so intense the body of one Vympel soldier was found with his helmet and visor completely melted to his face. One security officer at Beslan told me that at the end of the battle an enraged Alpha commando had cut the head off a terrorist and thrown it out a second story window. Spetsnaz soldiers confirmed this. No one could blame him.

Four months after the siege at Beslan ended, and the crowds and reporters were gone, Russian Prosecutor Mikhail Bobkov stated publicly that they had arrested a new suspect in the case. This man was reported to be Ingush, as were many of those who had taken the school. What was never reported in the Western news media were the dozens of other suspected terrorists who had since been tracked by government forces and obliterated throughout the entire region. In some cases, when confronted, these men holed up with hostages, just as they had at the school. The troops did not hesitate this time: no one came out alive.

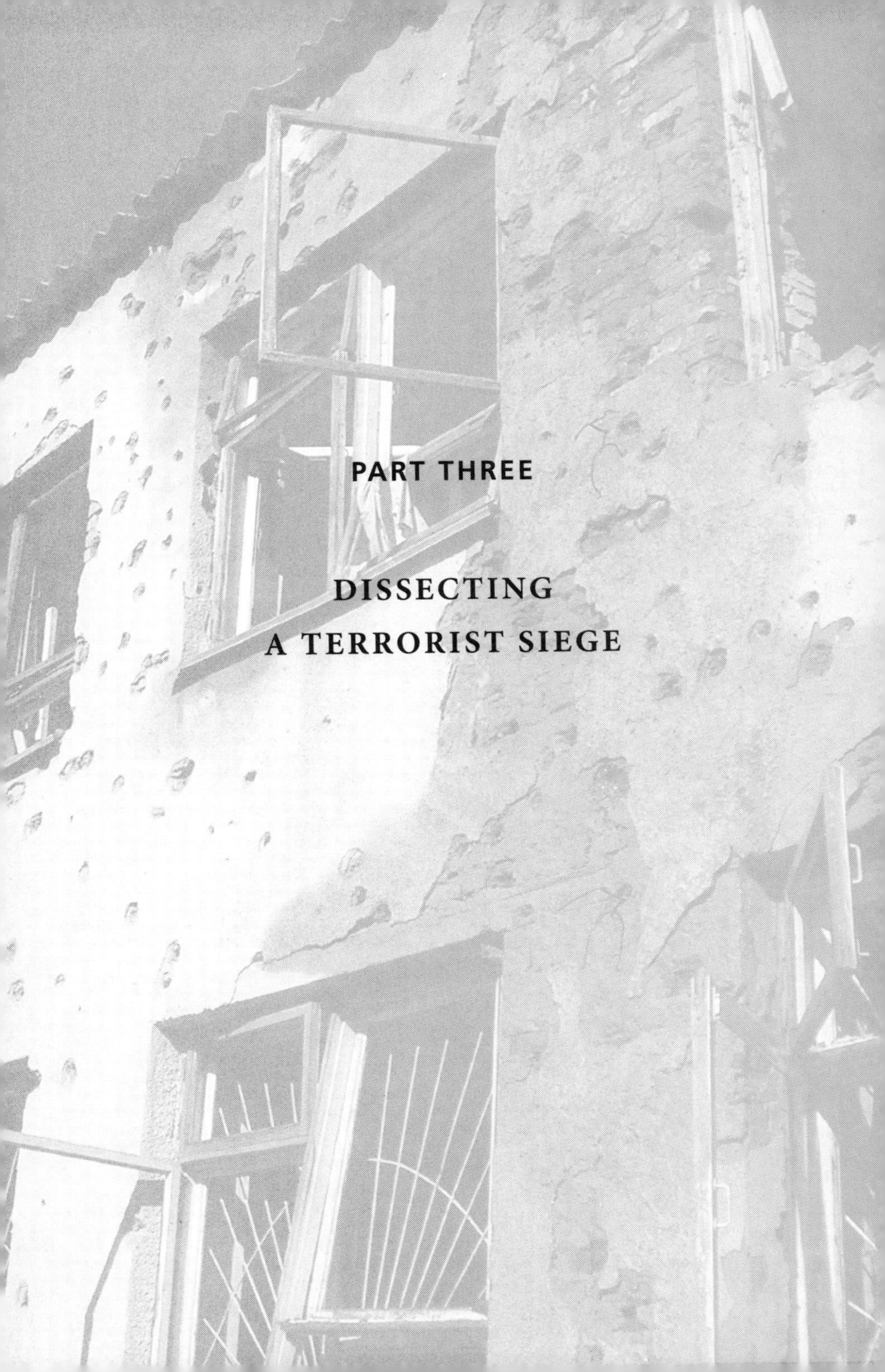

PART THREE

DISSECTING A TERRORIST SIEGE

Chapter Seven

The Terrorists' Plan at Beslan

When men of action cease to believe in a cause,
They believe only in action.

— Albert Camus

The terrorists had studied the Nord-Ost Theater outcome from 2002, and had learned their lessons well. At Nord-Ost, the terrorists discovered too late that they had committed a number of errors; errors that resulted in the successful storming of the theater by Alpha and Vympel, and at least one bullet to the head for each of them. The hostages had all been held in a single room. The explosives were pressure detonation - not pressure release or "dead man switches" – which would have ensured the detonation of the many bombs even if the bomber was killed. Also, the female terrorists in the room with the hostages were under strict orders not to detonate the bombs without an express instruction from the leader, who was seldom in the theater himself and had no direct communications with them. There was no ventilation either, which worked to the advantage of the use of gas. Ingress to the single area where the hostages were held was simple. The terrorists inside the theater, those with the hostages, had no gas masks. They would not make the same mistakes at Beslan.

The Beslan Middle School No. 1 was the oldest of the six middle schools in the town, and, unlike the others, had been built more than a century before. With additional sections having been added over the many years of its existence, it was a maze of rooms and interconnecting hallways. It was far from the simple, one-large-room design of the Nord-Ost Theater that had proved so vulnerable. All of the other schools in Beslan were of recent construction and simple design. They were all basic four-sided brick buildings, some with a central courtyard and one open end. In all, these would have been far too easy for government forces to assault, and far too difficult to defend.

Once again the news media got it wrong. Not one single depiction of the Beslan No. 1 school that I saw upon my return home was remotely accurate. A few had the right school, but published diagrams were missing half of the structure, leading American government and law enforcement agencies to believe that the challenge of securing and then assaulting the school was far less daunting than it was. Other news media sources printed a diagram of the Beslan Middle School No. 6. This depiction was even relied on by the United States Department of State, Diplomatic Security Service, and included in a PowerPoint presentation, in its effort to quickly educate U.S. law enforcement and government agencies on the situation that had faced Russian Spetsnaz.

A single, two story building in the shape of a squared off horseshoe, with the eastern end opening onto an interior courtyard, the simply designed No. 6 school stood on Oktyarbarskaya Street, one mile northeast of the No. 1 school. The renditions of No. 6's structure published for broad consumption were fairly accurate, even down to the running track next to it. The problem was that it was not the No. 1 school, which had no track at all and whose design was infinitely more complex. By the time I arrived back in the United States from the siege, some ten days after it ended, I had already been emailed a copy of State's DSS PowerPoint presentation. I was pleased to see that no time had been wasted in preparing to educate America on the siege. The problem was, there was significant inaccuracy in the slides I examined.

Thus, the school had been studied for some time by the terrorists. Their teams had obtained intelligence on it and the other schools in Beslan over a months-long period of time. With its proximity to the Ingush border, and its small population, Beslan was deemed ideal. Vladikavkaz to the south, with almost ten times the number of people, an MVD headquarters and enormous military presence, would have been too difficult. They were looking for a place that would offer itself up quickly, with little chance of immediate resistance. For a while they had considered seizing an orphanage in Beslan, one of the terrorists told some hostages. But that would have merely netted them approximately 160 children and adults. They were looking for a bigger score. The No. 1 School, with its special design and complexity, made it difficult to storm, and easy for several dozen men and women with explosives to control. It was perfect.

The terrorists behind the Beslan takeover knew, as Colonel Mikhail Ryabko pointed out, that in taking a school full of children they had upped the ante in the war with Russia to an unprecedented level. Col. Ryabko, a 20-year Spetsnaz veteran, is now the top advisor to Russia's Minister of Justice and one of those responsible for developing ways to deal with terrorist attacks like Beslan. "With the Beslan attack terrorism has just passed through a different level, to a different step," he said. And to have done so with a team whose members were drawn from other countries was a throwing down of the gauntlet to anyone who insisted Chechnya was merely a minor conflict within Russia's borders. In order to accomplish their ultimate objectives – to send a message to Russia that this war would no longer be confined to Chechnya itself – they had launched a series of suicide attacks in Moscow, the heart and soul of Russian government and financial power. The taking of Beslan, however, was to have the added effect of destabilizing already delicate relations between Ingushetia and North Ossetia, highlighting Russia's containment difficulties with that conflict.

According to many Spetsaz officers and government officials I met with, the terrorists were really comprised of two distinct groups or factions. Each of the factions had a different mission objective, and this caused conflict between them during the hostage ordeal. According to all, a number of them were "mercenaries." By this, they explained that while all were committed Islamists, the mercenaries had hired on to conduct a military terrorist operation, from which they expected to exfiltrate successfully and return home. Thus, they were "not there for ideology" or to be martyred, but ultimately for the money they were paid, and the terror they would cause. Of course all in the name of Allah. One Red Beret commando stated that the mercenary group "always had a completely different objective than taking hostages in a school." It was his opinion based on what he had learned from colleagues who had been on scene that assaulting the school was what the terrorists did when "something else went wrong." What this might have been, he says, no one knows.

Whatever the perceived objectives of the group in the school, Russian military and government officials are unanimous in their conviction that the terrorists at Beslan believed the school siege was merely part of a larger operation, that it was to have been a diversion of sorts. Some believe the main attack was to have come, once again, in Moscow; the target of two weeks of attacks leading up to Beslan. They cite this as one of the reasons why the terrorists, when initially contacted by negotiators on the first day, had no demands at all. It appeared they were waiting for some information or instruction from their leaders as part of the implementation of the grander plan, of which they believed they were a small but significant part. It was not until the other attack did not occur that relations among the terrorists, particularly between the two factions, began to deteriorate. Suddenly, with no other backup plan, more than a thousand elite commandos ready to attack, and behind them a crowd of thousands of armed and outraged citizens, the stress on them became extreme. Tempers were short and their abusiveness toward the hostages escalated. Many of them immediately wanted to begin seeking avenues of escape. Others, the leaders included, refused and ordered them to continue with the operation. By March 2005, other captured terrorists in and around Chechnya admitted that they had been part of a second plan to seize a government administration building in North Ossetia that same day. But when the school was taken, and military brought in seemingly from everywhere, their operation was aborted.

Fully two months after the siege, with ample time to debrief the captured Chechen Norpasha Kulaev, and conduct other investigations and raids in the region, the Spetsnaz were more certain than ever that luck was with everyone in Beslan when the terrorists' plans fell apart and only the school was taken. Russian officials are certain – and were from the beginning of the siege – that the terrorists had at least one, and possibly more, backup teams spread throughout Beslan. This tactic of simultaneous attacks is a trademark of al Qaeda, and the groups behind the Beslan assault had been well trained in this mold. A similar effort would be seen just three months later, on December 6, 2004, when terrorists would attack the U.S. Consulate in Jedda, Saudi Arabia. Though quickly put down by alert and reactive Saudi security forces, the original plan had been for several such coordinated attacks, all looking to maximize the number of hostages taken – and killed.

Back at Beslan the terrorists did, indeed, have support. Spotters in the crowd around the school were identified. Everyone from Alpha and Vympel to Rus officers who had been to Beslan assured me that the terrorist intel was "good." "They knew everything that was going on in the crowd and with government troops." It is not known whether the terrorists were set up by their leaders and this other operation was farcical and a ruse used to conscript them. Likewise, no one knows for certain if this grander operation had been planned but failed to be implemented. What is generally believed by the Russians is that, while one faction of the terrorist group at the Beslan School were committed *jihadists* willing to die for their cause, the rest of the terrorists entered the school that day expecting ultimately to escape. Chief Adviser to the Minister of Justice Col. Ryabko insists that the Beslan School situation was strange. "No one understood it, and it seemed the terrorists in the school didn't really understand what they had done either."

Several other Russian officials reported to me that when the mercenary faction of the terrorists realized that the others expected to die at the school, they began looking for avenues of escape. The first night some of them conducted forays out of the school to probe for any weaknesses in the lines of the government forces, or other gaps through which they could slip. Reports that when the "mercenaries" objected to this operation, three were killed, were never confirmed. Subsequent to initial interrogation of the sole, captured terrorist, Norpasha Kulaev, it appeared that the information I received had been correct: that for at least the ideologically motivated "martyr-terrorists", the school assault was always the plan, and that the "mercenary" faction had been "misled."

No matter their thoughts when they commenced the attack, the terrorists had arrived well prepared, carrying night vision goggles, sniper rifles, automatic and silenced weapons, and explosives. Spetsnaz team leaders said that they could not articulate just how many rounds of ammunition the terrorists had, the number was so great. Immediately upon securing the hostages in the gym, the terrorists booby-trapped almost every access or point of entry and exit in the surrounding school building, except the windows. Hostages would later report that eighteen bombs were rigged high up along the walls and basketball nets of the gym. From the videotape shot by the terrorists, and shrapnel spray patterns Yuri Ferdigalov and I inspected and photographed at length, it is clear that bombs had been rigged to both basketball rims or backboards, along the tops of the windows in the gym, and on the floor and to the hallway leading from the gym into the school. The windows had been broken throughout the rest of the school to neutralize the effects of a possible effort by government troops to use gas, as had been done so successfully at Nord-Ost. The terrorists brought gas masks along to defend against the possible use of gas. Once the windows were broken, desks, chairs and bookcases were stacked in front of them, which allowed ventilation, but hindered entry. The only exceptions were the windows of the gym, which were very tall and kept intact, causing the fearful overheating from which the hostages suffered.

Most booby traps used throughout the school were grenades, wired with intricate "webs" of tripwire, a system which is easy to configure, but difficult for even those employing it to disarm. The terrorists brought both F1 "heavy" grenades - with a lead body and a burst radius of as much as 200 meters – and smaller fragmentation grenades. Some were used early on to blow holes in the main floor of the building. They evaluated vulnerabilities and were concerned that the Spetsnaz would tunnel underground, breaching communications, accessing the ventilation system for a gas attack, or preparing an assault from below.

Having rigged the entryways with bombs, the terrorists spread throughout the school. Students were separated and held in different areas, such as the cafeteria, the library, different classrooms, and the auditorium, with some even in the industrial arts shop on the first day. Early on, women with small infants upset the terrorists, so they were put on the second floor. As a final measure they established sight or observation capability. Spotters were placed at windows and periodically on the roof, armed with RPGs and recoilless rifles. Their observations were coordinated with the information coming in from their observers with cell phones among the crowds surging about the school. The terrorist leaders were in regular contact with all of these operatives, who were able to give them real-time information on the movements and arrangement of the government forces. During the siege the crowd recognized three of these observers and killed them on the spot, denying the military forces valuable intelligence. At one point they located and fired a high explosive grenade at a Rus sniper team on the fourth floor of the apartment building immediately to the east of the school. They barely escaped as the entire apartment in which they were positioned exploded inward behind them. Three vehicles, all more than 100 yards distant were hit with rocket-propelled grenades. One, parked close to 300 yards away on the other side of the railroad tracks near the athletic club, was still smoldering when I arrived. Luckily, though two of the vehicles were occupied when attacked, no one was killed. One Alpha commando said that the Nord-Ost Theater siege "was a kindergarten compared to this."

It is now clear to Russian Special Forces that throughout the ordeal the terrorists inside were "listening to someone invisible," according to Col. Rodin. Though the leaders inside were highly placed rebel commanders, much of what took place was being directed from powers above even them via cell phone.

In all of this, the terrorists seemed to have not only applied the lessons of Nord-Ost, but cleaved closely to their training. The tactical training outline for al Qaeda's Saudi cells, written by the late Abdel Aziz al Mogrin - himself killed in June 2004 - appears to have been an integral part of the preparation and execution of the Beslan School plan. It is clear that the section of the tactical outline, entitled "How to Deal with Hostages," provided the blueprint for what the Russian Special Forces confronted. This tome of terrorism instructs its followers in every aspect of generating the greatest amount of fear, and attaining the greatest amount of death. It intones:

Separate the young people from the old, the women and the children. The young people have more strength, hence their ability to resist is high. The security forces must be killed instantly. This prevents others from showing resistance.

The terrorists wanted it well known that they had followed these instructions closely, killing the younger and stronger males very early into the operation, as soon as their usefulness had ended. While in Russia I had the opportunity to see a segment of videotape shot by the terrorists, with a group of men and boys lined up against a wall, kneeling with hands behind their heads, while masked murderers stood behind them just moments before gunning them down. This not only had the affect of eliminating the greatest source of resistance, but cowing the others, including the government officials, into complete submission and acquiescence. The only obvious security forces – the policeman and security guard – were killed within seconds at the outset of the attack.

The hostage-taking manual also advises: ***Speak in a language or dialect other than your own, in order to prevent revealing your identity.*** Reports from hostages published in newspapers indicated that the terrorists did not speak much, and usually only in whispers to each other, or communicated with gestures. By their speech among the hostages, many confirmed that some were Chechen and Ingush. The important aspect of the terrorists' compliance with this edict, however, was that the person they selected to conduct telephone negotiations with government representatives spoke Russian with no discernible accent, leaving the authorities to guess as to the composition of the terror force. This was a mistake that had been made at Nord-Ost. There, terrorist fear that the government would tap into radio transmissions saw them screaming at each other incessantly across the huge theater.

Mogrin's work also instructs terrorists to, ***Wire the perimeter of the hostage location to deny access to the enemy.*** This was the first, and one of the most consequential, tactical steps they took. While it was the consensus of Spetsnaz operators I met with that none of the hostage-takers was an expert at demolitions, it was clear that their knowledge was sufficient to hamper any assault by the commandos when the time came. Clearly, the bombs they rigged were at least good enough to explode – even if at times they did not want them to.

In determining whether to launch any operation such as Nord-Ost or Beslan, the manual provides five basic operational justifications for taking hostages:

1. ***Force the government or the enemy to succumb to some demands.***

2. ***Put the government in a difficult situation that will create a political embarrassment between the government and the countries of the detainees.***

3. ***Obtaining important information from the detainees.***

4. ***Obtaining ransoms.***

5. ***Bringing a specific case to light. For example, this occurred at the beginning of the cases in Chechnya and Algeria, with the hijacking of the French plane and the kidnapping operations performed by the brothers in Chechnya and the Philippines.***

With regard to the early hostage-taking incidents in and around Chechnya, numbers one and four, above, were present. Though the kidnappers were committed Chechen jihadists, their immediate and primary goals were to force the government to concede to certain demands – including the release of comrades then languishing in prison – and to get money, in some cases millions of dollars. As the Chechen conflict ground on, however, these efforts became more organized, more directed by Chechen command authorities, and consequently broader in scope and purpose. The taking of the Nord-Ost Theater was designed to make the government accede to demands that Russian troops be immediately withdrawn from Chechnya, to put the government in a difficult situation that would create a political embarrassment for the Putin administration – including countries such as the U.S. that had citizens inside the theater – and to bring the cause of the Chechen plight to light. These purposes would serve in the Beslan siege as well, though there appeared to have been no realistic expectation by then that troops would be withdrawn from the region, or that prisoners from earlier sieges would be freed. While some argument could be made that the purpose outlined in number three above could have justified the assaults on police headquarters and military bases in the region in earlier years, no one believes that any of the hostages taken in recent episodes had any tactical or strategic information. In fact, at both Nord-Ost and Beslan, it would appear that anyone who might have possessed useful information were among the first to be shot.

The terrorism planning guide also includes a description of the psychological makeup of those qualified for selection to a team of terrorist kidnappers. Had negotiators and government officials known this, it might have been useful to their efforts at Beslan. From the manual section titled, "Requirements Needed in Forming a Kidnapping Group," the following information on the commitment and viciousness of the terrorists in a siege may prove invaluable to American law enforcement in the event of a future attack. In no case did the Spetsnaz soldiers on the ground at Beslan think for a second that they were up against anything less.

Capability to endure psychological pressure and difficult circumstances. In case of public kidnapping, the team will be under a lot of pressure. Intelligence and quick reflexes are needed in order to deal with an emergency.

Capability to take control over the adversary. The brother is required to possess fighting skills that will enable him to paralyze the adversary and seize control of him.

Good physical fitness and fighting skills.

Awareness of the security requirements, prior to, during, and after the operation.

Ability to use all types of light weapons for kidnapping.

The manual further outlines how the hostage-taking team should be divided, and what each of the sub-group's roles is. Here, again, the terrorists proved themselves apt pupils with regard to the training they had received.

Protection group whose role is to protect the abductors. This function was fulfilled to an extent by the support teams of terrorists spread throughout the city of Beslan, and possibly ensconced high up in neighboring apartment buildings, as the Russians believe was the case. At Beslan, these units are known to have conducted surveillance of police, Spetsnaz and the people surrounding the school; though they may ultimately have failed in their mission to provide support to either an escape attempt or the execution of some other, grander, assault in the town.

The guarding and control group whose role is to seize control of the hostages, and get rid of them in case the operation fails. Here the group predominantly comprised of Chechens, Ingush and Russians was found. They were the ones charged with the duty of controlling, separating and – all too often – killing the hostages. When the government assault on the school began they were the first to engage the hostages as targets. The Arab faction had been in charge of fortifying other areas of the school, and fighting to defend it.

The negotiating group whose role is extremely important and sensitive. In general, the leader of this group is the negotiator. He conveys the Mujahideen's demands, and must be intelligent, decisive, and determined. Though, in this case the actual leaders may not have been the negotiators, they were clearly in charge and did not appear to hesitate to meet with former Ingusheti President Aushev, whom they knew would be a receptive audience. In no event, however, were the terrorists ever indecisive or undetermined in their handling of the government's negotiators or forces. That they appeared to have arrived at the school with little to nothing in the way of actual demands is more testament to their resolve to die in the school

– taking as many infidels as possible with them – than any indecision on their part.

The manual advises the hostage-takers how to conduct and control the negotiations. It encourages them to minimize the length of time that the negotiations are allowed to continue and advises them of the necessity of remaining calm at all times. It particularly warns them to be alert for signs of stalling on the part of the negotiators: ***In case of any stalling, starting to execute hostages is necessary. The authorities must realize the seriousness of the kidnappers and their dedicated resolve and credibility in future operations.***

At Nord-Ost, the government had successfully stalled a young and inexperienced Barayev, gaining valuable time with which to prepare and stage a successful assault. Barayev, for his part, had not executed any hostages as a result of government procrastination. At Beslan, the terrorists prevented any such opportunity. With no demands at all, they executed hostages with seeming abandon. The government was given no chance to attempt a stalling tactic, but was completely convinced as to the seriousness of the hostage-takers and their willingness to execute innocents; in this case children. By acting in this fashion, the terrorists had turned the tables: the government was prepared to do almost anything they asked, as quickly as it could. Only Putin's intransigent policy of not dealing with terrorists – and the sheer impossibility of accomplishing what they demanded – may have prevented officials on the scene from caving to terrorist demands.

The terrorist manual goes further in providing an outline of tactics to be employed in a hostage siege:

Security measures for public kidnapping. Though most typically employed in the kidnapping of individuals in public places, where the kidnapping group is completely vulnerable to everything from bystanders to the infortuitous presence of police, security or military, it was not without its application in Beslan. By Russian analysis, if the terrorists at Beslan had met unexpected heavy resistance, those positioned in surrounding buildings and streets would have immediately engaged, providing necessary time to break contact and attempt a run back across the border.

Detention must not be prolonged. The longer the siege drags out – even in the case of an individual kidnapping – the better the chances for the government to affect a successful resolution of the situation, even if that means storming the building.

In case of stalling, hostages should be gradually executed, so that the enemy knows we are serious. Again, this was one of the failings of the terrorists at Nord-Ost. In short, despite the heinous nature of their actions – and intentions – they were simply too civilized by Islamist extremist standards. Two years later, the hostages at the Beslan School would pay the price for this comparatively genteel behavior. Forced to sit outside and listen to the tortured screams of the hostages, of girls being brutalized and others mowed down or beaten for sport, no one at Beslan doubted the seriousness of those in control inside.

When releasing hostages such as women and children, be careful, as they may transfer information that might be helpful to the enemy. Here the terrorist leaders were careful. Few hostages were released, and each of those had a tactical purpose. The hostages to be released were young women with breastfeeding infants. They had seen little, and could not provide much more information than what had been provided by the rebels on the video. No one else was permitted to leave. Only Aushev was allowed into the school to meet with them. One has to wonder why they were not concerned about him leaving with critical intelligence to pass onto the - by then - anxious Special Forces.

You must verify that the food transported to the hostages and kidnappers is safe. This is done by making the delivery person and the hostages taste the food before you. It is preferable that an elderly person or a

child brings in the food, as food delivery could be done by a covert Special Forces person. The terrorists at Beslan came not only disciplined, but prepared. Between the food they brought, and the large amount of food they knew would be found in the school's cafeteria, they had no need to jeopardize their security, allowing the government an opportunity to drug or poison food or water, or to allow the troops to assault. In one hostage siege years before Beslan, Alpha had incapacitated the terrorists with drug-laced food. The hostage-takers at Beslan were not going to suffer from such negligence. That the hostages were given no food meant little, if anything, to them.

Beware of the negotiator. In such situations the negotiator for the government becomes the most important person. He is there to make every effort to see a safe resolution to the stand-off, or to help prepare a fast and bloody assault if he determines that is the only way to end the drama with the least loss of life. Here those inside the school were especially careful. One of the greatest frustrations for the government negotiating team was the terrorists' regular refusal to communicate at all. Hours on end they spent listening to the distant ringing of an unanswered phone. The terrorists talked when they wanted, how they wanted, and for as long as they wanted. There was nothing the Russians could give them, and so the hostage takers were in a position of power throughout the negotiations. One bereted captain told me that, "Negotiations were poor and hardly happened at all." "The government just wanted to stretch time, but mostly actual negotiations were only a couple of telephone calls, initiated by the terrorists when they were ready," he said. Only the proffer of a safe corridor back into Chechnya held any promise for a negotiated solution, and they seemed to be in no hurry to accept even that.

Still, they had studied the Russian Special Forces' history in handling these situations: they had to know they did not have long before the much-feared assault was launched. Even at Buddenovsk, with almost three times the number of hostages to deal with, a larger building, and being up against superior numbers of terrorists, the

Spetsnaz had shown their mettle and stormed the building. Yes, the elite troops were coming, and if the terrorists wanted a negotiated truce they would have to start talking. The only negotiator they were not careful about was Aushev, again raising suspicions as to why they would abandon mandated principles of controlling the situation for him alone.

Stalling by the enemy indicates their intention to storm the location. Not only the Russians, but every government with Special Forces counter-terror units to draw on, will attempt to stretch time out as much as possible. This is done for two reasons. From the government perspective, if the stand-off could be resolved quickly without bloodshed, there would not be a stand-off in the first place. As much as terrorists are trained to demand quick concessions, the government or police on scene are trained to draw the siege out to increase the chances that at some point, a peaceful solution will be negotiated. From the government side, a delay is as good as a win. For every minute a hostage is not killed, the probabilities of a safe end increase, or so we are all conditioned to believe. The other reason to delay is to allow the assault teams necessary time to prepare. They must determine – as best they can – the numbers, training, arms, and deployment of the hostage-takers. They must learn the positioning of the hostages. They must obtain and study the layout of the building, and confirm the presence of explosives. And then they must devise an assault plan and practice it. This takes time. In Alpha and Vympel's case it had never taken more than three days.

Beware of sudden attacks as they may be trying to create a diversion which could allow them to seize control of the situation. Well schooled in this principle, the terrorists reacted in full recognition of the likelihood of its accuracy. The terrorists in the gym when the bombs went off were – in many cases – killed or wounded. Others were dazed, and took time to come to their senses. These were the only ones who could have known what happened, and they were unable to use their communications equipment for some time to alert their comrades.

Above Archangel Team with freed slaves in Sudan. June 2003.
Front Row L-R: Yuri Ferdigalov, Darren Nardone
Back Row L-R: Mike Rich, John Anderson, John Giduck.

Above - Overhead view of school from apartment building to the east.

S.DAL / REUTERS / CORBIS

Hostages in gym. From terrorists' video.

Above Left- Seven year old Aida Sidikova climbs back into the gym after being blown through it by bombs.
Above Right - Within minutes the gym was engulfed in flames.

Volunteers and troops rush to aid victims.

YURI TUTOV. AFP. GETTY IMAGES

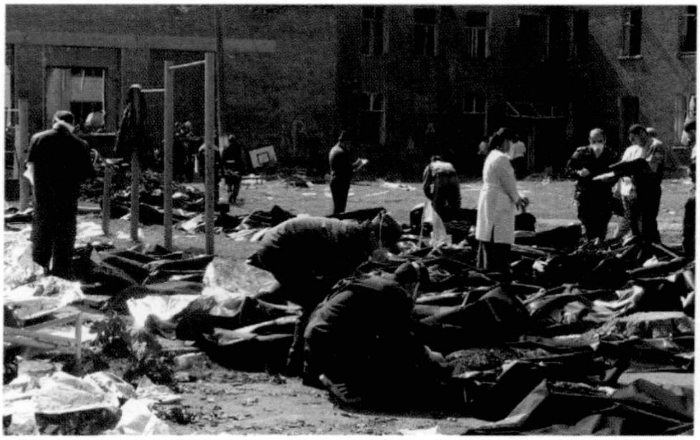

September 4, 2004. Bodies of victims taken from the school for identification.

PHOTAS. 3RD PARTY. GETTY IMAGES

Right - Troops and volunteers take refuge outside library.

OLEG NIKISHIN. GETTY IMAGES NEWS

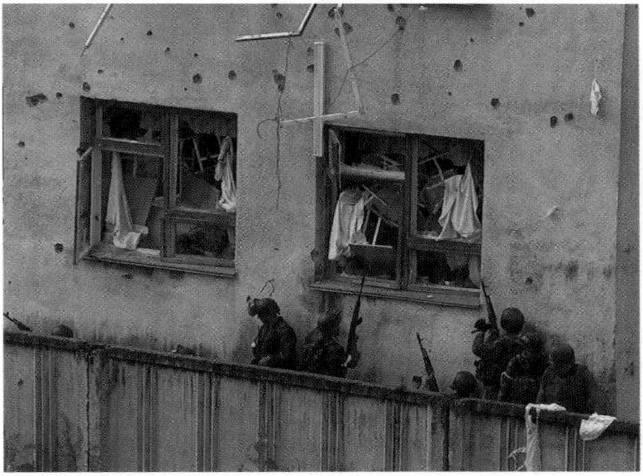

Vympel assault teams proceed west along south wall. The door they ultimately entered is to the left of the photo.

Gym from north courtyard.

JOHN GIDUCK

Open plaza where opening of school festivities took place (north side). Note small classroom building at far (west) end. JOHN GIDUCK

From rear (west) of school, view of cafeteria and theater (above it). JOHN GIDUCK

Below - Destroyed south wing. Last hold out of terrorists was shop on first floor and attic. JOHN GIDUCK

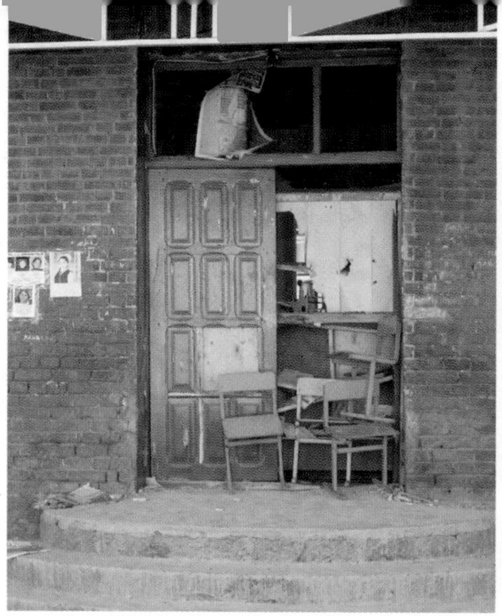

Above - Main entrance.
Never breached. JOHN GIDUCK

Above - South side doorway eventually breached by Vympel to enter school. JOHN GIDUCK

Looking eastward up alley along south side of building. It was too narrow to maneuver combat or rescue vehicles into south courtyard at far end.
JOHN GIDUCK

South side exterior wall. Vympel breached door at far left.
JOHN GIDUCK

Short hall around cafeteria (on left). Main hall of first floor connects from the right at the end. JOHN GIDUCK

Above - Northward up first floor hall. JOHN GIDUCK

Small corridor into west end of gym from main building. Note the balance beam. JOHN GIDUCK

Mouse Hole blown in eastern wall of gym for entry by Alpha

JOHN GIDUCK

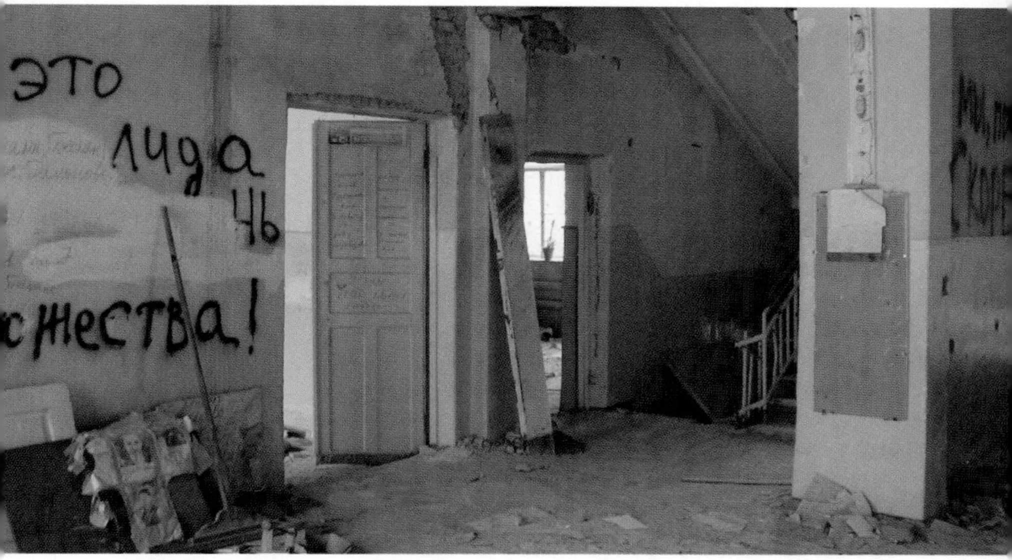

Above - Inside main entrance door (never breached) looking at north stairs. Library where weapons believed hidden through near door on left. JOHN GIDUCK

Library floor under which weapons were believed hidden.

JOHN GIDUCK

Looking northward up main second story hall. Commandos entered via stairs at far end. Courtyard was seen through windows on right.

JOHN GIDUCK

Wreckage of gym after fire.

MIKHAIL KLIMENTIEV. AFP. GETTY IMAGES

Below - Victims' bodies outside school. Day 4.

ALEXANDER KOROLOV. AFP. GETTY IMAGES

As for the others, the moment they had been expecting had come, or so it seemed: the government had used the ruse of collecting bodies on one side of the school to launch a surprise assault on the other side. Having been trained to expect this - indeed having been expecting it for two days - they reacted accordingly.

Combating teams will use two attacks: a secondary one just to attract attention, and a main attack elsewhere. Again, this is what the terrorists anticipated. Assuming that the explosions in the gym signaled a government assault there, many scrambled to pre-arranged and prepared positions throughout the school to await the main assault. Many of the Arabs – as well as others – fled to the fortified position they had built in the shop classroom. They had no way of knowing from what direction the "real" assault would come.

In case your demands have been met, releasing the hostages should be made only in a place that is safe to the hostage takers. The Chechens and Ingush have proven to be masters at successfully implementing this edict. On numerous prior occasions, they have successfully negotiated for buses, vans and helicopters to take them and their hostages safely across the border into Chechnya. Only one instance would have resulted in an ambush of government-supplied vehicles – Kizlyar – and there they had proven themselves quite prescient, detouring their own escape into the town of Pervomaiskoye.

Watch out for the ventilation or other openings as they could be used to plant surveillance devices through which the number of kidnappers could be counted and gases could be used. The terrorists at Beslan addressed this immediately upon securing the school. Numerous holes in the floor bore testimony to the grenades detonated, allowing them visibility under the structure to ensure that troops did not tap into the school communications, electrical, or ventilation systems. This also prevented the military from attempting an assault from underground. Such holes in a room off the main library later fueled the controversy over whether they had cached weapons there months in advance.

Do not be emotionally affected by the distress of your captives. There was to be no Stockholm Syndrome inside the Beslan School. The vicious, feral brutality of the terrorists saw to that. After dozens of hours of interviews in Beslan, Valdikavkaz and Moscow, I would not hear a single story of the smallest decency demonstrated by any of the hostage-takers to their captives. They had learned this lesson well, seeming to delight in the fear and degradation of those under their control.

Abide by Muslim laws as your actions may become a Da'wa. This is a "Call to Islam." It is shocking that any religion could have as its disciples, people who see the bloody, brutal killing of children, the rape of young girls and the outright murder of innocent parents and teachers, as acts of righteousness and divine justice, calling others to serve under its mantle. Perhaps the most telling indication of the complete disregard for human life inculcated into these grisly murderers came from Abu Bakar Bashir. The leader of Indonesia's radical Jemaah Islamiyah, Bashir was asked by a journalist in December 2004: "What would you tell the families of the 202 people murdered in the October 2002 Bali nightclub explosions?" Whether this attack had been planned to coincide with the taking of the Nord-Ost Theater has never been established. The terrorist leader's chilling response, told all. "My message to the families is, convert to Islam," he said.

Avoid looking at women. Here the terrorists failed miserably. It would appear they chose, instead, to follow the example of Muhammed in the seventh century, rationalizing the rape of enemy or infidel females as not violating the rules of Islam and a just god, which obviously pertain only to like-minded women.

Having been thus schooled, the members of the terror group were well prepared for the government's assault. Though some were both better trained and more experienced, it was clear they all had tactical knowledge. This fell within the dictates of al Qaeda's operations approach. With the leaders possessing superior knowledge, training, experience and ability in tactical situations, the others had little choice but to follow them. Basayev himself would later brag that he personally trained all of them in a two week course just across the border in Ingushetia. He had what he wanted, what his al Qaeda masters had trained him to create: a group of human bombs who would follow orders. One of the most difficult aspects for government forces in situations like Beslan is that communications among the terrorists go only in one direction, from leaders outside to lower leaders inside. This destroys any chance of persuading those inside to seek a different result. At the school, instructions were issued to the leaders inside from superiors in hiding elsewhere. The greatest apparent weakness was that, as a group, the terrorists had met not too long before the attack and trained together only briefly, so their ability to coordinate their actions during combat was diminished.

Colleagues from GRU, Alpha and Vympel confirmed that, to them – and despite the generally high level of training of the terror group's members – when it came to explosives the terrorists were all dilettantes. Though they used explosives, IEDs and grenades, none of them were skilled-demolitions experts, which resulted in unintended or premature detination of IEDs in the gym. According to a Special Forces veteran, it was actually lucky that the entire school did not explode the way the gym had. "The body count could have easily been much higher," he says. Despite this, the use of two women with suicide belt bombs secured to their waists sent an especially strong message to the Russian people and government. The assault on Beslan had taken place just one day after one woman blew herself and nine others up outside a Moscow subway, and only a week after two others boarded Aeroflot jets at Moscow's Domodedovo Airport, detonating their own bombs and killing all on board. The demonstrative presence of the two female shaheeds on the released videotape at Beslan put everyone on notice that the murder of all inside was a realistic outcome. Few believed the terrorists would just give up and vanish.

Adding to the overall stress level of the terrorists as they frantically sought a way out was the use of drugs. Norpasha Kulaev, after days of interrogation by the FSB, admitted that there was a system for their administration. Each morning all of the members of his group would take pills to remain alert and at the height of readiness. Some would receive injections. No doubt this added to the irritability of those overseeing the hostages, inciting even more extreme treatment. Kulaev claims to not know what the drugs were, but Russian experts believe they were some new generation of narcotic. Needles were evident around the school, lying amidst thousands of AK bullet casings, when I first examined it at the end of the battle.

No one disputes that the detonation of the first bomb in the gym was accidental. All of the hostages interviewed have said that it "just happened." There was no build up. One moment terrorists were talking, and then everything exploded. Some had been in the process of happily beating a hapless young boy. Even Shamil Basayev, the notorious terror leader still hiding in Chechnya, insists that a preemptive assault by the government troops caused the detonation in the gym, not his group's action. That it was not a planned government assault is clear: the troops were simply not ready and had already received orders to assault the following day, if Day Three did not see an end to the siege. Even President Putin said that, in this one instance, he was prepared to allow the terrorists a corridor to return to Chechnya in order to save children.

As for the terrorists themselves, if they were going to begin detonating the bombs as a diversion to escape, blending with the crowds outside, it makes sense that they would have done so at night. Darkness would have aided their efforts to slip unseen out of the building and into the throng near the school. The Russians had not set up any floodlights illuminating the building and surrounding areas at night. Escape would have been easy. The detonation of the bomb in the gym in the early afternoon of September 3 gave the Spetsnaz more than six hours of daylight in which to hunt and kill them, without having to resort to the use of Russia's cumbersome and often unreliable night vision devices. As it happened, the Special Forces commandos had much of the light they needed to hunt throughout the day.

If the terrorists had planned the detonation of their bombs either to kill all of the hostages, martyring themselves in the process, or as a distraction to screen their escape, it stands to reason that they would have simultaneously detonated all of the explosives in different parts of the building. Amidst the smoke, dust, debris and collapsing remnants of the building they could simply have stumbled out of their hides, dressed as hostages, and disappeared. It was clear no one was maintaining sufficient control of the people near the school to secure all those who came out. If their plan had been to achieve the highest possible body count, this would certainly have accomplished that objective.

Despite this, it is also clear that at least one faction within the terror group had something planned. Hostages reported that earlier in the day some of the terrorists had changed into more typical "civilian" clothing. Some of the men shaved their beards. Whether they had an intelligence source within the command post of the Russian government, or were preparing for their own attempt to escape, it is certain that they too, realized that no good end could come of the situation. They were at the end of what history told them was their grace period before Spetsnaz commandos would come raging in. Some hostages insisted that certain terrorists, including some of the leaders, were nowhere to be seen on the morning of the third day. Not only was Khuchbarov, the group's supposed leader, gone but the main negotiator for the hostage-takers, the one who spoke accentless Russian, was also nowhere to be seen. Many believed they had all escaped in the night. As it would turn out, the bodies of the three actual terrorist leaders would be identified in the aftermath. Vladimir Hodov and Magomet Yevloyev were clearly recognized. The third leader whose name has not been released – though definitely not Khuchbarov according to the Spetsnaz – was identified as well.

Former Spetsnaz commando and combat veteran Yuri Ferdigalov explains that it is a tactic sometimes employed by Russia's elite forces to cordon off an area, but leave a gap through which the terrorists can escape. Once gone with no more bloodshed, the Special Forces hunt them down with only two possible outcomes: death or capture. At Beslan, the masses of people pressing in on the areas around the school prevented any such escape. Reports of brief firefights as some of the terrorists probed the perimeter for escape routes during the first and second nights were evidence of the fruitlessness of any such efforts. But maybe, just maybe, some of the terrorists found that break in the ranks and slipped quietly from the school, leaving lower ranking members to take the full brunt of the Russians' rage.

For their part, however, what did the terrorists achieve with the Beslan siege? Their ultimate objectives may forever remain a matter of conjecture. Ministry of Justice adviser Mikhail Ryabko says that, "in every terror attack, everyone involved gets something." From this perspective, I found a number of Russian officials who believe that the oligarchs – those Yeltsin insiders who made billions of dollars looting Russia following the collapse of the Soviet Union, and who are now being hounded by Putin throughout the world – were behind the attack in Beslan, at least financially. This theory was being put forth by numerous Russian government officials in September, even as the Beslan siege was unfolding. It has been given a lot of thought by many in Russian government and military circles. When asked why the oligarchs, Russians themselves, with Russian cultural values and roots, would subsidize the attempted slaughter of almost one thousand Russian children, Col. Yuri Rodin replies: "The attacks are the last, agonizing gasps of a wounded and dying animal." Still, no one seems convincing and I wonder if they truly believe this themselves. No one can explain how it is these billionaire fugitives of Russian justice could possibly think they would benefit in their problems with the government by paying Muslims to murder children.

Other theories abound as to why the terrorists would have committed so heinous an act that they would risk losing the support of the entire world for the cause of Chechen independence. The truth is that, even if known, the reasons behind the decision to slaughter children would remain inscrutable to the Western world. One thing is clear, however; after years of seemingly pointless or failed bus hijackings outside of Chechnya, and the catastrophic Nord-Ost Theater siege with its numerous child hostages, Beslan was inevitable. Russian Special Forces' analysis of terrorism is accurate in one respect: the single common factor in all terrorist attacks is the desire for news media coverage. To the terrorists, worldwide television airing of their atrocities makes them heroes, and nothing can be gained without it. They never received this level of exposure in any of their attacks in Chechnya and neighboring Dagestan and Ingushetia. At Nord-Ost their operation failed, but what publicity they did receive was due to two factors: the large number of hostages, and, most important of all, the presence of children. At Beslan they sought to increase their media coverage by breaking what journalists saw as a record in terms of the sheer numbers of hostages. The unprecedented number of children was instrumental in driving Beslan as a media event. Having achieved that, they wanted the whole world to see, and remember. No one would ever forget Beslan.

Chapter Eight

The Government Response

You have never lived
until you have almost died.
For those who have fought for it,
Life has a special flavor
the protected will never know.
— U.S. Special Operations Assoc. motto

When I first returned to Moscow from the Beslan siege in September 2004, I was informed by several well-placed sources that none of the Spetsnaz or other military units, just across the border in Chechnya, had been deployed to the school. Not only were many of these units closer, but likely better trained, more experienced and certainly battle-hardened. It seemed to me that it had not been necessary for the Russian government to combine military units at the school that had never before worked together; a move to be avoided at all costs in critical incidents. A short distance away in Chechnya, there were integrated combat recon teams, comprised of members from all of the best Spetsnaz units. These men were well accustomed to operating together and could have not only been effective for their combat skills, but could also have acted in a liaison capacity between the different groups that had been called to the school, groups that weren't used to functioning as a single assault unit. This would have substantially reduced the conflicts inherent with any military teams working together for the first time.

I questioned two career Spetsnaz commanders about this, one GRU and the other MVD. They stated that in Russia, units would not typically be pulled out of Chechnya, or out of combat in general, to be used for other operations. When I pressed for a reason, they offered little real explanation, leaving the impression that this was simply a tactical mindset that no one questions. As it would turn out, this was not entirely true. Not only was one unit brought over from Chechnya – it was the first to arrive - but elements of both Alpha and Vympel departed their base at Khankala near Grozny, for Beslan. In the face of these facts, however, the same Special Forces officers I spoke to in September would later defend their contentions by pointing out that everyone obviously felt that they had more than sufficient troops with the few they did send, as many more were available but never deployed. Moreover, they informed me, the troops that were sent had been those sitting in the bases in rear areas at the time. No one in combat at the time was pulled out. The analytic center experts agreed: "The units that came down from Moscow were more than capable of dealing with the Beslan situation," they said. "Everyone else was just support."

Rus was the first Spetsnaz unit on scene. When Alpha and Vympel arrived it was determined that Rus would provide perimeter security and maintain their sniper positions. Once fully deployed Rus sniper teams were positioned in one of the homes immediately east of the school's large plaza, the same plaza the start of school festivities had been held on, and across which the hostages had fled when the terrorists first attacked. An Alpha team was in the house right next door, to the south. Rus snipers were also in the apartment buildings east of the school and behind the high fence along the south side alley. Alpha sniper teams took positions in the athletic complex buildings across the railroad tracks to the southwest. Other than its sniper teams, Rus was to be held in reserve, to back up Alpha and Vympel in the event the casualties they took depleted their combat effectiveness. But for the use of their snipers, they were never called into combat inside the school itself, leading one to believe that all of the Spetsnaz officers and analytic center experts had been right: once the fighting began Alpha and Vympel never felt the situation was so dire that they needed the help. It was also the contention of those I met that the FSB - most likely Alpha – had taken the lead in attempting to conduct negotiations with the terrorists, and would have continued to maintain that role despite the arrival of senior government officials and Dr. Raschal. Strangely, the only real exception to this was the use early on of a noted businessman in North Ossetia named Gutseriev as the primary negotiator for the government. The consensus amongst government officials was that they were happy to distance themselves from direct involvement and, thus, responsibility if something went wrong.

As mentioned MChS units were dispatched from Moscow and North Ossetia, as much because situations such as Beslan fell within their jurisdiction, as support to Alpha and Vympel.

One of the other early arrivals were units of the *Vnnutreye Voiska* or VV, part of what is known as the Interior Army. First established in 1919 under the fledgling Soviet Union, the VV was originally under the control of the NKVD, the precursor to the KGB. In 1954, with the establishment of the MVD – the Interior Ministry – VV was transferred under its control. The VV has always been comprised of two-year draftees, and easily recognizable by the letters *BB* in Cyrillic – or VV in English – on the shoulder boards of their uniforms, and the red band beneath the brim of their peaked caps. VV's main role throughout the Soviet era was to support local police, or *militsia,* with crowd control, riots, and to provide other forms of dissident suppression. VV also spent much of its time guarding food, ammunition and weapons depots, in addition to state factories and other facilities. The best of the VV were used as special purpose or SRT (Special Response Teams) units at prisons, functioning as high-end guards and escorts, particularly in the infamous gulag system in the outer reaches of the Soviet Union. Drawing on almost a century of experience in crowd control, they were tasked to provide outer perimeter security against the masses of people. They would prove to be far from effective in this effort.

One of the other units claiming the Spetsnaz title, that also appeared at Beslan, was a federal SWAT-type team known as OMON, for *Otryad Militsiy Osobogo Naznacheniya* or Special Operations State Militia. Though known by the nickname, "the Black Berets," OMON was not the only "special" unit of the Russian arsenal to sport that color headgear. Despite a completely different organizational purpose, in recent years OMON had been used in raids against tax evading corporations being taken over by the Putin government through the federal revenue service. OMON had originated as a result of the 1980 Olympics in Moscow. At that time the Soviet government determined that it needed to create yet another counter-terrorist unit in order to prevent a repeat of the massacre at the Munich Olympics just eight years before. This responsibility fell to the MVD, which created the Black Beret unit. By 1993 OMON forces totaled almost a quarter of a million, supported by light tanks and motorized divisions. Depending on the nature of their operations – such as counter-narcotics efforts in the Central Asian republics of the Soviet Union – at times they even had helicopters at their disposal.

Over the years OMON had been used to quell the uprisings in the Baltics in the early 1990s and other republics. Later, they had been thrown into various efforts to destroy the organized crime groups taking over Russia during the Yeltsin administration, and sometimes even functioned like SWAT teams and light infantry, depending on the country's needs. I personally had more than my share of unpleasant dealings with some of them while completing a master's degree in Russian studies at St. Petersburg State University. Their delight in rousting young men and women in the foreign students' dormitory in the middle of the night resulted in a number of tense situations compounded by threats of imprisonment for lack of cooperation. At Beslan, only the local OMON group was used, supposedly to provide perimeter security and act as a ready reserve force.

SOBR, for *Spetsialniy Otryad Boistrovo Reagirovaniya*, was the MVD's " Special Rapid Reaction Force." Another black beret unit, it is an extremely tough, dedicated and disciplined group of men, many originally from GRU Spetsnaz units. With several secret bases located around Moscow, I had trained with these elite commandos on a number of occasions, sometimes being run into the ground over daunting obstacle courses throughout the night. Among the best of all the units at hand-to-hand combat, they had served with distinction in Afghanistan, Chechnya and elsewhere. At Beslan, however, only the local unit was deployed.

Then, of course, there were the famed FSB counter terror units Alpha and Vympel. The best of the best. Though Alpha had undergone its difficulties and changes since the collapse of the Soviet Union, it was once again a formidable counter-terror unit. In addition to Vympel, it had previously worked with the MVD's Vityaz Anti-Terror group, and over the years I had become aware that the two units engaged in a lot of joint training exercises. At Beslan, a total of two hundred Alpha commandos were utilized: one hundred from the nearby detachment in Chechnya, with another one hundred brought down from their main base outside Moscow.

Vympel arrived at the siege with all of its skills in *diversion* at hand. These, of course, included direct action assaults, assassinations and kidnappings. It is little wonder Vympel is more typically described as a trained "terrorist" unit, rather than a counter-terror one. Vympel was deployed to Beslan in the same numbers and ratios as Alpha: one hundred from the local Vympel unit; one hundred from Moscow.

Once the units were in place, the local police that had been holding the perimeter and attempting to stabilize the situation were reduced to the role of mere helpers. One Russian MVD commander was not even sure that this role was official. What this caused, however, was the local police, heavily invested in the hostages and the outcome of the siege, to join the "volunteers" in their hostile vigil outside the school. When the hostages began running out of the gym following the detonation of the bombs and collapse of the gym roof, the police were among the civilians trying to carry them to safety.

Currently seen as the government's "Golden Child" of Spetsnaz, the Vityaz Anti-Terror unit was the only MVD Spetsnaz group to exist in regiment size. Reportedly receiving by far the greatest budget for training, infrastructure, weapons and operations, it is important to remember this was also the unit that had distinguished itself in the brief but bloody "rebellion" in 1993 when it conducted joint operations with Alpha. During that battle it retook the Ostankino Television Tower, giving control of the media and communications back to the Yeltsin government. As well, its members had endured countless tours in Chechnya where both it and its men had earned great distinction.

Vityaz is, to say the least, a multi-functional unit. Its teams serve not only as rapid reaction forces, but recon intelligence, hostage rescue, snipers and airborne troops. When Yeltsin emasculated Vympel – which had previously provided an underwater (UW) operations capability to the FSB – Vityaz not only took many of its veterans, but its UW mandate as well. Proudly operating under the Russian name for its fearless ancient warriors, Vityaz is mentioned here solely because it was not deployed to Beslan at all. It was explained to me that Vityaz was already stretched thin through massive deployments to Chechnya. It could not allow its remaining contingents to leave Balashikha - its main base east of Moscow - without adversely affecting its obligation to provide protection to the central government and the city. The belief that when the school was taken a second, larger attack was yet to come – most predictably in Moscow – was part of that decision. Someone had to stick around and be ready for a siege in the capital.

Selection for Alpha and Vympel typically required at least a two-year prior service with another unit, and passing a grueling test. In this, the two FSB counter-terror units were more like America's Green Berets, who must have served for a number of years in the Army before being eligible for consideration by Special Forces.[17] All of the other Russian Spetsnaz units are constituted by direct conscription. Each year as the new crop of 18 year-old draftees are processed, the Spetsnaz division commanders are given first choice from that pool. They typically look for those who are accomplished competitive athletes – particularly in sports with direct military application - and are the brightest academically, as well as politically reliable. The GRU Spetsnaz Brigades get first crack at these young conscripts, who are put into special training from the first day. Often the new draftees don't even realize that they are already in a Spetsnaz unit. Those who don't survive the training are shoved back into lesser units. Unlike America, historically in Russia service in a Special Forces group was not something you aspired to, it was something you were condemned to. Though this attitude has changed in recent years, and all manner of young men now clamor for the honor of becoming "Spetsnaz," the training continues to be unbelievably inhumane by Western standards, and many trainees die. The typical Russian attitude regarding training deaths is: "If he cannot live through this training, then he is no good to Spetsnaz anyway." Even more die in the

---

[17] The exception to this is in times of war. As well, recently the U.S. Army Special Forces have resurrected a program in which enlistees can qualify for a SF training program that usually takes at least two years before they are considered fully qualified.

many, ultra-secret deployments Spetsnaz seems to always be involved in. Also, unlike America until recent years, Russia has never suffered a dearth of military men with combat experience. They are always fighting somewhere.

Of those units – like the various MVD Spetsnaz divisions – that get direct conscripts for their required two-year service, entry into the elite club of special operations forces does not end with basic training. One can be a member of an elite unit like Vityaz, but still not have earned the right to wear the prized Blood Red Beret. The selection process to enjoy that distinction is another thing altogether, and many other units send their best soldiers for this highly specialized training and to win the coveted headgear. In Russia, if you have *ever* earned the right to wear the beret, you are then authorized to wear it throughout your entire military career, no matter what other unit you might later serve with. Thus, someone from a unit that wears a black, green or tan beret – or no beret at all - may still wear his red beret as a signal of distinction and elite service and accomplishment. This would be like a former Special Forces sergeant doing a tour of duty as a basic training drill instructor – as often happens in the U.S. Army – but still being permitted to wear his green beret rather than the well-known Smokey the Bear campaign hat.

But earning the right to wear the special berets in elite Russian units is no small feat. It first begins with months of training, during which the overwhelming majority of trainees are weeded out. The final day of testing requires months of preparation. Like running the marathon in the Olympics, many will commit an entire year of arduous physical preparation to survive it. Few pass it the first time, and I have met the soldier in Vityaz who holds the dubious distinction of having gone through the final day of testing more than any other: a record 8 times before passing. This last day of selection begins with a torturous run in full battle gear. No less than 12 kilometers are covered through shin deep mud, forest and rivers, up and down hills. Those already in the unit – with their red berets – run alongside, in front and behind. Every two kilometers fresh Red Berets are waiting to take over, to force the would-be commandos into an impossible pace. Periodically, the group is forced to drop to the ground and crawl, sometimes with only their hands and feet touching the ground. Men who appear to be weakening are made to carry comrades on their backs. The battle gear is heavy, and the helmets they are made to wear weigh 26.4 pounds (12 kg) alone. If anyone falls more than 50 meters behind the rest of the group, he is automatically pulled out. He can try again next time.

As the grueling run ends back at the Balashikha Base, the candidates are immediately forced through the daunting Firestorm Obstacle Course. I have been through the 12 kilometer run, and spent more than my share of time almost dying on that damn obstacle course, while tanks drive alongside blasting deafening rounds across the course. Almost a dozen piles of burning tires mix with the smoke from the big machines' cannons to completely disorient anyone trying to negotiate that course. Red Berets stand about laughing, tossing concussion grenades among the trainees. Occasionally someone is hit by one of these. No one cares.

At the end of the course, everyone who has made it that far is lined up. Each man's AK must fire; the same weapon he has dragged through mud and water all morning. The gun with which he has just clambered over, through, and under the oily smoke and flame engulfed obstacles. If it fails to fire when the trigger is first pulled – no matter the reason – he fails. There is no appeal. After this, the survivors undergo a series of exhausting physical fitness and skills tests. Rappelling, grenade throwing and martial arts are among them. Their effort to wear the famous beret culminates in an inhuman, all-out hand-to-hand combat test for fifteen full minutes. During this time each would-be commando faces a fresh soldier every two minutes. These are the men already in the unit, who have already survived this day of torture. The rules are simple: if the Red Beret veteran fails to give his all to knock the recruit out completely, he loses his beret and must undergo selection all over himself. As for the recruits, all they have to do is keep getting to their feet. There are no mouthpieces and seemingly few men from these units have their own front teeth. The first time I was exposed to this torturous process, only seven of more than 300 who had started the selection process graduated. I was immediately reminded of the old Barry Sadler song, *Ballad of the Green Berets*: "One hundred men we'll test today, but only three win the green beret." For Russia's would-be commandos, three out of a hundred would be an exceptional showing.

* * * * *

Back at Beslan, elite manpower was not the only military resource deployed. Four Mi8/MT "Hip" attack helicopters were quickly flown to the Vladikavkaz airport. These assault aircraft are armed with rapid firing cannons as well as missiles, and can carry six to eight man assault teams. With the ability to deliver up to twenty-four men in total, it is surprising that not a single one of them would carry anything more than its flight crew. The advantages of fast rope teams from the Special Forces units deployed to Beslan were ignored by the Russian command. The Mi8 helicopters were used, at most, one or two at a time for overhead surveillance. From the start they were mostly all kept on the ground at the airport some eight miles away. At no time were fast rope teams prepared or placed on board to use for a possible roof assault. Before the end of the first day, the terrorists would fire upon the circling choppers. Fearful that they would be shot with rocket-propelled grenades, they withdrew to the nearby airport and the vodka factory where they awaited further orders. Not until the battle erupted on the third day were they ordered back within any proximity to the school.

What the men of the Special Forces and other units encountered when they first arrived in Beslan was enough to chill the strongest heart. The Beslan School is a large brick structure, built in 1889. As with buildings of that period, it is comprised of rather narrow corridors, tight turns and fairly small rooms. From overhead it looks like a large, right angled "W" whose arms stretch to the east. The left arm of the "W" is shorter than the other two, and from the center arm, a long white building wing extends to the left, or north. Of greater concern was the fact that, due to the age of the structure, no decent floor plans were available to the assault teams, from which to begin planning an operation.

With approximately 1,200 hostages in the school, and likely 20 times that number of spectators, armed "volunteers," and local police outside, half of the town's total population was at that school. The police and regular military did little to preserve order or control the crowd, often adding to the danger and incendiary mood of the local citizenry. These people would respond to verbal insults and challenges of the terrorists who constantly shouted from windows. Random shots fired by the terrorists into the courtyard and toward the surrounding crowd on the north side of the school would be met with provocative taunts from a mob that quickly returned fire. At one point a man in camouflage stepped out of the crowd into the north courtyard and fired his AK47 on full automatic in an arc, at the building.

According to every Spetsnaz officer and government official I spoke to, at the beginning the terrorists had no demands. They had to be pressed continually before they finally came up with the few demands they would ever make: (1) To meet directly with the presidents of Ingushetia and North Ossetia; (2) For the terrorists arrested in the June 2004 assaults in Ingushetia to be released; and, (3) For Russia to withdraw all troops from Chechnya. It is both Col. Rodin and Col. Stepanovich's belief that the "mercenary" faction within the terrorist group was not ready to make any demands or conduct any negotiations, as they had not expected to be placed in the situation in which they found themselves. The fact that the terrorists had no initial demands, and then subsequently ad-libbed ridiculous ones they knew would never be met, should have served as a warning to the government forces that a contingency assault plan needed to be put in place quickly. Sadly, that warning went unheeded, and the absence of demands during negotiations became the death knell for 338 innocent people.

These same two colonels both said that the government was going to assault. They insisted that within the Russian government and elite military circles, "there are NO negotiations at all; the only reason for negotiations is to help set up the military assault." This is obviously a recent policy, as prior hostage incidents are replete with examples of negotiated releases of victims and safe corridors into Chechnya for the hostage-takers, sometimes even in government supplied helicopters. Perhaps this non-negotiation policy was a result of recent history and the Russian government's new realization that prior efforts at peaceful resolution only resulted in more and bigger hostage sieges. Whatever the reason, both Spetsnaz veterans were adamant that the fact the hostages at Beslan were children "means nothing." Even GRU and SOBR Major Konstantin Komarov said this to be the case. When Komarov said this to me the first time I asked him if, being the father of a 10-year-old boy himself, he agreed. Could he support such an approach if his own child were a hostage? I knew he was devoted to his son. Komarov, who is disarmingly slight of build and academic in manner, surprised me with his unhesitating answer. "Absolutely," he said.

From the moment I first arrived in Moscow on my way to the siege, Spetsnaz insiders not deployed to Beslan said they knew the assault would occur in less than one week, and that that timetable would depend on developments throughout. For instance, if it appeared that the terrorists could be persuaded to release more hostages, or to accept food, water and medicine, the government would have played that out longer, in order to get as many hostages as possible out before the assault. Immediately after the siege, all government and military sources I spoke with confirmed that the decision had been made "at the highest levels," that the building would be stormed early in the morning of the fourth day. Spetsnaz always assaults early in the morning while the enemy is at his lowest alert level. Under cover of darkness, but with dawn just around the corner, this provides many hours of light in the event the battle rages for any length of time. The only thing that would have delayed this decision was a change in the status by the end of Day Three, such as the terrorists releasing the hostages and accepting the government's offer of safe passage back into Chechnya. As there was no top-level government official who had taken sole charge at Beslan, speculation was that Putin himself had made this determination.

The negotiations themselves had not gone well from the start. Accurate accounts of how the secretive negotiations proceeded are virtually non-existent. Journalist Nabi Abdullaev correctly points out that since the efficacy of negotiations can only be judged from the negotiators' version of events, it is difficult to assess how truly effective they were. He reports that former Ingush President Ruslan Aushev, who was successful in having 32 women and infants freed – and who was the only civilian actually to go into the school – says critical time was lost in negotiations at the beginning of the stand-off.[18] Aushev indicates that this is always the time to build positive momentum. He recalled that the terrorists had eventually imposed a three-day deadline on the government meeting their demands, and, just as with Nord-Ost, time was of the essence from then on. That he lays the blame for this at the feet of the government is interesting. How he felt they were to have held discussions with terrorists that refused to answer their phone and thereby gain "momentum," is confusing. It should not be lost on anyone that the terrorist leader Magomet Yevloyev – himself the actual "Colonel" cited by journalists and a former major in the Russian MVD – was Aushev's security chief during his term in office as president of Ingushetia.

Abdullaev further points out that there were contradicting reports coming from the different negotiators during the crisis. North Ossetian President Dzasokhov was quoted as saying that the hostage-takers demanded the release of their jailed comrades from a prior raid, and then for the withdrawal of Russian troops from Chechnya. Dr. Raschal, whose presence the military officers there saw

---

[18] All references to journalist Nabi Abdullaev from "Beslan, Russia... Terror in the Schoolhouse!", *Homeland Defense Journal*. Sepember 2004, Vol. 2, Issue 9, 28-35.

as questionable, denied that the terrorists ever made any demands. Of course, Raschal's claim is likely more reflective of his limited involvement and single telephone call with the terrorist negotiator, than the fact that demands never came at all. Aushev, in an interview on *CBS' 48 Hours*[19] said that the terrorists made seven or eight demands, the greatest being for Russia to end the war in Chechnya and withdraw all of its troops.

The government also seriously erred in its release of inaccurate, and grossly underrated, figures on the numbers of hostages inside. Russian dissembling in such circumstances – Chernobyl and the *Kursk* being just two of the better known – seems at times to be almost pathological. These intentional lies adversely affected not only the temperament of the terrorists but the course of negotiations as well. Both the gunmen and the citizens of Beslan reacted to the obviously false numbers as an indication that the government was attempting some subterfuge; an effort that was sure to get hostages killed. But Lev Dzugayev, spokesman for North Ossetia's president, insisted that no one had intentionally reduced the numbers. "This was not misinformation or silencing of the truth," he was quoted as saying by Abdullaev. "We just could not get it in our heads that this is possible – more than 1,000 people taken hostage!"

But even this reaction – if true – bespeaks an institutionalized compulsion among Russians to create their own reality when confronted with unpleasant and unwanted circumstances. Even if Russian officials were incredulous at the numbers in the school, the fact they felt free to manufacture their own more palatable figures is symptomatic of a wanton and reckless disregard for the lives and safety of the very citizens they are pledged to protect. Moreover, history tells us that the numbers at the Nord-Ost Theater just two years earlier approached these proportions. The fact that the Beslan School's registry showed 895 student names should have been

[19] January 22, 2005.

sufficient to prevent such a grievous tactical error. What makes this statement smack of the worst kind of deceit, however, is the fact that at Buddenovsk, Pervomaiskoye and Kizlyar, the numbers of hostages were several times those actually held in the Beslan School. A Russian government official's public statement on September 6 that they had in fact intentionally lied about the number of hostages does not bode well for the truthfulness of Dzugayev or the fate of Russian hostages in future incidents.

Indeed, the negotiations had not started out well. On the first day the terrorists had delivered a message with a cell phone number. But between Putin's refusal to deal with the terrorists at all and the government's seemingly intentional reduction in the hostage estimate, the terrorist leaders were incensed. Throughout the ordeal, government negotiators would call and call, but the terrorists refused to answer.

According to Aushev, even once the fighting began communications with the terrorists did not end. In the midst of the chaos following the explosions and the fleeing hostages, he insists he called the hostage-takers and "asked them to stop firing." The *Novaya Gazeta* newspaper quoted Aushev as saying, "They said that they had stopped their fire and insisted that it was us who fired. We gave the order through our channels: 'Cease fire!' But there was this idiotic 'third force,' these armed militia [volunteers] that decided to free the hostages themselves." The terrorists, just as confused, thought it was the troops' assault that had incited the violent chaos. "And then it started," according to Aushev. It appears that the terrorists may be a bit generous with regard to their own behavior. No one I spoke to who was at the scene noticed so much as a single moment when the terrorists stopped shooting mercilessly into the fleeing and unarmed hostages. Why the terrorists, many of whom had relationships with Aushev and his family, would not have listened to him if he had ordered – or implored – them to stop firing is just as baffling.

Most of the Spetsnaz officers I spent time with agreed that there had been no detailed immediate action plan to fall back on in the event the terrorists began killing hostages in number. In typical Russian fashion, they explained that while there was "some type" of plan for what the Spets units were to do if that occurred, it was not a complete plan. No standing order had been issued for the units to act upon the occurrence of a particular, triggering event, such as the detonation of bombs or the killing of hostages. They explained that, according to the Russian bureaucratic mindset, the existence of "some" plan allowed the top commanders to argue that they did not fail to anticipate the event, and also to defend themselves by rationalizing: "Who could have anticipated this?" That they had already stood by as a number of hostages were gunned down on Days One and Two is certain. What they were waiting for, we will likely never know.

Everyone well recognized that conceding to the terrorists' demands – any terrorists' demands – only assured more such situations in the future. Abdullaev wrote, "...this understanding of the potentially violent outcome, which demands the utmost preparedness and resolve from those involved, was not properly communicated down the chain of command. The accidental explosion forced both parties of the conflict to act in ways that unexpectedly led to massive additional casualties among the hostages." Abdullaev goes further in asking, "whether the fear of accepting responsibility for responding appropriately to the kidnapping and murders by authorities at all levels may have exacerbated the incident and contributed to the tragic loss of life?"

The Special Forces officers I spoke to would say that Abdullaev's rhetorical question was dead on the mark. The experts at the analytic center were clear: "No one was in charge. No one was in charge, and no one wanted to be." They insisted, however, that this ultimately worked in Putin's favor, "as he never made any decisions, nothing could be blamed on him." Other military officers agreed. Col. Rodin said, "At Beslan there was no single person." Justice Ministry adviser

Col. Ryabko – while declining to comment on Russian decision-making at Beslan – agrees that in terrorist sieges there should be a single command unit or organization. That unit should have only one leader. All other units must be subordinate to the command unit, and its leader. The leader must handle both control of the tactical situation and the main assault. No representatives of any other departments should be shown to the public, news media or the terrorists.

Col. Rodin, however, went further to say: "From the start the government controlled the arrangement at Beslan, but too many departments were involved. MChS, SOBR, MVD, FSB, the Army, all were thrown into the situation. Everyone wanted to be a hero, but no one wanted to be responsible." This occurred at all levels of the government. According to Alpha's Stepanovich, "When the siege occurred, local government officials hid so they would not be in the public spotlight and could avoid responsibility for anything. While the local government and police were trying to push this thing uphill all the way to Moscow to avoid responsibility, the leaders in Moscow were running for cover."

The notorious Russian "maybe" was also present in the government's failure to secure ambulances and have medical teams and hospitals standing by. Much like Nord-Ost, the Russians seemed hard-pressed to commit such life saving resources, when "maybe" they wouldn't be necessary, "maybe" the terrorists wouldn't kill too many of the hostages, "maybe" this would "all work out and then we would have gone to all that trouble for nothing." One thing they were wrong about was the notion that *maybe* there would be no need for a lot of ambulances. When hostages, burned and bleeding from shrapnel, bullets and the fire spreading through the gym, began streaming out there were no ambulances to attend to or transport them. As with Nord-Ost, area hospitals were not ready. The military forces, largely concentrating on the growing battle, were incapable of saving the victims in any great numbers. Ironically, it would be the volunteers who had caused so many problems that would drag them to safety, often across open ground after they managed to escape the school. This would be a fitting end, as it is entirely likely that but for the wild behavior of those volunteers, many of the hostages would not have been injured or killed in the first place.

Nevertheless, when the bullets began to fly countless civilians from the crowd raced into harm's way to whisk the wounded away, placing them in their own cars and speeding them to hospitals. It would be some time before ambulances, finally alerted to the carnage, arrived and made their way through the masses of people and cars obstructing the narrow streets leading to the school. In many cases, private transport vehicles and ambulances were able to get through only due to the citizens physically pushing obstructing cars out of the streets. That these were their own cars parked in the way did not seem to diminish the pride most felt for their contribution.

It was apparent to everyone that the terrorists had set the siege up in a way that eliminated any possible outcome other than the two most revolting to the Russians: either accept defeat and let them go free, or see the deaths of hundreds of children and innocent adults, living forever with the blood of those victims on their own hands. That the Russians' ultimate hope was the former is of little doubt. They had successfully pulled this off in several prior bus and hospital hostage incidents outside of Chechnya. Why not here? Why not with the eyes of the whole world on them?

Despite the paralysis of leadership the Russian forces were suffering, planning still went on. Alpha and Vympel largely split duty at the school. Each of the counter-terror units was divided into three shifts. Each unit's men rotated eight hours on watch at the school, and eight hours stand-down time. With this schedule in place, they began training for a potential assault. The other eight hours were spent at the distant Vladikavkaz building. Though no detailed assault plan had yet been completed, this was the closest building in design to the Beslan Middle School No. 1 they could find. It was here that they began training to storm the building.

The use of paralyzing gas was considered, just as it had been at Nord-Ost. To the Russians this is a virtual panacea in hostage-taking situations, and in almost two solid months of interviews of military experts I found only one who felt the use of gas would not have been effective at Beslan. When asked if the terrorists' selection of the Beslan School, with its warren-like hallways and rooms, as well as the separation of the hostages, would not have eliminated gas as a viable tactic, Russian military officers scoffed. "You just have to use more in a multi-prong, coordinated attack," one says. "Beslan would have just been treated as a number of smaller Nord-Osts, with each unit initially treating its assault as a completely separate effort once the gas was administered." Col. Ryabko is of the opinion that the use of gas can never hurt. "Don't ever be afraid to use gas grenades," he opines. When pressed, others who agreed with Ryabko softened this somewhat by saying that only sleeping gas should be deployed rather than the paralyzing gas of Nord-Orst, in order to prevent accidental death to hostages due to adverse reactions. Still, Spetsnaz across the board believe that if both hostages and terrorists are asleep the number of dead will be limited.

One of the harshest realities that had to be accepted was that with the pedal detonators in the gym, there was no way to neutralize the bombs they were attached to. They were going to explode once an assault began, and there was nothing anyone could do about it. People would be killed. As it turned out they were detonated anyway. However, Russian experts argue that far fewer hostages would have died if the bombs had gone off due to the terrorists falling asleep, their feet slipping from the detonators' "safety" pedals, with no one awake to begin shooting. When confronted with the fact that the terrorists had brought gas masks, Ryabko responds by saying that even if some of the terrorists did not succumb to the use of gas, with all of the hostages asleep it would have been impossible for them to carry the sleeping hostages as human shields, as happened throughout the school during the battle. Finally, he argues that the use of sleeping gas prevents the assault teams from having to address the problem of panicked hostages racing about. "At Beslan, if everyone had been asleep they wouldn't have been shot in the back trying to escape," he contends. Based on his more than 20 years of experience in Russian Special Forces, he adds that this is one of the problems with flash bang or concussion grenades used by counter-terror forces to enter a building or room. "You never know how the hostages are going to react, and children will panic, running right into the line of fire."

Of equal importance is that the Russians were doubtful that the pedal detonators were actually wired "hot" to the bombs. From the intelligence they had gathered from those hostages that had escaped or been released, they were becoming convinced that – perhaps – these terrorists were not looking to die inside the school, as they had said. If the pressure release or dead man switches were phony, it offered the Spetsnaz an opportunity to save a great many of the hostages. The information on which these evolving conclusions were based was scant. For one thing, they indicated that the men mainly wore masks. "This is always a sign that the terrorists do not intend to die inside," a SOBR officer said. When they show their faces openly they are not worried about being identified while escaping, or being captured at some later time. They know they are not leaving there alive. Moreover, they had reports that the two women inside – despite wearing suicide belts – had their hair dyed blonde. Haling from regions where indigenous ethnicity produces almost exclusively dark haired people, this, too, was a sign that they hoped to evacuate the school and disappear into the fairer Slavic population of Ossetia.

When they came, no one knew for certain what caused the explosions. Just days after the fight was over, Major Komarov was certain that Alpha had not incited the detonations by assaulting. It was his belief at the time that a terrorist had accidentally set off an IED. It was later reported to me by Russian colleagues that the Special Forces had a surveillance tape that depicted the terrorists arguing about whether to remain or attempt an escape, just before a bomb detonated in the gym.

When the explosions occurred, there was still no clear, critical incident command hierarchy, and no one to give the "Go" order to the units to launch an assault. As always, communications were bad among the various teams surrounding the school. Some waited for orders, some hesitated before assaulting. Amidst it all, the enormous crowd was a violently chaotic mass of humanity. Those Spetsnaz officers at Beslan are certain that there was some level of plan in place, but that not only was it insufficient, the teams "never received a *go* order from the authority in charge." The response was "chaotic, inconsistent and undisciplined," one intones. It was clear the Russian authorities had failed to prepare for a violent outcome prior to their own slowly evolving assault plan for the next day.

The detonation of the gym itself was a complete accident. People were shocked. The citizens outside started to fight. Soldiers from South Ossetia, the breakaway Georgian republic so enamored of Russia, leapt into the fray, the only disciplined, combat experienced "volunteers" within the crowds. Russian troops came from the training and rest areas. They did the best they could, lacking hard information on the school's design. Journalist Nabi Abdullaev found one FSB Spetsnaz officer who believed that up to the time the fighting started, they had put together a viable assault plan: "We planned a very good operation. There would be no such casualties, for certain. But there was no order. Everyone was afraid to take responsibility. We are professionals, but those who made decisions were not prepared." Whether this is true, or this one officer was attempting to cast their preparations in the best light, one thing is for certain: Inside the terrorists seemed to be suffering no such problems. They were ready. And waiting.

Komarov, still a consultant to Russian Special Forces, corroborates that the troops on duty started shooting immediately upon the gymnasium bomb exploding, though they did not assault it. He says that within a short time the others came up and began firing behind them: "It only took the other teams five to six minutes to arrive, and so were shortly behind." While the on-duty group may have started shooting right away, they held their positions for some time before attempting to storm the building. Those on guard waited, using the opportunity to get into the positions from which the assault was tentatively planned for the following day.

Once the Spetsnaz units decided to assault, events spiraled quickly into even greater chaos and violence. Within 30 minutes of the explosions, and with the terrorists shooting down into the fleeing women and children, at least two of the Mi8 helicopters could be seen circling impotently overhead. Still leery from the terrorists' earlier efforts to shoot them down with RPGs, they refused to come too close. By then, ambulances in addition to privately owned vehicles were beginning to arrive to transport wounded to hospitals and clinics; though in such a rural region, these were few and ill prepared for what they faced.

Vympel was the unit mainly on duty at the time of the explosions. Its men attempted to disarm the elaborate and sensitive filament spider webs attached to bombs across the doorways. Eventually, Vympel would simply have the main door on the south side of the building blown out by a non-exploding tank shell, giving them immediate access to the stairway leading to the second floor and the basement. Alpha, though either on stand-down or training at the remote building, was on-scene as quickly as they could get there. Some Alpha teams, on duty in the residential homes to the east, immediately went racing across the plaza to the north side of the school. They joined their Vympel brothers in attempting to enter the building from various positions. One Mouse Hole charge blew a three-foot by two-foot gap in the east wall of the gym, allowing soldiers to enter and children to escape. The bottom ledge of one of the cathedral windows on the north side of the gym had been blown out by the bombs inside and the Spetsnaz rescuers, together with other soldiers and citizen volunteers, used it to help the children simply run through.

By 4:20 p.m., medical first responders began entering the building and the word went out over the international news networks that the siege was over. Then, in the midst of attempting to douse the fire that had consumed the collapsed gym ceiling, and establish triage efforts in the north side courtyard, fighting broke out again. More bombs exploded and several terrorists appeared in windows firing down onto the crowd of helpers. Some terrorists escaped, and others were shot down in the hallways at close quarters. The fighting continued throughout the day.

Ultimately, the government reported that 29 terrorists were killed, and 3 captured. Later the government would alter the story, saying that two terrorists had been captured, and one other killed by the crowd. Still later it was reported that only one terrorist had been caught and interrogated, the other two having been dragged from military vehicles by the crowd and torn apart. No one seemed to have his story straight. In all, the crowds would reportedly claim the lives of three of the tormentors that had held their children captive, murdered their friends and family. Of the supposed "captured" terrorists, originally there were rumors that one was a policeman in North Ossetia, but of Ingusheti heritage. Whether he was a terrorist, or a hostage at some point, as he claimed, remains to be seen. He claimed to have been kidnapped by the terrorists while they were driving through Beslan in the early morning, when he stopped them for looking suspicious. He said that he had escaped, and was supposedly the original source of information on how many terrorists there were. The last I heard, he was being questioned but was not in custody. Obviously, he had been dropped from the "captured terrorist" list. Russian dissembling was clear from the beginning.

Despite these reports, the government has not admitted to having captured anyone other than the Chechen Norpasha Kulaev. He was the only one who surrendered; the others died at the hands of the Special Forces commandos. However, the government sought to avoid admitting that they had even him. On Monday evening, September 6, shortly after an official report aired stating that no terrorists had lived, Kulaev was shown on Russian television. Visibly injured, he verified that the group's leader, whom he too claimed to be Khuchbarov, had led the raid. However this was not an autonomous operation for him, or the other leaders, as they had been in constant cell phone contact with Chechen leader Shamil Basayev, as well as with Aslan Maskhadov. Kulaev stated that he had asked Khuchbarov why they had to take a school, and was told: "Because we need to start war in the entire territory of the North Caucasus."

Though President Putin made a connection between al Qaeda and the two downed airliners the week prior to Beslan, four days after the siege ended he had not made any public statement that this was the case with the school. Nevertheless, Beslan Police Deputy Chief Oleg Tedeyev was adamant: "They were so well trained, the highest level," he said in establishing a direct link with the notoriously well-trained al Qaeda terrorists.[20] In analyzing the assault and siege, other Russian authorities and the Special Forces recognized that the speed, timing and efficiency with which the school was taken bespoke the kind of training and planning once taught in the al Qaeda training camps of Afghanistan. Even three days after the drama ended, the Putin government was still incapable of putting on a coordinated front.

Of all the statements from military pundits and Special Forces veterans the world over, representatives of Britain's elite SAS – the Special Air Service - were the most supportive of the Russian Special Forces in their handling of the Beslan siege. The United Kingdom's 22 SAS is the unit with the greatest amount of actual, real world, counter-terror combat experience. They virtually wrote the book on counter-terror operations. Unanimously, the international news media cited expert opinions from these almost peerless commandos that the Russians appeared to have done just about everything they could under near impossible circumstances. The British veterans from "the Regiment" all said that they didn't know whether any other unit could have done any better.

---

[20] As reported in papers throughout the world, including *USA Today*, Tuesday, September 7, 2004, p. 9A.

Despite the SAS's generosity, the Russian government's response still appears to have been the worst of all possible planning. It allowed everything to come apart at once. It also proved the disaster of throwing different units together without distinctly different tasks, or without integrating the teams adequately. Even the combining of local Alpha and Vympel units with their big-city counterparts, with no substantial history of training together, was no better. The failure to first – before anything else – put together an effective emergency contingency assault plan, and properly instruct all units in what to do upon the occurrence of the triggering event, was largely responsible for much of the catastrophe that followed.

Chapter Nine

Aftermath

Russia has a unique capacity
for attracting the world's attention.

— Alexis de Tocqueville
19th century

When we first arrived in Moscow in September 2004, Major Konstantin Komarov was waiting at the airport. He hustled us to the Vnukovo domestic airport in south Moscow, completely on the other side of this massive city, notorious for its slow moving traffic. We had to attempt to get a flight to Beslan. If no flights were available directly into the Vladikavkaz airport, just minutes from Beslan, we would have to fly into Magaz. That airport, positioned a long way from the city for which it is named, is a new, state of the art facility whose runways can handle the biggest aircraft in the world. This includes the largest heavy bombers any air force can muster. The problem was that its main runway sat just fifty yards from an unguarded and unfenced Chechen border. One way or the other, Yuri and I knew we were going to get into Beslan. During the long, nerve-wrackingly slow drive across Moscow we had time to get an update on the situation. During our flight over, Konstantin had been in touch with his Spetsnaz comrades to determine the state of events in that remote village.

While focusing on negotiating the snarled capital traffic, eyes screwed up in concentration, he told us that the government was certain that the rest of a larger group of terrorists was holed up somewhere in Beslan. He said that was how the terrorists in the school expected to escape, and who they had been trying to get to. He said this was also the reason the government sealed the borders and closed off the city: it believed there were still other terrorists inside and trying to escape. Clearly, this had been the government forces' experience in numerous prior Chechen-led hostage sieges. To barricade themselves in a large, sprawling and complex building with hundreds of hostages, with the support of other teams elsewhere in the city, was a key part of the terrorists' playbook; and they appeared to be following it step by step. Hearing this gave us hope. If the government's concern was people getting out, they might not be so concerned with an American trying to get in.

* * * * *

That the terrorists were well armed to carry out the Beslan operation is without doubt. The commandos were up against the worst, a formidable display of weaponry. After the school was secured, Alpha and Vympel recovered, among other things, the following:

- approximately 30 AK47 7.62 x 39mm assault rifles;

- AK 74, 5.45 mm assault rifles;

- GP 25, 25 mm under-barrel grenade launchers;

- Dragunov 7.62 x 54 sniper rifles, with 10 round magazines;

- Three 7.62 x 54 mm Kalashnikov PKM machine guns;

- 5 RPG 18 "Fly" anti-tank rocket launchers – these 64 mm rockets are single use disposable weapons. Once armed by extending the arming tube, they cannot be repacked, and must be fired. They are capable of destroying 150 mm armor up to an angle of 60 degrees;

- 5 RPO-A Schmel (Bumble Bee) "fire throwers" – these are 93 mm infantry type rocket launchers that fire a rocket containing a napalm-like liquid that ignites on impact;

- 5 Makarov 9.2 x 18 mm handguns;

- MON-50 directional anti-personnel mines, with a 50-meter range of focused destruction. Many of these were used to detonate the homemade explosives manufactured by the terrorists;

- F1 heavy hand grenades – designed for defensive purposes and to fortify positions, as well as to set up ambushes and for booby traps. They have a 200-meter burst radius;

- RGD-5 light hand grenades – these are assault grenades with a 25-meter burst radius, often used as booby traps; and,

- IEDs from handmade TNT, obtained by boiling cannon shells for the explosive, then wrapping it in bolts, nails, screws and other pieces of metal.

Since the disaster at the school, the government's response has been one of rationalizing that it was not their fault, that "no one could have predicted this action on the part of the terrorists, as we were going to wait it out." Both Stepanovich and Rodin – again corroborated by other Spetsnaz officers - say this is "crap." It seems clear that the decision had been made that an assault would have taken place on Day Four, absent a complete surrender by the terrorists, or an agreement to accept the government's proffer of a safe corridor back into Chechnya. It had been done before. Despite this short timetable, however, Stepanovich insists that while they were prepping the assault plan for the following day, they had nothing else "real" in place.

One week after the fighting stopped, 105 people were still reported missing. The identities of 239 of the hostages killed had been established, but 90 bodies remained unidentified. Four months later all of the hostages had been identified. Final numbers officially reported by the government were 338 dead and 700 wounded, including 161 children. Of equal importance were the eleven men from the Alpha and Vympel units, who died attempting to save the hostages. Ten others who had been with support units like SOBR, Rus, OMON and MChS, also lost their lives in the battle, several from "friendly" fire as they ran through the maelstrom of bullets coming from the crowd in an attempt to rescue hostages fleeing the building. Additionally, 30 soldiers were wounded in the fighting, 18 from Alpha and Vympel. Stories of incredible heroism in the long hours of the hellish gun battle are proof of the courage of the Russian elite forces.

Two weeks after the end of the Beslan siege a Chechen rebel web site published an email letter purportedly written by terrorist leader Shamil Basayev. According to Kavkazcenter.com, Basayev claimed that his *Shaheed Brigade Riadus-Salahina* was responsible for the carrying out of several recent "successful militant operations." In addition to bestowing credit upon himself for Beslan, he claimed responsibility for the Moscow metro bombing that killed ten just one day before, as well as the two bombs which killed all 90 on board two commercial passenger jets the week before. Basayev's unabashed pride in these operations did not keep him from expressing his feeling that the outcome at Beslan – not the siege itself - was a "terrible tragedy." He placed the blame for the massacre squarely at the feet of President Vladimir Vladimirovich Putin, claiming that the Russian forces had planned to storm the building from the very beginning, no matter what transpired, and that the "freedom fighters" had not detonated any explosives until after the government assault. "The Kremlin vampire destroyed and injured 1,000 children and adults, giving the order to storm the school for the sake of his imperial ambitions and preserving his own throne," Basayev wrote, referring to Putin.

Basayev's letter went on to say that his hostage-takers had demanded Russia stop the war in Chechnya immediately and withdraw its troops. As an alternative, they had insisted on Putin's "immediate resignation as president." Referencing a separate letter he supposedly had delivered to Putin through two intermediaries, Basayev insisted that he had offered the Russian president "independence in exchange for security," agreeing to stop financing any groups fighting Russia and the cessation of the formation of "military bases" on Russian soil. As a final conciliation, he claimed to have offered that Muslims in Russia would take no armed action against the Russian Federation for 10 to 15 years. In anticipation of the government refusing to meet his terms, he warned both Russia and other nations of the consequences of not supporting the Chechen and Muslim cause: "We are not bound by any circumstances, or to anybody, and we will continue to fight as is convenient and advantageous to us, and by our rules. Chechens are fighting Russia only – for now." This could signal an increase in the internationality and multi-cultural dimension of terrorist groups, and could be a harbinger of terrorist group composition the U.S. may yet face on its own soil.

Basayev's letter may shed some light on the preparation and operational capability of the Beslan terrorists. In it, he claimed to have personally conducted a ten-day training course for the hostage-takers in a forest some 20 km (12 miles) from the very town in which they would launch their horrific assault. Both Komarov and Russian Special Forces officers on scene lamented that for the most part it was obvious the terrorists were "well trained and professional," while the majority of the support forces, local police and military were "dilettantes compared to them." While visiting a Spetsnaz garrison in March 2005, I was told by two officers who commanded sniper teams at Beslan that even "the terrorist snipers were very professional, they were very good."

It would only take until December 2004 before information became public that al Qaeda linked Islamist terrorists, with connections in Chechnya, had set up a training camp in southern Somalia, right up against the border with Kenya. The *Nairobi East African Standard* newspaper reported, in the week before Christmas, that the camp, at a place called Ras Kiamboni, was being used to recruit and train extremists for the al Qaeda affiliated terrorist group, *Al Ittiyad*, and that Kenyan border guards were well aware of it. Reportedly, this camp is heavily funded by wealthy businessmen stretching from Kenya to Kuwait, and, at 45 square miles in size, is capable of supporting both the jihadists and their families. Reportedly, the jihadist trainees are told that they are part of the global jihad, and they will be going to Chechnya to fight upon completion of their training. This is most telling of what the Russians may have been up against at Beslan.

* * * * *

Aside from the loss of life, the deepest wound of the terror attack was psychological. MVD psychologist Marina says that even though North Ossetia is in a war zone, there was still deep psychological injury caused by the siege. MVD Major E.I. Tatarshin agrees. "Nord-Ost in Moscow was horrible, but Muscovites have already accepted its horror and moved on," he says. "In Beslan that will not happen. Two years ago a huge avalanche wiped out two entire villages nearby in the Caucasus Mountains. They have never been rebuilt. The people here believed that was the worst, most terrible thing that could ever happen. Now they know Beslan is."

The individual hostages themselves have received the best medical and psychological care Russia has to offer. And assistance has not been limited to Russia. From the moment the first hostages were freed, government resources inundated them with treatment, both physical and emotional. By the time of my return to Beslan in November, two months after the siege, many of the hostages had been taken from the area. Most of the children had been sent to special treatment centers in Moscow, Sochi, Rostov-on-Don, Ukraine and even Israel. Some of the children had been whisked away before their parents could even see them, in some cases before they even knew their children were alive.

When I reached Vladikavkaz on my way to Beslan in November, a team of Israeli psychologists had already been there for a week, setting up a treatment center for those child hostages who had remained or returned in the interim. I was told it was their intention to remain in the area for several months, doing what they could for the hostages and their families, and training their Russian counterparts to continue with the therapy after their departure. Israelis were invited to come to North Ossetia because the Russians see them as being able to relate to their plight. To them, the Israelis live with terror every day, and have therefore had to deal with it realistically. Still, according to Major Tatarshin, "every culture, and even every region within a single culture, is different. How the people from each area deal with the psychological stress of such a thing will vary." Nevertheless, Russians view Israel as the one country capable of understanding what they have been through, and that has necessarily developed techniques in treating the consequences of such experiences.

For better or worse, the political trauma for Russian officials was far less than the psychological injury of the victims and townspeople, though the officials may not see it that way. When I first returned to Moscow in September, well after the siege ended, I asked Rodin if he believed the incident would weaken Putin. His response was prescient. "Putin will not be weakened by this politically. It only appears to be so in the news media; but in a number of ways this will strengthen him and give him opportunities he will use," he predicted. Before I left him in Moscow, this was already proving to be true. Within a short time, just as Rodin foretold, he had used this assault as an excuse to gain control of a number of groups, and consolidate ever more power under the presidency. His continued appointment of ever more *siloviki* – current and former security services agents – to top government positions, has had the effect of increasing his power, while at the same time rendering his administration ever more mono-faceted. Having previously emasculated the Federation Council, the upper house of the Russian parliament, Putin used Beslan as an excuse to move on the Duma, the more powerful and independent lower house.

Little protest was expected. Not only was Putin delivering the "secure and strong Russia" the Russian people yearned for after the chaotic and tumultuous Yeltsin years, but he already controlled the three major television channels in the country.

Moreover, Putin's popularity with the Russian public has not been diminished as a result of either the Chechen War or the increased number of terrorist attacks. Though no official statistics are kept - or at least none are released - estimates of casualties of the Chechen War put the number of Russian soldiers, Chechen fighters, civilians and police wounded or killed at 100,000. The number of Russian military and police killed alone is estimated at 25,000, with statistics showing that approximately one million Russian soldiers and "police officers" (i.e., MVD troops) have seen service in Chechnya. Even after Beslan, Putin's approval rating never fell below 66 percent, and his United Russia party continues to drive much of the political affairs in the country.

As I was leaving Moscow for home in late September 2004, one FSB officer explained that already the "big debate" was over who was responsible for the debacle that resulted at Beslan. He agreed that there was no clear-cut chain of command operationally, and to the extent there was any chain of command at all, the head did not have any real power or authority over others at the school. "The whole thing was a leaderless mess," one officer from Vympel reported. "This mess was the biggest reason for many hostages dying." Another laid the blame squarely at the feet of the very officials likely now conducting the investigation: "Government officials did all they could to avoid responsibility. This only happened because representatives of government troops and headquarters were paralyzed and wouldn't decide to do anything. They tried to do everything but make a tough decision." Rodin saw much of the same, saying just days after the drama ended that those in power were already forming small conspiracies to protect each other, blame others, and cover up what really happened. Just one day after the Beslan crisis ended, Putin addressed the nation on television, admitting Russian law enforcement's "failure to recognize the complexity and danger of processes going on in our country and the world as a whole," and "to react to them adequately."

Contrary to many news reports, there were no demonstrations against Putin when he went to visit the survivors at the end of the siege. In general, the people of Beslan were pleased that he had taken so active an interest and had come to visit them. Predictably, though some individuals tried to incite a public response or provoke assaults across the border into Ingushetia, there were no formal protests, and certainly no public ones. While many journalists might chalk this up to the increasingly iron fist with which Putin rules Russia, the local citizens I spoke with appeared genuinely happy with his presence and his handling of the ordeal. They seemed to think that he is their only real answer to the problem with Ingushetia and Chechnya. To the extent there is any sentiment against the government for its handling of Beslan, it is that the troops should have attacked on Day One, or Day Two at the latest. Even in expressing this criticism, most still acknowledge that the crowds likely made this impossible.

There is little useful information likely to come from the Putin commission now formally investigating the Beslan crisis. At first refusing to have any official inquiry, Putin was quickly assailed by the international press, in addition to an affected Russian public. However, his choice to have an investigation conducted under the inestimable influence of his own political crony and appointee, Federation Council Chairman Sergei Mironov, is hardly likely to result in anything beneficial, including objective, valid and much needed criticisms of the government and its handling of the crisis. The official head of the Federation Council's commission investigating Beslan is one Aleksandr Torshin, Vice Speaker of the League of the Federation of Russia. Hardly coincidentally, Mironov is Torshin's boss.

The investigating commission set up by Putin is not the only one looking into how the crisis happened and what went wrong once it started. Both the North Ossetian Parliament and the North Caucasus branch of the Prosecutor General's Office have launched their own, or supplemental, investigations. Nevertheless, with everyone largely subordinate to an increasingly powerful and autocratic president, little is expected to come from those efforts either. It is a virtual certainty that all useful conclusions to be drawn from Beslan – in the hope of preventing the deaths of children elsewhere in Russia and the wider world – will have to come from experts' independent analysis and the application of those lessons to their own countries, security systems, and laws. "Putin's commission won't find anyone guilty of anything and won't draw any relevant or significant conclusions," one career government official confided. "Their only real effort is to compel people to forget this. Though America is interested in Beslan, Russia has already lost interest."

Aside from the efforts of the commission, Komarov said that the government had announced it would be giving huge budget increases to both Alpha and Vympel. Putin called this a major overhaul of the nation's security and police infrastructure, including "a complex of measures aimed at strengthening [Russia's] unity," and the creation of "a new system of forces and means for exercising control over the situation in the North Caucasus." The increases would allow them to train up to the level of anti-terror capability necessary in today's environment of ever-increasing sophistication and funding for terrorists, or to the very level of incidents they have been called on to handle after years of languishing. They will be "whole new units of great capability," he told me. When asked, Komarov explained that this did not mean different units would be formed, or that current team members would be dismissed and replaced by new, better-trained recruits. He said that the units of Alpha and Vympel would remain staffed as they were, but that they would be receiving the money to engage in much better, more intensive, and sophisticated training, much like Delta and SEAL Team Six. No mention was made of Vityaz, SOBR, or OMON, rendering this improvement the sole province of the FSB. Part and parcel of this, as stated by the president in a public address, will be the added creation of an "effective crisis-management system, including entirely new approaches to the work of law enforcement agencies." Clearly, Putin's message is that Beslan only proves that he needs even more power concentrated under his presidency. By early 2005 the MVD had already vastly expanded its responsibilities and taken definitive steps to create highly trained, rapid response assault teams. The Interior Ministry has established new operational groups to control the entire Southern Federal District of Russia under the greatest threat from Chechnya and its Islamist terrorists already moving outside Chechen borders. More than a dozen early operational exercises combined units of OMON, SOBR and the Red Beret units of the Dzherzhinskiy Division, along with units of the regular army operating under MVD command for the first time. Efforts to protect infrastructure by these units has included assignment to more than 400 sites throughout Russia seen as potential terror targets. These include schools, railway stations, airports, universities and hospitals, as well as more than 100 nuclear power plants.

Though Putin has clearly used Beslan to take the next step in a years-long power grab, he has not been without influential detractors. In addition to receiving scathing criticism from many in the international news media, two weeks after the Beslan tragedy ended Mikhail Gorbachev, the former president of the Soviet Union, and Boris Yeltsin, the former president of the Russian Federation, simultaneously assailed Putin for his hard-line policies in Chechnya as well as his continuing consolidation of power over all Russian government and national institutions within the Kremlin. None of this criticism, however, has stopped those in power from moving quickly to point the finger at others.

By Friday, October 15, 2004, three police officers in Ingushetia had been charged with criminal negligence, ostensibly for allowing the terror group across the border into North Ossetia. It did not go unnoticed that only Ingush were found at fault for this systemic failure. I was later informed that each of the accused was a top law enforcement official who was charged simply for being "generally responsible" for the terrorists crossing the border. This prosecution, coupled with the firing of the FSB's Valeriy Andreyev, represented the sum total of sanctions mandated by the government in the first months after the incident.

That Putin's commission accomplished little more than laying blame for the massacre on a few irrelevant scapegoats was already being seen long before it had completed its investigation or issued any report. The week of January 24, 2005, saw a commission, pandering to its presidential master, criminally charge two more career MVD officers as the supposed masterminds behind the Beslan siege. No one seemed to notice that these men were merely administrative clerks. Three others were being investigated, and two more – deciding not to wait around for a pre-determined guilt verdict – had disappeared. After a decade and a half of studying Russian history and working in and around that country, I was not surprised. No one really expected the commission to issue any findings of value, or even suggest ways in which the governmental infrastructure should be improved to prevent and deal with such problems in the future. Putin had already done all that he intended to; all that he felt was necessary. And he didn't need anyone telling him how to run the country, or fight the Chechens. The commission was already fulfilling the very goals for which it had been formed: it had found a few inconsequential scapegoats and its members were going to hang the fault of the entire mess on them. That seven men, all career officers in the Russian Interior Ministry, would give up their lives to assist Chechen terrorists murder Russian children was preposterous. None of them had even been at Beslan. This was beyond the pale, even for Russia.

The commission was beginning to resemble the Stalinist show trials of the 1920 and 30s: mere theater with the final act predetermined by a powerful dictator. The members of the commission themselves were inextricably linked with the Federation Council, now a body largely handpicked by Putin. Moreover, the one part of the government responsible for protecting the country from terrorism - the FSB – is not only Putin's former employer, but the source of most appointments in every branch of the Russian government for more than the past four years, and several of its top people were commission members. It was appearing highly unlikely that the commission would find significant fault with anyone in power; those most responsible for the complete failure of the Russian security system. Certainly, no one at a senior level had been held accountable. In a nation in which everyone in power lives off the spoils of the corruption that position brings, those selected were clearly scapegoats, the lowest people whose convictions would be guaranteed to deflect attention and outrage from those who could really have prevented Beslan. The same ones who could prevent the next assault, but likely will not.

By the beginning of March 2005, after the date by which the commission's report was first scheduled to be released, Beslan Commission Chief Aleksandr Torshin reported that they had answers to everything except whether terrorists had hidden weapons in the school in advance of the attack, exactly how many terrorists there were, and what the composition of the group was. Somehow, after months of concerted investigation by Russia's top officials and with a virtually unlimited budget, they had only missed the most important answers surrounding the Beslan attack. I wondered who they had been talking to. Moreover, by that same time reports were being made by some of the Beslan townspeople that several days after the siege ended they had found a ditch filled with hostages' clothing, hair, a live grenade and other evidence. It had all been put there by government officials, clearly demonstrating to the people of Beslan they had no intention of gathering evidence, of conducting a real investigation. When the townsfolk contacted the MVD and reported this ditch full of evidence government agents arrived and quickly packed it up, transporting it out of Beslan. What became of it is unknown, though it is unlikely to have received any better treatment than its unceremonious dumping in a hole in the ground outside of Beslan.

By the time I arrived in Beslan in September, just as the dust was settling, Lydia Tsaliyeva, the Director of Beslan Middle School No. 1, was being blamed for virtually inviting terrorists in and taking no preventive measures. Still others accused her of being complicit in the assault; claiming she must have arranged the painting and remodeling of the school the summer before to allow the terrorists to hide weapons. Using the Russian diminutive for her name, graffiti around her office declaimed such things as, "Lida – Sellout. Couldn't you see where they put the weapons?" Still another charged, "Your place is in hell, Lida. God will punish you." The most graphic recited such obscenities as "Lida, you fucking bitch, you suck cock," "Lida you should die," and "Do you hear the children crying?" What seems to be lost on the grief-stricken is that Ms. Tsaliyeva herself had been a hostage, along with her sister and three of her grandchildren. Videotape taken by the terrorists, and shown on CBS months later,[21] clearly depicted Ms. Tsaliyeva imploring the terrorist leader to at least allow the women with babies to leave, and not to kill any of the children. What is even more ridiculous is that, while much of the world may not have been aware that she was a hostage prior to CBS' airing of this tape, the people of Beslan – those laying the blame for the siege at her feet – knew it from the very beginning. Ms. Tsaliyeva, injured in the initial assault, remained hospitalized weeks later. Six months after the siege she was still in hiding, fearing for her life.

Just as ridiculous are claims that those working on repairs to the school over the summer were Chechens, or had Chechen sounding names. The majority of those engaged in this effort were teachers at the school, along with some local construction workers. One was the Dagestani brother of the school's custodian. Either a now vengeful

---

[21] *CBS 48 Hours*, aired Saturday, January 22, 2005.

Ossetian public does not care, or no one in the government has seen fit to explain this to them. Each and every person who worked on the school in the summer was interrogated and cleared by the FSB. More than two months after the horror at Beslan, such outlandish accusations had not waned, and what few Ingushetis remained in the Ossetian provinces, as well as throughout Russia, were living in fear for their safety.

Undoubtedly the terrorists were successful in exacerbating or inflaming – to some degree - already seething ethnic animosity between the North Ossetians, on the one hand, and the Ingush and Chechens on the other. In fact, despite all of the issues surrounding the Chechen War and the regular terrorist atrocities committed by the Chechens, the Ossetians' hostility is aimed more at the Ingush, with whom they share a long border. Though no real reprisals occurred, many expected attacks by the Ossetians at the end of the Orthodox forty-day mourning period. These never came, in part due to the tightly sealed border and huge troop presence ordered by Putin as preventive measures against a repeat of the violence that occurred in 1992. Then, they had only been fighting over land.

Thus, it is clear that the political fallout for Russian officials will be virtually non-existent within Russia itself. And internationally, the Beslan School siege has served to legitimize perceived Russian hegemony in the North Caucasus, removing it from the moralistic microscope of the UN and the international news media, where it has been for years. Just as clear, is the fact that the Chechens now recognize that this atrocity not only failed to serve their purpose, but may have gone far to erode their support in the international community.

Seizing on this unexpected opportunity, Putin, in a national address on September 6, foretold the potentially dark and gloomy days ahead for Russia and those dealing with her. Borrowing a line from Joseph Stalin, the iron-fisted dictator of the Soviet Union who engineered the murders of 30 million citizens in the 20 years leading up to World

War II, Putin intoned: "We showed weakness, and the weak are trampled upon. Some want to cut off a juicy morsel from us while others are helping them. They are helping because they believe that, as one of the world's major nuclear powers, Russia is still posing a threat to someone, and therefore this threat must be removed."

Putin's statement came just two days after I received the ire of a noted Spetsnaz commander over America's harboring of a top Chechen leader, as well as Britain's hiding of another. With my ears still ringing from this man's wrath, it was not lost on me what countries Putin was talking to. Indeed, he left no room for doubt as to whom he saw as complicit in such occurrences in the big picture. Arguing the need for "legality and toughness" in dealing with Chechnya and refusing to negotiate with terrorists, he pointed a finger directly at the West for harboring and comforting these criminals: "A patronizing and indulgent attitude to the murderers amounts to complicity in terror." Just who were the Russians talking about, and who could possibly believe the U.S. and Britain would give aid and comfort to terrorists?

Ilyas Akhmadov, the exiled Chechen administration's putative foreign minister, had fled to the U.S. two years earlier, arriving on U.S. soil on Thursday, September 26, 2002. Once there, he immediately requested political asylum, which the American government granted. At the time, the Russian government's outrage at the United States for providing refuge to one of its domestic terrorist leaders was hardly tempered by its ability to exploit the defection, declaring through Kremlin spokesman Aleksandr Yakovenko, that such a move by a top Chechen guerilla was "indicative" of the fact that the Chechen terrorist leadership was "starting to realize that their terrorist cause is doomed."

Earlier that year, the 42 year-old Akhmadov had drawn the interest and sympathy of numerous nations for the cause of Chechen independence, during a tour of such cities as Prague, Berlin and Washington, D.C. In June 2000, just before President Clinton's Moscow summit with Russian President Putin, the political science-trained guerilla leader was permitted to meet with Secretary of State Madeleine Albright where he outlined his peace plan for Chechnya. All of this proved too much for the Russian government, inciting Putin's Foreign Minister to lodge official complaints with such nations as the Czech Republic, Germany, and the U.S. for granting a fugitive terrorist virtual foreign dignitary status. To the Russians even today, U.S. behavior relative to Akhmadov is tantamount to them providing refuge to Usama bin Laden or any of the terrorists in Iraq currently on the American "most wanted" list. Despite this, the following year, 2003, Akhmadov was reportedly permitted to brief U.S. State Department officials on the Chechen perspective of the status of the conflict.

Equally outrageous to the Russian government is Britain's support for Chechen terrorism. Not only has Chechen "envoy" and accused former terror leader Akhmed Zakayev enjoyed asylum in that country – free to travel to and from Brussels and Oslo on a regular basis – but so has fugitive oligarch Boris Berezovsky. Most recently, in November 2004 it was released that a London court had granted political asylum to Andrei Krotov, a Russian conscript soldier who had fled his unit in Chechnya, eventually making it to the United Kingdom. Britain's highest judicial authority on such matters, the Immigration Appeal Tribunal, accepted Krotov's contention that he had deserted because Russian troops were committing atrocities in Chechnya, and he was not in a position to refuse an order to participate. Justice Ouseley, writing for the court, said: "There were numerous credible reports of human rights abuses and atrocities committed by federal forces. . . . We conclude that at least during this period [when Krotov was deployed there] breaches of those basic rules were widespread." The court's decision, which was handed down in May 2004 but kept secret until November, served to further inflame relations with the Putin administration.

In the U.S., Akhmadov had been enjoying political asylum since the fall of 2002. He regularly attempted to interject himself into American politics, lobbying for U.S. support of the Chechen cause.

The taking of hundreds of children in Beslan drew him out once again. Knowing that the Western cultures would accept no excuse for the willful slaughter of hundreds of children, the Chechens seemed to decide they had no choice but to go on the offensive in the media war over Beslan. Proving his continuing support of Chechen terrorists, Akhmadov did not denounce the murder of so many young innocents. On September 6, following Putin's statement to the press in Russia, Akhmadov boldly said to the *New York Times*, referencing the 200,000 Chechens estimated to have died in both wars, "You must agree that the elimination of one-fourth of the population is not the struggle against terrorism. On the contrary, it is something that leads to the growth of terrorism."

Indeed, one Chechen website seemed to agree with this self-styled emissary of peace, rationalizing the assault on the school by saying that the Russians had killed 42,000 Chechen children in the war, necessitating that some Russian children die as revenge. What the world did not notice about Akhmadov was that he established himself in America exactly one month before 800-plus hostages would be taken at the Nord-Ost Theater, including hundreds of children. His presence in America well coincided with the Chechens' need for a received dignitary to rationalize their cause to a horrified world after Nord-Ost. With Beslan, he appears to have continued in this capacity.

One of the other nations that Russian officials believe is harboring and supporting Chechen terrorism is Turkey. A Muslim nation, Turkey has not only a long-standing enmity with Russia and its predecessor, the Soviet Union, but is typically aligned with the United States on many international issues. Just three months after Beslan, on Sunday, December 5, 2004, President Putin made an historic visit to that country, the first official visit to Turkey by a Russian leader. Putin seemed to be successful in his efforts to co-opt some Turkish cooperation, or at least the appearance of it. Dangling the carrot of increased trade with Russia's growing and powerful economy,

Putin listened as Turkish President Ahmet Necdet Sezer recognized the great advantage in "moving cooperation and relations between [their] two countries toward a multifaceted partnership," and his commitment to cooperate with Russia in its fight against terrorism. Just days before the meeting, in a demonstration of good faith, Turkish authorities had arrested nine suspected Chechen militants and another three pro-Chechen Turks. It was released publicly that they had been linked to al Qaeda. For Turkey, a nation of people, many of whom trace their ancestry to Chechnya and other parts of the North Caucasus, and whose secret service has long been believed by Russian authorities to actively support Chechen terrorists, this was a big victory for Putin.

Also on the international scene, Putin has benefited from an America that has started to see things its way with regard to Chechnya. In exchange, Putin has begun to reciprocate. In October 2004 he called on the international community to mobilize its resources to support the American-created Provisional Government of Iraq. In a message to Prime Minister Iyad Allawi, Putin wrote that Russia and Iraq were "tied by traditions of friendship and cooperation that have been developed over many years."

* * * * *

While a number of the terrorists appear to have gotten away with the Beslan attack, the aftermath for them has not been enjoyable. As was predictable for Alpha and Vympel based on past practice, they quickly went to work once the battle at the school was over. Both the Interior Ministry and Federal Security Service put out a wide and aggressive intelligence net, learning that a number of the terrorists were holed up in the city of Nazran, a small town in Ingushetia, located a short distance from the Chechen border. Archangel's Spur Team had spent weeks there the previous year, providing security consulting and assessments to the numerous humanitarian aid organizations forced to move their headquarters away from the daily combat in Chechnya. IDP camps abound, with thousands upon thousands of people forced out of Chechnya. There they sit in tents with dirt floors, many a short drive from their former homes reduced to rubble by the constant fighting. When the MVD's Special Forces attacked the terrorists in Nazran just two weeks after the school's own horrific battle ended, the terrorists once again seized hostages. This time the hostages were a family whose home they fled to for refuge. The government wasted no time. The assault was rapid and the battle raged for six hours. The entire family and all of the terrorists were killed. The house was destroyed.

Other, similar incidents would occur in the months following. On October 22, eight alleged members of Hizb ut-Tahrir al-Islam (Islamic Liberation Party), a radical Islamic group from Central Asia, were arrested in east Siberia on charges of terrorism and membership in an extremist organization. Included among these was the group's leader and founder, Alisher Usmanov, who was already on the international terrorism wanted list, and who at the time of his arrest was carrying explosives and al Qaeda training manuals and information. The Russian government also claimed to have evidence these men were planning terrorist sieges in which hostages would have been taken. Additionally, they were suspected in prior attacks, including bombings that killed civilians. Earlier in October, 11 suspected members of this group had been captured in the central Russian city of Nizhni-Novgorod. The end of October marked a year in which rebels and terrorists in Chechnya had killed more than 500 police and Interior Ministry troops. Despite this, the government managed to thwart 52 terrorist attacks and captured or killed 193 terrorists.

Throughout November and December, government crackdowns on suspected Chechen and Ingush rebels and terrorists continued. Putin's promise to increase the forces necessary to protect the country was being put into effect. As part of that effort a secret proposal had already been made to Russia's parliament for the government to adopt a policy of taking terrorists' own family members as hostages in response to a Beslan-type siege. In November, information was released by U.S. intelligence that al Qaeda had been planning to set up bases in Chechnya for years. The FSB also learned that more than 80 new suicide bombers had been trained abroad to attack Russia. The deputy mayor of the capital of Dagestan was assassinated on December 1, the second murder of that city's deputy mayor in three years. The U.S. State Department declared that Russia was not safe for Americans. Russia's problems with terrorism raged on.

In early January 2005 more than 100 government assault troops, backed by five armored personnel carriers, surrounded a house holding five suspected terrorists from the June 2004 assaults that left close to 100 people dead, including almost 60 police and troops. Wasting no time, the government troops assaulted right away, killing all five. These men were believed to have been planning still more terrorist attacks in the area. Later that month Russian forces barely stopped a second Beslan-style siege of a school in Southern Russia when numerous raids by Special Forces in Dagestan, to the east of Chechnya, thwarted their plans. In one 15 hour firefight in Makachkhala, Dagestan on January 16, 2005, one Alpha officer was killed and another severely wounded.

Not everyone was happy with the outcome of Beslan. Frustrated over government intransigence and a seemingly ineffectual commission investigating the tragedy, by mid-January 2005 distraught parents and grandparents of children who died there blocked a major highway on two occasions in protest. Among their demands was that the North Ossetian President Aleksandr Dzasokhov resign.

As for the purpose behind the school siege, the terrorists seem to have been successful in very few respects. Admittedly, they did manage to gain the attention of the international news media they so desperately sought. However, every mass murderer, serial rapist and natural disaster in the world accomplishes the same to some degree. Contrary to their hopes, the attention they drew has been far from positive, and even their previous supporters among journalists and foreign governments have turned an increasingly cold shoulder to their cause. Perhaps the world has finally begun to see what Russia has been claiming all along: the Chechen militants are vicious terrorists of the worst stripe. Perhaps, for once, the Russian government has not been lying.

Certainly, the Muslim terrorists who took the school failed miserably in their goal of inflaming and maintaining increased tensions between North Ossetia and Ingushetia, or between North Ossetia and much of the rest of affluent Russia, namely Moscow. Although in the immediate aftermath of Beslan, historically poor relations between North Ossetia and Ingushetia seemed on the verge of quickly deteriorating into armed conflict, the region has since stabilized, or at least returned to its prior uneasy state. Russian authorities have now released information obtained from interrogations of the one captured terrorist, Norpasha Khulaev. According to Kulaev, the leader, Khuchbarov, had insisted that the school in Beslan be attacked because they needed "to start a war in the entire territory of the north Caucasus." In this, they enjoyed no success at all. Reports that during the siege some Ossetians had crossed the border, surrounding Ingusheti villages and demanding the release of the hostages, were fanciful. And while the border between the two regions has been largely shut down since the incident - now guarded by regular army rather than MVD "police" forces – this reflects no great deterioration in relations. Tensions between those two regions have always been high, and trust between the two peoples non-existent. I had experienced this first hand in the summer of 2003, when we were forced to cross the border at that very spot every day. Tense and heavily guarded, it was clear that there was no love lost between the people of the two republics, and our hosts on the Ossetian side refused even to greet the federal security agents who met us just inside Ingushetia each morning.

Of course, there have been a great many reports of cross-border violence since Beslan. I have also been assured that every single Ingush living in Ossetia fled back across the border, and not a single one remains in the entire region. Reports also abound that some

Ossetians, many of whom lost their entire families in the school massacre, have been crossing the border secretly looking for victims on whom to vent their rage, and that Russian troops had to quell a North Ossetian attack on Ingush villages immediately after the end of the school siege. These are more rumor than fact, and I have personally seen no evidence of it. Whether true or not, however, the terrorists fell far short of their stated objective of dragging both the Ingush and Ossetians into the war, and expanding the conflict into those regions.

And just as with Beslan, the terrorist group behind *all* of Russia's recent horrors has failed to achieve any of its goals over the past year. Kadyrov's assassination in May 2004 did not destabilize the situation in the North Caucasus, and the Russians not only managed the election of his replacement, but Alkhanov has been moving forward with his governance since the inauguration. Neither the plane, metro, nor bus attacks in Moscow achieved their desired purposes either. There has been no mass public hysteria. People have not stopped using public transportation, and Domodedovo airport continued its operations with barely a hiccup. Unlike in America, the downing of commercial aircraft did not seem to affect the economy at all, and Russia has engaged in no hyper-reactionary restructuring of its entire air transportation security system. Certainly Russia experienced no mass demonstrations against the Kremlin along the lines of what Spain suffered after the terror attacks there over the spring of 2004.

Rather than weakening Putin, the Beslan attack seems to have not only made him more popular than ever with a Russian public yearning for a final solution in Chechnya, but provided him the justification he needed to increase further his power base and control in the country; all in the name of counter-terrorism. He has appointed his closest friend, Dmitri Kozak, as the new envoy to the Southern Federal District – covering the North Caucasus region – bestowing on him greater powers than ever before. Additional FSB and MVD anti-terror units have been placed throughout the North Caucasus region, gaining Moscow a greater foothold for controlling all events there, and forcing local units and law enforcement to stand back. The biggest weakness that allowed Beslan to occur – the overall governance structure of the entire region – has been recognized and will be repaired, no matter how Draconian the measures. The United States, in light of its own far-reaching conduct and legal sleight-of-hand in making the U.S. Constitution disappear while enemy prisoners appeared out of nowhere in the recent years of her War on Terror, has been in no position to object. Russia, despite a year of unprecedented terrorist attacks and numbers of victims killed, has continued to move along with one of the strongest economies in the world today. For them, it has been business as usual.

As for the Ossetians, despite their positive opinion of both Putin and the Special Forces in responding to the school crisis, they do to a degree blame Moscow for Beslan. To them the battle is between Moscow and Chechnya, with North Ossetia sitting - like a neutral country – in the middle. And just as with many non-combatants in war, they are the ones suffering. "We get caught in the middle; as the Chechens send demands to Moscow, Moscow ignores them and North Ossetia suffers," one Beslan resident told me. The psychologist Marina, after meeting with numerous of the local police trying to deal with the emotional aftermath of Beslan, confides that this enmity exists to such a depth that the North Ossetians even saw the subway attack in Moscow the day before as giving Muscovites their due. "This is not a feeling toward all Russians, but only Moscow," she says. "Ossetians feel that the Muscovites got what they deserved. They hate the affluence and arrogance of both the government and the people in Moscow." Still, the Ossetians continue to hate the Ingush, as they have for centuries, but realize that they do not want another protracted battle as happened between them in 1992.

Yuri, a cab driver in Beslan, puts it all in perspective: "Everyone is welcome here. We do not blame anyone," he says. "We want to be friends with everyone: Georgians, Russians, Americans, Ingush and Chechens. Only journalists are not welcome," he laughs. With his friendly demeanor and beaming smile, made all the brighter by a mouth full of gold teeth, he is perhaps the best ambassador of peace Putin could hope to find in this troubled region.

Chapter Ten

Russian Hindsight

Russia is a riddle,
Wrapped in a mystery,
Inside an enigma.
— *Winston Churchill*

Russians are not typically a people who take great pains to keep their opinions to themselves. However, when urged to articulate what America must do to prepare for a possible assault on her own schools, even the most vocal become strangely humble. They know what is at stake. "Security in schools should be a large system," Special Forces commander Sergei Lisyuk says. "The first and most important part of the system must be the information and intelligence system. Officers should have agents to collect information at all times." He is not unrealistic about the changes this would entail. "This would be a large deviation from how schools have historically viewed themselves and their mission," he admits. "But if they do not adapt to the times, and recognize the threats they are now under, they may not have children to teach." He encourages school administrators to listen to security experts, and to accept the reality of the potential danger they face. To keep their children safe in order to educate them, they must take on – at least to some degree – a tactical mindset. For the threat to the safety of children has grown far beyond crossing the street in front of the school and falling off the monkey bars. Indeed, it has grown far beyond even the threat of Columbine-esque weapons wielding students intent on revenge for some imagined wrong, or child molesters lurking about school grounds. It is a whole new threat, brought on by an enemy of unprecedented viciousness and capability.

To ensure the safety and security of the school's charges, Col. Lisyuk says the second tier in the school security approach must be technology, specifically surveillance and counter-surveillance. He and others in the Russian Special Forces community believe that the answer is not just men with guns, but trained, professional awareness. "Each school needs skilled counter-surveillance and counter-intelligence professionals," they tell me. "Not just men with guns who can shoot." But if prevention is not successful the school must still be able to fall back on physical security measures. "The entire school compound should be fenced, with iron doors at all exits, entrances and gates," Col. Lisyuk says. "Gates should be electronic, operated by remote control. Different sections of the school should be designed to close electronically so they can lock off the various sections in order to reduce the number of victims in a takeover," he explains.

Just as important a factor are the employees. Teachers cannot afford merely to focus on their academic subjects anymore. "Every employee in a school should be ready for everything, trained in everything," he asserts. "For example, in Japan teachers should be trained in how to respond to an earthquake. No one can afford school administrators and teachers who cannot react to any type of emergency. Look at Columbine in America. Since then there have been other incidents, and many others stopped before they occurred. I would think by now American teachers would have had to learn how to deal with students armed with guns and bombs."

Komarov, though a former career Special Forces officer, holds a doctorate in psychology. He believes there are limits. "I and my colleagues have studied the Israeli school model and decided it will not work in Russia, it will not be effective," he says. He explains why this approach for the protection of children, so successful in Israel, cannot be exported: "Israel only had to harden its schools as targets against simple fanatics, not professional diversion teams like the Chechens and Ingush. The people Russia is up against are good enough that they will do good intelligence gathering and find the weakness in the security system." Even Lisyuk agrees that the better the security, the more trained and armed defenders are put into schools, the greater the likelihood the terrorists will merely send their own better trained, elite forces against them. Komarov has another concern: "If you make schools barricaded like castles, it will cause psychological harm to children. Children all want freedom and the ability to move around all the time." Still, children throughout history have had to adapt to worse than some increased restrictions. And what will be the psychological harm to those who experience the horrors of a terrorist takeover? How quickly have the survivors of Beslan overcome their emotional trauma?

Of real relevance is how the Russians view their own performance in handling the Beslan siege. In many ways, rather than directly confronting their own failings, government officials have chosen simply to forget Beslan and move on. Journalist Nabi Abduallaev reports that "municipal authorities across Russia announced that they have boosted security in schools, dispatching police officers to guard them during the class hours and providing the schools with electronic systems to alert police of possible terrorist attacks." Nothing could be further from the truth. Increased security at schools in Russia is virtually non-existent. To the extent that schools in Moscow and St. Petersburg can afford it, most have hired a single guard armed with pepper spray. That two armed men present at the Beslan School when the siege began – one a police officer - were no match for armed and trained terrorists, having been overwhelmed by superior weapons and numbers, seems to be lost on school and government officials. Nor has there been a great public clamor from parents to be better prepared for the next siege. "We are not concerned about another school siege, because the one thing we have learned is that the terrorists do not do the same thing twice," is a shocking opinion heard from some government officials. When I point out the numerous bus hijackings in Ingushetia and Dagestan, seizures of entire towns and military posts, kidnappings, hospital seizures, bus and metro bombings in Moscow and St. Petersburg, not to mention the three successful apartment bombings in Moscow in September 1999, I receive little more than an inscrutable Russian shrug. It is as though in their inimitable way, the way of a culture that has survived two thousand years of cruelty, of gazing out over the brooding and endless Russian steppe and grey skies, and 74 years of communist brutality and oppression after that, they believe they will simply outlast this grief as well.

Russian officials point out, however, that in schools around the country, entry and exit points are now better controlled with regard to both children and adults, especially in kindergartens. Of course, schools in the universally poorer regions outside the economic beneficence of Moscow and St. Petersburg cannot afford even a lone guard and will remain completely open and vulnerable to attack. In some of the bigger and more affluent cities, parents are raising money themselves for surveillance systems. One official maintains that 70 percent of all schools in Moscow now have them. Of course, none of this would have stopped the terrorists from gaining control of the school in Beslan. These efforts would not even have slowed them down.

The Russian military men, on whose shoulders fall the responsibility for handling such situations, are far more realistic. They accept the painful realities of such incidents and what must be done to overcome them. For instance, many in the Russian military questioned whether the pedal release detonators were real, believing them to be dummies designed to instill terror in both the hostages and the public. They contended that was the only reason the terrorists filmed them and sent the videotape out to negotiators: to serve a prohibitive effect on the government assaulting. The military men analyzing the situation did not believe the terrorists intended to kill themselves and would not have wired detonators to the bombs. If correct, this lends credibility to the hostages who reported that one of the explosives had simply fallen from the basketball net and exploded on impact. When I pointed out to the Russians that if they had guessed wrong, they would have caused the loss of many lives in an assault, they respond with chilling accuracy that if the pedal detonators had been live, then people were going to die anyway. There was simply no way to prevent their detonation. They contend that under that circumstance one has to accept those losses and devise a plan to save as many of the others as possible. Otherwise, everyone dies.

The Russians believe that in order to devise a plan that will work when confronted with situations like Beslan, you must first understand the nature of the terrorism the world is now dealing with. The Justice Ministry's Col. Ryabko points out that terrorism is a business, and a very profitable one at that. It is – and has always been – used like a secret military by countries, organized crime groups, and even some of the world's largest religions over the course of history. Whether the act of a particular group is deemed terrorist, or the patriotic accomplishment of a dangerous operation behind enemy lines by brave men and women, depends entirely on which side of that operation you find yourself. Colonel Lisyuk agrees. "Imagine you are with an American Green Beret group. You have been ordered to infiltrate deep into a foreign country and blow up a facility which will result in the deaths of many otherwise innocent people, or assassinate a key member of that country's government," he theorizes. He explains further: "You will do everything to complete your mission, down to the last man. To you, you are a member of an elite group carrying out your nation's orders to protect your own national security. You are a hero doing something that takes the courage of a hero. But to the people of that country, you are a terrorist and you have done exactly what terrorists do." Ryabko emphasizes that no one can afford the luxury of looking down on the Arabic or Muslim terrorists as less than human, or less than ourselves: "Terrorists are acting exactly as you would be as a member of your Special Forces," he tells me. "They are just like any soldiers, with satcomms and connections to their headquarters command." The difference is that unlike forces of an established country, they do not have even the fig leaf of operating under international law, or recognized "norms" of conflict.

Ryabko goes further to explain that though different countries may have different languages and cultures, all use the same methods. The reasons for his success as one of the leading Spetsnaz commanders, and now as a top government adviser, are obvious when he points out, "This is what we all do, and have always done. This is what the CIA, KGB, Special Forces and Spetsnaz all do." He believes that we cannot possibly begin to be successful in fighting the terrorists, in responding to their attacks, until we understand them. By that he means understand them from an objective perspective, not the over-moralizing viewpoint we all want to adopt. In explaining this, he hones in on both the Russian and American tendency to see today's terrorists, and their Muslim fanaticism, as stupid, uneducated, misguided and undisciplined. He warns that they are committed, creative and, in most cases, extremely well trained. As he says this, the words of another officer with one of the first regular units to arrive at Beslan echo in my head: "We were amateurs compared to them." Lisyuk makes the same point: "Terrorism now is the biggest threat, it's like a state within a state. Some representatives of our governments just do not get this. Terrorists use the same systems as the government. They are trained in the negotiation techniques of law enforcement and in how to counter them. They are trained to complete their mission no matter what."

However, Col. Ryabko sees a critical weakness in the individuals who comprise the Islamic extremist terrorist groups. "They are brainwashed, they all too often become zombies, acting as though they are on some narcotic," he says. This also makes them extremely dangerous because, "They will carry out their missions like robots," he says. However, he also believes that tactics are available to exploit that weakness. "With brainwashed zombies, you have to reprogram their brains, give their brains something else, something new or different to react to," he contends. One tactic the Russians are insistent must be developed and always ready for implementation, is the use of gas. I am assured by more than one source integral to the operation in Beslan that its use was assured if there had been an opportunity for an assault by government forces. While much of the world viewed the outcome of the Nord-Ost Theater siege in late October 2002 as a disaster, the Russians see it as – and in truth it was – an unprecedented success of epic proportions. But for the use of gas, most, if not all, of the more than 800 hostages would have died there. Again, the Justice Ministry's Col. Ryabko is the most articulate in detailing the tactics and philosophy that must be adopted to deal adequately with seemingly impossible tactical circumstances. "Gas is always something to be looked to as a tactic against terrorist-hostage situations," he patiently explains at his dining room table late one night. His ever-present bodyguard, a young man from Spetsnaz identified only as Pyotr – whom I have met on previous occasions - gazes at me warily. He is clearly unhappy to be called to this duty late at night, sitting uncomfortably in a business suit that scarcely conceals muscles forged on the torturous Russian obstacle courses. The obvious years-long association between his charge and me means nothing to him.

Another career Spetsnaz officer who had been at Nord-Ost recognizes that despite Russia's obvious program to develop the optimum gas for such uses, the substance employed at Nord-Ost was too powerful. "It should not be paralyzing gas, just sleeping gas," he opines. The exact composition of the gas used at that theater is one of the best-kept secrets in the world. Despite knowing top commanders in three units deployed to that desperate barricade, and having two high ranking Spetsnaz officers – both long time friends and both on site at the theater – speak at Archangel's debut International Anti-Terrorism Conference in 2004 on that very topic, I still do not know exactly what the gas was. No one in the American government does.

Other Spetsnaz officers agree. From a Russian perspective, the use of sleeping gas can never make a situation worse. They explain that at Beslan, if gas had been used in the gym and the pedal detonators had been activated, far fewer hostages would have died. If they had all been lying down amidst each other, unconscious and unmoving, there would have been fewer injuries and far fewer fatalities from the bombs. Moreover, it is impossible for terrorists to move hostages around as human shields if they are unconscious, hanging limp in their arms. This makes gas an effective tactic even if the terrorists have gas masks, as those at Beslan did. As it turned out, many hostages were held tightly between the terrorists and their would-be rescuers from Alpha and Vympel. That many of those hostages lost their lives is testimony to another Russian Special Forces tactic and acceptance of the unpleasant reality of such dilemmas: a hostage in that circumstance is already dead; take out the terrorist quickly at all costs, even if it means shooting the hostage. This point was made painfully clear when I trained with these men to deal with airline hijackings after 9-11. If Russian forces have access to firearms, and a terrorist holds a hostage in front of him, they shoot. They shoot fast, and they shoot a lot. If the hostage lives it is through sheer fortuity, as their only focus is to make sure the terrorist is killed quickly and cannot threaten others. In the aftermath of Beslan, the bodies of terrorists were proof of this. Many appeared to have been blown apart by bombs or grenades. I was quickly disabused of this notion. Most had been so riddled with bullets as to have been literally shot to pieces. In a couple of cases, their human shields fared little better.

When asked what they would do to prepare schools for a terrorist assault, if they had an unlimited budget – or if they "had America's money," as most of them pointed out – many included installing "special neutralizing equipment." Specifically, they advocate a delivery system for gas as a preventive measure. Rather than wait and be forced to improvise gas delivery in the middle of a siege, they feel it is important that a system be set up long before an assault occurs. They do recognize that nothing is a panacea, and that such a tool has its problems. One such problem is that if bombs inside the school can be detonated electronically or via radio signal from outside the school, there can still be maximum devastation even after the introduction of gas. Still, they contend that it is one more tool that, more often than not, can be used effectively and will save many lives. When told that American cultural values would likely revolt at the notion of setting up systems to gas our own children, they are compelling in the argument that if everyone is unconscious, fewer people will die, and the only reason to deny ourselves this tactic is our refusal to accept reality.

The Russians offer another argument in favor of the use of gas. One consequence of the hostages having been awake when the bombs went off and the battle began at Beslan, was that they panicked. If they had been asleep they would not have been running around, inciting the terrorists to begin shooting them. Even after government forces initiated a concerted rescue effort and assaulted the school, hostages were still racing everywhere, getting in their rescuers' line of fire. A number of commandos and other government troops died as a result of their inability to fire for fear of hitting fleeing hostages. How many hostages were killed by friendly fire is unknown, but in the fog of that battle, the odds are that at least some did. This is also the main reason the Spetsnaz advise against the use of concussion or flash bang grenades in such operations. They believe that they can only be used in a quick assault where the entire battle will last mere seconds, like the bus hijackings of the 1990s. Anything more complex will not, they feel, provide any real advantage, and in fact will act to the detriment of the success of the assault. "With such grenades as concussion or flash grenades, you cannot predict or control the reaction of the hostages," Ryabko says. "They are only good for immediate entry."

At Beslan grenades were not used and not distributed to troops. They were afraid the children would panic. Just as important, other commanders point out that at Beslan no one was completely certain where all the hostages were. Intelligence from inside the school was limited. The assault team was afraid that the use of concussion grenades, when not all of the terrorists were in the same location at the time of the initial assault, would warn them and provide them valuable time to prepare a response, perhaps killing more hostages. Given the complexity of the school's design, there were too many rooms, walls, and different floors; there were nooks and crannies everywhere. These are always factors to consider in deciding to use diversionary devices. As the advantage of using such a building was one of the major lessons learned by the terrorists after Nord-Ost, it is almost certain that it will be repeated in every siege involving large numbers of hostages. The al Qaeda-trained Chechens and Ingush had already enjoyed some success with buildings of this type at Buddenovsk and Kizlyar. At Beslan they perfected the technique.

Though the terrorists selected a building of great complexity, broke windows and had gas masks to mitigate the effects of a gas assault, the Spetsnaz were not diminished in their intention to employ gas, and employ it successfully. In response to concerns over the maze-like corridors and rooms of the Beslan Middle School No. 1, they responded that with gas – unlike concussion grenades – the assault is planned as though it is really a lot of little Nord-Osts, rather than a single building and a single assault. Each room and area of the building was assigned to a separate team. Each team had, as its first priority, the deployment of gas and the assault of that one section, and the rescue of those hostages. This was to be a coordinated attack of all assault teams, with everyone hitting the building at once. Any terrorists who fled the area they were occupying at the time, would run into the next assigned team and its adjacent sector, dividing them and allowing for more efficient tactical elimination of them.

Col. Ryabko insists that with America's ability in the development of technology, we must bring these resources to bear for law enforcement purposes. "You must increase technology for better, less lethal gas and its delivery," he says. "And law enforcement must be ready to use it." He points out darkly that all real technological advances come from either Russia or the U.S. Many others use our developments for their own purposes, and all lethal technology in the world originated with one of our countries. If we are not using our technology to thwart the ungodly purposes our enemies are putting it to, we are merely setting ourselves up for failure. And with that failure comes death. On the other hand, he warns that in today's age of rapid information dissemination, "everybody knows everything about technology. When some company develops something new, it is exhibited and advertised and then everyone knows about it and can get it." This includes the terrorist groups that study us. "Technology alone is not the answer," he says.

At Beslan, the commando units assigned to the assault followed the same steps that had been devised for Nord-Ost and prior hostage incidents. This has become doctrine throughout Russia's elite forces. Russian Spetsnaz officers are adamant that this approach is necessary for the rescue of as many hostages as possible and the resolution of any terrorist hostage siege. The outline is simple and, perhaps, ingenious in its simplicity:

1. Use negotiations to stabilize the situation;
2. Use negotiations to delay and prepare an assault;
3. Develop an assault plan;
4. Practice the assault plan;
5. Assault.

I am assured that with this approach America will give herself the greatest chance of not only successfully resolving a terrorist siege, but also sending the message to other terrorists that we are ready, we are capable, and we will act. No matter what the plan, several top officers from SOBR agree, you can never be weak in the face of terrorist demands. "If they are made to think the forces arrayed against them are incompetent, they will win," the tall colonel who looks like Jaws says. "Only through strength can you survive. Only through your strength can the hostages survive." Still, Col. Lisyuk gloomily warns, "The U.S. and all other nations will have the same result as in Beslan. It cannot be avoided. There is going to be a battle, and people are going to die. Government needs to deal with the big issues surrounding terrorism. Everyone else can only be as prepared as possible for the battle."

But not all the Russians' advice is applicable to American society or the constitutional principles upon which our lives and freedoms are based. More than a few Russian government officials advocate strongly the arrest of the families – and even the friends – of the terrorists as soon as their identities are known. They relate that in a number of instances the terrorists will identify themselves. Intelligence will provide this information in others. As soon as the names of the hostage-takers are known, their families should be rounded up and taken to the site. They can be put out in the open, and threatened with their own execution if any hostages are killed. For this, the Russians advocate a team of professionals ready to analyze, identify, and locate the families of each terrorist. Komarov served this role at Nord-Ost, in addition to providing psychological profiles of the terrorists as background investigations quickly identified them. At the very least the family members can be neutralized as a source of support for the terrorists. The Russians believe that such a policy may have a deterrent effect on terrorist plans to take hostages in many instances; knowing that their own families – who they often care deeply about – will be the victims of retribution.

I am told that this approach has proven successful in other countries. In the mid-1990s a Turkish passenger ship was taken, and the Turkish Secret Service rounded up the hijackers' families. The terrorists let all of the hostages go free. In recognizing that such a policy may offend the sensibilities of many countries – and their legal codes – the counter-terror experts I met with insisted that it should be done by the government only in total secrecy. In Beslan this secret was a poorly kept one. Almost as soon as the crisis began, Russian intelligence analysts were working feverishly to determine the identities of at least some of the hostage-takers. Failing in this attempt, up to 40 family members of Chechen rebel leaders Aslan Maskhadov and Shamil Basayev were placed in custody at the Russian military base in

Khankala, the same base from which several of the Spetsnaz units had deployed. Ilya Shabalkin, the Russian Security Services' spokesman in Chechnya, insisted this was merely to protect them from attempts at retribution by friends and relatives of the hostages.

In addressing the question of how America can best prepare for a Beslan-type assault, the Russians demonstrate the genius of simplicity for which they are so well known. Many of them believe America would not be nearly so susceptible to such an attack, convinced that the American people are far more alert than their Russian counterparts. "In the United States, neighbors watch out for each other a lot more," one officer tells me. Colonel Lisyuk believes that the geographic and historical status of the U.S. is a deterrent to major terror operations on American soil: "The United States is an independent continent. It is a nation of law and law enforcement. And the U.S. has had more than 200 years – a great deal of time – to establish its traditions. As with its INS system. It is not in a new state of evolution like Russia and the former Soviet republics."

Part of their belief in this regard is that since American society does not suffer the endemic corruption of Russia, accomplishing such an operation would be much more difficult for terrorists. In drawing this conclusion, they are focused on the fact that with regard to both the suicide bombing of the two jet passenger airliners and Beslan, the terrorists got to their objectives by bribing security officers. "I am a full colonel in the Special Forces, yet I only make the equivalent of $350.00 per month," Yuri Rodin admits. "In the Russian system, every officer looks right away to make additional money from his position. If that is all I make, imagine the salary of someone like a lieutenant." He laments, "If the government doesn't care any more than to pay someone a wage they cannot live on, this type of thing will continue to happen." Yet, for all of their honesty and objective self-evaluation, they fail to realize that on 9-11, nineteen hijackers managed to bring down four separate aircraft without bribing anyone. The common occurrence and general acceptance of bribes may have made the terrorists' jobs easier in Russia, but its absence would not have stopped them.

Nevertheless, the Russians – who often eschew the American dependency on technology to solve every problem – believe that simple vigilance is the single best tool to prevent a terrorist attack on a school here. "The main idea is to be alert and prevent the appearance of strangers in and around the school," I am told. "The best way to anticipate and make a preemptive strike is to collect good intelligence and do everything possible to prevent it," Col. Lisyuk agrees. With this advice, emphasis on good and active counter-surveillance and counter-intelligence is once again seen. As numerous officers from Russian Special Forces told me: "The terrorists did not just happen on the Beslan Middle School No. 1. They had done their reconnaissance months in advance. They looked at and studied every school and building in the area. They studied the surrounding neighborhoods and buildings. This was planned down to the smallest detail. If someone – anyone – had seen them and reported it, this could have been prevented. No children would have ever died."

Though the point has been made that these terrorists are often well trained and professional in carrying out their attacks and pre-operational planning and reconnaissance, that does not mean that common people cannot be of value in being vigilant and aware. History has provided numerous instances of average people taking notice of seemingly innocuous incongruities, and having the courage to act on them, thereby thwarting crimes or attacks. If reported, authorities must learn to trust and act on the observations of their citizenry.

In Southern Russia, an area that had already seen its share of attacks and hijackings, the police and government forces would very likely have responded if someone reported a specific school was being surveilled. After 9-11, American authorities would probably pay attention to reports of someone planning to fly a plane into a building, just as they act quickly on information regarding students planning Columbine-type assaults on schools. The question remains whether authorities are alert enough, and open in their own view of a broad terrorist threat, to act on reports of potential attacks other than those already experienced. Once this high level of alert is achieved by everyday people, it must be maintained. And it must be maintained so long as we are at war. This does not mean walking about suffering the effects of stress from virtual paranoia, but merely learning to adapt to the usual high level of awareness all parents demonstrate for the safety of their children all the time, every minute of every day. Parents all over America never falter in watching out for kidnappers, child molesters, vicious dogs and fast moving cars around their kids. Increasing the number of perceived threats to the children of our nation will take little real effort. Israel accomplished this, and its citizens have lived like this for decades.

For the Russian men who had to devise a plan to deal with the terrorists at Beslan, a high level of alert was the best thing the townspeople could have maintained as a preventative factor. It is the one thing the people of every nation, of every region and city in the world, must maintain. To them, it is the only thing that would have prevented it from happening in the first place. But when I ask what is the most important thing for America to keep in mind when *responding* to a terrorist siege similar to Beslan, one intense lieutenant colonel from SOBR, a man with a Gulag haircut and military bearing so ingrained it seems to seep from his pores, looks about the office of the secret base on which we are meeting. No one says a word for a long while. I can barely make out the sounds of soldiers training outside in the rain, and the distinctive pop of AK rounds going off in the underground shooting range beneath us. His eyes are distant, seeming to focus on faraway battles in Nagorno-Karabakh, Chechnya and other wars they have seen. He is a veteran of the 9th GRU Spetsnaz Brigade, and too many years in the elite Rapid Reaction Force. How does he answer that question? How does he tell America what the single most important thing to do is when the terror comes to her schools? For a moment he is back with us, blue eyes flashing while he mutters the only answer anyone could ever have. "Do whatever it takes to save the lives of the hostages, of the children," he imparts. "Nothing else matters." He lost friends with Alpha and Vympel at Beslan, men with whom he had survived those other, long ago wars. At Beslan, they had been true to that code. They did whatever it took. And in doing so, gave all.

* * * * *

Still, the one thing everyone in America wants to know is: what are the chances of it happening here? In asking this question, what they really want is for someone to tell them it can't, or won't, happen here. The truth of the matter is that it can and very likely will. Schools meet a number of terrorist criteria in selecting targets. In hitting a single school, they really strike a number of targets: symbolic, economic, and psychological. With all this for the picking, there is no better way to bring America to her knees, to cripple her economy, to strike real psychological fear and insecurity into her heart, and at the same time assail the one thing that stands as her hope for the future, than to take her children. Nothing else could be so devastating.

And who might come and deliver this evil to us? Who must we be aware of and prepare for? In October 2004, one month after Beslan, the news services reported unconfirmed intelligence that in July up to 25 Chechen militants slipped illegally across the border from Mexico into the U.S. Coming – as it did – right after the siege in Russia it seemed that everyone was on high alert. *The Chechens are coming! The Chechens are coming!* was the sudden battle cry, harkening back to the alert of our own Revolutionary War period when other invaders had come to terrorize our families. Immediately, everyone across America wanted to know *if* they were coming, and *if* they were here to attack our schools. They wanted to know how we could identify them. How we could be ready where Russia had failed?

The truth is that the Chechens are already here, and have been for quite some time. Since the collapse of the Soviet Union, the United States has received hundreds of thousands of immigrants from the former Soviet republics. Many came on visitors' visas and simply stayed without permission. Lax and under-funded immigration controls made this not only possible, but easy. Many entered illegally. Still, many more are here because we are a nation of immigrants and opened our arms up to them, in many ways naively clinging to our own Cold War belief that inside every Russian was an American waiting to get out, and that all we had to do was free them from Communist tyranny and they would be exactly like us. Since the collapse of the Eastern Bloc more than a dozen years has passed, and we have come to recognize that this belief was never true. Some people will never be like us. With the Chechens, the American government backed the wrong horse, and we are only now attempting to close the barn door long after that horse has gone.

Despite the dissolution of the U.S.S.R., and the resurgence of the Russian Republic as the new Russian Federation, we have continued to play a game of one-upmanship with its leaders. Despite what has been written and lamented in the news media, financial assistance to Russia has been small, almost non-existent. The U.S. has consistently ranked embarrassingly low on the list of trade partners with that nation. The Disney Corporation spent more money on its new park in Paris than the U.S. ever gave to Russia.

Politically, we made every effort to rub the Russians' noses in the humiliation of their Cold War defeat. The Russians have never understood this behavior on the part of America. They saw themselves as the victims – that is, the survivors - of 74 years of Communism, not the defeated architects of it. Successive U.S. presidential administrations have used America's superior political position in the world – and its far superior economic power – to ensure the mighty Russian Bear does not ever rise again and threaten a cowering world with its enormous size and voracious appetite. The U.S. quickly co-opted as many of the former Soviet Republics as it could, dragging as many of those into NATO as possible. The Baltics – Estonia, Latvia and Lithuania – all nations we refused to ever acknowledge as part of the Soviet Union, are now ours. Poland has quickly regained the national memory of its own democratic history from the 18th century and joined the West. The Czech Republic, with a rejuvenated Prague, is the new cultural and economic center for Central Europe. And we are even now fighting over the future of Ukraine. We also sought to let the Russians know we could threaten them from any point, improving our prior strategic position in Turkey with efforts to gain footholds in Georgia, Kazakhstan and Kyrgyzstan.

And while positioning our chess pieces around our former enemy, we also have leapt to the aid of almost anyone who has come in conflict with her. *The enemy of my enemy is my friend*, is an ancient strategic doctrine the U.S. has followed. In the 1994-1996 conflict in Chechnya we jumped strongly into the debate with both feet on the side of the Chechens. Our own knee-jerk reaction to Russian militarism was that anyone who wanted to secede from Russia had to be good and right, and the Russians – with their long history of oppression – had to be wrong. And the Russians did not disappoint, allowing lack of military discipline to result in their own atrocities committed on Chechen citizens. But this was only part of the story, and neither the Western news media nor Western governments bothered to recognize the culture of the Chechen people, their own behavior and atrocities.

I have seen hours upon hours of videotape taken by the Chechens themselves, captured by Russian Special Forces from those wars. The films depict what the Chechens do to anyone they capture, whether young girls, innocent civilians or simple Russian foot soldiers; even other Chechens and Muslims. These tapes show the grisly memorialization of Chechens gleefully torturing their captives. Some films show the hapless victims being shot in different parts of their bodies, and then asked how it feels. It is reminiscent of the Nazi medical experiments on Jews. Others are made to hold their fingers out so a gun can be put to them and the fingers shot off one by one. Teenage girls are tortured, girls who could not possibly have any military information of either tactical or strategic value. When they have had their fun, the Chechens ultimately force everyone onto the ground, and while the camera pans in for a close-up shot, they place a knife to the captive's neck, push it in and slowly saw the head off, while the condemned gurgles on his own blood as the knife is pushed through the windpipe. It is a slow and horrible way to die. Sometimes they cut the prisoner's head off with an axe. However they manage it, when they are done, they clap and play music, dancing about with the severed head in their hands, tossing it back and forth while their children look on.

Since 1994, and certainly again when the Second Chechen War began in late 1999, America has maintained a policy of support of the Chechen people and their supposed cause of independence. We have ignored who and what they were and who they are aligned with. We have been so busy embracing them as the enemy of our enemy – Russia – that we have failed entirely to recognize the applicability of another military doctrine: *the friend of my enemy is also my enemy.* In the case of the Chechens, their deep alliance and complicity with Muslim extremist terrorist groups should have alerted us to the fact they were a people to be guarded against, not embraced; certainly not welcomed into our homes. And despite the fact our intelligence agencies missed completely the approaching collapse of the Soviet Union – after their failure to predict the fall of the Berlin Wall two years earlier – as well as the attacks of 9-11, is it possible that they also failed to notice the history of the Chechens, the rise of militant Islam there, their assistance to and association with the Taliban of Afghanistan, and the presence of al Qaeda ringleaders in that region of Southern Russia?

And so we welcomed the Chechens. We have given at least one top Chechen "rebel" political asylum, and watched happily as our closest ally – Britain – followed suit. We have decried Russian hegemony on the world stage at every opportunity. And we have allowed Chechens to enter the U.S. for years.

After Beslan I was asked repeatedly if America and American law enforcement needed to begin watching out for Chechens entering the country, if there really was a connection between them and al Qaeda and other terrorist groups. My answer was that the leaders and planners of al Qaeda were not - and have never been - stupid. America's reaction to the attacks of 9-11 was the most predictable thing in the world. Once again, just as half a century before, the sleeping giant rose up and directed its considerable might against an identified enemy. Government and law enforcement resources were brought to bear against a recognizable enemy to ensure that it never happened again. Arabs, Arab Americans and almost anyone who looked remotely as though he – or she – could have come from any part of the world in which Islam was the predominant religion were quickly under scrutiny. If they fit the stereotyped profile by a naïve American public, they were suspect. The common citizens of America, too, began to watch and monitor the behavior of those who in any way resembled the 19 men who brought four commercial passenger jets down within minutes of each other.

The Arabs of al Qaeda knew this was sure to happen. They knew investigations would be conducted to identify Arabs who learned to fly, took scuba diving lessons, or karate. We wanted to know who belonged to which groups and sects of the Muslim faith, who lived where, was seen where, or acted suspiciously in airports. In anticipation of all this, al Qaeda had already stacked the deck in its own favor. Prior to September 11, 2001, they had been moving Chechen associates into the U.S. The American government's policy was sympathetic to the Chechens and, once again due to our blind ignorance of certain geo-political realities in that part of the world, we sought to support them, to help them find a new life. What's more, the greatest benefit to al Qaeda of the Chechens is that the majority of them are not dark skinned. They do not look Arabic. Not that there are no dark-skinned Chechens, but the majority have the pale skin tone of "Caucasians" in America. There are even a good number of Chechens with blonde hair and pale eyes. One of the few distinguishing features of the Chechens is one that would go completely unnoticed in the U.S., with its hodge-podge of commingling ethnicities. The Russians call the Chechens "the long faces," as a result of their relatively long, angular noses and jaw structure. In a country in which the Slavic race predominates – a race that isn't even recognized in the West – this characteristic is easy to pick out.

Ironically what we in the West call Caucasian – by which we typically mean Anglo-Saxon white – in Russia means dark-skinned. There, if someone is identified as looking *Caucasian*, they are part of the *chyorniy* or "blacks" of the country. So, to say Chechens are *Caucasian* in the precise sense of the word as Russians define it, is untrue. For the region of the Caucasus, and the dark skin of the people whose roots are there, they are unusually light in complexion. This would allow them to move easily through American society without drawing the attention that their Arab brethren would and do. Moreover, there are few urban areas in America that have not seen a large number of Russian – or more precisely former Soviet – immigrants. Though that country had more than 190 distinct ethnic groups, and though their own communities are chauvinistically divided in the U.S. - and often within a single city in the U.S. - to Americans they are all just "Russian."

So, in a nation that is fighting a War on Terror against the Arab Islamist extremists of al Qaeda, the presence of terrorist operatives in the personage of white skinned, "Russian" immigrants goes unnoticed. Moreover, though their visa applications to emigrate from Russia do indicate their Chechen heritage – something which no doubt helped them gain access through the U.S. State Department – once here their passports merely identify them as Russian citizens. And not only does the FBI, and the INS- or ICE in its current permutation – fail to track them, but they have not traditionally identified them as a potential threat and so completely lack the capability of doing so now. Quite simply, countless Chechens have entered the U.S. – legally and illegally - and slipped unseen into the stream of our society. Recently

I was even told that based on Russian tracking, the U.S. Embassy in Moscow continues to issue visitor visas to no fewer than 30 Chechen males between the ages of 35 and 45 every single month. These are the very men who were combat age in the First Chechen War. If true, how many get issued to those Chechen males young enough to be veterans of the current war is anyone's guess.

Even if efforts were initiated to determine who these people are and where they have gone, it is unlikely that very many agents of even the FBI's Foreign Counter-Intelligence unit can recognize the difference between a Chechen surname and an Armenian, Azerbaijani, Ukrainian or even a Russian name. The only special agents in the Bureau who might have that capability are those who once staffed the highly specialized Russian Organized Crime (ROC) squads in eight cities of the U.S. In a sad irony, this expertise has been ignored and lies dormant, as these agents have long since been re-assigned to fight the War on Terror against the Arab threat. In short, the federal government, in the myopia of its efforts to fend off our dark-skinned, Middle Eastern, Islamist extremist enemies, has neutralized one of the greatest assets it ever developed: its own experts in Russian, Eastern European and Central Asian organized crime.

For all of these reasons, it was unusual that an intelligence report would receive wide public attention when 25 Chechens illegally entered the U.S. Cited as having come from a single source, and so not verified, it begged the question of why Chechens would have to attempt to do so illegally in the first place. One colleague informed me that it was because they were known organized crime figures; the Chechen OC groups being some of the most successful and inarguably the most brutal of all the ROC gangs. Historically, they have specialized in drugs and murder-for-hire, and most recently have used their extensive connections to the Taliban of Afghanistan to import heroin into Southern Russia. With the proceeds they have helped fund al Qaeda and continued their own war, all in furtherance of expanding that war into neighboring regions, thereby creating an ever growing pan-Islamic state.

In the midst of all this, petty Russo-American squabbling has continued. In 2002, the U.S. sent the 10th Special Forces Group into Georgia, setting off an almost incendiary reaction among the Russians. Russian colleagues informed me that a *sub rosa* agreement was quickly struck between George W. Bush and Vladimir V. Putin: Russia would provide the U.S. some intelligence and not otherwise object to American operations in Afghanistan, and would even lay off the U.S. and its coming invasion of Iraq. In exchange America would pull its Green Berets out of Georgia and stop calling Russia to account for its actions in Chechnya. This information was brought to me and to Archangel Chairman, Special Forces Sergeant Major (ret.) Andy Anderson while training in Russia with the Vityaz Anti-Terror Spetsnaz unit in the fall of 2002, during the time the crisis was developing. 10th group presence was subsequently confirmed by associates who were there. However, as things are wont to go between the U.S. and Russia, neither completely lived up to its side of the bargain. Russia did provide the U.S. with important intelligence in Afghanistan, including the locations of key Taliban forces, as well as information on Iraqi intentions to attack the U.S. in the months prior to the war. And George Bush did publicly make the connection between al Qaeda and Chechnya, providing Putin with the first formal acknowledgement of Russia's own war with international terrorists. Other than that little else was accomplished between the two countries. We kept our military in Georgia, and Russia made great hay out of the inappropriateness and supposed illegality of the U.S. going into Iraq.

Only recently has the United States government begun, for the first time, to acknowledge consistently that the Russian efforts in Chechnya may indeed be part of their own fight against a terrorist sect within their own borders. Prior to this, the Bush Administration, and that of Clinton before him, always saw the Chechen issue as a non-religious fight for independence by a minority long discriminated against by the Slavic Russian government. This belief led the U.S. to rally its allies in decrying Russian behavior in Chechnya, turning the conflict into a humanitarian rights issue, and deserving of the meddling of the international community, including the United Nations. However, no matter what is occurring on the world stage, one fact is certain: if the government is concerned about a mere 25 Chechens entering the country illegally, we should all be worrying mightily. For the number of Chechens in this country is already in the thousands, including a top leader we welcomed with open arms. The fact that, prior to September 11, 2001, there were many Chechens already in the U.S. is without doubt. That by September 2002, when we let Akhmadov in, they had an effective leader in our midst is more than a little troubling.

Subsequent to Beslan and the unconfirmed intelligence report of the 25 illegal Chechen immigrants, the FBI and Department of Homeland Security issued a joint report to law enforcement and educators across the country. This report, containing the U.S. government's initial position on what occurred at Beslan and how – including what we must do to prevent it from happening here – was far too little, far too early. From the information provided by FBI/DHS, the U.S. Department of Education issued its own letter to every single school district in the nation. Obviously, all of these efforts at quelling public concern were a direct result of the siege at Beslan. Whether they were, in any way, connected as well to the report of the Chechen infiltrators over the summer is unknown.

Dated October 6, 2004, and signed by the Deputy Secretary of the United States Department of Education, the Honorable Eugene W. Hickock, the letter opens by stating the reason for which it was penned: "The recent terrorist attack against a school in Beslan, Russia, was obviously a shocking incident worldwide." It goes on to acknowledge the fear that the incident struck in the hearts of everyone in America: "Understandably, the horror of this attack may have created significant anxiety in our own country, among parents, students, faculty, staff and other community members...." However, the overall purpose of the letter was to alleviate concerns that such an incident could or ever would happen here. In a passive tone, it encouraged school administrators to consider their respective "protective measure guidance" for responding to such attacks, and attempted to soothe concerns by assuring everyone that neither the FBI nor DHS are "aware of any specific, credible information indicating a terrorist threat to public and private schools, universities or colleges."

From there the letter offers advice on remaining vigilant to the most obvious – almost ridiculously so – *indicia* of intelligence gathering efforts by terrorist groups, in the faint hope that this alone would prevent assaults on our schools. That the very signs of terrorist attack preparation are depicted as virtually identical to the behavior of everyday child molesters – signs that every parent would, or should, already notice, sending them scurrying to school principals and police – is not mentioned. The terrorist groups we are combating – and that our school officials are now joined in the battle against – are well trained, military level tacticians. They would make every effort at effective pre-operational intelligence gathering, and are highly unlikely to ever be caught in such amateurish behavior as described in the letter. This reality seems to be lost on most everyone, but the Russians understand it all too well. The FBI has downplayed the recovery in Iraq of a computer disk containing information on the design and structure of six schools in the United States. Found in the possession of one of Hussein's Ba'ath Party members, the information detailed schools in California, Florida, Georgia, Michigan, New Jersey and Oregon. Another person, supposedly a student, was found with the same information on other schools. The FBI has assured everyone that they are certain this data had been downloaded from the internet to help prepare Iraq for emergency planning for its own schools. What they base this certainty on is a mystery.

Assuming this conclusion to be true, the fact that it demonstrates that even bureaucratic school administrators in the Middle East, belonging to a despotic regime with which the U.S. is at war, know they can find critical information on how individual schools in the U.S. are prepared to respond to emergencies like hostage seizures is frightening. That the FBI and DHS would find some peace of mind in this conclusion is astounding. After years of working with that fine agency and some outstanding agents, I find it hard to believe it is true.

Moreover, recent intelligence efforts have determined al Qaeda terrorists continue planning to enter the U.S. illegally, and that Arabs have already been taken into custody crossing over surreptitiously from Mexico. Taken together, this is more than sufficient grounds for all U.S. schools to be operating on high alert. Still, perhaps the most troubling statement of all was the conclusion of the Department of Education letter. In closing, Deputy Secretary Hickock sought to alleviate any concerns by assuring us all that "the information provided by DHS and the FBI … was not generated by any threats received by U.S. educational institutions." The fact that terrorists carried out this heinous act in Beslan should be warning enough. If we wait until specific threats are actually received by us before taking necessary steps, it may already be too late.

PART FOUR

PREPARING AMERICA FOR BATTLE

Chapter Eleven

Preparing America's Schools

Proudly you gathered, rank on rank to war;
As you heard God's message from afar;
All you had hoped for, all you had, you gave
To save mankind – yourself you scorned to save.

— John Stanhope Arkwright
"Old Valiant Hearts" 1919

In attempting to prepare the American psyche for the worst possible terrorist act– the taking and killing of our children – we must all shed the veil of civility and luxury in which we conduct our lives. Americans, school officials, military planners and law enforcement commanders must ask a number of questions about our own ability to handle an assault of this type, on children, bringing to bear both the most volatile and paralyzing mixture of emotions, tactical reality and government policy. The preparation of our country is not merely the preparation of our law enforcement and military. It is the preparation of our nation; of every man, woman and child who claims the title of "American." It is the preparation of every citizen and school employee, but most importantly, of every parent across our great nation.

In part, this means every person accepting the responsibility of being a tiny but integral cog in a nationwide intelligence network, ever vigilant and alert to signs of danger to our schools and our children. It also means educating ourselves as to the inestimable task of our police, military, firefighters and paramedics so that we are well versed in what they will be doing when the terror comes to visit us, why they are doing it, how long it will take and what the chances of success are. In this way, these men and women, who together comprise the last citadel of freedom for our country, can go about their unenvied duties without the distraction of unanswerable questions by panicked parents and everyday citizens who are only then confronting the reality of terrorism for the first time.

This is not the kind of war fought only by those valiant souls who everyday don a blue uniform bearing the Stars and Stripes on the shoulder, or who pick up an automatic rifle and shrug weary shoulders into an overloaded rucksack. It is a war that either will be fought by all Americans, or one that will consume our nation. For it is our very way of life that the enemy sees as evil, and is intent on destroying. As it is, every one of us lives the American dream. It is therefore every one of us who is a target of terrorism. We are all therefore – quite literally – in a fight for our lives.

In trying to help people prepare for that fight, it is impossible to create exhaustive lists of all that must be done to enable law enforcement and citizens alike to be ready for every aspect of every possible terrorist attack. The purpose of this Part IV is to provide more insight into what went wrong at Beslan in the government's handling of the crisis. But more importantly, it is to offer some basic recommendations as to ways we, as Americans, can use our greatest strengths – both in terms of resources and people – to deal with the possibility of an assault against our schools. If the following sections do nothing more than incite discussion and independent analysis, help each of you think of other and better ways to prepare, then they have accomplished all I could hope for.

Training with Law Enforcement.

Law enforcement must be contacted and solicited to provide training for schools to deal with hostage and assault situations. Relevant police departments must begin preparing programs and providing training for local teachers and school officials (including parents). Schools must work hand-in-hand with them to consider and develop protocols for mass emergency situations and to share knowledge of the chronology of events to be anticipated in a hostage situation.

Lockdown Drills.

School authorities must establish emergency lock down procedures that are current, well constructed, and ready for immediate action in the event of a terrorist siege. This is one area in which security experts agree. No longer can we respond to every problem by sending our children into the parking lots or fields outside our schools. In the terror attacks of the future, this is where the assailants can most easily position shooters and car bombs, which necessitates not only lockdown procedures but planned collection points and evacuation routes different from those historically used for fire drills.

According to Vityaz Col. Sergei Lisyuk, our efforts toward developing the ability to lockdown students should include electronically wiring the gates that are already used to divide and separate school hallways after hours, to automatically come down when a certain alarm is sounded. This will isolate and divide terrorists, making it impossible for them to move to other areas of the school, prepare their defenses and establish fortifications. It will have the added benefit of greatly reducing the number of hostages. The unfortunate consequence of this measure, however, is that it may increase the likelihood that those few hostages they end up with may be executed in retaliation.

School Diagrams.

Police must have school blueprints, floor plans and diagrams. Do your local police have – or have access to – detailed school building blueprints, building diagrams or floor plans during breaks, off hours, weekends and late at night? Police have many tasks to perform, especially as they all attempt to prepare for terror attacks in the U.S. School officials must assume the responsibility of preparing this material and getting it to police in advance of an attack. Such efforts are of tremendous value in any type of attack or other potential crisis, such as floods, mud slides, earthquakes and fires.

Tactical Videotaping.

School officials should videotape walk-throughs of the entire school and have them available for police - or deliver them to the police - keeping a copy for themselves. All copies should be kept in a safe place, off the school grounds, that can be accessed outside of business hours. For this reason, bank safe deposit boxes are not appropriate storage sites. School principals' homes with second or third copies stored at designated teachers' houses would be viable repositories, so long as school officials did not make it widely known where these were located or how many copies had been made. It is important to remember the terrorists will do their preparatory work as well.

Communications.

Establish channels of communication between law enforcement and local schools. Are the channels of communication between the relevant police department or responding agency and the local schools well established, open and functioning? Do school officials know whom they should be talking directly to in the event of a terrorist attack or other catastrophe? Has this been discussed with the police chief or sheriff in your area? Make these contacts now and develop, with their assistance, a list of protocols and priorities to follow in the event of such emergencies.

Additionally, radio protocols must be developed for school bus drivers. Few targets are as attractive as school buses for not only capturing large numbers of children, but providing unquestioning access to a school in vehicles which can surreptitiously hold large numbers of people with myriad weapons and explosives. While codes can be developed for radio calls, the problem is that all too often people who are not accustomed to using codes on a regular basis will forget them in a moment of crisis or panic. Make certain radio dispatchers are alert to any communications which do not include expected or known information, and are not afraid to call authorities if they are received. Do not, under any circumstances, ask the driver to clarify something that was just said. It might have been her only attempt to let someone know there was a problem, and the ignorant request that the incongruous transmission be cleared up could get the driver killed and tip terrorists off to the fact their plot has been uncovered.

School Security and Surveillance Systems.

Many schools see increased camera and video security systems as the answer, or at least part of the answer, to any crime or threat on the grounds and building. The ability to monitor the goings-on in a school, or to know what threats or attacks exist and in what sector, can be crucial information. All too often security cameras serve little purpose other than to protect the school district against the ever-present threat of litigation by students and their parents. But in making the decision to spend five, six, or even seven figures, on such systems, be wary of the fact that if and when a school - or mall or office building - takeover occurs, it will happen fast. The terrorists will be in quick control. And they will then have the benefit of those security systems. Attempting to dismantle or destroy them may be met with the killing of hostages in retaliation. One of the most important tactical considerations is never to keep such surveillance on the roof. No matter what else, do not deny our FBI, police or military the one avenue of approach that terrorists would be unlikely to ever use in assaulting a building. Our own forces may need to use the roof to breach the building in an assault against terrorists.

Schools and police should also coordinate use of security systems and surveillance cameras. America has prepared its schools' security for threats from within, designed to protect property and life from students acting in an aggressive fashion or stealing property. For this reason they are usually directed at corridors and doorways throughout the school. If taken over, the existence of these systems will only provide the terrorists with a significant advantage, eliminating the need for dividing their forces throughout the school to monitor ingress points. Though the Russians correctly point out that all such school security systems should have their controls in another building – allowing them to be switched off remotely – disabling the cameras can and will incite an early conflict with the terrorists. Anticipate that any terrorist group, aware of the existence of the camera system, will first demand it be turned back on. Failure or refusal to do so will likely result in the early executions of some hostages.

It is possible to rig schools with recessed and hidden cameras, with both the monitor and control of the system outside the school building. This might deny the terrorists even the knowledge of the existence of the camera system and give law enforcement the advantage of remote viewing of terrorist movements, numbers, fortification and hostage location. Certainly, gambling casinos in Las Vegas and throughout the gaming cities of America have highly developed systems which could be put in schools, allowing terrorists the false belief that they have total control of the cameras, while law enforcement controls another, hidden system throughout the school. For the corporations who own high stakes gambling operations, where money is the only thing at risk, such systems are well worth the cost. These systems are very expensive, but what value do we place on our children's lives?

The difficulty with using such a system in America, is the fact that major expenditures by school districts – expenditures of the tax dollars of the citizenry – are typically public record, if not subject to an absolute duty of public disclosure. Never underestimate the amount of intelligence gathering that is done by Islamic extremist groups prior to launching an operation. Recently, a number of terrorists arrested for committing some of the bombings and attacks around the world in the past few years admitted that in selecting sites and planning attacks, fully 80 percent of intel came from public sources, often the Internet. If you have made such information public, especially if it is posted on your school, school district or town website, you can be certain they will know exactly what they will find upon entering the building.

Schools and Counter-Intelligence.

As pointed out, terror groups will conduct a significant amount of intelligence gathering on possible target schools long before a single one is selected, or an operation mounted. Al Qaeda's *The Military Series Manual* or "Manchester Document" is clear on the subjects of both surveillance and counter-surveillance. As the Department of Education pointed out, the intelligence gathering phase is the time most critical to stopping them. It is also the time when teachers and parents are of the most value. Counter-intelligence efforts should not stop at just keeping an eye out for anyone suspicious watching the school. In America we live in a nation of transparency. Our Constitution mandates that the government – which at all levels exists to serve the citizens – must be open about how it discharges its duties. Most public records are open to anyone, on demand, regardless of residency status. The problem with this is that there is an enormous volume of information – information that the vast majority of citizens would never think to access – available to evildoers in our society. Things like plans, diagrams and blueprints of buildings sit in county and city offices, available for inspection by anyone who asks. Information on security systems that may have required a permit for installation await anyone who wishes to learn where the alarms are, where the cameras are positioned. Not surprisingly, the Manchester Document even informs its al Qaeda readership that fully 80 percent of all necessary intelligence can be gathered from open sources.

Every single school in America should take the time to find out who has asked to see these records. If the local government offices – the ones that perhaps happily provided those records to would-be terrorists – refuse to provide this information, then you must look to the same laws that allowed the enemy access. At least bi-annually each school should file a Freedom of Information or Open Records Act request to learn who has sought information on their buildings and systems. Every state in America has passed legislation requiring the disclosure of virtually all government records. Do not let the bad guys use our laws against us.

Arming Our Schools.

There are many things that can be done to yet improve the security of our schools and the children whose safety they are charged with. When I would ask various Spetsnaz commanders what they would tell America to do to make the schools safer, I was often met with a chuckle and the corresponding question: "Are you asking what we would do if we had America's money? An unlimited budget?" Relative to most nations, we do have an unlimited budget to bring to bear. If we choose to do so. But the question with regard to both money to be spent, and how far we are willing to go to make our children safe, is purely a function of the risk level we perceive. We have long since known that someday, some terrorist would take over a U.S. aircraft and very likely fly it into a building. We had been warned of this, and our intelligence and federal law enforcement agencies tracked information on it for years. Those of us who chose to stick our heads in the sand – suffering from the American affliction of *ostrichitis* – had only to look at all the airport security and wonder why it was there. It was there because we believed someone would try to do something horrible with a plane if we did not prevent it. Yet we – as citizens – chose never to look at the true nature of this threat. We all knew we had security because evil men wanted our planes. If that security had been taken away, no one would have doubted the risk. Yet, as citizens, we chose not to concern ourselves with the fact that these same people, who wanted our planes so badly, might attempt to breach our security and take them anyway. Nothing could have been more obvious.

And, despite the catastrophic losses of 9-11, our airline and airport security is still not even close to what it could be. We fuss and moan when security takes too long. We are incensed that we are selected for special screening. Women are outraged that other women might touch the edges of their breasts when ensuring no passengers have weapons on a plane. Recently, the Transportation Safety Administration was forced to announce in the national media that women would no longer be touched there, publicly broadcasting the limitations of the allowable searches. At that moment, every terror cell in America was experimenting with hiding non-metallic weapons in the areas of women's bras that were suddenly declared off limits. Since the two jetliners came down in Russia everyone, even after passing through a metal detector, gets completely and competently frisked in a search for possible weapons. The same happens in Germany and elsewhere. In Russia male passengers are searched in this fashion by male and female agents alike. No one cares, and everyone is sent quickly on his or her way.

The same is true of our schools. We know terrorists like to hit schools, for nothing is as devastating as large numbers of children in harm's way. They have done it again and again. If you did not know it before, Dave Grossman's excellent Foreword to this book certainly brought that point home. We also realize that no nation would be as devastated as a soft and pampered America if its schools were seized and children murdered. We also know we are a prime target for virtually every Islamist extremist group out there. So, how is it we have yet to pull our heads from the sand, take a long gander about, and start doing something about it? And if we are to start, how far are we willing to go? Are we – as so many have predicted – going to sit imperiously upon our moralistic laurels and refuse to do those things that violate certain opinions we hold dearly, but that have been built upon the luxury of a completely safe and secure existence? Are those who oppose gun ownership ready to have parents and teachers armed, or for every school to have patrolling teams of Special Forces to defend them, every single day of the school year?

I think we are not yet ready culturally to embrace the majority of things that could most ensure the safety of our children. The Russians suggest strenuously that as each new school is built a gas delivery system be installed that can knock out everyone in the building in the event of a terror-hostage standoff. This could be done today, in schools already built. They advise to spend whatever it costs to have school security systems that automatically shut down solid metal doors, and lock internal and external doors throughout the school, when an alarm is activated. This would have the very beneficial effect of denying terrorists complete control of the school, separate them from each other, and limit the number of hostages they take. But such systems are expensive. Are we ready to spend the money? If not, what will it take?

For little cost we can train and arm those already in our schools. Many would be happy to receive this training at their own expense. Teachers and school administrators could undergo a certified and approved training program, allowing them to retain their firearms in the school. Parents could do likewise, just as many parents already travel to and from their children's schools with the very concealed weapons they are legally authorized to carry, though under most states' statutes not in schools. Could armed teachers and parents prove an effective fighting force against 50 well-trained, combat hardened and committed terrorists with automatic assault weapons and explosives? Unlikely. But their presence and ability to fight back might just save some lives, or force the terrorists to alter their plan in the initial attack, denying them complete control of the facility and thereby preventing many from ending up as hostages and facing the same fate as the children at Beslan. It is likely that all of those parents and teachers who choose to fight will die in a hail of gunfire. But they will leave this world having fought nobly and well, saving the very children on whom this nation depends for its future and its survival.

A final possibility is to deploy armed fire teams in every school in America. At minimum numbers, this could be done with three men. In light of low military pay, each school could hire former Green Berets, SEALs, Force Recon Marines or Rangers, for $50,000 per year. They could be equipped with the latest automatic weapons, smoke and flash bang grenades. They could have silenced handguns, and all of the tactical gear they could possibly need. They would work every hour school was in session. They would be present in the school during major sporting events. They would have three months every summer to obtain additional training, certifications, and qualifications, so they were prepared to save lives in everything from floods to hurricanes to earthquakes. And they would stand ready for any terrorist that wanted to try seizing their school.

From a military perspective, it takes minimum numerical superiority of four to one for an attacking force to rout out well-entrenched infantry. When the defenders are elite commandos, defending a heavily fortified position that ratio rises to at least 9 to 1. With three men in each School Fire Team (SFT), this would require a force of no fewer than twenty-seven terrorists to have even a chance at seizing control of the building. And America's special operations forces are legendary for their ability to take on numbers greater than even that.

Career Green Beret John Anderson says that three well trained men with a single SAW (M 249 bipod mounted, belt fed, Squad Automatic Weapon) would never be taken by ten times their number. Moreover, this military doctrine and assault ratio typically applies to combatants holding a position in areas under enemy control. These ratios have proven true in battles where the enemy could take its time, sending assault after assault against beleaguered defenders. In an American school, where police, SWAT, FBI and possibly even military will be mustered and on-scene quickly, this ratio would by necessity be even higher, making the SFT model even more viable.

No one would know the school building, grounds, recesses, vulnerabilities and defensible positions better than Special Forces operators working and training there every single day. No one would be better trained and prepared psychologically to give our children every possible chance of surviving such an ordeal, than these brave men from our military. They could be required to undergo law enforcement certification and work hand-in-hand with local police. They could even come from the state police, or the National Guard. An additional benefit would derive from the constant interaction between young students and the elite of American society which might just result in more and more of our young men and women choosing to serve in the armed forces as they go forward in life.

Most importantly, the entire program could likely be implemented for a total cost of $250,000 per year. For most schools – even those in lower socio-economic areas – this would be a tiny fraction of their annual budgets. Per taxpayer or parent, it would be pennies per year to fund. If we were willing - and did not let previously existing personal attitudes and local politics get in the way - we could ensure that Beslan will never happen here, and that the terrorists who are at this very minute plotting how best to hurt America, will pick a target other than our children.

Despite the efficacy of this approach, many parents will revile at the notion of heavily armed commandos patrolling the halls of their kids' schools. But that is largely because we are just not yet ready, we have not suffered enough. As both American school security officials and Spetsnaz soldiers have pointed out to me: it is first going to take a big body count of children before Americans are going to be willing to abandon their sensitivities and opinions, and demand anything and everything be done to save their children.

Reality Check.

School officials and parents must be prepared for the realistic possibility of such an occurrence. As pointed out by both Dave Grossman and Deputy Secretary of Education Hickock, in his October 6, 2004 letter, reality should not strike fear in the hearts of every parent and schoolteacher; though, they should be concerned. Without a realistic understanding of the threat, we cannot begin to prepare ourselves. And such preparation must be done mentally and psychologically first. Only then can we begin to prepare tactically and fiscally, for the protection of our children will require the financial support of the public.

Chapter Twelve

Preparing Law Enforcement

Whoever fights monsters should see to it that in the process he doesn't become a monster.

— Nietzsche

Though they prepare mightily everyday, a situation like Beslan would force our nation's law enforcement to confront circumstances and tactical hurdles unlike anything they have ever seen before. It will be a war. As a war, they must prepare to deal with factors that are not part of everyday police work, no matter how terrible or difficult.

Mental Preparedness.

Law enforcement must mentally prepare for threatened, brutalized, and possibly executed children. We can never suffer another Columbine. Police must be prepared to risk their lives to save the children if and when the time comes, as many of the brave commandos of Alpha and Vympel did on September 3, 2004. Make no mistake about it, when it comes – as prophesied by Col. Lisyuk – *there will be a fight and people will die.* If you, as a law enforcement officer or soldier are not certain you could risk your life in a Beslan-style attack, and if necessary give your last breath to save a child, then you should start looking for another line of work. One of the epiphanies I had when first arriving in Beslan was the jarring realization that fear was, indeed, the one thing the attackers needed the most. Much as the Nazis depended upon each individual's fear as they marched thousands into showers from which deadly gas poured during World War II, all the while guarding them with only a few armed men, so the terrorists at Beslan benefited from the same paralyzing effect of fear.

Even with bombs going off, close to a thousand children is a formidable amount of physical force if directed against you. The fear is what controls everyone; the fear is what enables evil to affect these horrors. For years Archangel Chairman Andy Anderson has said that he wasn't afraid of dying, that he "was looking forward to the ride." After 25 years as a Green Beret, having seen some of the worst things human beings could do to one another, he said "I have a few questions I want answered when I get there." Until Beslan, I had never understood his thinking. I had always opted for my own life over death. At Beslan I suddenly understood what he had been talking about all those years. I knew when I walked out of that place that I would never hesitate to fight, shoot, and kill were I ever to stumble onto a similar scene. For the first time in my life, dying would not bother me. Killing perpetrators of such horror would bother me even less. I would not now hesitate to draw a weapon and shoot. Even in America where everyone lives in fear of criminal prosecution and civil litigation over every action we take, I would no longer hesitate, whereas before I might have. For once again, fear – even the fear of ridiculous lawsuits – will only play into the hands of the terrorists.

Deluge of Terrified Parents.

Be prepared to deal with a huge volume of constant contact by parents and relatives. Set people up to interface with them, keeping the decision-makers, who will be under enormous stress and suffering from information overload, well away.

What To Do With Reporters?

Be prepared to deal with a huge volume of constant contact by news media. Is local law enforcement ready and able to deal with a tidal wave of news media reporters, including constant questioning, and bombardment with accusations of incompetence? Is local law enforcement sufficiently, tactically prepared to recognize that everything they say – and everything that can be seen – will be aired on local and national television? Any small piece of information that gets out will give both the terrorists inside the school and their colleagues elsewhere, with whom they may be in touch, real time intelligence on how well the situation is being handled by authorities, sometimes revealing crucial weaknesses.

Crowd Control.

Train to maintain position and discipline in the face of surging and panic stricken crowds. Local law enforcement must be sufficiently prepared and equipped to create and maintain a secure, impenetrable perimeter around a school in the face of emotionally charged, highly volatile and possibly threatening parents and relatives of hostages. They must be prepared to maintain this perimeter despite the fact that their own children may be in the school. Local law enforcement must maintain their posts, keeping crowds, news media, civilians (possibly armed) and maybe even other terrorists from surging toward the school in the event of a Beslan-type impromptu battle. If the officers who are holding this perimeter have children in that school they, too, must remain in position.

Cops' Kids Can Be Taken Too.

Create protocols on what roles officers will assume if their own children are hostages. Ensure that local law enforcement officers are prepared for the task of remaining professionally focused and well functioning, should they find themselves dealing with a terrorist siege at a local school or church which might involve their own children, relatives, or others they know personally.

Train To Kill and To Rescue.

Train realistic, extreme close quarters combat and precision shooting. During the fight at Beslan, terrorists held children in front of them with knives to their throats and guns to their heads when assault teams entered the school. A number of them were killed by having their throats cut, or were shot in the battle. In a situation like that, casualties are a foregone conclusion. However, much as the one SOBR lieutenant colonel pointed out, you must do everything possible to save the hostages, to save the children. Much of what you can do needs to be done now. Train hard and train realistically. For many, if not most, in law enforcement this means abandoning decades-old shooting techniques and positions. The standardly accepted combat handgun techniques are inadequate for the terrorist battles of America's future. Traditional law enforcement "defensive tactics" – self defense – systems must be supplemented with real, close quarters oriented hand-to-hand combat training that prepares police for mass attacks, weapons disarming, and the integration of handgun and unarmed techniques. Be realistic. How valuable is it to practice falling to your back and wrapping your legs around a terrorist in the now-famous "guard" position? How realistic is it to attempt such a move in a tight school hallway with automatic weapons and grenades going off all around you? Do you really think that squaring off with a terrorist and delivering head-high karate kicks is going to work, or that you'll ever be given the chance or the distance to even attempt such a move?

Close quarters combat is fast, terrifying, ugly and brutal. There are no rules. You must be able to bring to bear the techniques you have trained on loose and broken ground. On ground that is slick with blood. You will not have an opportunity to "stretch out" before fighting, and it is a waste of time to train any fighting technique that requires a warm-up before you can use it. This type of combat takes place at a distance of inches, not feet, and sometimes there are not even inches between you and some psychotic murderer trying to kill you and children. To survive it you must have comfort with pain and comfort with proximity. You must have a commitment to total violence, and a commitment to total victory. The Russians have a decades-old hand-to-hand combat system that incorporates all of these realities and needs of a soldier. It was developed for soldiers in combat, and is not considered to be either an "art" or a sport. It is a system of combat. They train hand-to-hand every day, up to 15 hours each week. As distance in combat decreases - as they are forced to go from rifle to pistol to knife to bare hands - they get stronger and braver, not more scared and uncertain. This is the type of training that is necessary for America's own heroes to survive a Beslan-type battle.

No Going Back.

Train to use maximum force of violence – NO RETREAT. In a siege of this type, there can be no going back, no withdrawal. Whatever the outcome of an effort by police to storm a building, it will pale in comparison to what the fallout will be if assault teams of law enforcement or military are withdrawn, and the terrorists permitted to reassert control over the hostages.

Cops As Spies.

Law enforcement in America has long since entered an era where police can no longer simply be police. The organization and sophistication of even pedestrian level criminal episodes has rendered this notion obsolete. Dave Grossman points out in his inspiring book *On Combat* that we are now at a point where our military functions increasingly like a police force, and our police more and more like soldiers. Certainly, the increase in the drug trade in the United States, and its ubiquitous presence in every community, has been a significant factor in this role reversal. Many police and sheriff's departments have intelligence units, or officers with intelligence gathering responsibilities. While the U.S. Constitution does place important limits on the ability of police simply to gather and maintain information on its citizens, the gathering of crucial intelligence is not only permitted, but absolutely essential in properly addressing a terrorist siege inside the United States.

As has been seen in many instances, it is the doctrine of al Qaeda, HAMAS and others to ensure that additional units or teams remain in the vicinity of a barricade site. This may be done for support of the terrorists inside, for communications, command, intelligence, and tactical assistance, or for diversionary purposes. It may be that the first incident being responded to is not the primary attack, but a distraction, allowing another team to launch the primary assault with greater effect elsewhere; or an attempt to draw or drive more victims to the site of the ultimate attack. No matter what the purpose, the existence of other terrorists presents a situation that is both a challenge and opportunity to responding law enforcement. The first objective is to prevent the terrorists from assuming tactically useful positions in the surrounding crowd and area. Their efforts to gather and communicate intelligence must be defeated. This is the counter-intelligence role. The second objective – and just as important – is to locate, identify, and neutralize these people. If captured, government officials must quickly obtain what intelligence they can from the prisoners and see to it that information is integrated into the development of their own assault planning. Any information will also aid the negotiators in their efforts. For many, this is a whole new aspect of the police duty to "serve and protect."

Law enforcement agencies cannot afford to just assume they can perform this counter-intelligence role if and when the time comes. Each must ask itself whether it has sufficient covert operations or undercover capability, and officer resources, to place important intelligence gatherers in the crowd surrounding the school perimeter, or to observe nearby buildings in the event associates of the hostage-takers are in the area and developing intelligence. Have these people been truly and well trained in the shadowy skills of surveillance, counter-surveillance and protective surveillance? If not, efforts in this area should be developed. A group of former British SAS soldiers run a school out of a safe house in the United Kingdom. Listed as the Professional Bodyguard Association (PBA), they impart some of the finest tactics in this field available outside of federal government training. They have even trained a number of our federal agencies and military units. The basic course is three weeks of grueling work in cities and towns all over that country, and is highly recommended to any law enforcement agency needing to further develop these skills.

Helicopters.

The military accepts the use of helicopters as an absolutely crucial aspect of many different types of operations. Even the news media recognizes their inestimable value in transporting personnel to critical areas quickly, depositing people in small, otherwise inaccessible areas. In the recent flooding from the tsunamis in South Asia, helicopters were the most sought after piece of equipment in the rescue and recovery operations.

Yet law enforcement has run behind the curve in adopting this unique piece of hardware and implementing it in less conventional operations. For the most part, this has been due more to fiscal considerations than any failure of police to recognize their value. While some departments do maintain choppers and pilots, few, if any, have ever prepared fast rope teams to be inserted from them, or even an "air assault" type landing and insertion capability for their SWAT teams along the lines of that used by the Air Cavalry.

Helicopters are not a complete answer to anything, and they come with a number of inherent problems. For one, they are expensive, both to operate and maintain. Helicopter pilots – especially those with law enforcement credentials – are few and far between. Moreover, they are dangerous, have an unappealing crash rate, and training such techniques as rappelling or deploying from them is certain to result in many injuries and not a few deaths. But we are far beyond the point where America can afford to continue making every decision for her survival constrained by a pathetic and naïve social expectation that nothing bad ever happens to anyone and undertaking anything risky is negligent. As a culture in which parents are now deemed unfit for allowing their children to straddle a bicycle or venture into the backyard without a helmet, elbow and knee pads, hockey gloves and an orange vest, we will resist subsidizing our police to prepare to repel terrorists in such dangerous ways with our tax dollars. We will continue to sue everyone we can think of each and every time something unfortunate - something unplanned - happens while making those preparations. This obstructionist attitude will continue until the first school is seized and its children murdered. Only then will we realize we lacked the tools, resourcefulness, and skills to deal with it.

I have spoken with a number of security officials and administrators from different school districts. They are painfully aware that the things they would like to do – that they know have to be done – to be prepared to deal with a Beslan in the United States, would never be tolerated by school boards or parents. They would be reviled in the media for even attempting them. But to a person they say, "That will be the case until the first school is attacked, and there is a big body count of children." Only then will America wake up to the reality of the situation and what must be done to prepare for what is certain to happen again.

For the Russians' part they are somewhat defensive over their failure to effectively use the helicopters they had at Beslan. When the battle began, none of them were in the air. Two were landed at the nearby BMK Vodka Factory and the other two at the Vladikavkaz Airport. They rationalize their failure to have kept them on station, i.e., in the air, because when they were first deployed on Day One the terrorists shot at them with assault rifles and RPGs. Rather than be shot out of the sky, they were moved to safety. Yet at no time thereafter were they ever ready to fly, nor were they kept in the air at a distance, ready to exploit the great ability of a helicopter to arrive on scene in moments. Most notable, however, is the fact that they never put troops in them. The Mi8/MT choppers they had are military assault aircraft, with both cannons and machine guns controlled by the pilot. They carry up to eight men, fully equipped. With two in the air at all times, and two more ready to launch on five minutes notice, the Spetsnaz could have had fully 32 commandos ready to rappel onto the roof of the school before Alpha and Vympel even began their assault. Rather than have to fight their way upstairs – and all the time that took while hostages were being moved and executed – these men could have conducted a lightning raid from above, affecting a vertical pincer movement with the assault teams on the first floor.

According to some of the Russians, this type of assault would not have worked. They disagree with American military tactics, refusing to see the almost unlimited versatility and applicability of rotary wing aircraft. One response I received in Russia, while discussing tactics that should have been employed at Beslan, was, "Helicopters with fast rope teams can be used, but if using them, no other teams can enter the building but them, to avoid friendly fire." This inability to think tactically in a vertical fashion, but merely in a horizontal one, is baffling. The Russians insist – contrary to earlier information I received and the reputation of the Russian military in general – that the assault teams did have good communications. They are certain that every single member of Alpha and Vympel had his own comm's system, and that they could not only talk to other members of their own teams, but to the members of the sister unit's teams as well. With such communication systems in place, there is no reason not to use helicopter borne assault teams in a coordinated attack. To do so is no more dangerous than having different teams assault a single floor from numerous positions simultaneously.

Another argument against the use of helicopters I heard was that they are too noisy. "With helicopters you lose the element of surprise due to the noise," one Spetsnaz officer told me. Though with a Special Forces unit that was not deployed to Beslan, he was still defensive of his comrades who were there. "You cannot approach and surprise the enemy, they know you are coming. It is always better to try to come up through the steam vents rather than down from the roof." Despite the fact that this argument flies in the face of a military doctrine that is as old as Sun Tzu and *The Art of War,* that sees an advantage in always fighting from a position of superior height, even this concern is irrelevant once the battle has begun. When the bombs started going off in the gym, and everyone everywhere was shooting, not only would the sound of the helicopters have been muted to a large degree, but there was no surprise left to be had. The Beslan battle was not an offensive strike designed to catch the hostage-takers off guard. The battle was joined; everyone was already on full automatic. The noise of the helicopters would have been no greater detriment to the government forces than the covering fire on the ground under which the men of Alpha and Vympel were advancing on the building. Moreover, military tactics have well established that a low flying, fast moving helicopter is virtually undetectable to an entrenched enemy until it pops up, seemingly from nowhere, flaring to deposit its troops. And if the helicopters had been heard, it could have very likely resulted in the terrorists refocusing some of their attention on the approaching sounds of whirring blades, taking that attention away from the shooting of innocent children.

The general Russian negativity toward the use of helicopters in such circumstances was unexpected. They feel that fast rope teams are "too fancy" and take a lot of training. Commanders repeated concerns that they can be easily shot out of the sky with a single RPG, and that, in any event, they must be used with a combination of other things and never alone. They feel that at Beslan, after the explosions, the arrival of choppers with deployable soldiers would have been even less effective. Yet Russia is a nation that has historically suffered from little money being spent – or at least appropriately spent – on its military. Russia's airborne troops have few jumps and must practice landings by leaping backwards out of moving trucks. Special Forces rarely have any HALO[22] parachute experience, and training budgets are a fraction of those in the United States. It is little wonder they eschew tactics that require large expenditures of money. Still, over the years I have met many Spetsnaz veterans of the Chechen War who recount stories of having been saved from horrible ambushes by helicopters. I am

---

[22] High Altitude Low Opening.

left with the conclusion that, perhaps, they see helicopters as good for little more than moving troops into and out of open battle zones.

In any event, helicopters – though expensive – are a tool that can and should be employed if possible. If a law enforcement agency already has one, it should be prepared for deployment. If, in the midst of a battle to rescue hostages, it is determined the helicopters are not beneficial or will be too jeopardized, they do not have to used. Certainly, they can be used to convey the seriously wounded to area hospitals more quickly than land based vehicles, particularly – as the Russians have now experienced on two occasions – through streets clogged with cars due to the interest the siege has drawn. One thing is certain: they cannot be used if they are not available. Putting these machines in the air has other benefits as well. After all, the Russians – as I pointed out to them – had them at Beslan for a reason. They can provide aerial observation, direct fire, and coordinate communications from a superior vantage point. And they can carry the fast rope teams to be used at a moment's notice if called upon. However, for all of the advantages helicopters and the assault teams in them possess, they are of little use if the teams lack the ability to breach the roof of a building for fast entry. In most instances any door to the roof will be wired with explosives, barricaded or guarded, with an ambush surely waiting.

Coming Through the Walls - Explosives.

One of the things the Russians are adamant that American law enforcement must develop – and the American public must be prepared to accept – is the use of explosives to breach walls, floors and roofs for quick entry. Alpha is famous for its Mouse Hole Charges that blow holes in walls just large enough for single troops, fully outfitted in tactical equipment, to move through quickly. The explosion itself is sufficient to have an immediate effect on anyone within a small radius. The paralyzing impact of the explosion provides the assault team sufficient time to move commandos through the hole and begin engaging the enemy. When coordinated with simultaneous entry from other points, it is a devastating tactic, and was used with great success in the gym at Beslan. The Russians are nonplussed that most of American law enforcement has, at best, weak charges that can perhaps breach a door lock. They correctly point out that terrorists will always have the existing points of ingress under surveillance. Security camera systems would go far to help them with this in schools in America. As well, windows will be watched, and both windows and doors likely wired with explosives. Any assault team will have to come in unexpectedly, with maximum force of violence. Though they are careful to always attempt this type of entry at points where hostages are not concentrated, the loss or injury of one or even a few hostages must be accepted as a necessary consequence of saving the rest. Still, to the Russians, wall breaching charges represent an important enough capability and tactic to make the expense of training and development of materials more than worthwhile.

Are They Better Off Asleep?

Though a generally revolting notion to Americans culturally, we may have reached the point where the federal government and law enforcement weapons firms must start working on developing gas that can be used effectively in hostage situations. After 9-11 a proposal was made that all commercial aircraft be outfitted with sleep inducing gas capability through the air conditioning systems. In the event of an attempted hijacking the use of gas would put everyone outside of the cockpit to sleep. This met with strong – even outraged – opposition. Obviously, the death toll and infrastructure damage of September 11 were insufficient to budge the sensibilities of Americans in confronting certain tactics, no matter how effective.

The Russians have accurately pointed out a number of reasons why the use of gas cannot hurt a situation, merely help it or be of no consequence. Perhaps it is time we gave it due consideration. At Nord-Ost the Russians employed what is believed to be a fentanyl-based agent some have referred to as M-99. Known since the 1970s, the effects of fentanyl are well recognized, though its development was halted in the U.S. as possibly violative of chemical warfare treaties. I am also informed by experts in the chemical and bio-weapons fields that fentanyl is difficult to weaponize, making suspension for delivery difficult. While fentanyl or other currently existing agents may be too powerful or life threatening, milder sleeping substances can certainly be developed for tactical use.

Other Non-Lethal Weapons.

While the use of non-lethal weapons by law enforcement might embolden terrorists holed up in a school with hostages, the efficacious deployment of these new, high technology arms could have just the opposite effect. As 9-11 and the past several years of *intifada* suicide bombings in Israel have made abundantly clear, many terrorists look toward the benefits of martyrdom, so long as it accompanies the deaths of non-Muslims. For this reason, they do not fear the one thing that has been a constant in wars since the formalization of nation-states under the Treaty of Westphalia in 1648. That one thing is death. It is a human constant we have come to recognize and rely on, not only in preparing our own forces for battle, but in predicting enemy behavior as well. The absence of a fear of death in this new enemy requires – and will continue to take – some adaptation of traditional tactics. This does not mean, however, that these people do not fear anything; they are simply committed to dying for their cause. And where their fear lies, so must we attack.

The three greatest fears of an Islamist terrorist are: (1) Being caught in the safe house before realizing the opportunity to wreak his terror in the planned operation; (2) Being arrested, tried, convicted and put into an American prison for the rest of his life; and (3) Dying to no actual purpose, which is what occurs in their minds if that death comes at the hands of law enforcement or security officials and in a time, place and means not of the terrorists' choosing. Thus, even if the terrorists know that law enforcement may – or will – assault with non-lethal or less-than-lethal weapons, their use may still be highly successful. Obviously, the desires of the terrorists notwithstanding, the use of non-lethal weapons can dramatically increase the likelihood of hostages' lives being spared. This is an entire development in American military and law enforcement armaments where the Russians lag far behind.

Though not designed to be a comprehensive overview of the advances in technology in this field over the past few years, or a complete array of such tactical devices available to law enforcement today, some brief mention of the current state of non-lethal devices may be beneficial. As pointed out by John and Mark Alexander in an excellent review of these weapons over the past few years, technological innovations have led to improvements in "aerodynamic stabilization of flight for beanbags and baton rounds have increased in accuracy...."[23] Other innovations have seen the alteration of certain compounds to reduce injuries, which not only prevents suspects from being gravely injured but can save hostages' lives altogether. "Distraction devices, quite popular and effective in many dynamic entry operations, incorporate loud noises, flashes of light, and sometimes rubberized pellets," according to the article. The authors go on to say that, "Some newer multi-functional grenades are incorporating fuel air explosives for blast overpressure, flameless sparks, multiple explosions, and offensive odors in the mix." Advances in chemical sprays and delivery systems have greatly increased the range in which such substances can be used and their effectiveness, providing increased standoff distance to police.

As well, weapons and equipment that take advantage of everything from light and sound technology to nervous system interruption, in the form of tasers, have been enhanced. Even the Defense Department has gotten involved, engaging in research into laser beam weapons whose heat delivery can neutralize an enemy due to the excruciating pain that is created, even from ranges of hundreds of meters. No matter

---

[23] John Alexander and Mark Alexander, "Emerging Less-Lethal Weapons," *Tactical Response*, Vol. 3, Number 4, Fall 2004, p. 62.

what the cost, because they have the ability to eliminate a terrorist threat while at the same time giving the rescuers the greatest chance to save lives, those weapons must be developed to their fullest potential. And it will not only prove beneficial in terrorist sieges, but in all law enforcement operations throughout the country. With the availability of this technology, there would be no more public outrage due to police shooting teenagers, retarded kids, innocent motorists, or disabled and bedridden old people – as happened in Denver in 2004 – just because they thought the person might have looked from a distance like he had a weapon. Whether funding for these weapons comes from the Department of Homeland Security, some other branch of the federal government, or state and local taxes, research and development must be funded now.

Where Are You Practicing?

Police must use the time now to locate buildings identical or similar to their most likely terror targets, in which to practice assaults. As each law enforcement agency begins to look at its own ability to respond to a terrorist-hostage siege, every likely target must be identified. In most jurisdictions this is not too difficult, and police have long since noted the likely targets within their areas of operation. The next step in the process is to find a building that is identical, or similar, to each of those identified targets. This is crucial in practicing for an assault of that target building during a standoff. If you wait until after a group of crazed extremists has taken a large group of people in a church, mall or school to begin looking for something similar, it will be too late. And it may not be found in your jurisdiction. If you have a building that appears to have no match anywhere, get in touch with the architect who designed it. That person or firm will know what other, similar, buildings were designed on that model by them, or what other similar buildings exist anywhere in your area.

The third step is to practice in the actual target buildings whenever possible. Whether you are a rural county sheriff's office, or belong to a SWAT, SERT, SRT, or SORT team – or any of the other permutations of tactical units – you have to practice regularly. Not only do tactics have to be developed and used, but also the team must regularly operate together if it is ever to have a chance of doing so successfully in combat. Many private building owners are only too happy to have groups of armed policemen use their buildings for such training. If not enamored of the idea of you training there, gently explain that their building has been identified as a potential terrorist target, and you are looking to prepare to save lives should it become necessary. Nothing could be more important to either the target building owner and its residents, or the police, than to allow them the opportunity to become extremely well versed in its layout. And few owners or tenants are put out by a regular presence of police commandos on the premises, sending would be criminals and plotting terrorists far down the road.

Likely Targets.

You should already know what these are in your jurisdictions. Gather drawings, blueprints, schematics, floor plans and walk-through videotapes of all public buildings in your jurisdiction. Encourage all schools, churches, office buildings and other places of public accommodation to prepare these for you. If you cannot maintain such records, have the building owners or tenants keep copies in an easily accessible, safe place, away from the building itself that can be reached during off hours and weekends. Do this now, before you need it. It is a certainty that if 100 percent of all law enforcement agencies have this information prepared for 100 percent of all high probability targets, the relevant agencies will have important information available in all of the terrorist - and other extreme criminal - incidents to which they must respond.

For smaller or more rural areas, this is not too difficult a task. For larger cities, for example New York, this effort must be broken down into the various boroughs and precincts, with each subdivision responsible for further dividing this need down to the patrol sectors. In some cases it may even be necessary to delegate this responsibility to officers on a per street or block system.

Can You Handle This?

Psychological preparation is everything. The first rule of special operations is, "humans are more important than hardware." Do not fight with the slightest worry over your equipment. The same, unfortunately, is true for human life. If, in the midst of an assault with an all-out pitched battle you kill a hostage, accept it and move on. Do not linger over the dead, and not even over the wounded or dying. Others coming in behind you will have that responsibility and can attend to the injured. You are the tip of the spear, and if that spear is pointed in some other direction, even if for an instant, the result will be disastrous. If you do not constantly move forward, always engaged and staying in the battle, more will die. Afterward, get professional help. Dave Grossman is the greatest living expert on this necessity. Read his books, and follow his advice. This should be done in advance of facing a terrorist horror, and as part of everyone's mental preparation. The more you know before you throw yourself into the holocaust, the better able you will be to handle it.

Command Replacement.

One of the other realities with regard to psychological factors impacting combat effectiveness is the ability of the commander to deal with the horror of the circumstances. Unlike the military, police officers rarely confront situations where people may be murdered in large numbers. Most go their entire careers without ever confronting terrorists, or people being tortured before them, or severed heads. The likelihood of someone becoming psychologically paralyzed by the abomination of such conduct is high, and each law enforcement agency must be prepared for it. We cannot afford to suffer from the shock and paralysis the Russian government officials at Beslan displayed. As the Spetsnaz commanders all stressed: one person must be in charge. And it must be a person capable of dealing with the situation and making difficult command decisions. Often, the results of which will be the deaths of innocents. What if the commanding officer cannot handle it? What if the acts of the terrorists are so disgusting and indescribably inhuman that the designated commander becomes ineffectual? Nor can rage become a decision-making factor.

There must be a process by which that person can be quickly relieved of command if the appalling nature of the situation renders him unable to make sound decisions, and make them quickly.

Reserve.

Do not ever forget the prediction of Colonel Lisyuk: there is going to be a battle, and people are going to die. If that does not happen, all the better. But it is the reality you must be prepared for, both mentally and tactically. If it does occur, you must have a force held in reserve. The ready reserve unit serves two important purposes. First, it is there to back up the assault force if they are overwhelmed by the terrorists, and greater numbers and weapons are needed. Second, and in many ways more importantly, they are there to take over as soon as the fight is over. This is a doctrine that is always implemented in military operations. Warriors – no matter how experienced or brave – have their limits, physically and psychologically.

When human beings are engaged in combat they undergo extreme changes in terms of both mental and physical functioning. Many internal systems peak at extreme levels, others shut down entirely. No one understands this survival response better than famed combat expert Dave Grossman, and his books *On Killing* and *On Combat* describe these processes in great detail. Anyone in the combat arms professions should read them, and then re-read them every single year they remain on the job. Combat is stressful, and the alteration of our internal systems, not to mention the demands of combat itself, are draining. Once the fight is over all of these systems crash; they shut down and the person who was involved in the battle – the same warrior who just moments before was battling mightily with courage and unbridled energy – collapses. He collapses physically, mentally and emotionally. This is why counter-attacks are so often successful in military operations.

As soon as the fight is over, the moment your school and your children have been delivered from evil, the assault force must stand down and the ready reserve take over. Though it is hard for any warrior to stand by while the battle is joined by his comrades, the men and women of every agency must be disciplined to do exactly that. For once the fight ends, the assault teams are at their most vulnerable. They cannot deal with the horror and suffering of the hostages, nor can they competently handle the disarming of explosives. At that point they should not even be allowed to move around areas that may be booby-trapped. Some of the terrorists may be hiding, others who appear dead may be simply waiting to attack or detonate explosives. It is at this point that mistakes are made. And when mistakes are made people die.

Psychological treatment and recovery must begin immediately as well, and this means withdrawing your brave warriors from the scene of the holocaust. No matter how tough, disciplined, trained and courageous, they are still human. And very few human beings can or will handle the trauma of such an engagement easily. This is one reason why snipers should never be allowed to approach the body of a person they have taken out from long range. Just as with the men of Alpha and Vympel I met: not a single one was unaffected by what they saw and did, by being among those who walked out of the Beslan School, while so many others would not. The faster the assault team is removed from the site of the battle, the sooner and faster they will be back on the road to combat effectiveness, and mental health.

Equipment.

The following are some guidelines on essential kit law enforcement should have at the ready, always replenished, during a hostage siege.

Ammo! Bring as much ammunition as possible. As discussed, once the battle is on you cannot afford to withdraw, or worse, DIE, for lack of an ability to shoot back. More importantly, the hostages cannot afford it either. They will pay with their very lives for every mistake in preparation you have made.

Retired U.S. Army Special Forces Sergeant Major John Anderson spent the first 25 years of his adult life in special operations. Then he spent the next ten years training and supervising the Department of Energy's special response security teams at a nuclear weapons plant. He well knows the realities of combat. He insists that U.S. law enforcement must change its attitude and policies regarding numbers of rounds carried by officers if they are to have a chance in a real terrorist battle. By illustration he points out that most SWAT snipers will arrive at a tactical situation with 60, 80, maybe even 100 rounds of ammunition. They have been trained and conditioned to be ready for anything; but that conditioning is within the parameters of a typical barricade-hostage scene in America.

When SWAT is called out in the United States the overwhelming majority of barricades involve a single hostage taker, often someone distraught holding his own family. No one anticipates more than one or two rounds ever actually being fired. The worst that is usually confronted is something like a bank robbery gone bad. Even then, with few bank robberies involving more than two criminals, the number of shots to be fired by a sniper is extremely low. But in a pitched battle - in combat - that all changes. Sergeant Major Anderson points out that in a situation like Beslan, if a sniper had 120 rounds he would be good for no more than four minutes of actual battle. That is 30 rounds per minute to take out targets and provide covering fire for the assault teams and escaping hostages. For the shooters in those teams, the number of rounds expended will be much, much higher. The battle at Beslan went on for 10 hours, with no less than eight hours of intense fighting. With that as a standard, all departments need to re-evaluate their ordnance issue and devise methods by which shooters can be resupplied during a fight.

Body Armor. With modern technology, the ready availability of body armor is crucial. There should be sets brought for every single assault team member. No one should ever have to share a vest, or trade off with others during shifts on the perimeter. This is not much of a problem with American law enforcement and military. Whether during a guard or perimeter shift, training shift, or rest period, every single responder should have body armor with him, if not actually on him, at all times. This includes paramedics and any others who might be designated to enter the inner area or breach the building to retrieve the wounded. If possible, body armor must be carried for hostages as well. If, as in Beslan, you are forced to move them through fields of fire that are being – or may yet be – actively engaged, they should be provided adequate cover. In that event, police must be as brave as the men of Alpha and Vympel, covering the running forms of the hostages with their own bodies, taking the bullets meant for the innocents.

Drawing You In. In no event should anyone be permitted to touch the terrorists, whether wounded or seemingly dead. This is for sound tactical reasons. When dealing with men and women ready to die for their cause, you cannot adequately ensure they have not booby trapped themselves in the heat of the battle. If they are dead, and have not exploded, they should be left exactly where they are – untouched except for two rounds in their heads – until after the bullets have stopped flying and EOD professionals have had an opportunity to take their time examining them, and possibly disarming IEDs. Only after that can their bodies be removed.

Over Penetration. Do not use weapons with over-penetration potential in buildings. Typically, the newer the building the less the inner construction material will absorb rounds. This is an aspect of combat that American police and military are generally well versed in.

Obsolete Technology. Shotguns are 100-plus year-old technology. Though most shotgun rounds do not suffer an over-penetration problem, they do suffer an horrendous accuracy problem. With hundreds of innocents about, they are virtually useless. Leave them at home for the next bird hunting season.

Concussion Grenades. Notwithstanding the Russian perspective on their use, they can be very valuable. Though the Russians were capable of viewing the complexity of the Beslan School building as merely a number of small Nord-Osts - still allowing for the successful deployment of gas - so, too, could the same approach be taken with the use of flash bang or concussion grenades. In America, where gas is unlikely to be available, concussion grenades may be the next best thing.

Communications. Communications must be good, working and compatible with all responding agencies. Before a building is stormed, this must be checked and re-checked. This was one of the greatest weaknesses in police and fire crews responding to the Twin Towers: their radio systems were incompatible, making it impossible for each department to learn what the other knew. This resulted in many unnecessary deaths, and to this day that problem has not been corrected. Do not allow your jurisdiction to suffer from so great a deficiency. Even if it means doing nothing more than going to Radio Shack to purchase cheap multiple unit systems that can be shared in a crisis, do it now.

Other Equipment. What gear is viable and relevant will be known once you have developed some understanding of the nature of the siege. Included in this should be an ample supply of handcuffs and flex cuffs. Make certain the flex cuffs are pre-threaded, with the tongues inserted through the locking eyes. The Special Forces learned, through training and experiences regarding Afghanistan, that trying to lace these through in the heat of battle, with adrenaline raging through the operators' systems, is next to impossible.

Night Vision. Everyone should have NOD (Night Optical Devices) with them, at all times. Just because it is 5:00 o'clock in the morning when you launch your assault does not mean they won't be needed. Likewise, as at Beslan, a seemingly stable situation does not mean that it will not unexpectedly and instantaneously fall completely apart. When that happens you will be forced to assault, with only the gear on your tactical vest at that moment, and it may be well into the night before you are finished. Moreover, if electricity has been shut off inside, you may find yourself in the dark recesses of a building, in rooms with no windows, or a school basement. You can bet the terrorists will have night vision capability. So should you.

Gloves. Though many shooters will not want them, and many combat firearms instructors teach that they should never be used, there are times when gloves may be an essential tool in saving hostages. If explosives are detonated, there will be large pieces of the building, splintered furniture and twisted metal and rebar that will have to be negotiated, bent or moved. Some items may be burning hot to the touch. You may have to punch through a window, bend fencing, or tear out an obstructing metal window frame. Though you cannot possibly anticipate all of the times that you might need hand protection, you can anticipate the one item of equipment that will allow you to deal with them all.

First aid kits. Everyone should have them as part of their tactical gear, secured to their tactical vests or harnesses. From years in hazardous training and other dangerous undertakings in places like Sudan and Russia, I have learned that some simple first aid items are extremely light, take up little space, and can save lives. Super Glue can quickly close any wound that requires stitches. Tampons are the single best item for stemming blood flow from deep wounds. Small needle nose pliers are not only useful as a mechanical tool in an emergency, but can serve as clamps for uncontrollable bleeding to major arteries when hemostats are unavailable or already in use. In such circumstances, don't worry about germs. If the person lives he can deal with it later.

Footwear. Everyone should have on good tactical or combat boots, with the laces tucked in. At Beslan, when I first entered the school, you could barely negotiate it. Between the bombs and grenades of the terrorists, and the RPGs and bullets of the rescuers, the collapsed ceiling in the gym and elsewhere, and the barricades that had been set up during the siege, the school was a warren of twisted wreckage, boulders of building material and blown out floors. Moving through it was like leaping from one unsteady, slippery rock in the middle of a rushing stream to the next. Rebar and metal framing tore at me like thorn bushes. Even with an excellent pair of tactical boots on, and no one shooting at me, I could barely walk through many areas. For the Russian troops, who eschew the ridiculously poorly made and uncomfortable army boots they are issued in favor of athletic shoes or sneakers, it must have been near impossible. In the U.S., I have worked with enough SWAT teams to recognize that most have not been conditioned to completely secure their laces. In Beslan, you could not have moved fifteen feet in any direction without snagging exposed laces on something and falling flat on your face, maybe flat onto a booby trap; or having the knots pulled loose, leaving you to move with laces trailing behind. Combat is not the environment in which to stop and tie your shoes. For every operator, such basics are essential: double knot your boot laces, twist and tuck them in tight, then wind electrical tape around to secure them. Remember that mistakes may get someone killed. It could be you, a teammate, or an innocent.

Stretchers and Body Bags. The unfortunate need and use for these is self-explanatory.

Water. Combat is exhausting. You will need water and lots of it. Remember, once inside you will not be coming out for a rest. It could be ten hours or more. And even if you don't need it, the hostages you save will. At Beslan, many parts of the school were oven hot. Added to this was the heat from the fire consuming the gym, other explosions and even heated rifle barrels. Fear and adrenaline alone will cause your body to perspire at exaggerated rates. You must have water to allow you to remain an effective fighting tool.[24]

---

[24] For a complete examination of the physiological responses to combat, see Dave Grossman's books *On Killing* and *On Combat.*

Reality Preparation.

No matter what decisions you make in preparing your teams, make sure that training is as realistic as possible. Follow the military training doctrine of injecting unexpected contingencies or problems into the mix. One of the problems with America being a nation dependent on technology is the failure to realize that in combat, the greater the technology the more things there are to go wrong. And go wrong, they will. The Russians frequently have to work without comm's or with poor equipment. What will your teams do if suddenly your radio systems fail, or worse, the terrorists themselves have jamming devices? What if one of your men is captured with a radio and you must keep from communicating important information over the air?

Though the Russian people are our technological equals in some areas – and our superiors in others – they do not have access to the ubiquitous layers of technology that Americans do. They are most often forced to develop low technology solutions to major problems. To illustrate the differences between our cultures, for years I have told the story of the space race between the United States and Soviet Union in the 1960s. Both countries were spending untold billions – if not trillions – of dollars in putting men in space, to be the first on the moon. At about the same time, however, they both encountered an identical problem: pens would not write in zero gravity conditions. The United States spent even more millions of dollars in today's money to develop a pen that wrote upside down, in zero gravity, in negative gravity and underwater. They proudly sent this new writing implement up in every one of their space capsules. Facing the same problem, the Russians sent pencils.

Here is the genius of simplicity that often makes the Russians formidable opponents. And both of our nations have seen instances where our mighty technologically advanced military and security forces have been completely waylaid by low technology solutions. Look at our experiences in Vietnam and those of the Soviet Union in Afghanistan. Each is an instance where a poorly educated, technologically inferior enemy stopped a superior military cold. What of 9-11, where a few small knives were able to defeat millions of dollars worth of security equipment and manpower? Each of you may, someday, have to find a fast low technology answer to a problem when lives are at stake. This is the necessity of reality training.

Another important aspect of preparing realistically is abandoning American law enforcement's complete reliance on technology in all aspects of combat. In centuries past combat was waged in very close quarters, at hand-to-hand combat range where each warrior could see the fear in his enemy's eyes, feel the heat from his body, smell his blood and his breath as he fought to take the very life from the enemy. Hand-to-hand combat skills were at their zenith, and martial artists the world over continue to study the ancient ways, believing fully in the superiority of those systems. A succession of technological advances over millennia – from spear to bow to musket, rifle, cannon, artillery and finally missiles - have expanded those distances more and more. We have long since lost the ability to psychologically withstand the stresses of up-close combat, and no one has made a greater study of this than Lt. Col. Grossman. As he points out in both of his books, both psychological and physiological stress levels increase dramatically as the distance in which battle is waged decreases.

In preparing for terrorist-hostage sieges you are girding your loins for battle with an enemy that has demonstrated not only his success, but his superiority, at simple low tech combat. He has achieved all of his great victories with relatively simple methods, bombs, firearms and knives. He thinks he is more comfortable than you inside a building with tight corridors. He has seen people's heads being cut off, and in some instances will have done it himself. The blood, gore and human suffering witnessed at extreme close ranges do not bother him. He yearns for this. He is on familiar territory in close up combat. You must be as well; indeed, you must be his superior. As the British SAS is fond of saying: "Your worst has got to be better than their best." All this means that American law enforcement and military alike have got to improve their close quarter combat skills and approaches to deal with this reality. In the 1960s and 1970s America's tunnel rats – men who were forced to go down into Vietnam's fearsome tunnel network armed with merely a knife, handgun and flashlight – developed a shooting system for close work in which the pistol was held in a combat ready position, close in to the chest to prevent disarming. In the confines of many buildings it would likewise be impossible to "present" the firearm at arms' length, out away from the body as is taught by the Isosceles, Chapman and Weaver shooting stances of old. These are decades-old fighting systems designed for a completely different type of combat environment. And do not think for a second your SWAT team will simply "roll right over the bad guys" as I have heard numerous tactical commanders say, rationalizing their refusal to train realistic hand-to-hand combat skills, or integrating those skills with close quarter handgun techniques and transition drills.

Accepting the necessity of developing this next generation of combat techniques is not enough. They must be trained and trained hard. Each and every shooter must be able to shoot with extreme accuracy and speed. These are the skills that make each person – whether soldier or policeman – capable of saving lives and the skills that give him the confidence to move to the sound of the gunfire. The skills that make him able to kill the person holding a child up as a shield and not hit that child. Through years of travels and training others I have seen an increasing reliance on the *spray and pray* approach to weapons discharge in combat. This is what technology, money (to buy bullets) and fear of close quarters combat do to a warrior. For those who attempt to delve into the world of realistic combat training in today's terrorist environment, do not be surprised if all your good intentions and efforts are stopped by some bureaucratic range master because you are training something he does not know, something that is not part of the current spate of antique shooting and moving techniques, and is therefore something he is threatened by. No matter the obstacles, close quarters shooting and hand-to-hand training must be developed to deal with realistic terrorist conditions. Every tactical team member must not only be an expert at both skills but at integrating the two seamlessly when bullets are flying. U.S. Special

Forces have recently been turning to the Archangel Group for this new, combat essential system and law enforcement needs to as well.

Multiple Terrorist Doctrine.

Until Columbine, few in law enforcement had stopped to contemplate a gap in their doctrinal planning and development. Until then police would never move through a room or area of a building that had not been thoroughly searched and secured. This helped prevent criminals in hiding from ambushing police from behind. With Columbine – and the resultant casualties, some even occurring as police painstakingly searched every nook and cranny of the school – the Active Shooter Doctrine was developed, which compels law enforcement to move to the sound of gunfire, toward the armed assailant in times of emergency and ongoing killing without regard for the areas he has transgressed. Just as the Active Shooter Doctrine was developed to deal with a new threat to America's children, so must we all now develop yet a new and more sophisticated model for our police: the Multiple Terrorist Doctrine. The terrorists are well aware of the post-Columbine protocol currently used by police across the nation, if not the world, now. Yet that doctrine is only applicable in situations like Columbine; where you do not realistically believe there could be other shooters lying in wait for law enforcement to come racing to the rescue of the children. In a situation like Beslan where you are confronting numerous terrorists, all of whom are part of a well-prepared plan to maximize hostage and police deaths, you must deal realistically with both the need to move quickly to the sound of gunfire, and at the same time secure the areas you have moved through, so as not to be ambushed from behind. Stop and imagine what the outcome would have been for Alpha and Vympel at Beslan if they had raced through the school's corridors, barely looking into each room, all on their way to the sound of terrorist guns going off? The numbers of dead, already too high, would have been greater still. It took Columbine to come up with the new doctrine we have in place in America today. Don't wait for our own Beslan to prepare for an altogether different scenario.

Chapter Thirteen

Combining Forces

Who Dares Wins.

— British SAS motto

From a tactical perspective, the debacle at Beslan School No. 1 is more akin to our disaster at Desert One in Iran in 1980, than Nord-Ost, or even Columbine. At Desert One an untested Delta Force (1st Special Forces Group Operational Detachment – Delta) was saddled with the logistical and tactical nightmare of too many branches of the military sticking their hands in. When it was decided that too many of the CH 53 Pavelow helicopters, necessary to evacuate the hostages and team members, had fallen out, the mission was aborted. When preparing to extract, one of the helicopters struck a C-130 transport plane, causing an enormous explosion and killing eight servicemen. Too many groups that had never before worked together, and whose doctrines made them incompatible, were integrated for nothing more than political considerations. This resulted in many months more of detention and torture for the hostages, the death and humiliation of the rescuers, and a devastated psyche for America. Groups of diverse units, which had never trained together, were forced to operate together in a combat environment. This situation was exacerbated by the injection of unanticipated variables, followed by a catastrophic and unexpected explosion that cost lives. The loss of lives, chaos and sense of defeat at Desert One was surpassed in Beslan only by the ages of the victims, the number of dead, and the sheer horror of the circumstances leading to it.[25]

At Nord-Ost, the assault team developed a plan, worked together and executed it almost flawlessly. It was the government's refusal to recognize its duty to the lives of its citizens that resulted in its failure to alert local hospitals and have ambulances standing by; the only reason why 129 hostages died needlessly. Had this one small step been taken, the Nord-Ost Theater assault would have gone down as the greatest hostage rescue of all time; likely never to be surpassed. Columbine involved two active shooters, with a school full of victims, but with hundreds of responding law enforcement officers from a variety of agencies and without a clear leader with courage and conviction, doing nothing but standing fast as children died. Had Alpha and Vympel simply stood by on Day Three when the explosives detonated unexpectedly and the terrorists began shooting fleeing hostages, there would at least have been some similarities.

Is U.S. local law enforcement prepared to work with the FBI, FEMA, its own state WMD/CST,[26] and even the National Guard if necessary in responding to such a situation? Have they worked out a critical Incident Command System (ICS)? Have they trained together before? Have they done any of this with sister jurisdictions that will likely respond? What is prepared as between the local police and fire departments? Are private ambulance services a part of the critical incident response plan? Is your police department ready to subordinate itself to another law enforcement agency if that other is better trained or more experienced in SWAT, hostage negotiations and rescue? These are all questions that have to be asked and the answers addressed, long before the siren sounds on a hostage siege.

Develop Critical Incident Command System with other agencies.

Establish immediately a Critical Incident Command System (CICS or ICS as it more commonly known) and see that everyone follows

---

[25] See *Inside Delta Force*, Eric Haney (New York: Delacorte Press, 2004).

[26] The Weapons of Mass Destruction/Civil Support Teams are full time National Guard units based in every state.

orders according to it. It is best to enter into formal, written agreements between jurisdictions now, so that each entity understands its role in the event of a terrorist siege or attack. Do not tie your role to ego. If a sister jurisdiction is better equipped and prepared to deal with a situation, give them the authority to lead others, yourself included. Learn to ask for effective assistance. Honestly identify needs and deficiencies, then request backup.

Here, law enforcement must be prepared to adopt and follow the Special Forces model. In the U.S. Army's Special Forces, operations are carried out by ODAs – Operational Detachments Alpha – or A Teams, as they were previously known. On each ODA is a captain, who is the team leader, a chief warrant officer, who is the number two in command and the intelligence specialist, and ten other men all at sergeant grade. When an operation is being planned, and even when the operation is being conducted, the most knowledgeable person is in charge. It may mean that the youngest and lowest ranking sergeant on the team is the person with the most expertise or experience in a given area or tactic. If so, everyone defers to him. In this way, the mission always has the greatest chance of success: ability is put ahead of politics.

Law enforcement agencies must develop much the same approach in dealing with a terrorist situation, especially with other jurisdictions and agencies. Even the FBI must come to accept this. If you are confronted with a group of terrorists from Algeria, and you find you have a rookie officer who spent time in the French Foreign Legion, Peace Corps, U.S. Special Forces, or was a missionary there - someone who knows the people, culture, language and issues - he should be made one of the most important assets not only in your operational planning, but in your execution. He should be consulting and briefing the negotiating team. He should be involved in the tactical assault planning, and he should be made ready to go with one of the first teams to make direct contact with the hostage-takers. If a terrorist is captured before an assault of the building takes place, he should be integrally involved in his interrogation.

Much the same approach must be taken with "competing" law enforcement agencies. First, all agencies must stop thinking of each other as the competition. When terrorists come to take our children, everyone will have to work together for the good of those children, not in furtherance of some self-serving interests in the political aftermath. If you belong to an agency that has only recently created a SWAT team, and have a neighboring department that has not only had one for years, but that tactical unit has had dozens of successful operations, then you should bring them in and defer to them. Take their advice. Let them lead. This does not mean that you are absolving yourself of responsibility. In the Special Forces the captain and warrant officer can always countermand what the young trooper is advising. So must you continue to exercise your ultimate authority if you believe that what is being planned, prepared, or recommended is irresponsible or negligent. But that determination must be made in a professional, objective manner, not as a result of feelings of inadequacy relative to another group of professionals you think you are in competition with. There is only one group you are competing against: the terrorists. And the stakes are high.

Once that is all sorted out and a particular agency is determined to be in charge, it must remain so. There can be only one organization in charge, and from it only one person in command of it and all other agencies: that is, a single leader, no matter how many groups, departments and representatives of different levels of government are present. And that person must have absolute autonomy. In Russia, this lesson was learned the hard way. At Beslan there was no single person. The Russian military commanders I spoke with acknowledged that there had been no control over the various units, each with its respective loyalty to a different branch of government. They said that a single unit, under that one leader, should handle the main response to a terrorist situation like Beslan, with all other groups subordinate to it. When the time came to assault, "Too many units did their own thing, without coordination or supporting each other," one Spetsnaz officer admitted. As was seen, this lack of coordinated effort was also a significant factor in the lack of crowd control, with the "volunteers" injecting themselves into the equation at every turn.

If, in the American system, the FBI and its Hostage Rescue Team (HRT) will assume operational command in the event of a true terrorist siege, realize that there will be a delay in their arrival on scene. As many FBI special and supervisory special agents have pointed out time and time again: "The FBI is never the first on scene to anything; we are never *first* responders." In the situation of a school siege, local law enforcement will be on site, possibly for hours, before FBI and HRT arrive. HRT's target time for arrival inside the continental U.S. is measured in hours, not minutes. In the meantime, the chain of command among the first responding units must be sorted out quickly and followed. For these reasons, the Russians believe that the FBI's model, with its centralized HRT, is unworkable. Those I spoke with were of the opinion – in the face of the likelihood of terrorist assault in the U.S. in the near future – that smaller HRT teams, or other units or forces must be distributed around the country, prepared, trained and ready to go. Those other units must come from our local agencies.

Multi-Department SWAT Team Model.

We live in a country of seemingly increasing costs of living and taxes. A significant factor in both the reality and perception of these increases is the economic fallout from the 9-11 attacks. Democrats and Republicans alike enjoy claiming or blaming the status of the economy on the party that serves their ends, in their never-ending campaign at self-serving pedantry. The truth of the matter is that the U.S. economy is an enormous, complex, living organism. Like any organism, it has a natural cycle that it follows, with both upswings and downturns. No political party or president of the country can any more ensure an economy on a never-ending upswing, than you can keep your own body from never being tired or falling prey to illness, no matter how perfectly you live and healthily you eat. And much like your own body, the economy is highly susceptible to trauma, and both the short and long term consequences of great trauma can be devastating to it, causing untold side effects.

On the 11th of September 2001, the U.S. suffered a trauma of enormous scale. And though comparisons have been drawn to the attack on the U.S. at its naval base in Honolulu, Hawaii on December 7, 1941, they are only alike in terms of numbers of Americans killed and the surprise of the attack. But it was not the numbers of Americans killed on 9-11 that caused such a great and far reaching impact. Between job accidents, car accidents, murders and natural causes, the U.S. sees many more of its citizens die every single day, than were killed by the terrorists. As well, we are a country of such breadth and enormous population that the loss of several thousand people from the job market would not have been noticed. Not noticed, that is, but for the way they perished and the locations of their demise. These factors caused such great a trauma that it has rocked the U.S. economy to this day. Company growth, new jobs and the stock market have all been dismal – or, at best, tentative and scared – ever since. And it could not have come at a worse time. When the attacks on that day came, the American economy was already well into one of its natural and irresistible down turns.

It is for these reasons that the American public feels like it is facing ever-increasing demands on their pocketbooks, at a time when they have the least to give. The war in Afghanistan, the ongoing war in Iraq, the strains that have been put on families and the economy as thousands upon thousands of military Reservists and National Guardsmen are snatched from their civilian lifestyles and jobs, have made this all the worse. And yet, our government, from the federal to the state levels, still does not have the necessary financial resources to battle the terror we all still face. There is no place this is truer than with our local law enforcement.

By and large local law enforcement has been devastated by the military call up. We have learned – all too late – that many of the same people who served in the military, and continue to meet obligations to the service of our nation by holding rank in the Reserves and National Guard, are also police officers. From a humanistic perspective, this should come as no great surprise. The transfer of many officers to full time military service has decimated law enforcement agencies. And, under the Uniform Services Employment and Re-Employment Rights Act[27] they cannot replace those men and women, having to hold their positions for their eventual return. This has resulted in our police forces – already under-staffed and under-funded – having even fewer resources than ever before at a time when they are being called upon to do ever more. No longer do we simply demand of them our protection, the stopping of crime, the crushing of drugs and gangs in our communities. Though we have not relieved them of any of those duties, we also now expect them to keep us safe from an even greater enemy intent on the destruction of our very society. Yet in dropping these expectations squarely on their shoulders, we have not given them the tools or resources to accomplish the tasks laid before them.

One of the true necessities for all law enforcement agencies across America to deal with increasing violent threats to them and us is a special response, tactical unit. Though generally known by the term SWAT – for Special Weapons and Tactics – these tactical teams are also known variously as SERT, ERT, SORT, SRT and others. But no matter what moniker is laid upon them, they are all the Special Forces of the law enforcement community. First they are a team, trained as such, tested strenuously and demanding of peak physical condition and superior combat skills. They deploy as a team, a single fighting unit that spends more time with each other than any of their other colleagues, and sometimes even their own families. In the event of a terrorist attack, it is these men – and increasingly women – who will be thrown on the front lines, who will be the ones to storm the doors of the school in which the terrorists are hiding, holding our children. They will be our Alpha and Vympel. And, as Colonel Lisyuk forewarns, they will be the ones who die.

---

[27] 38 USC Section 4301, *et seq.*

Yet in America our ability to commit to establishing and funding these necessary units of superior tactical ability is sorely lacking. According to Larry Glick, long time head of the National Tactical Officers Association, of the approximately 16,000 law enforcement departments in the United States, only 2,000 of them have 50 or more officers. Moreover, of all of those, only 58 percent have tactical teams at all, and of those, there are only 245 full time tactical teams. The rest are reserve units. These function much as our military Reserves do, with officers who have otherwise full time police duties, called upon to return to their headquarters, meet, get briefed, gear up and then deploy in the event of a critical incident. This not only means that they have less training time than their full-time comrades, but have a longer response time when called upon.

And of those many reserve SWAT units, the majority has only ever functioned alone. They have little enough time and money to get together to train as a single unit as it is; they completely lack the resources to integrate training with sister jurisdictions. Yet, just as we saw at Columbine and on 9-11, when the terror comes to visit, tactical units from departments in neighboring counties and cities will be called upon. In the face of this reality, and until all police departments are given the resources necessary to train, equip and field full time tactical response units, they must look to expand their delivery capability to the extent possible.

One of the best ways this can be accomplished is through the development of multi-agency SWAT teams. Though the formation of such integrated units can present problems, from liability issues to chain-of-command insecurities, the ultimate product is of such value as to make them essential to the preservation of our society in the times ahead.[28] In promoting both the necessity and efficacy of multi-agency tactical teams, writers Jim Weiss and Mickey Davis point

---

[28] For an excellent presentation of this, see Jim Weiss and Mickey Davis, "Multi-Agency SWAT: Delaware Tactical Unit," *Tactical Response*, Vol. 3, No. 4, Fall 2004, p. 16.

out that 50 percent of barricade situations result in shooting where SWAT teams are not present. When SWAT teams are on site, there are shootings in less than 2 percent of the cases. In the Delaware, Ohio multi-agency unit, as detailed in their fine article in *Tactical Response* magazine, the authors explain how this can be done with little budget. In Ohio, each participating agency provides the necessary equipment to its respective officers, and contributes whatever gear it can for the entire team. When no longer needed or used, this equipment – always on loan – reverts to the donating agency. Other budget concerns are resolved by the individual police departments being financially responsible only for their officers. In this way, each jurisdiction enjoys the benefits of a highly trained, well-equipped tactical unit, drawn from a greater law enforcement population, thereby increasing competition for positions and performance ability. Yet they are each only burdened by the financial demands of a few officers.

Overall command authority is housed under the member-sheriff's department, as it is considered the top law enforcement agency in that area. However, any number of other models could be successfully employed, including rotating SWAT commanders from the various organizations. In order to make this function successfully, and to ensure commonality of purpose and function, written joint-operations agreement should be entered into. These agreements should delineate all of the formational and operational aspects that have been agreed, including minimum qualifications for selection of new members. Training demands should be included, requiring each agency to ensure that its members are available for scheduled team training sessions. Finally, triggering events for activation should be spelled out, with a single individual bestowed the authority to call the team out.

While the Delaware, Ohio group demonstrates merely one successful model, this concept can be exported across the country in any number of variations, providing exponentially greater tactical ability to every jurisdiction. If one can approach the issue of potential terror attacks from the belief that every police agency should have a committed SWAT team, then it is a foregone conclusion that the 245 who already have them, do need them. Jurisdictions without even a reserve unit can form one with neighboring counties and cities. Already existing reserve units can join with other reserve units to drastically increase their delivery of well-trained law enforcement and weapons in response to critical situations. And those that already have full time units can go even further, creating as formidable a force as anything the military can produce in times of crisis and national defense. The FBI has a similar program with local law enforcement, but that does not mean that local departments should not recognize the need for their own multi-agency forces to be deployed under their own command and control. You can never be too prepared, and redundancy of force deployment is a good rule to go into combat with.

This model is not only applicable to law enforcement. Fire departments and paramedics all find themselves in virtually the identical situation: most are volunteer and not full time, all are under-funded and under-staffed, and every single one will have to work with sister departments in response to a major incident. The same types of training and joint force units in those fields need to be formed and readied against that which is yet likely to come.

Teammates, Not Competitors.

At the first International Anti-Terrorism Conference held in Lakewood, Colorado, the opening speaker was a retired Army Special Forces officer, a former head of various highly classified operations for the U.S. government, who had recently retired from the position of head of Homeland Security for the State of Alaska. He was also a proud recipient of our nation's highest award for bravery: the Congressional Medal of Honor. Mr. Drew Dix is a tall, spare and reserved man. With his sparkling eyes, beard and stoic demeanor, combined with his height and military bearing, he looks like a cross between Charlton Heston and a modern day Abraham Lincoln. After decades of serving our country, from fighting in the jungles and cities of Vietnam to running a top secret naval operation on the North Pole, from advising the president on terrorism to doing the same for the governor of Alaska, Drew has seen it all. He possesses an understanding of the terror threat and our nation's ability to address it that is both broad and deep. Yet at the conference he had only one message to deliver at a gathering of several hundred of the top counter-terrorism experts from the many federal agencies, military personnel, and police involved in this war.

That message was that in order for our nation to survive this war, everyone in every agency and military unit must shed himself of the historic turf battling and parochialism that resulted in the very intelligence failure that allowed 9-11 to happen. No longer can FBI and CIA afford to hide information from each other. The then-fledgling Department of Homeland Security had to be welcomed as a teammate by all other agencies, and different branches of the military had to stop competing for every single dollar and piece of new equipment, instead learning to objectively recognize the strengths and weaknesses of each. In short, to combat the terrorists successfully, all of these agencies have to stop combating each other, for the terrorists are surely working together toward our destruction. With our destruction as the common goal that has brought *them* together, how is it that our survival has not yet served as the common goal necessary to bring *us* together?

According to Drew Dix, it is crucial that every single agency, department and group involved in the War on Terror develop relationships and protocols with each other. Every one of us – no matter where in that list we fall – should seek out and establish some connection with the local CIA office, FBI supervisory special agents, DHS, TSA and JTTF representatives. Though they are often criticized – and sometimes rightfully so – for refusing to share information with sister agencies, you may find unusual teammates in the local CIA officers, who may be willing to tell you what they can if you just make the effort.

The nationwide JTTFs (Joint Terrorism Task Forces) have gone far to assist in this fence-building, but all too often remote departments or under-staffing on the federal side keeps this from happening. Also, at a local ATAC (Anti-Terrorism Advisory Council) meeting, there may be upwards of 150 agencies and departments represented, with only one CIA person. He or she may not even be able to disclose whom they really work for. Find them on your own, talk to them, meet with them and try to help them as much as they help you.

The necessity of developing some contacts and relationships with "other" agencies, however, should not preclude each governmental entity – law enforcement in particular – from doing the same with their counterparts in neighboring jurisdictions. These comrades-in-arms will still represent those groups with which you share a common mission and experiences, the ones you will interact with the most, and those that you will call on first in response to a critical incident. The same goes for paramedics and fire departments. Train, prepare and develop protocols for joint operations. The life you save could be your own, or that of a child.

Chapter Fourteen

Citizen Soldiers

This is life, and none of us are getting out of it alive.
And for most of us our deaths will be horrible,
and will come long before we think we're ready.
We must decide now how we will face death when it comes.
For only through that knowledge
can we then decide how we would live.
— *The Author*

Where do you think all those great FBI agents, CIA intelligence officers, Green Berets, Secret Service Agents and international experts come from? They are all part of – and at one time were nothing more than – the average citizenry. There is no greater resource in the world than Americans. I often lament the loss of certain characteristics of American society found in eras like World War II; before our society indulged its puritanical need to quantify and credential everything to the point where you can't do a workout without either an expert trainer or a master's degree in exercise physiology. In the 1940s we drew our courageous Smoke Jumpers – men who would parachute into a raging forest fire with nothing more than a shovel and neckerchief – from college kids looking for summer work. Our military, recognizing the tremendous resource that was the American people in a time of great need, did not hesitate to give direct commissions to common citizens who could contribute to the war effort. In this way, movie executives might have found themselves suddenly on par with men who commanded entire armies.

And where do we think the most daring and mysterious of all came from? The OSS, forerunner to both the CIA and our vaunted Green Berets, was an organization started by a Wall Street lawyer, commanded by a lawyer, and populated with lawyers. That organization took a group of silk-stocking attorneys - and all of the tremendous analytic power they possessed – gave them some military training, taught them how to shoot, parachute and kill up close, with knives and their bare hands. Called Jedburgh teams, they were then dropped behind enemy lines in teams of merely three, where they caused incalculable damage to the German war effort.

Police and government officials can only know so much. Each of you may be completely well versed in the gangs in your area, the drug dealers, the taggers and prostitutes. You may be on a first name basis with pimps, wife beaters, drunk drivers, and meth users, all of whom you have no doubt arrested on numerous occasions. But that does not prepare you to be experts in foreign and arcane languages, the Koran or Wahhabism, or know the difference between a Shi'ite and Sunni, or identify the differences in their belief systems, or why these beliefs ever developed in the first place. You likely don't know what country the Tamil Tigers operate in, or even the era in which Muhammad lived. Prior to reading this book, you likely were unfamiliar with the culture of Russia and her regions of Chechnya, Ingushetia and North Ossetia. You probably haven't ever been to Afghanistan, the Philippines, Sri Lanka, Indonesia, Algeria, Rwanda or Sudan, or even recognize why knowledge of those countries could become important in dealing with a terrorist-hostage barricade situation.

Every single law enforcement agency has such professionals in its jurisdiction, and their areas of expertise range from international affairs to hostage rescue and tactics, even negotiations. Some are experts on the foundations of Islamic extremist terror groups; others have an in-depth knowledge of the Koran. There are men who worked for the U.S. in Afghanistan in the 1980s as well as recent years. There are ex-Green Berets, SEALs, snipers, Force Recon Marines. There are professors, Russian speakers, Chechen speakers and Arabic speakers. Seek these people out now and have them at the ready. The heroic notion of the Minute Man, so ready to race out the door to defend and protect his home, family and way of life against violent invaders runs hot through the blood of every American; indeed, through the blood of everyone who has come to our country to live, work, raise a family, and create a better life.

You cannot be expected to be an expert in all of these areas, nor is that required. The odds are that you can find people in your area who do have a significant level of knowledge, if not true expertise, in every imaginable discipline and subject matter. Determine who the available experts on terrorism-related subjects are now. Contact them and talk to them. Establish relationships with them and know that they are on call to you 24 hours a day, every single day of the year. Many would be willing to volunteer their time; many others are now in the private sector, looking to make a living, but would not fail to heed the call to arms if their help was needed in an emergency, especially in their own hometowns. Just look at how Dave Grossman responded to the Jonesboro, Arkansas school shooting as described in the Foreword to this book. He wasn't looking for money or fame; there were no medals to be awarded. He was only looking to help. There are many like him in this respect. Know who they are and what they think. And know that you can get them quickly to your on-site command post if their expertise can be beneficial.

There are enormous amounts of untapped resources and expertise throughout the U.S. And should a Beslan or Nord-Ost type siege come to you, consultation in many of these areas may be crucial to you not only understanding the history, violence potential, goals and customs of these people, but in knowing the likely timetable you are up against, what the effective negotiation techniques may be, and what type of training and weapons they likely possess as you plan an assault. Conduct your vetting process now. If you wait until hostages are being stood up in the windows of an elementary school, you will not have the time to find these experts, nor the ability to cull through the thousands of volunteers and judge the veracity of their claimed expertise. And if you try to locate them then, you will have little choice but to do so by broadcasting your need for them over television and radio, tipping the hostage-takers off as to your efforts and your weaknesses.

Take the opportunity now. Contact your local chapter of the Special Forces Association, Special Operations Association, SEAL/UDT and Ranger associations. They all possess men of incredible military training and experience, most of whom have gone on to other civilian careers. But the knowledge and experience is still there, like the Minute Men, waiting to be called to service. Stop by the colleges and universities in any proximity to you. Remember these people need only be close enough to get to you, on-scene at a hostage situation. A several hour drive will make them available in ample time in most cases. Call the FBI and CIA, see what resources they both have within their own offices, and what other assets they've developed that might be of service. This is in no way an exhaustive list. With a little effort and imagination, you can have a veritable army of such warriors awaiting anyone who comes to your town.

In a time of crisis, when homes, families and our way of life are yet again threatened, these warriors will not let you down. Only you will have failed if that time comes and you do not have those Minute Men to turn to, because you failed to create that brigade of defenders in advance of the attack. As the biblical question asks: When did Noah build the ark? *Before the rains came.* Draw on your civilians now.

And for you civilians out there who possess expertise in an area that may be of use to your local police department in a crisis – any crisis – get in touch with them now. No matter how hard they try, they may not be able to find you. Send your police chief or sheriff a letter and resume detailing what benefit you might be to him. Make sure you include your address and all of your phone numbers. If you move or change numbers, send him a new resume, so he can have a single document with all pertinent information on file at all times. You may not hear back from him, but it will be a resource he can draw on when the time comes.

America As A Warrior Culture.

The most common criticisms of Americans typically involve our violence and love of guns. Even Americans assail this as a tremendous cultural weakness. But what is not recognized is that this supposed obsession with firearms and violence is only a weakness in a society that enjoys the luxury of the greatest, most unprecedented security in the history of the planet. Most Americans have lived their entire lives never knowing war, assault, hunger, poverty or even a serious economic downturn. Until 9-11, many of those same people had wallowed in the self-indulgence of their own vapid and vacuous lives, focused merely on jobs and salaries, 401K plans, movies, glitz, the drama of reality shows, and Hollywood stars. Now, though most Americans have gone back to ignoring the realities of the world, we remain a nation under threat. A nation in which any day could see a debilitating assault on our children, our government and us.

This disturbing atmosphere is causing our country to return to an appreciation of the warrior. Make no mistake, America is a culture, society and nation, founded on the creed and ethos of the warrior. From the early settlers who hacked out a civilization from the wilderness, battling the warrior race they found living here, to modern times, we are a people unalterably devoted to the notion of the warrior. Starting as early as Rogers' Rangers and the French and Indian Wars, to the Minute Men, Daniel Boone, and Davy Crockett, through our cowboy era with the romance of a lone, self-assured man never hesitating to bring justice with fists or the famed Colt revolver, we have worshipped the warrior. In World War II we had the Big Red One, the elite and courageous Marines of the Pacific Theater, Rangers, the 101st and 82nd Airborne Divisions, and the OSS. All were brave men who picked up arms to do what had to be done in a world gone crazy with murderous lust. In Korea, the Frozen Chosen were among the many who braved the harshest circumstances and environment for the cause of liberty, not only for Americans but so that everyone in the world could enjoy the liberty and self-determination of America. Vietnam brought us the Green Berets - "men who mean just what they say"[29] - and an entirely new ethos of elite warrior that would sustain us through the turn of the century.

Until the collapse of the Soviet Union and the end of the Cold War, the United States was the first and only nation formed upon the principles of individual freedom and civil liberty. It was the only country that raised the inalienable rights of every single citizen above all other considerations. Yet, somehow, Americans today have forgotten on what anvil the guarantee of those rights was forged. It was the anvil of violence, of combat, of a people fighting for those liberties against tyranny and oppression, and we have continued to fight for those rights with almost every single generation of Americans since 1776. Since the inception of our nation, rarely have we gone even thirty years – a single generation - without being engaged in war. From the Revolution, to skirmishes beyond, the War of 1812, the War with Mexico in 1846, the Civil War, the Spanish-American War, World Wars I and II, Korea, Vietnam, Grenada, Panama, the Persian Gulf War, Afghanistan and now Iraq. We are a people who carved freedom out of an unyielding world of despotism, and ensured its sanctity year after year, with a gun.

But the warrior spirit of America is not found merely in her military during times of war and crisis. For the military is nothing more than an organization comprised of common, everyday American citizens, men and women alike. And it is those very people who carry the warrior code forward. As a country, the United States has, in aggregate, more martial artists, boxers, wrestlers, scuba divers, mountain climbers, sky divers, shooters, extreme skiers, hunters and motorcycle

---

[29] From *The Ballad of the Green Berets* by Barry Sadler.

riders than any other. As though these activities – which require a warrior spirit and love of danger – are not enough, we seem to invent more, and ever more dangerous, activities each day. To this very day, more than a quarter of a millennia later, we are a people in search of the constant demands of the warrior lifestyle, forever testing ourselves, our courage and our limits. The same cultural ingredient that results in the errant violence for which we are so roundly criticized, also breeds ever greater numbers of men and women who possess the positive qualities that it produces. This is the backbone of America, and our greatest single resource.

What this means to law enforcement and those other officials who will find themselves bearing the responsibility of responding to a terrorist hostage crisis, is that you have at your fingertips scores of fellow citizens eminently capable of providing you with much needed assistance. They will take the tasks given them seriously, and will not waiver. They will not shy from danger to themselves, knowing their friends, neighbors and fellow citizens are at risk at the designs of our enemy. They will be outraged that creatures of terror would come here, would invade our homes and attack us. They will come racing to the sound of the battle from the far reaches of our great nation, just as thousands upon thousands did to New York and Washington, D.C. on 9-11. And they will provide a resource that you cannot do without.

Despite this ready abundance of manpower that will arrive after a terrorist attack occurs, it can be exploited to its full advantage if sought out now; before terrorists come racing into the parking lots of our schools. For in this great treasure trove of humanity, you will find search and rescue experts, pilots, scuba instructors, jump masters, rappelling and mountain climbing aficionados. If you live in a jurisdiction that has had to arrest and prosecute one of the many civilians who have made careers of being public nuisances by climbing quickly and effortlessly up the sides of skyscrapers, seek them out. Have them show you how and solicit their agreement to help law enforcement if and when the time comes. Have them provide training to your SWAT teams. If your jurisdiction has bodies of water and waterways, make sure you know who the local boating experts are, former naval sailors, SEALs and divers. Talk to those who own and rent ski-dos and jet skis. You should seek out and find people like Steve Bronson in Virginia Beach, a former Naval Special Warfare expert and Master Chief, who runs a training organization called Tactical Watreborne Operations. Or men like Sergeant Joe Bail, commander of the Chester, Pennsylvania SWAT team that has developed waterborne counter-terror capability for his group's eight miles of Delaware River shoreline. No matter the jurisdiction, targets and terrain in which you operate, you will find experts who can assist you. One thing our history has proven: in an emergency you can always count on an American.

One organization has already gone a long way in creating a network of professionals, from all walks of life, who can contribute critical services and information in the event of an emergency. The American College of Forensic Examiners International is a global organization with thousands of top people in all areas of government, law enforcement, military, academia and the sciences. Through its College of Homeland Security it has put together Emergency Preparedness and Response Teams in every major city and each state in America. Everyone involved is a volunteer, and membership in these teams is divided into numerous areas of expertise. Whether you are a law enforcement officer, military commander, government agent or citizen looking to get involved, this group should be contacted as a resource in the event of a terrorist attack or other critical incident.[30]

Doctors On Hand.

Create a network of hospitals, ambulance services and medical professionals. Law enforcement should already know what those

---

[30] The American College of Homeland Security can be contacted at 800-423-9737 or through its website at www.acfei.com.

agencies' plans are for creating a temporary critical care and triage facility, how it will be staffed, and what their needs will be in a crisis of large proportions. If they've never considered creating such a temporary mobile facility in a time of crisis such as Beslan, get them to start thinking about it now. As well, you need to know how they are going to get emergency patients to area hospitals, and how those hospitals will be alerted to the crisis. If you ask them these questions and they don't have answers, then they need to get to work. If you have not already, conduct training drills and exercises in coordination with them.

Outside of the area hospitals, networks of doctors should be developed in advance. It does not matter if they work in a tiny clinic or are retired. It does not matter if they do not practice trauma medicine. Be they psychiatrists, plastic surgeons or internists, when bullets start flying and hundreds of people are wounded from falls, shrapnel and rounds, you will be able to make use of anyone who has ever been to medical school or had extensive medical training. Find out if anyone in your area is a former Green Beret medic. As the saying goes, they are the best doctors practicing medicine without a license, and they may well be the coolest heads you've got if your school, mall or church turns into a combat zone. The same goes for nurses. I know of one school nurse who spent years in the emergency unit of a Philadelphia area hospital, situated in one of the highest crime areas in the nation. Find her, and those like her, and press them into service.

Psychological Preparation.

The best thing that law enforcement, government and even the media – if it can ever be conscripted into helping America deal with terrorism rather than shaming it – can do for the public at large is to prepare everyone for a school siege that is terribly gruesome. As horrific as the images of Beslan were to the American people, they were merely that: images. Most have already forgotten the name of the town and the school; others have a scant recollection that it ever occurred at all. When it comes here, it will be terrible, and it will be happening to us. We must be ready, mentally as well as tactically. The Israelis live with this reality every day. We must put aside our naïve American expectations and unrealistic hopes of a happy or peaceful resolution. If on 9-11 the terrorists had gone to the trouble to begin negotiations with FAA officials, all of America would have held its collective breath, desperately believing it would all work out. Today, we know better.

We have to prepare now for the realities of the siege of a school, day-care facility, mall or a church, or any other gathering place which will offer highly emotional and symbolic targets for terrorists. We must also be ready for such an event to be merely a diversion for something far bigger and far worse, as impossible as that may be to conceive at the time. None of us, not the military, government, law enforcement or public, can lose sight of the fact that the trademark of al Qaeda is multiple, simultaneous, coordinated attacks. It may not be one school. The constantly referenced "chatter" has indicated for some time that when it comes – if it comes – it may be up to four schools in a single city, or a number of schools throughout the country. Will you be ready?

Broad Preparation.

When I asked Russian experts what the most important things were for America to learn from Beslan, I was frequently told that the number one thing was preparation. Not only psychological preparation is important, but physical, tactical and mental preparation of everyone. This means that every single person in America, including parents, teachers, students, police and government officials, must be ready, must be alert and must be able to respond to terrorism anywhere and everywhere, at all levels. As a people we must become our own best resource and be ready to act at once, not cowering like victims of abuse, sitting back and waiting for our own government forces to try to figure it all out, to come save us. They pointed out that terrorists decreasingly take hostages in the conventional sense, they "take people and then kill them." To the Russians, at best hostages can be viewed as short term prisoners on their way to execution. Russia's experts I spoke with insist that everyone must recognize when they find themselves in the middle of a terrorist takeover that the time to act is right then, immediately. The hostages' only real opportunity for survival is during the confusion of the initial assault. They insist that terrorism is everyone's problem, and every single citizen in America must accept his and her responsibility for dealing with it: "Act or wait to die are your only real choices."

Chapter Fifteen

Preparing a Tactical Response

The society that draws a line between its fighting men and its thinking men, will find its fighting done by fools and its thinking done by cowards.

— Sir William Francis Butler

Before government and law enforcement can even begin to sort out the overwhelming and countless factors when dealing with a situation like Beslan, they must first have a model that allows them to put all that they are confronting into some sort of framework. This allows them to begin sorting not only the situation they are facing into different categories for planning and response, but dictates what everyone on our side of the fence must be doing from the outset. We all must realize the simplistic genius of the Russian 5-stage plan for dealing with terrorist-hostage sieges. Nothing could be simpler, or more effective.

Don't View a Terrorist Siege Through a Soda Straw.
According to a number of top ranking Russians I met with, if and when a Beslan-type siege occurs here, it would be a mistake to study only the school situation as though that were the problem. In Russia, the problem – only a part of which was the operation against the

school - included the buildup to the siege, as well as the entire area of the city of Beslan. This will be the same should an assault occur in the U.S. Col. Ryabko points out that he perceives that in America, such an incident would be well responded to by law enforcement, but that all of that focus would be on the school. He says that the U.S. must adopt the tactical approaches of Russia and Israel, recognizing that the most visible actions of the terrorists – as in a school seizure – represent merely one part of the entire terrorist operation, and that there may be a great deal of activity elsewhere in that city. The first incident may be a diversion, with a greater effort to be launched once government resources are committed there.

In Israel this is a foregone conclusion. As soon as the tactical units receive word of a terrorist assault, a number of the responding teams do not go anywhere near the site of the attack at all. They have long since realized that whoever the assailant, and whatever the nature of the terrorist action, there are other support or control teams in the vicinity. Sometimes these people are within blocks of a human suicide/homicide bomber, nervously fingering a remote control detonator in the event the sacrificial lamb loses his nerve at the last moment. Or, they may be controlling a second attack, to be launched as soon as the first responders arrive on the scene, grotesquely increasing the human carnage and destroying the ability of the authorities to help those already victimized. Either way, they know associates of the terrorists will be in the area, and they begin hunting them immediately.

This approach is supported completely by expert analysis of al Qaeda organization, training and operational dictates, found in such documents as the *Al Qaeda Manual*, also referred to as the Manchester Document. The Manual was found in a computer file described as "The Military Series" related to the "Declaration of Jihad," by the Manchester, England Police Department during a search of al Qaeda member Nazih al Wadith's home on May 10, 2000. The author is uncertain, though most likely Ali Mohamed, a/k/a Ali Abu-al-Saud

Mustafa, a former Egyptian army major thrown out of that country's military for his radical beliefs. After his overtures were reportedly rejected by the CIA, he managed to immigrate to the U.S.

After a time Mohamed found his way into an instructor slot in the U.S. Army Special Forces. After taking a leave in 1988, during which he traveled to Afghanistan to fight the Soviets, he was discharged from the U.S. Army as well.[31] Mohamed is believed to have recruited and trained many al Qaeda operatives in America during his stay, and was eventually indicted as a defendant in the Nairobi, Kenya and Dar-es-Salaam, Tanzania embassy bombings. Classified for a time, the Manual was ultimately introduced into evidence against him at the trial on March 26, 2001.

Weapons Choice.

Do not use weapons with over-penetration capability, especially in modern buildings with easily penetrable walls. Shotguns are of little use in such circumstances: they won't penetrate body armor and they are not precision delivery weapons. As Lt. Col. Dave Grossman frequently says, "Why would anyone want to bring two hundred year technology to a hi-tech battle?"

Eavesdropping.

Have boom and directional microphones and receivers available to intercept terrorist communications. If Beslan and Nord-Ost are repeated, and they simply yell to each other rather than risk law enforcement tapping into their comm's systems, you must be ready to pick it up. On the other hand, equipment necessary to invade those comm's systems must also be on hand, along with skilled operators. This should include the ability to jam cellular phone frequencies, both to frustrate terrorist communications and to prevent remote detonation of IEDs. It is important to keep in mind, however, that

---

[31] See, *inter alia*, Todd M. Rassa, "Lessons From The Al Qaeda Training Manual," *Police Marksman*, January/February 2005, 17.

for every act that is taken against the terrorists in a siege, there will likely be an equal and opposite reaction. That reaction will usually involve the deaths of hostages. While it is important to maintain this capability, in most situations greater intelligence derived from eavesdropping will far surpass the value of blocking the enemy's communications entirely. At Beslan the terrorists collected all of the hostages' cell phones. Numerous calls were made to several Arab countries on those phones by the terrorists during the siege.

Series of concentric secure perimeters.
This is one of the most important tactical principles, and clearly one of the greatest errors committed by the Russians at Beslan; one that led to many other problems. The Russians were weak in controlling both ingress and egress. This collapse of discipline and clear tactical duties of the various assigned units allowed civilians with weapons inside the perimeter. The soldiers could not have known whether these were part of the other terror teams they believed were holed up in the city. These citizens could have just as easily turned to the Alpha and Vympel commandos and started shooting them. Also, when the fight began, those escaping the school were not controlled or contained in any fashion, allowing terrorists to blend with the crowd, slip through the cordon and escape.

Establishing hard, outer and inner perimeter security is essential. Immediately upon the occurrence of a terrorist assault or siege, law enforcement must isolate the building at issue and get all civilians out of that building – where possible – and all surrounding buildings. You must make sure there are no bombs, sniper or observation posts or positions anywhere in the area. Beslan must be used as an opportunity for America to prepare for what is to come, just as 9-11 has been studied by other countries in anticipation of a similar attack on them. At Beslan the terrorists had backup and people outside the school monitoring troop movement, position and activity, and passing that intelligence on to the leaders inside the school. Any movement of police outside a siege site must be completely secret, with no one able to report it. This includes the news media.

The ability to thwart surveillance being carried out by terrorist support teams outside a siege site is made all the more challenging by the existence and availability of technology that allows anyone to conduct surveillance. For this reason, civilians must be kept outside a minimum radius. While the Russians correctly point out that it is impossible to devise a single standard or distance for all situations, they advise it can never be less than 500 meters. You also want to keep TV cameras away that will feed intel to the terrorists. My recommendation is that, at a minimum, law enforcement should follow the same guidelines that are applied for bomb removal from public buildings or areas. Even these distances may have to be increased. Keep in mind that with modern technology, one can be a safe distance away from a bomb blast, but still well within sight of the rest of law enforcement responding to a scene, and even the location of the bomb itself; especially with hi-tech viewing and listening devices.

Staging Areas.

Establish both CP (Command Post) and staging areas for medical treatment and coordination. Be certain the CP and the medical areas are completely removed from the news media, and each other. Do not allow someone with a superficial, or even a self-inflicted injury, to gain proximity to the command post. You must also provide a treatment area and facilities for psychologists to help citizens. This, too, must be kept away. Nothing is more important than isolating the hostage site and preventing any information being passed to the inside, which happens all too often with the news media. Remember, the information that journalists most want to air is the very information the terrorists most need to know.

Crowd Control.

Without doubt, America and every other country have a lot to learn from the failure of the Russians to maintain control of the crowds around the school. That failure began as a single fallen domino, which gained momentum and became a grievous factor in every subsequent decision and action during the siege, all the way up to and throughout the battle. From the start, the crowds – as crowds do – began gathering at the scene of the terrorist assault. The fastest responding tactical unit took at least three hours to arrive. A lot of people can converge on one spot in that amount of time. Like a fistfight on a playground, there is a strange, almost telekinetic signal that goes racing out to every human being in a broad area when there is a crisis. The police did nothing to stop them, and may have even been glad for the company, so overwhelmed were they by the extreme nature of the situation.

When Rus first arrived, they were too intent on taking over from the local and MVD police units, and attempting to establish a perimeter around the school – an inward looking perimeter – to deal with the large and growing hordes of people. And there were too few of them. Had they attempted to disperse the mob, or even move them back a great distance from the school, they would likely have met with resistance, even violence. Upon their arrival they were challenged vocally by heavily armed, and in some cases intoxicated, locals. These townspeople screamed that government troops were not needed, that they themselves would not leave, would not allow the Rus commandos to get their kids killed. Rus did the only thing it could do, at the same time the worst thing it could have done. It allowed the crowds to remain.

Every single person I spoke with - government officials, military commanders and Beslan citizens alike – insisted that the volunteers, or the "militia" as they had come to call themselves, did nothing but make the situation worse. As with many mob scenes and human group dynamics in general, the vast majority of locals recognized the danger these armed helpers posed; recognized the fact that they not only could and would make things worse, but also would get hostages killed. The volunteers were in the minority. Yet even as a minority their numbers were still enormous, and they were the ones armed and the ones who were the most vocal. *Izvestia* quoted one FSB officer at Beslan as saying, "The militiamen could not be disarmed and sent home. This could have ended up in a conflict between the police and civilians."

As always happens, those with cooler heads remained silent, while the irate villagers ran with the emotional inertia they had created. The presence of the remaining citizens behind them merely added to the circus-like atmosphere. Unable to lose face and withdraw in front of scores of their fellow townsfolk, the militia members provoked the terrorists at every opportunity, shooting their weapons without control, further inciting panic. *Homeland Defense Journal* reporter Nabi Abdullaev quoted one witness as saying, "Unfortunately, after the militiamen were allowed to stay in the security perimeter in the first hand, getting them out of it was impossible." This gave journalists, thick as flies, the environment they needed to maneuver around, secure critical camera angles and broadcast important information. Moreover, the journalists are reported to have further incited the passions and hostility of the crowd, especially those armed. Numerous Beslan residents told me of journalists asking incendiary questions designed to ignite hatred of the Ingush and incite some violent remonstrations against them, including those inside the school. When the battle finally began on Day Three, the Spetsnaz soldiers said they felt like nothing more than living shields between the crowds and the terrorists. One thing is certain however: no matter the inflamed nature of the siege, outside of the terrorists the group most hated by everyone was the reporters.

Some in the Russian government and military believe the potential exists to employ groups of civilian volunteers in a way that would have prevented the mob scene at Beslan. Turning, once again, to the use of *trained* citizens working with law enforcement, they believe that such groups of locals would have a calming effect on their neighbors, instilling confidence in the handling of the crisis. The Rus leaders also felt this could be a viable device, but advised that police should be careful to use those civilian "assistants" who belong to the same ethnic group as the majority of the on-lookers looking to be controlled. The overall impact of such civilian groups, working under the imprimatur of law enforcement – but without arrest authority – would be a great asset in keeping a crowd under control and cordoning people well away. From the perspective of Spetsnaz tactics, this would also allow the tactical commanders to create that gap the Russians will sometimes look for to allow the terrorists to slip away, alleviating an unwinnable situation and offering a secondary team or group of teams the opportunity to monitor and track them if they manage to escape. *Izvestia* quoted that same FSB officer as agreeing there was potential value in conscripting the volunteers: "...they could have been put to better use as a security cordon in the outer ring and the militiamen would be better in keeping away the crowd than soldiers, and they would not allow the gunmen to get out of the cordon. Of course, it is vital that the militiamen have a commander, appointed by the headquarters, who would see that the militia performed their assigned mission without obstructing the work of the professional soldiers and professional first responders."

The tactic of creating a hole for terrorists to slip through is of dubious use in America, where authorities would never risk trading a bad situation for a worse one. Moreover, unlike in Russia, terrorists surrounded in the U.S. have nowhere to flee, rendering this tactic of little, to no, practical value. Still, the inapplicability of the Russian tactic of creating an escape hatch for terrorists, in no way negates the overall usefulness of preparing civilian support groups to add manpower to police resources in the event a siege were to occur.

But for these groups to be effective, they have to be prepared in advance to perform their duties in such a crisis, and recognize that they exist as the government's – or law enforcement's – agents for the purpose of interacting with the population. In the course of fulfilling these duties, they would be perfectly situated to gather information from people in the crowd, conduct surveillance and counter-surveillance, regularly reporting to law enforcement.

Still, the great downside to such a program is the same weakness the Russians pointed out with the composition of the crowds themselves at Beslan. "Too many of the people there were police and military who were from that town. They had loved ones and friends in that school. In a town the size of Beslan you cannot use local forces, there are too many local relationships," I was told. "You must use forces from neighboring areas." If the police and military from the Beslan area were so emotionally overwrought to have been part of the problem and not the solution, what value could untrained and undisciplined citizens be? And of America and her citizens, how well would we deal with something like this in our own hometowns?

Determine Who is Too Emotionally Involved.

In deploying police, search and rescue teams, or any other types of professionals or volunteers, evaluate their skills, discipline and ability to function as professionals. Nothing will incite uncontrollable emotions more than the threat to one's children. In Russia, the local police were poorly trained, worse shooters and emotionally involved. Police in America are great men (and women), but they are not supermen. Everyone has a breaking point, or circumstances which will keep them from performing at their best. The threat to the life of loved ones ranks high on this list. If lawyers are ethically precluded from representing loved ones in cases of significant consequence, and doctors cannot operate on their own family members due to the misjudgment such emotional attachment can cause, how effective do we expect police to be as they stand a post outside a building in which their own children, nieces and nephews, spouses or neighbors, are being held?

Don't Let 129 People Die Unnecessarily.

Alert all possible medical assistance. With a terrorist situation involving large numbers of hostages, immediately alert area hospitals and clinics, and get as many ambulances and paramedics on hand as possible. Be certain a staging area is established that can be reached by the emergency medical vehicles and keep all traffic clear of that area and the routes to the hospitals. See that medical first responders and doctors in area hospitals are alerted to the types of injuries the hostages will likely be suffering from when they come in.

Sectors and Vectors.

Establish areas of responsibility and fields of fire. Determine and control those fields of fire. At Beslan there was too much uncontrolled shooting, which endangered both the hostages and the rescuers. This principle is basic, simple and all too often overlooked.

One Shot, One Kill.

Set up snipers at once. Keep them in the loop at all times. But most important of all, after giving the "Shoot" order, commanders need to stop talking to them. The stress of such situations is difficult enough without a nervous command officer chattering into their ear pieces as they attempt to take shots which could save or kill all inside.

Don't Shoot Until You See the Whites of their Eyes, Or Not At All.

From the outset there must be a "No Shoot" order issued to every single law enforcement officer on scene. There can be no tolerance for any weapon being discharged within hearing range by civilians. In fact, there can be no noise whatsoever that could possibly be construed as a gun or incendiary device. This means no backfiring vehicles, loud doors slamming, or practicing of building assaults within hearing distance of the terrorists. Remember, if you can purchase directional microphone receivers on the internet, so can the enemy, and they are likely sitting inside trying to pick up intelligence from the conversations of the people on the inner perimeter. With such devices, they will be able to hear you practicing storming the building from a long distance.

With a building siege, NO ONE can be shooting at the building from distance except designated snipers. The outside of the Beslan School was riddled with bullets from mass shooting at a school that contained more than a thousand hostages, including countless children, spread out in various locations. Also, this complete lack of fire discipline caused the deaths of a number of commandos who were shot from behind by overzealous locals. Men will do brave things to save hostages, especially children, but cannot and will not do them if being shot at from the front, and behind.

Things That Go Bang in the Night.
Anticipate the fact that all entry points of the school will be wired with explosives. If you do not have an EOD team or expert on your staff, develop a relationship with one from a neighboring jurisdiction. Make certain they have training and experience with more than just detonating suspect devices with a water cannon, as most law enforcement agencies do. The time may well come where they will be called upon to disarm intricate booby traps at doors and windows, or to rig their own charges to blow holes in walls to insert tactical teams, and through which to extract hostages. If no one in law enforcement has this ability, find someone with military training. You can always contact the nearest army base and seek their assistance in additional training.

There's No Time Like the Present.
When a group of terrorists take a school or other public place, there are a number of things that all must be done "first." One of the most important, however, is to immediately establish a contingency assault plan. Have a clear, standing order of what every person is to do in the event of an unexpected catastrophic event – a triggering event - including simple dictates on when teams will "go" on their own upon observing the occurrence of that event. These rules of engagement must be clear, concise and not subject to interpretation. Everyone must know when to "go" on their own, and when they should wait for an order. Moreover, there can only be one person on scene with the authority to issue that order. Be ready to assault at any moment. Terrorists may choose to initiate their own agenda and timetable. Remember, if they have no discernible plan or demands for their

own extraction, they intend to die in there. And they do not intend to die alone. You must be ready to respond immediately to the killing of hostages.

Once the contingency assault plan is in place, begin work on an assault plan.

Tactical Assault Plan.

Develop a tactical assault plan as quickly as possible. Though it may not appear so to many in the West, every Russian military person I met with was adamant that in doing this, it is absolutely essential to account for the percentage of victims as a result of that plan. Even while insisting that the use of Mouse Hole charges is a viable and necessary tactic, the government forces were intent on assessing whether any hostages would be injured by the explosion, and did their best to place them in a way that would provide them the tactical advantage they needed, while putting the victims at as little risk as possible. Though the Russians do not have an established number or percentage of predictable losses that dictates whether an assault will be attempted or not, they are deeply, almost soul-wrenchingly concerned over the fate of those innocents. The number of young men who gave their lives using their bodies as shields for the children is proof of that.

The Assault.

Once the decision to assault is made – whether as a reaction to a triggering event or as a surprise attack - you must go in like Delta and SEAL Six. This means *maximum force of violence.* There can be no holding back, no hesitation, no stopping, and never a withdrawal. A lesson that was learned from Columbine, as children and one teacher lay bleeding to death while SWAT teams painstakingly cleared and secured every part of a large school, is that where children are involved, concern for personal safety of the assault force must assume a far lower priority than normal. There are worse things than dying; such as watching close to two hundred children being shot, blown up and burned to death, or walking among their small lifeless bodies in the aftermath, wondering why you are alive but they will never have their chance in life. When you assault, hit the building hard, move as quickly through it as possible, and toward the sound of battle, or the known positions of terrorists. If good building floor plans are available, develop phase lines to provide safety from friendly fire when using multiple, simultaneous assaults. Most importantly, once the assault begins, American law enforcement must realize that at that moment, and until that battle is ended, they are no longer police but soldiers in a war.

After making my first presentation on Beslan for the Minnesota State Fire Chiefs Association in Minneapolis - "A Terrorism Symposium: Sustaining Our Vigilance – Now More Than Ever" - just a few days before returning to that school, I was approached by Brooklyn Park Police Lieutenant Steve Pearson. Lt. Pearson was in charge of police security for the conference, in addition to being an internationally known bomb and drug dog trainer. He came up to me the morning after my evening lecture. Handsome, with a wry smile and ready wit, he became quickly serious about the issue of American police storming a building in which hostages are being held. He told me that with regard to my comments on the tactical necessity and propriety of Alpha and Vympel having entered the Nord-Ost Theater and put a single round in the head of every terrorist, including those who appeared to be unconscious from the gas, he did not believe any American cop would take such action. In my speech I had stated that, despite the fact the international news media had vilified the Russian assault teams for this conduct, it had been completely necessary. I said I was content in the knowledge that American forces would do it, only better: using two bullets instead of one. Perhaps this showed the biases of my own professional experiences, more weighted toward military than law enforcement in tactical training and planning. Lt. Pearson told me that after my talk he spoke to at least a dozen cops at the conference from different departments. To a person, every single one of them said that not only would they have never considered doing it, but that their departments would have never allowed it.

In the case of Nord-Ost, a group of rescuers entered a building containing hostages, with terrorists, perhaps, asleep from gas that had not even rendered all of the hostages asleep. These terrorists had their hands on the detonators of belt bombs containing several kilograms each of high explosives wrapped in nails, screws, bolts and nuts. The very notion that the rescuers would not have immediately eliminated the ability of these terrorists to give a quick yank on the handles of these bombs, in the only way certain to neutralize them, was frightening to me. American law enforcement, and perhaps more importantly the American public, the legal system and the news media, have got to get it through their heads that such situations are not pedestrian level criminal episodes committed by the socially misunderstood, where less-than-lethal force should be used and a suspect afforded all his rights. These are attacks on American soil and American citizens by enemy combatants. Rather than the least possible amount of force, the greatest force available must be brought to bear against them if the lives of the innocent are to be saved, and the deaths of the rescuers are to be prevented.[32] National legislation must be passed granting all responders to a terrorist siege – once that status has been declared by the appropriate authority – to use deadly force with full immunity from civil and criminal prosecution.

Even federal courts have acknowledged the different nature of these combatants and the legal process which they are due. Law enforcement, if called upon, must recognize that these will not be crime scenes whose evidence must be painstakingly preserved, but battle scenes which do not, and will not, allow rescuers the luxury of worrying for even a moment about the existence of sufficient proof for a conviction. We cannot forget that the terrorists do not plan on sticking around for the trial.

---

[32] See also definition of terrorism at 18 USC Section 2331. The State Department definition is "Premeditated, politically motivated violence perpetrated against noncombatant targets by subnational groups or clandestine agents, usually intended to influence an audience." Also see, "The National Strategy for Combating Terrorism," February 2003 at www.whitehouse.gov and he State Department's annual report, "Patterns of Global Terrorism," at www.state.gov.

In planning rescue operations of this type, the Russian Special Forces always estimate they will lose three to five men for every terrorist killed. To all of you in the combat arms professions, stop for a moment and imagine what that means. Imagine the courage it takes for those men to go willingly into a conflagration in which their own superiors believe their chances for survival are that bad; and yet, in which they still fully expect ultimate victory. While the Russians have far exceeded those statistics in all of their operations against terrorists, the numbers serve as a reminder that they are planning an assault, a battle, under difficult circumstances in an impossible war. And when it happens here – again - we must all give the heroes of our own law enforcement, and the military, all of the freedom they need to win that battle. And we must give them our support. Just as we did for too short a time after the 11th of September 2001.

Intelligence gathering, surveillance and counter-surveillance.

There are a number of ways in which law enforcement must expand its strategic and tactical approaches to terrorist situations. One of the first, and most important, is in surveillance and counter-surveillance. The Russian experts I met with stressed that everyone must realize that in a hostage siege such as Beslan, the terrorists inside the school are not the only ones present. Even in the case of the seemingly daily suicide bomber in Israel, that person does not act alone but has command, support and observation teams nearby. For this reason the Israelis have developed an operational approach which has their own teams sweeping through a several block radius immediately upon the commission of such an act. At Beslan, the terrorists did, indeed, have numerous associates in the crowd around the school, at observation points in surrounding buildings, and elsewhere in the city. American law enforcement must have its own trained surveillance and counter-surveillance teams in any crowd of onlookers surrounding the site of siege or attack.

In a terrorist siege local law enforcement must have sufficient covert operations or undercover capability and officer resources to place important intelligence gatherers in the crowd surrounding the school perimeter, or to observe area buildings, in the event associates of the hostage-taking terrorists are in the area and developing intelligence. Counter-intelligence, which now labors under the term *Foreign Internal Defense*, is crucial, and those cast with its responsibility must be vigilant. They should take photos of the crowd to be developed, blown up and studied. The British SAS, renowned for its own surveillance and counter-surveillance skills, teaches that hundreds of such photos must be taken and studied. For what you cannot see while "group looking" at a crowd, will become obvious as you study picture after picture. What to the living eye is just a sea of humanity, to the lens is a moment frozen in time, thus allowing the identification of the same person in the same position talking on a cell phone, hour after hour and day after day. As well, someone who reacts quickly to a camera pointed in his direction, attempting to turn or hide his face, is clearly someone you will want to talk to.

Counter-surveillance agents should also be schooled in basic sniper principles. This will allow them to find those areas further away that offer some of the better points of observation. The terrorists will not use the best points, knowing that military or law enforcement snipers will find them quickly, setting up their own positions there. But the second and third tier choices will be utilized. Counter-sniper training will allow you to find those other positions, directing your agents' focus outward, toward the surrounding buildings and other points providing decent elevation and clear lines of sight. Keep in mind that these support terrorists do not need or even want to be able to see the entire scene, but merely the one point or arc of view they are assigned. It may be that at predetermined times, one of the terrorists inside the siege building will go to a designated position to communicate through prearranged signals to one of these support people. Some will be placed in buildings looking outward or across at law enforcement, not inward at the barricade site.

As resources in all law enforcement agencies are tight, and budgets strained, many may be able to draw on civilian support teams or reserve officer programs that already exist. People conscripted into providing this assistance should be as thoroughly vetted as officers themselves. However, taking advantage of such civilian volunteers will expand the capability of the department and provide it with a valuable tool in responding to a terrorist incident. It is important to remember that if found by the surrounding crowd, these terrorist observers may be killed on the spot by angry mobs, as at Beslan, denying police critical intelligence.

Law enforcement must also be prepared to access other types of information. In the intelligence community, TECHINT is the term applied to technologically obtained intelligence or information. In the case of a terrorist siege of some duration in America, we must be prepared for exactly that same effort. The Russians correctly point out that not only do American intelligence agencies develop substantial intelligence by monitoring and tracking Internet sources, websites, chat rooms and email, but even schools and law enforcement have learned to do this in the aftermath of Columbine. If terrorists seize a school, we must recognize that they will not be isolated and alone, making decisions only according to the best judgment of the leaders of the terrorist team. Those leaders - though they may be somewhat highly placed in the organization - have already been sacrificed by the leadership above them. Those top-level leaders will not risk the team in the school losing its nerve, or otherwise making decisions or judgments which put at risk the goals they are attempting to achieve through the siege. If the government shuts down telephone and even cell phone communications, or if the terrorists are afraid they can be monitored, they will resort to Internet communications either through computers they will bring with them or the school's computer systems. This will provide crucial access to their intercourse, and the ability to attain this access must be developed and ready in advance of an assault on our schools.

Access ventilation systems.

One of the things the Russian Spetsnaz do well in terrorist-hostage situations is determine unconventional and innovative methods for gaining access to the barricade site. This includes not only buildings, but buses, trains and the like. To preserve the effectiveness of these methods they cannot be listed here. However, in training with Vityaz, I have been amazed at the creativity and speed of their operations to storm both buses and airplanes, often using such simple devices as 2 x 6 inch planks which are smashed into the windows, then laid on the ledge while commandos race up them, ducking inside with weapons at the ready. They have applied this same ingenuity to other means of gaining access to buildings. They blow Mouse Holes into walls, come in through sewers and look for opportunities through ventilation systems. While the ventilation ducts themselves – or any of the other avenues of ingress – are not always solutions, it is important that all possibilities be explored. Each siege must be approached from the perspective that there is a way in that will surprise the terrorists. You only have to find it. The Russian elite units have developed many ingenious methods of entering buildings, often requiring no more equipment than a board, a pole, or each other. American forces can be no less innovative.

Where possible, look for answers to these puzzles for the buildings you have identified as prime targets now, well in advance of a take-over. At each school ask the maintenance servicemen. This also helps you develop rapport with critical school personnel, whose constant presence and acute eye for the condition of the building will act as an early warning system in the event it comes under surveillance or is probed for vulnerabilities. With only one exception, no one knows the school and its secrets better than these men. The exception to that are the children. Find out where the more innovative and mischievous ones have been caught doing things or hiding in the inner recesses of the structure. Talk to them. By communicating adequate appreciation for their deviousness, there is no telling what you might learn.

Access building communication system.

Though terrorists are increasingly sophisticated in both their methods and equipment, you can afford to leave no stone unturned. If a school is taken, the fixed communication system must be accessed. You will need to know where cables are run, where the system is centralized and how to invade it. You will need to be able to do this surreptitiously, so as not to incite a hostile and violent reaction, which could cause the hostages to suffer. Though it is less and less likely that any terror group would use the in-house communications of the school, you never know and cannot afford to miss the intelligence-gathering opportunity it would present.

Call experts for assistance.

As discussed in detail earlier, once the siege is on and you have some understanding of who the terrorists are, where they are from, what languages they speak and religion they belong to, when you have heard their initial demands and have developed some idea of their ultimate goals, get in touch with your network of experts. Get them to the scene and have them brief you and all other critical personnel – especially negotiators – as to what you are up against, and how the situation is likely to play out. As Sun Tzu wrote two and a half thousand years ago, "If you know the enemy and know yourself, you need not fear the results of a hundred battles."

Helicopters on station at all times.

If you are going to use helicopters to aid in an assault, they must be on station at all times. That means in the air, not sitting passively at a nearby airport. If there is even a possibility of using fast rope teams to assault the roof, at least one helicopter must be in the air at all times as well. Do not wait until *you* are ready to assault, as the terrorists may push your timetable up.

Do not separate jointly operating agencies.

All responding agencies must be integrated, and work together. When using departments or units with little to no joint training, or operating experience, do not deploy them in such a fashion as to keep them completely separate. Vympel and Alpha rotated "on duty" status, back and forth, taking turns surrounding and securing the school. When the assault occurred Alpha was either on stand-down or training at the remote building, and took quite some time to respond. Once it did there was little synergism between the two. Rus and SOBR were not integrated at all. The best approach in the U.S. would be to assign to each post an equal number of police from, for example, two different departments. Only rotate half off and on at a time, keeping half the team to brief and re-integrate those just coming back on post. This type of rotation ensures experiential and situational overlap. This will allow the officers to develop some working relationship between the departments, and also allow for continuity of on-scene observations and reports by never standing an entire team down, replacing it with one that has had no information or experience with the situation throughout the previous shift.

Negotiation vs. Non-Negotiation Dilemma.

When this happens in the U.S., it will be local law enforcement responding initially. It will take the FBI's HRT hours to arrive, and still more hours for Delta or SEAL Six, if they are called in at all. It is erroneously believed that the Posse Comitatus Act prohibits U.S. military from functioning on U.S. soil. This is a holdover from the early colonists' experience with British soldiers in our towns and homes. In recent years, however, drug trafficking and terrorism have started to blur those lines, seeing our military aiding America's law enforcement efforts. Since then such joint operation efforts have migrated into the areas of global organized crime and homeland defense, always with the requirement that for any operation on U.S. soil the tasked military unit be placed under the command of civilian law enforcement. In a terrorist siege inside America, this will be the FBI. Whether a terrorist siege such as Beslan will result in our best counter-terror units being deployed to save American children remains to be seen.

Russia's 5-Part Tactical Plan[33] will have to be implemented. When all this occurs, the U.S. will be confronted with a conundrum for which it is completely unprepared. The U.S., much as with Russia, has a federal policy against negotiating with terrorists. Once it is determined that a hostage taking incident is a terrorist one, and not one of civilian crime, the federal government will assume jurisdiction. This means agencies like the FBI and FEMA will be in charge. Military units like the fifty Weapons of Mass Destruction, Civil Support Teams (WMD/CSTs) will be deployed under FBI authority. Yet, in all situations of hostage taking within the United States – whether involving local or federal law enforcement – the strategy, the doctrine, indeed the inviolable rule, has always been to negotiate. Unless hostages are being killed, we will always negotiate with them. But the question is, how will the contradiction in policies be resolved in the event of a Beslan-type incident within our borders?

The U.S. government has done an admirable job of holding fast to its policy of non-negotiation in its dealings with terrorists outside the borders of the U.S. The terrorist incidents we have seen inside the borders have been ones of immediate violence, which have come without warning, leaving no opportunity to negotiate. The only tactical aspects have been the clean up afterward. Yet what will we do when everything in the law enforcement and FBI playbook is based on negotiating with hostage takers, doing everything possible to quietly resolve a stand-off, but their bosses in Washington refuse to allow them to do so? Indeed, can the president afford to refuse to negotiate with terrorists in our own country – holding our own tiny children's lives in his hands – while all of America clamors for nothing more than the safety of its innocents? What will happen when our own thousands of armed citizens refuse to stand down when ordered, and form a perimeter around a school; not to attack the terrorists, but

---

[33] (1) Negotiate to stabilize the situation; (2) Negotiate to draw time out to prepare an assault plan; (3) Develop an assault plan; (4) Practice the assault; and (5) Assault.

to protect them from American law enforcement and military? How delicate is our balance on this precipice, and how much of a push by terrorists will it take to see our policies and tactics topple over?

And what of the American public? We are a nation of terrified people, who have already witnessed the tragic consequences of our law enforcement unprepared for such situations as Waco, Ruby Ridge and Columbine. No one has forgotten the debacle at Desert One in Iran in 1980. We have witnessed in recent years our military's inability to quickly track and locate such threats as Noriega and bin Laden, to deal decisively with the insurgency in Baghdad, or even to prevent Navy SEALs from drowning in botched insertions in Grenada. We have learned to have scant faith in our intelligence community's ability to warn of 9-11s, the state of WMDs in Iraq, or to proactively address a predictable Islamic insurgency in Iraq upon the toppling of its despotic leader.

We must be prepared for the very real possibility that America's people would not stand idly by and allow federal and state police to make their own decisions regarding the lives of innocent children in a Beslan-type siege on American soil. Who in Oklahoma would not have given anything they owned if Timothy McVeigh had been willing to negotiate and possibly resolve his grievances peacefully, before blowing a truck loaded with more than 5,000 pounds of ammonium nitrate under the Alfred P. Murrah Federal Building in Oklahoma City? What parent in Littleton, Colorado does not wish that Harris and Klebold had simply taken hostages and then allowed a negotiated resolution? And which of those parents will have any faith in local police and the FBI the next time their children are being killed, or being threatened with death; remembering all too clearly an overwhelmed Colorado sheriff stammering into a news camera about being outnumbered and outgunned, while hundreds of cops and federal agents held their positions outside the school, listening to the screams of children being mowed down by two other children?

Is it even possible that in the face of all these grisly outcomes, Americans will tolerate the government's refusal to negotiate with terrorists when our children's lives are at stake? This is a reality – and a predictable one – for which the U.S. government and both federal and local law enforcement may be unprepared. How will they deal with surging masses of terrified parents, positioned behind the police and military, all exercising their 2nd Amendment right to bear the very arms they are empowered to own? What will be the resulting conflagration when the severed heads of children are thrown from windows due to the president's refusal to meet initial demands, or to communicate directly with the terrorists as they demanded of Putin at Beslan? All of America must prepare for this, and decide now what our policy will be. Once done, we must all then be prepared to live with its consequences.

And what of America's approach to negotiations in general? The entire FBI and law enforcement approach to hostage – or critical incident negotiations as it is now called – must be reviewed and remodeled. It is inapplicable in regard to the current threat our country faces. It is solely based on an ethnocentric approach to psychology and American criminal behavior. Law enforcement must be circumspect in allowing psychologists to dictate negotiations once a hostage taking occurs. Trained to diagnose and empathize, many may not be up to the task of dealing with professional torturers and assassins. The terrorists we must prepare for do not, and will not, fit neatly into the DSM, the *Diagnostic and Statistical Manual*, upon which mental health professionals rely to categorize, and thus understand, those they confront. When dealing with this new threat, the DSM will not give anyone a useful or predictive psychological profile. Their profile has already been cast by countless acts of terrorism. They intend to kill people. What more do we need to know?

Terrorists are not like conventional American criminals. In fact, they are not criminals at all, but enemy combatants intent on destroying our country and our people. In hostage or barricade situations, the criminals for whom our current negotiation policies have been developed tend to quickly realize their hostages are more of a burden than anything else. They want to get rid of them; and after a couple of hours they want to see a peaceful resolution to the standoff.

The people we must now prepare for are religious zealots, brainwashed automatons, whose very indoctrination training and seething hatred for us, and for their hostages, will render them impervious to the best-intentioned psychological pandering. In many cases the terrorists have been raised from birth to accept and even yearn to see human death and suffering – particularly the death and suffering of non-believers. Of infidels. They are cult created psychotics, artificially constructed sociopaths for whom hostages serve their very purpose and whom they *do* want to kill. Only they want to kill them at the time and manner of their choosing for maximum effect. They have already chosen the place.

Russian Justice Ministry official Mikhail Ryabko points out that the terrorists at Beslan had no initial demands at all. Russian officials, recognizing that it is normal in every hijacking or hostage situation for there to be initial demands, were unprepared to deal with a complete lack of requests. This gave them nothing to work with. He elucidates that, whether political or financial, everyone in a terrorist siege tries to get some type of benefit. But in a situation where the government cannot convey any benefit to the hostage takers, it means they already have everything they want. And that does not bode well for a peaceful resolution. Know what it will mean if you confront silence from the hostage-takers when attempting to initiate communication with them as the Russians confronted at Beslan; and what you will do if it continues.

Ryabko further explains that it is exceedingly difficult to "fight a situation when the people you are fighting are under a cult." He believes it important for Americans to recognize that some people use psychotropic drugs to prepare themselves "to do anything asked or ordered of them; but these terrorists are the most dangerous because they are ready for anything, and can and will take life easily without them." Their religious faith and zealotry is their drug, and there is none stronger. Negotiators must be ready for groups who see their barricade and hostage seizure just like – as one Russian officer articulated – a team of our own Green Berets carrying out a mission. Hardly a receptive group to typical negotiating techniques.

In some cases the terrorists may look for their own escape, but this cannot be relied on. Increasingly, in recent years they have no exit strategy; they never planned one and didn't need to. They intended to die. American law enforcement and government officials must recognize that for the terrorists, the only acceptable "peaceful" resolution involves them escaping. This has happened time and again in Russia, where they have negotiated and obtained air and ground transport and a safe corridor into Chechnya. Yet in the United States there is no nearby safe haven for them to flee to. Mexico and Canada will not accept them, and they cannot transgress the oceans that border us to the east and west. Furthermore, since 9-11 we will never give anyone aircraft in which to make an escape. And they know all this. They will not allow themselves to be sent to an American prison, and there is no negotiating an escape for them. They already know what the outcome will be. Out of all those involved in such a scenario, we are – perhaps – the only ones refusing to accept what that outcome will be.

They also know the United States' negotiating techniques. Every single one of them has been trained in what to expect from American law enforcement and its negotiators, and how to respond at every turn. "Active listening" skills, as used by the FBI and taught to law enforcement all over America, are not going to cause them to think someone on the other end of the phone really feels their pain or cares about all the injustices life has wreaked upon them. They will use these against us. They will laugh at what, to them, is the pathetic obviousness of it all, while using it to their advantage. We can no more get them to feel something for the hostages than a negotiator could sit on a phone and persuade a pig farmer to recognize the error of his ways, to convert to vegetarianism and not slaughter his hogs at market time.

Everything we do must be reworked. We must realize – as the Russians have – that negotiations in a terrorist–hostage siege only serve the purpose of allowing the assault team time to prepare to storm the building, to gather intelligence, to get everything in place. Negotiators can only stretch the time until the inevitable happens. From this point on, in terrorist situations negotiators can only be looked to as a tool of the tactical unit; no longer can they be a possible alternative to it. If successfully utilized, they may allow us to get a few of the hostages out, while the terrorists look to buy time as well. This may lower the ultimate body count a bit, but that will be all. Ultimately, in such scenarios the negotiator's job will become – as Russian Spetsnaz doctrine dictates – to talk the terrorist over to the window.

The terrorists, for their part, know this and will play the game too. They will release the odd hostage from time to time, knowing that so long as they do the authorities will not assault. They will continue to do this until they feel they have got everything in place on their side: whatever that might be. For this reason, even this use of negotiations has its consequences. Of all the criticisms laid at the feet of the Russian government and military for Beslan, in the aftermath the only real lament of some of the people from that town was that the government did not assault right away. Using negotiations to drag out the ordeal in the faint hope of a happy ending did allow the government forces some time to prepare. But, just as important, it provided the terrorists much needed time to establish their own plan, build and fortify defenses within the school, and wire the entire thing with explosives. Perhaps the days when we could afford to stall off the tough decisions in the hope that things would all turn out swell are over, and we must now invest ourselves in being prepared to assault at once. Perhaps many traditional negotiating techniques have become obsolete in light of the current war we are waging and must be prepared for. Therefore we must begin developing new methods for talking to this new enemy, adding to what we already know and use.

Still, in every terror-hostage taking we are compelled to see that the game is played out. For, to the terrorists, that is exactly what it is. We must understand that there will be a body count. These people are never going to just come out with their hands up: every negotiator's goal; indeed, every negotiator's dream. If our tactical forces attack right away, taking away the terrorists' opportunity to fortify their positions, then the presence of negotiators becomes inconsequential. If the decision is made to live with such increased fortifications, then the negotiators' only purpose is to stall for time. That is all the Russian negotiators were really doing, and everyone knew it. At least the terrorists and the troops both knew it.

As difficult as it is, it is important that all potential and future hostage-takers see that we will not accede to their demands; instead we will always fight. The negotiators must realize that they cannot save all of the hostages, but they can help save some. This is why you do not see hostage-taking situations in Israel anymore. Today the terrorists just walk in and blow themselves and others up. They do this because they realize that is how it will end up anyway: with them dead. Israeli commandos will move in quickly and kill them. America must begin exploring other tactics that offer at least some promise of success. The rule in U.S. law enforcement is never to bring family members of the hostage-taker to him. But the Israelis, and now the Russians, use this as a regularly employed successful tactic. Immediately upon identifying any of the terrorists, their families are rounded up and taken to the siege. Only they are brought there with the threat to their misguided relation that each will be killed in front of them; one for every hostage killed. In Israel the government confiscates the property of the terrorist's family, and they are thrown into the street, punished for the crimes of their son or daughter. Since Beslan, federal legislation in Russia has even been quietly introduced by the Minister of Justice in an executive session of the Duma, the lower house of Parliament. According to Justice Minister Chaika, even if the terrorists accede to this tactic and surrender, the government should still destroy their families' homes to send a message to all others contemplating the same thing.

While these methods may be constitutionally untenable in America, they reflect the fact that there are tactics which can and must be devised to deal with future terrorist assaults, and which have a better chance of success than the methods we currently employ. None of them will be gentle, but they are necessary. For who can name a terrorist-hostage situation in which the terrorist actually did release his hostages and walk sobbing into the arms of law enforcement, as American criminals do?

But this is not to say there is nothing the terrorists want, even though those desires may not fall within the more typical hostage model. Russians involved with the Beslan negotiations and assault plan are universal in emphasizing that for American preparedness, we "must always remember, one of the first goals of terrorists is to get information to the news media." When asking military leaders who were involved in Beslan and other hostage situations borne of the Chechen War what their best recommendations are for America to be prepared to deal with a similar incident, they all stress that our negotiators must realize that all terrorists want to be famous and seen as heroes. However, they are adamant that the negotiators must make them realize that they will get no press, no fame, and that no information will get out that will make them heroes. They must be made to understand that they will "die like pigs," with the public never having known much about what they did or wanted.

This approach, in a nation such as the U.S., with its 1st Amendment and institutional and unquestioning acceptance of the media's "right to know" everything, would have inherent problems. But that does not mean there is nothing to learn from it. In such a situation in America, it would be more important than ever before for police to control media's access to the scene and the terrorists. Whether through severing the terrorists' communications capability, or agreements with media representatives, the flow of information would have to be dramatically limited. This would defeat the terrorists' goal of gaining broad publicity, and eliminate their ability to gather important intelligence through their own viewing of media reports on government response. In doing this, however, police and public alike would have to be ready for early hostage executions, for the terrorists will then have their first demand: access to the media. If we cave to that demand, we will have just created a far worse situation, guaranteeing the deaths of many more hostages.

If media control is accomplished, and if we prove capable of overcoming the immediate consequences of this tactical approach, the terrorists would be forced to begin listening to our police, rather than us listening to them. If we can determine that the families of the terrorists attacking us are in the Middle East, diplomatic pressure can and should be brought to bear on the host country to round them up, threatening them with whatever sanctions are legally tenable in that system of jurisprudence.

Russians largely believe that American preparedness and elite units would have been able to successfully handle Beslan. However, U.S. law enforcement, military, and school communities are turning a blind eye to a terrible reality if they are content to sit back and preen in the confidence of that preparedness. For there is no school in the United States, including our military academies, that would have had the personnel, numbers, weapons and training necessary to thwart 50 trained terrorists armed with automatic weapons. It is true that the Russian government, police and military committed a number of errors at Beslan. Many of these were due to culture, doctrine and tactics peculiar to that country and would not have been committed by our professionals in the U.S. Despite that, even if each and every one of those things had been done right, the outcome at that school would likely not have been any different at all. That is the thing that frightens me the most.

* * * * *

In Russia the emphasis has been more on the term *anti*-terrorism than *counter*-terrorism. This does not imply a complete distinction between preventing terrorism and responding to it. I met with a former SEAL recently. This man was a plank owner in SEAL Team Six, and one of the original Red Cell members. To his mind, there was no such thing as anti-terrorism, because, as he put it, "You can never prevent a terrorist act from occurring; the best you can do is prepare how you will react to it."

To the Russians, anti-terrorism implies exactly that preparation. It means hardening targets, training, conducting intelligence and anticipating the very terror attacks that are likely to occur. If we examine terror attacks in the past – again applying Dave Grossman's axiom that the best predictor of future conduct is past behavior – then we are left with a clear picture of what those targets will be in the future, in America. From Israel, to Indonesia and Turkey, to the Philippines and Russia, the targets have been few. They include kidnappings, schools, discos, buses, subways, trains, trucks, ships, markets (malls), places of worship, planes and hospitals. Though this is not an exhaustive list, it provides real insight into the favorite targets of the terror groups we are up against. These are the things they have attacked, and will attack again. And most of these exist in virtually every part of the United States, no matter how small the town or remote the county. You may be in a rural county high up in the Rocky Mountains with no ships, but there you will have a municipal airport or ranchers with crop dusters,[34] cross country

---

[34] Crop dusters were one of the types of assault craft and bio-chemical weapon delivery platforms intelligence had indicated might be used subsequent to 9-11. In the months following those attacks, CIA officers and FBI agents canvassed the country, meeting with farmers and ranchers everywhere to alert them to this possibility.

trains every hour, buses and major bus routes, interstate shipments via semi-trailer, schools, a hospital and likely even a shopping mall. You may even have a big lake with a casino or restaurant on a large boat or ship, a target with precedent in the world.

As part of your anti-terrorism efforts, you must look at all of these potential targets now, and formulate your response to each. As with other aspects of anti-terrorism that have been discussed throughout this book, if 100 percent of the law enforcement agencies prepare their responses to 100 percent of the likely targets, we will most probably be ready for 100 percent of the future terror attacks in our country.

In accomplishing this, we must realize that no one can do it alone. Law enforcement officials must divest themselves of any elitist attitude they have, which preclude them from working effectively with the communities they serve. Know what your resources are and draw upon them now. Perhaps the single greatest asset in our anti-terrorism efforts comes from the mothers of school age children. The media has been making great hay of the social evolution of these women from "Soccer Moms" to their self-styled role as "Security Moms." Many might see the presence of insistent mothers walking their children into and out of schools everyday, holding their hands until the moment they are forced to leave them, as just more targets to combat-ready terrorists. But they are already serving a different and grander purpose. Just as the Russian terror experts I met with said, the best thing that can be done to be ready for an attack, or to prevent one altogether, is to be alert. To be prepared. The terror groups we must be prepared for conduct months of intelligence on numerous potential targets before selecting one. If they are presented with one school which sees scores of young mothers driving their children to school and walking them inside every morning – meeting them in the same way at the end of each day – ever alert and vigilante, they may just move on. There are too many schools that see bus loads of children driving up to drop off their charges, who are then left to wander into the building on their own. Other than the bus drivers, there are no – or few – adults outside surveying the school grounds, looking at the doorways to ensure no one is there who does not belong. The terrorists will choose the latter, and not the former, every time.

Whether these moms are watching out for traffic threats to the kids, logging the frequency of police presence around the school, the speed of cars through the school zone, or simply being alert to possible child molesters or even school bullies, the fact is they are there. They are there in number, and they are watching. They represent the single largest and most motivated security and intelligence force our country has. And they do not cost a single dollar. I can easily imagine the havoc these women could wreak on terrorists in this country if one of their schools were targeted. Unlike Beslan, as soon as the threat was perceived, some would be on their cell phones, calling local police and husbands, many of whom would be within seconds of the school with guns. Some, already in their vehicles, would escape while others rammed the groups of terrorists with their SUVs as they took positions around the school. Some might flee on foot, taking refuge in areas throughout the school. Still others, likely armed themselves, would simply pull their guns from ready purses and shoot some of them down.

No one can realistically believe that a small group of enraged mothers would be an effective counter-force to a larger group of heavily armed, well trained, jihadists taking over an American school. Nor that they would likely possess the skills to ascertain sophisticated surveillance activities. But just because you cannot do "everything" does not mean that you should not do what you are capable of. Terrorists are human, they make mistakes too; and if committed citizens like the mothers of our children are there every time they make a mistake in their plotting against our children, we will be able to stop them time and again. Also, with adequate training these same parents could have a significant and maybe even decisive effect on the success of an initial assault against a school, or provide important intelligence once the authorities arrived. All women should take a sex assault defense class at least once each year anyway, and twice is better. Not only do such classes provide important information on improvised weapons, but many teach their students to observe and mentally log descriptions of criminals or suspicious persons. From this training women can learn basic counter-surveillance techniques, how to move away from an aggressor, use of their cars as weapons and even firearms. Mothers who are serious about their "security" roll must provide themselves the necessary training to act in that capacity if and when the time comes. Companies like Archangel, and others, offer training in how to function as a hostage if ever taken, and how to gather important intelligence in case you are released early on. Just as I have described necessary training for American law enforcement and teachers in order to adequately deal with this new threat, so too must America's mothers prepare for the possibility.

Would these brave ladies likely die themselves? Absolutely. And we are no longer a country that can afford to treat as reckless those who take a stand, who refuse to let the evil aggressors have their way, all in the faint and naïve hope that if we all just do nothing it might turn out okay. 9-11 proved that is not the case. Beslan ensured that no one should ever believe that again. The words of Sergei Lisyuk should ring in our ears everyday for the rest of our lives: "There is going to be a battle. People will die." Some causes are worth dying for. The lives of our children and the freedom of our nation are chief among them. The character of Charley Waite, played by Kevin Costner in the movie *Open Range*, perhaps expressed it best: "There's a lot of things that gnaw at a man worse than dying." From this moment on, indeed since 9-11, we are all little more than passengers on United Flight 93 that crashed in a lonely field in western Pennsylvania. We can never again allow terrorists to take control, to gain a foothold, to achieve their ends. We must fight, and we must bring the fight immediately. If all we can do is die to save others, to act as a deterrent against future attacks, to show the world of shadowy Muslim extremists that we as a people speak with one voice in saying we will not go quietly into the night, then we will have had an impact grander than anything we could ever imagine. For without this, without our willingness to fight and to sacrifice, we are surely doomed.

These committed and fearless women - and everyone else in society who accepts this role and fulfills his or her duty to the safety of our community - will provide us with the knowledge, information and warning that we will need to prevent an attack if possible, and respond to one if necessary. Coupled with all other efforts of our police, government and military to prepare for the terror surely on its way once again, this will make us a most formidable opponent. Just as Sun Tzu wrote so long ago: "What enables the wise sovereign and the good general to strike and conquer, and achieve things beyond the reach of ordinary men, is *foreknowledge.*"

Chapter Sixteen

How Great the Threat?

Nye tak strashun Chyort, kak yevo maluyute

"The Devil is not so horrible as it exists in paintings."

— Old Russian Proverb

An America Unprepared. The problem up until now is that to most Americans – despite all of the terror attacks on our fellow citizens, on our property, and despite 9-11 – the very notion of Islamist extremists coming here to kill us remains a distant and unrealistic thought. The average person does not get up every day and seriously contemplate that the bridge he is about to drive across on his way to work, or the office building he is about to walk into, the mall or restaurant she will have lunch in, the school or day care her children will merrily clamor into that morning, may well be the target of a terrorist attack. Moreover, Americans have not been given the information needed – in the context required – to recognize this as not only a realistic and serious concern, but an inevitable one.

For most Americans Beslan is something distant, far away and unreal. We tend to view most things that way, that happen to others around the world. When 9-11 occurred thousands of Russians placed flowers outside the U.S. Embassy in Moscow and wept for our loss, for what that atrocity meant for all of humanity. I received phone calls and emails from friends in countries all over the world. When Beslan happened we noticed it merely because it periodically interrupted the Kobe Bryant sex assault trial on TV. We did not grieve for the Russian children as they had cried for us. It is beyond most Americans' conscious thinking that there is an inextricable connection between the very basis of Islam, the attacks on the Pentagon and World Trade Center, Afghanistan and Beslan. A direct and causal connection exists between terrorists' rage at the West and the war they are today waging in Southern Russia. Most of us are incapable of realistically appreciating that Beslan was little more than a dry run of operations they intend to soon be running on American soil, against American targets, American children.

Few Americans have any substantive knowledge of the history of Islam, and the growth of modern radical extremist Muslim groups in the modern world. For if they did, they would see a direct and incontrovertible path of violence headed in our direction, not unlike the visible trail of a missile as it soars unerringly toward a great jet airplane flying so far above the fray that it does not think to look for threats racing toward its soft underbelly. In order to understand the threat we face today, what the terrorists are planning for America this very minute, some grasp of the history of Islam and its impact on the world is essential. As Dr. Mary Conroy often lectures: "A people without a knowledge of history, is a people with amnesia." For too long we have suffered this malady, and it has now proven to be a deadly affliction.

It has become popular and politically correct to publicly tout Islam as the "religion of peace." Though the vast majority of Muslims live peaceful lives, it remains a faith steeped in a foundation of violence. Today, there is no other single common factor in the wholesale slaughter of innocent men, women and children around the world than the perpetrators' conscription into the Islamic faith. And when a terror attack occurs, the average, everyday Muslims living in America are all-too-quickly seen on television decrying the non-Islamic community for blaming them for the acts of the terrorists. Their only response is that the consequences of the terrorist attacks should not be taken out on them. In this, they too prey upon the sensitivity of Americans to claims of discrimination and bigotry. Strangely, what seems to never be heard is an outright condemnation of the terrorists' atrocities. For a single religion to spawn so much hatred, so much inhuman capacity to commit violence against the innocent – even if those innocent are the citizens of a perceived enemy nation or culture – there must be a cause. That cause cannot be the preaching of tolerance and peace so often ascribed to it.

Muhammed's Early Life. The religion of Islam was founded by Muhammed in the 7th century A.D. Born about 570 A.D. in the city of Mecca, Muhammed, or the "Praised One," was seen as a prophet of Allah, or God. During the years of his life and his ministry, his commitment was not to love, peace and understanding, as was the case with the historical Jesus Christ almost six centuries his senior. Rather, much of Muhammed's life was dedicated to a never-ending search for vindication, for revenge against those who had disdained him in his early years.

The term *Arab* refers to a collection of peoples from the Middle East and the Arabian Peninsula. Though largely genetically unrelated, this broad term came to include all the various tribes from that region of the world. Up until the time of Muhammed's birth, many Arabs believed they were descended from Ishmael, son of Abraham of the Old Testament. These were the Moaddites, and Muhammed's ancestors fell into this category. Most of the rest claimed ancestry from the upper lands of the southwestern corner of the Arabian Peninsula, which is modern day Yemen.[35] This distinction between the two groups of people haling from this region of the world would continue until modern day.

---

[35] For an excellent history and analysis of Muhammed and the Islamic faith, see Serge Trifkovic, *The Sword of the Prophet: Islam History, Theology, Impact on the World*, Boston, MA: Regina Orthodox Press, Inc., 2002.

Despite the seeming similarity, the two groups historically viewed each other with some enmity, mostly due to the common disconnect between societies of settled farmers (the Yemenites) and those of the nomads (in this case the Moaddites), not unlike the schism between the mountain and lowland Chechen clans. Within the custom of the nomadic people of the Arabian Desert, vengeance, the blood feud, and an unrepentant willingness to decimate rivals was prevalent. Often violence served to recompense injury to one's honor, to gain or retain such possessions as livestock and pasture, as well as win women. In many ways in that early time, aggression was a mainstay of social relations. So long as it was committed against those outside the clan, robbery and murder were not even looked on as being inherently evil or wrong. However, in the time before Muhammed and the growth of Islam, Arab women were free persons, eligible to select their own mates, own and dispose of property, and even divorce.

Muhammed was born Abu'l Qasim in the city of Mecca. His father, Abd'Allah, had died some months before his birth. Haling from a poor family, his recently widowed mother would face severe struggles to survive with her only child. She suffered from hallucinations, and died when Muhammed was six. At that time, Muhammed's rearing fell to a grandfather, one Abdel-Mottaleb, who passed away some three years later in 579. Muhammed had a wealthy merchant-uncle, Abu Taleb, who then accepted the responsibility of raising him, turning him into a camel driver for his caravans. Thus, growing up on the fringes of a society that largely scorned him, author and religious historian Serge Trifkovic, writes, "Muhammad's later bitterness towards the establishment of his native city and its social and spiritual structure reflected the sense of powerlessness felt by a resentful young man."[36]

Much of Muhammed's early adulthood – and later religious doctrine – was defined by a battle between a group of Ethiopians

---

[36] Ibid., at 25.

who threatened Mecca and an assemblage of defenders commanded by his uncle. At the age of 25, the sight of bloody combat so terrified him that he fled the battlefield. Ostracized and criticized for his cowardice, he was forced to make a living as a shepherd, the lowest position on the social strata. Over time he became an assistant to a traveling cloth merchant, which found him in the city of Hayacha. There he met a 40 year old widow, Khadija, and went to work for her; this time as a camel driver. He quickly ingratiated himself with the wealthy Khadija, and eventually became her business supervisor, and then her partner. He later agreed to marry her. For the next ten years he focused his efforts on growing her business ventures and gaining wealth by his own devices.

The Creation of Islam. While he enjoyed a fairly affluent life, Muhammed was continually outraged at his abandonment and rejection by his own people in Mecca. This was fueled by his own clansmen, who deemed his social ascendance via an exploitative marriage to an elder woman to be an embarrassment. With free time being the benefit of a successful business, Muhammed was known to spend much of it wandering the hills around Mecca, perhaps meditating, perhaps plotting the comeuppance of his own people. Whether he suffered the hallucinations of his mother is unknown. What is known is that Muhammed did spend a great deal of time meditating in a trancelike state. At the age of 40, in 610 A.D., Muhammed confided to Khadija that while he was sleeping a great being had appeared before him. In later versions of this experience, he claimed the vision to have been the angel Gabriel, who told him that he, Muhammed, was the Messenger of God, or *rasul Allah*. He later adopted the title of Prophet or *Nabi*, and from that point until his death he benefited from revelations that he claimed were the direct messages of God. Sometimes during his revelations, Muhammed manifested physical symptoms such as hearing certain noises, perspiring or falling unconscious. These would lead historians years later to question whether he suffered from epilepsy.

Throughout his life as a prophet, Muhammed and his followers held the messages he delivered from God in their collective memory, rarely reducing them to writing. During the time before Islam, the predominant deity was the moon god, who was referred to as *Al-ilah,* chief among the gods. Over time this reference would be shortened to *Allah.* Muhammed's adoption of this single, known and comfortable term for the supreme deity made conversion of his polytheistic tribesmen all the easier, effectively merging more than 300 recognized gods into a single, supreme being: "There is only one God, Allah, and Muhammed is his Prophet."[37] Muhammed's first convert was his wife, Khadija. What limited knowledge Muhammed had of the then-spreading Christian faith allowed him to interpret his own messages from God as those of the Christian and Jewish prophets, like Moses. He argued his divine authorization to deliver these messages to all others. It was not until three full years from his first revelation that he began to receive regular messages from Allah, prompting him to begin preaching in private. By 613 he had gathered enough of a following of listeners, and had gained enough confidence, that he began conducting his ministry overtly. At first his teachings were more suggestive than commanding. He attempted to persuade all who would listen to submit themselves to Allah, to know the end of the world and Judgment Day, and to recognize the rewards of the pure and the damnation of sinners.

The growth of his flock was slow, with the next converts after his wife being Zaid, his slave and adopted son, and his cousin Ali, the son of Abu Taleb, the wealthy uncle who had raised him. Abu Bakr, his life long friend and companion, followed in the faith. By the time his following reached 39 individuals, mostly young men, they were meeting at a house together, often praying as a group. It was at this time that the practice of touching their heads to the ground in subservience

---

[37] Muhammed would later abrogate this section of the original Koran, saying that this had been an interpolation of Satan, giving them forever the name the "Satanic Verses." See Trifkovic, pg. 31.

to God became a regular practice. The contingent of followers had reached 70 before the leaders of Mecca became concerned and organized some form of opposition to him. Up until that time they had tolerated Muhammed with quiet derision, never taking him too seriously. As his influence grew, they came to see in him and his doctrine a groundswell of criticism and rejection of the very lifestyle of Mecca. They believed that his preaching of the Judgment Day was nothing more than a criticism of their decadent way of life. The rejection of Muhammed by the Meccans, an open wound that never seemed to heal, turned cruel. Over time the very people whose favor he had spent a lifetime attempting to garner openly persecuted him.

While the treatment of Muhammed by the people of Mecca was harsh, it was not violent as is contended by Islamic history. Not a single life was taken. This would not be reciprocated by Muhammed in the years to come. One of his greatest detractors was Abu Jahl, who believed Muhammed's behavior to be more a political power play than religious conversion. He led a mob against Muhammed, but his influential uncle Abu Taleb intervened and Muhammed was allowed to leave the city in humiliation. Taleb attempted to convince his fellow tribespeople that Muhammed was insane and should be pitied, rather than reviled. Nevertheless, Muhammed took refuge in the caves of Mount Hira and worked to spread his word to any and all passersby. During this time, his claimed ethereal encounters became more and more extravagant. He related that he had been visited by other angels, had traveled through the seven heavens and had met the other prophets, including Adam, Jesus, Moses and Abraham. He had met Allah personally and been instructed in the proper manner of worship.[38]

For years Muhammed did not condemn or even question either the Jewish or Christian faiths. He did not appear to see them as incompatible with his own calling, believing instead that he was the

---

[38] See Trifkovic, pg. 32.

modern equivalent of those prophets who had come before him, and that followers of both of those older religions could attain salvation through him. However, in 620 A.D., at the age of 50, this position would undergo a complete conversion when he confronted the growing hostility of both Christians and Jews in his hometown of Mecca.

In 619, his own Quraysh tribe was becoming increasingly intolerant of him, incensed that he now sought to convert strangers. In this same year his uncle Taleb died, as did his wife Khadija some months later. With all protection from the ruling establishment of Mecca gone, he departed for the nearby city of al-Taif. Rejected there as well, he negotiated some measure of protection from the head of another clan in Mecca and returned to the city. Though still unwanted and reviled, things began to turn around for him in 621. At that time he managed to conscript twelve visitors from the city of Yathrib, some 200 miles to the north. After complete conversion, they all pledged to return to Yathrib and pass on his message. The following year he was greeted with 75 converts from that city, all of whom pledged to defend him. With this foundation, he directed his converts in Mecca to leave that place, and their own clans and families, and relocate to Yathrib with him. It is claimed that this may have been instigated, as well, by the fact that the council of tribal elders in Mecca had convened to try him for various offenses. Coincidentally, after learning this, he received the first revelation from Allah authorizing him to attack the Meccans. It seemed Allah did not appreciate the Meccans threatening his prophet.

Muhammed left Mecca with another 70 *muharijun*, including Zaid, Ali, Abu Bakr, his own father-in-law, and his son-in-law Omar. Trifkovic cites Muhammed's arrival in Yathrib on September 24, 622 as the beginning of the history of Islam, and from that time that city became the home of the Prophet, *Medinnet el Nebi*, which would later be shortened to Medina.

Upon arrival in Medina, Muhammed first had to settle the ongoing disputes between the three groups comprising its population.

This took four and a half years and one victory in battle, after which time he became the absolute ruler of the city. Despite this, his military and political efforts, coupled with the fact that his *muharijun* disdained the notion of working for a living, left him woefully short of funds. Besides, his followers were eager to exact revenge for their humiliation at the hands of the Meccans. With Allah's sanction, Muhammed led three raids on passing caravans, all of which ended in failure. But then in a complete surprise, the Medina Muslims had their first victory in 624, in part due to the fact they chose to attack during the holy month of Ramadan. It would seem that this, too, had been authorized by Allah. As time would go on, the one and only God would intercede increasingly on Muhammed's behalf to help establish his legal and political power base, as well as to justify his actions in administering to his own personal and familial life. Not the least of these would be Allah's divine intervention in allowing Muhammed to marry a seven-year-old girl, bring his many wives to heel at a time when they became unruly, and marry his own adopted son's wife, whose youth and sensual beauty drove him mad with lust. This same coincidental appearing of God would also authorize the torture of captured enemies and the mass rape of women who were not Muslim, practices that would be continued in the millennia to come.

The turning point for Muhammed and the Muslim faith came just two months later in the year 624. Confronted with a force led by an old Meccan nemesis, two to three times the size of his own following of 300 holy warriors, Muhammed scored a shocking victory at the town of Badr. It was completely unprecedented in the Arab culture for anyone to drift so far from tribe and family as to actually engage them in armed combat. However, Allah had spoken, telling him that, "Islam hath rent all bonds asunder." This would be the beginning of Islam's demand of blind obedience, and complete devotion and loyalty, effectively setting itself up as the substitute to all family, clan or other relationships. From this point on, Allah became a vengeful and angry god, insisting upon "instilling terror into the hearts of the unbelievers...."[39] As Muhammed's campaign of robbery and looting progressed, he amassed great wealth. When arguments began to break out over the distribution of the spoils, Allah spoke, dictating how all plunder would be divided, but insisting that fully one-fifth of all such wealth be given to Muhammed.[40]

From this point on, Muhammed's personality took on a decidedly sadistic turn. He had his nemesis' head thrown before him, and beheading became a regular practice in future forays. Throughout a campaign of battles against any and all that were not already converts, he would kidnap many, becoming wealthy through ransom payments. Some were tortured and murdered; others enslaved and sold. The means of torture seemed without limit in terms of creativity, and women were raped freely. Poets - the cultural social commentators of the time - who were critical of him were ordered killed, one stabbed to death as she nursed an infant child. It was through these fits of anger over any criticism that poetry and music were both swept outside the realm of pious living. From this point, his thirst for retribution and blood only grew. He engaged in a campaign of ethnic cleansing, ordering the death of any Jew who fell into his followers' hands. He attacked and expelled two of the remaining Jewish tribes in Medina. A third tribe was slaughtered outright. His men engaged in an orgy of rape and murder.[41] Allah beamed proudly down on the followers of his word.

In 627, when Muhammed was approaching 57 years of age, the Meccans decided to destroy him and his troublesome following once and for all. An enormous army of 10,000 marched on Medina and laid siege to the city. After lasting only two weeks, they were disheartened and withdrew, giving Muhammed yet another landmark victory for not only the battle, but also his claimed blessed state with the

---

[39] Koran, 8:12, Trifkovic, pg. 36.

[40] Koran, 8:42, Trifkovic, 37.

[41] Trifkovic, pg. 43.

Almighty. Flush with victory, he attacked the last remaining Jewish tribe in the area around Medina. Of those captured, he offered them the choice of conversion to Islam or death. Approximately 900 individuals refused to convert and were beheaded. Of the others, he did not demand actual spiritual conversion, merely that they recite a pledge to Allah and Islam, calling it the Surrender of the Tongue. Others were tortured, some burned alive and, of course, the women taken as the spoils of a great victory. By now, Muhammed had gone from a quiet preacher to an absolute and despotic ruler.

Ironically, it would be Muhammed's insistence on merely verbal obeisance – not actual, intentioned, spiritual conversion – that would allow for the rapid spread of Islam throughout the Middle East and its neighboring regions. By 628, he decided to make a pilgrimage to the holy site of Mecca himself. The Meccans quickly reached an agreement with him to allow Muhammed and all of the Muslims to come the following year. In Mecca, fear of Muhammed had been growing with many conversions to Islam and departures for Medina. Still, Muhammed was determined to subjugate the city that had for so long trivialized him. In January 630 he led an army of 10,000 on his native home. Upon arriving at the city gates, the Meccan leaders met him and surrendered to his complete authority. Muhammed would die of illness soon after in the year 632 A.D.

Expansion of Islam. Muhammed's lifetime of revelations, messages from God and edicts to his followers were not collected and written down in a single document called the Koran until about 650 A.D. Throughout his lifetime, however, he had created the model for relations between Muslims and the rest of the world for time immemorial. Allah had told him – and all true Muslims – "Fight those who do not profess the true faith till they pay the jizya (poll tax) with the hand of humility."[42] The followers of Islam were condemned to a life of seeing the world as a never-ending conflict between themselves and the unbelievers of Christianity and Judaism. The words of

---

[42] Koran, 9:29, cited by Trifkovic, 51.

Allah and Muhammed would forever ring in their ears: "Kill, kill the unbelievers wherever you find them."[43] Thus, the problem with Islam is, and shall ever be, that religion's belief that the words and acts of Muhammed provide the single "valid standard of morality" by which Muslims shall deal with infidels for all time.[44]

From Muhammed's lifetime, the expansion of Islam was rapid in terms of both spiritual conversion and conquered lands. Muhammed's autocratic rule over Islam was followed by the reign of the four caliphs, each his original follower. Umar, the second Caliph, who ruled the faithful from 634-644 A.D., took all of Arabia, the Western Sassanian lands and the Byzantine provinces of Syria and Egypt. The remainder of Persia followed soon after his death. Then in 636, under Caliph Uthman ibn Affan, the Byzantines were beaten by the forces of Islam at the Battle of Yarmuk. Jerusalem fell to them two years later. The Persians were finally defeated in 642, and northern Egypt was subjugated the same year.[45] The forward march of Islam would continue for years, consuming all in its path.

Engulfed in the growing pan-Islamic world were numerous Christian holy sites. In 1095, Pope Urban II began the First Crusade, ostensibly to rescue these sites from Muslim control. Then from 1099 to 1187 the Crusaders fought for, captured, and held Jerusalem. The Second Crusade would begin within that time frame, 1147-48. In 1187 the Islamic leader Salidan retook Jersulam from the Christians, instigating the Third Crusade to take it, yet again, from 1189 to 1192. The Fourth Crusade was fought from 1202 to 1204, and the Fifth came in 1212. The Sixth Crusade, from 1228 to 29 left no doubt that the world would forever suffer the conflict between Muslim and Christian in the Holy Lands of Judaism. Still, there came the Seventh Crusade from 1248 to 1254, and the Eighth in 1270. But Islam was far from defeated, and the forces of this mighty religion continued in

---

[43] Ibid., 51.

[44] Ibid., 53.

[45] Ibid., 91.

a quest for new lands and followers. By 1300 the Ottoman Empire was established, spreading the influences of Islam further and further. It was at this time that the indigenous people of modern day Kosovo would be forcibly conscripted into the faith, forever casting them into a continuation of the enmity between Islam and Christianity, only now with Kosovars and Serbs inheriting the legacy of hatred. The regions of Persia, Iraq and Iran were brought under direct control between the early 16th and 18th centuries.

By 1517 the Ottomans captured Egypt and Syria and created a protectorate over the holy places of Arabia. Palestine fell under their control, where it would remain until 1917.[46] While the religious conflicts of the Middle East and North Africa spilled out into Europe, the perpetrators of the Crusades began expanding into the New World. In 1607 the first permanent settlement – formed by the progeny of the Crusaders - was established in America, at Jamestown, Virginia.

The forces of Islam would not suffer their first major defeat in more than one thousand years until the Treaty of Karlowitz in 1699, when they were forced to relinquish many of their European territories, including Hungary to the Hapsburgs, creating the Austro-Hungary Empire. While the colonies in the New World were expanding, and battles for control over the North American continent only beginning to foment between England, France and Spain, Islam began to turn inward, commencing a centuries-long period of increased asceticism. In 1735 the Wahabbi movement, devoted to the purification of Islam, began in Arabia. Less than forty years later, in 1773, the tribe of Saud – a Wahabbi sect – captured Riyadh, and once again the expansion of Islam began throughout the Arabian Peninsula. Oil would not be discovered under the sands of Saudi Arabia until 1936, locking the United States into an eternal battle with Islamist extremists to ensure its own industrial development and survival.

---

[46] Much of the information in this section is taken from the chronology of Islam, entitled "Timeline of Terrorism", *Inside Homeland Security,* Vol. 2, Issue 6, Nov/Dec 2004, published by the American Board for Certification in Homeland Security. For a copy of this excellent timeline contact them through www.acfei.com or call 800-423-9737.

Roots of Global Terrorism. By 1801 a fledgling United States would be drawn into its first direct conflict with Islamic forces. Muslims in the region of Tripoli, Libya had been regularly raiding Europeans traveling in the area, demanding tribute to the Barbary Rulers, believing that it was a cost of doing business in the region. They rationalized that it was their duty under the Koran to attack all who denied Muslim authority. Over time they took it upon themselves to raid American parties traveling in the region as well. The U.S. government did not agree with the Europeans' practice of acquiescing to this blackmail, hence an early argument for funding of the U.S. Navy at a time when many wanted nothing more than a coastal defense force: "Millions for defense, but not one cent for tribute." Tripoli declared war on the United States over its refusal to pay this poll tax.

In 1882, another event which would cement the bonds of allies, and ensure the burn of hatred for centuries, took place with the first wave of Jewish immigrants into Palestine. These wandering nomads, in search of religious freedom, would not find any measure of self-determination or assured existence until after World War II.

The First World War would forever cast the world in a battle over religion. Though fought from August 1914 until November 1918, several key events took place within the span of its destruction of much of Europe. Under the 1917 Balfour Declaration, Great Britain took Jerusalem from Turkish rule, recognized the right of the Jews to a home in the land of Israel, and opened the Temple Mount to outsiders for the first time in history. After the war the presence of the Jewish immigrants, and control by the Brits, began to cause the region to disintegrate into much anticipated strife. In 1928, the Wailing Wall incident took place when Jewish worshippers traveled to the wall to pray. Lacking permission from the Muslims controlling the Wall, violence broke out, leaving hundreds dead and injured on both sides. The fighting worsened, and in 1929 Arabs massacred virtually all of the Jews living in Hebron. By 1932 the nation of Saudi Arabia was founded by the Saud family, giving legitimacy to Islam as the controlling force in a new Wahabbist nation-state.

By 1939 Britain was calling for the creation of separate and independent states for both Jews and Palestinians, drawing the opposition of both groups. World War II began this same year. By its end in 1945, millions of Jews had been summarily murdered. Even before the war was over in Europe, however, Egypt, Syria, Lebanon, Transjordan, Iraq, Saudi Arabia and Yemen would form the Arab League and declare their intention to defend Palestine against the Jews and their allies. At the close of that war, the United States and an already threatening Soviet Union would divide the world into two spheres. In so doing, many nations were created or placed under control of the countries allied with these two superpowers. Ultimately, these same two countries would become the two greatest targets of Islamist terrorism.

Modern Terrorist Threat. Within two years of the end of World War II, November 29, 1947, the newly minted United Nations voted to partition Palestine into separate Jewish and Arab states, with disputed Jerusalem declared an international zone. The Arabs rejected the UN plan, and six months later, May 14, 1948, the nation of Israel was established. The following day, May 15, 1948, outraged Arabs began the Arab-Israeli War when they invaded their new neighbor, pitting the Jews of Israel against all of Egypt, Syria, Lebanon and Iraq. This war would continue until 1949. Over the ensuing three years, approximately 150,000 Jews would flee their home countries of Iraq and Egypt for Israel. Many would die in clashes with Arab opposition forces. The U.S., already a supporter of the new Israeli state, would become preoccupied with the Korean War during this period, 1950-53.

But the Israelis – intent on ensuring the horror of World War II never again happened – engaged in aggressive action of their own, moving into Jerusalem and attacking Palestinians. The United States protested this action at the UN, garnering it neither success in that forum, nor any gratitude from the Arab states. In 1956, large groups of Arab terrorists invaded Israel and threatened its ports in what came to be called the Sinai Campaign. That same year Yassir Arafat founded the terrorist organization, al Fatah. A second Arab-Israeli War was launched.

Again, while the U.S. was immersed in a war in Asia – 1959 to 1973 - to stop the forward expansion of communism, events in the Middle East continued to spiral out of control. The Palestine Liberation Organization (PLO) was formed in 1964, and Palestinian attacks began shortly thereafter. Israel responded with raids against West Bank towns in 1965. This established the Arab strategy of using attacks against Israelis to provoke reprisals against Palestinians. Israel took control of the West Bank, Gaza Strip, Sinai and Golan Heights. That same year, 1967, would see an as yet unknown Usama bin Laden, inherit millions of dollars when his father died in a helicopter crash in the United States. In June of that year (June 5-10, 1967) the Six Day War was fought when Arabs invaded Israel from Egypt and Jordan. Israel destroyed the Arab air forces and annexed East Jerusalem, earning it ever more hatred from the Arabs.

In 1968 Arab outrage at the existence and expansion of Israel continued, ignoring the fact that much of this was the result of their own behavior. Yassir Arafat became the leader of the PLO in this year, beginning decades of terror against the U.S. and Israel. In 1967 alone, he would be the architect of more than 200 terrorist attacks.

On June 5, 1968 shoe-in presidential candidate Robert F. Kennedy was assassinated by Sirhan Sirhan, a Palestinian outraged by Kennedy's pro-Israeli stance. The U.S. had suffered its first Islamist terrorist attack on American soil. It would be decades before we even realized it.

From this point on, the world would begin to see the export of Islamist extremism. One month after Kennedy's assassination, an Israeli El Al flight from Rome was hijacked and flown to Algiers. On February 18, 1969 terrorists attacked another El Al jet at the Zurich airport. One pilot was killed and another wounded. Six months later, August 29, saw a TWA flight out of Los Angeles hijacked and forced to land in Damascus. In the final three months of that year, El Al offices in Brussels, Athens, and Berlin were attacked by terrorists armed with bombs and grenades. Between 1969 and 1970, 560 raids were launched from Lebanon into Israel.

The 1970s saw a dramatic escalation in terrorist assaults around the world. In February 1970, on the heels of the El Al attacks, a bus was hijacked in Munich, West Germany. One hostage was killed and eleven injured. In June, terrorists failed in an attempt to assassinate Jordanian King Hussein. On September 6, 1970, a total of 400 hostages were taken in simultaneous hijackings of flights out of Amsterdam, Zurich, and Frankfurt. All the planes were flown to airports in the Middle East and blown up. Beginning the next day, from September 7 to 9, Palestinian terrorists again engaged in a series of coordinated hijackings. One Swiss, one British and two American planes were taken over. America and her citizens were increasingly becoming targets of Arab terrorism.

Between May and July 1972, several attacks took place. A Belgian commercial jet was hijacked. Lod airport in Israel was attacked, leaving 24 dead. A Tel Aviv bus station was bombed, with 11 killed. Even an oil refinery in Italy was attacked. On September 5, 1972, nine Israeli athletes were murdered and another eleven taken hostage by Palestinian terrorists at the Munich Olympics.

1973 was a banner year for terrorism. On March 2, Black September – one of the terrorist groups responsible for many of the attacks up to this point – assassinated the United States Ambassador to Sudan, along with other diplomats at the Saudi Arabian Embassy in Khartoum, that nation's capital. The following month, Israeli commandos launched an operation into Beirut, killing three PLO officials they claimed were behind the Munich hostage taking. The Yom Kippur War started on October 6, when Israel was, again, attacked; this time by Egypt and Syria. It would not end until the following year. On December 17, 1973 an airport in Rome and Pan Am Flight

202 - heading for Beirut and Tehran - were attacked. Twenty-nine people were killed.

In November 1974 the United Nations passed Resolution 3236, recognizing the right of the Palestinian people to independence. It recognized the PLO as their sole representative. Pandering to Arab terrorists would do little to protect the Western nations behind this effort, early proof that they cannot be negotiated with or appeased.

In December 1975, angry over a reduction in oil prices and increase in production, Carlos the Jackal and members of the Popular Front for the Liberation of Palestine (PFLP) raided OPEC headquarters in Vienna, Austria. Three were murdered and 62 hostages taken. The terrorists negotiated an airplane and $40 million dollars ransom, and escaped. Just six months later, June 1976, the PFLP and Baader-Meinhof Gang joined forces to hijack a French commercial jet, taking 258 passengers hostage.

Islamic Jihad was founded in 1979. In February of that year, the U.S. Ambassador to Kabul, Afghanistan was kidnapped and killed. On November 4, 1979 the Iran Hostage Crisis would begin when fundamentalist Islamic revolutionaries and students overran the U.S. Embassy in Tehran, Iran. This was a direct attack on American soil and American sovereignty. Fifty-two U.S. diplomats were taken hostage with demands that the U.S. send the ailing Shah – then in America for medical treatment for terminal cancer – back to Iran. My friend Ken Kraus, a Marine guard, was shot in the stomach at close range with a shotgun, while fighting in the hallways to defend the embassy. He was the only person allowed to be medevaced out. The hostages would not be freed until the inauguration of Ronald Reagan as president, exactly 444 days later. Other Americans began to be kidnapped and killed throughout the Middle East, and the world.

With Arab terrorism and Islamist extremism gaining momentum, the Grand Mosque in Mecca, Saudi Arabia was attacked on November

20, 1979. Two hundred-fifty were killed; many of them tourists. Hundreds of pilgrims to the holy shrine were taken hostage and 600 wounded. One month later, upon the invasion of Afghanistan by Soviet troops, Usama bin Laden and his associate Mohammed Atef became involved in the Mujahideen rebellion. Throughout this war, the United States – largely through the CIA – helped organize, train, arm and lead the Afghani forces against the Soviet Union. The Taliban and al Qaeda were born of this conflict, ultimately turning their capability against America. Throughout all of these decades since Israel's birth, and in the years to come, Arab terrorists targeted Jewish schools and buses, forcing the development of a siege mentality in every aspect of Israeli life. In April 1980, Islamist terrorists followed up their rebellion by seizing the Iranian embassy in London. This would serve as the public début of the heretofore-secret British SAS who, in a lightning raid, freed the hostages. Two were killed.

The following year, in May 1981, Pope John Paul II was shot in a botched assassination attempt by Mehmet Ali Agca, a Turk. He claimed to be a member of the PFLP. Though there is good evidence that Bulgarian intelligence, and ultimately the KGB, was behind this attempt due to the Pope's support of the Polish Solidarity movement, the fact that they chose a Muslim extremist to carry out this attack is significant. Several months later, on October 6, Al Jihad assassinated Egyptian President Anwar Sadat.

In 1982 Lebanon invaded Israel. Simultaneously, the PLO launched repeated attacks in the Galilee area of northern Israel. On July 19, the President of the American University in Beirut, David Dodge, was kidnapped. Strangely, he was released, and then kidnapped again. The second time he was tortured and killed by Hizballah. The following month witnessed a bomb planted by terrorist Mohammad Rashid explode on a Pan American flight over Hawaii, killing one and injuring many. America was again attacked. Again, she failed to notice.

Less than a year later, on April 18, 1983, a car driven by Radical Islamic Jihad suicide bombers destroyed the United States Embassy in Beirut. Sixty-three were killed and another 120 injured. The U.S. State Department had denied the embassy guards the ability to have ammunition in their guns. America rolled over and went back to sleep. That same year, on October 23, 1983, a truck packed with 2,500 pounds of TNT smashed through the gates at the U.S. Marine barracks in Beirut and exploded. Two hundred forty-one Americans were killed, along with 58 French soldiers. Again, we scarcely noticed. Two months after that, December 12, another truck bomb killed six and wounded dozens at both the U.S. and French embassies in Kuwait. France would begin a policy of pandering to Muslims to avoid further assaults.

During this time, the Soviet-Afghan War rolled on. Usama bin Laden moved to Pakistan in 1984 to fund and help organize 20,000 Mujahideen rebels. The U.S. was supplying more than $250 million per year for this effort. In March, CIA station chief William Buckley was kidnapped, tortured and murdered in Beirut by Islamic Jihad. Famous Navy SEAL commander Mike Walsh would miss the opportunity to protect Buckley by minutes when delayed for a meeting. He was the last to speak to him by phone and would be forever haunted by his friend's death. Then again on September 20, 1984, a bomb was detonated at the U.S. Embassy in Beirut, killing 23 and injuring 21, including both the American and British ambassadors. The final effort of the terrorists to make headlines in 1984 would come in December, when Kuwait Airways Flight 221 was hijacked. It was flown to Tehran by Islamic Jihad members, including close associates of bin Laden. The hijackers demanded the release of 17 terrorists arrested in the 1983 bombing of the U.S. and French embassies in Kuwait. Ultimately, Iranian troops would storm the plane, arresting the hijackers. Two passengers were killed, but the Iranians let the terrorists go free.

The year 1985 saw the beginning of a new campaign of terrorist bombings, kidnappings and hijackings. In April a bomb exploded outside a restaurant frequented by U.S. soldiers in Madrid. On June 9, U.S. professor Thomas Sutherland was taken hostage in Lebanon by Hizballah. He would be held for five years. Just days later, on June 13, a TWA flight from Rome was hijacked and taken to Beirut. The next day, another TWA flight out of Athens was also hijacked and flown to Beirut. One hundred fifty-three people were held hostage and one American Navy diver murdered. From Lebanon the aircraft was flown twice to Algiers before finally relanding in Beirut. It would take Israel releasing 435 Lebanese and Palestinian prisoners to achieve the release of the hostages. This siege was recreated in various forms in numerous movies.

Later that summer, desperate to help its citizens in captivity, the U.S. began secretly selling weapons to Iran in exchange for the release of American hostages, channeling the funds to the Contra rebels fighting the communist Sandinista regime in Nicaragua. Keeping to the bargain, Iran released Benjamin Weir, Martin Jenco and David Jacobson. The Iran Contra Scandal would later rock the American political world and the Reagan Administration.

In August a Volkswagen loaded with explosives was driven into the main gate of the U.S. Air Force Base at Rhein-Mann, Germany, killing 22. In October 1985, only 59 days later, PLO terrorists seized the cruise ship *Achille Lauro* at Port Said, Egypt. More than 700 passengers were taken hostage, and one American, wheelchair bound Leon Klinghoffer, was shot and pushed over the side into the ocean. The remainder of the hostages would not be released until the Egyptian government provided the terrorists with safe haven, after demands for the release of Palestinians imprisoned worldwide failed.

The following month, an Egypt Air flight was hijacked by Abu Nidal in Malta, leading to a 30 hour standoff. And another month later, in December 1985, both American and Israeli check-in counters were attacked at the El Al Airline offices in Rome and Vienna. Exploding grenades in both attacks killed 20 people. The terrorists were working for the Libyan government. That same month, on December 12, all souls on a chartered DC-8 carrying 248 soldiers from the 101st Airborne Division and its 8-member crew perished when the DC-8 crashed during takeoff in Newfoundland. They were returning home from a Mid-East peacekeeping operation. Terrorism was suspected.

In April 1986 a bomb was planted under the seat of a TWA flight out of Rome. Four Americans were killed and nine injured. Three days later, the LaBelle discotheque in West Berlin was bombed by terrorists working with Libya. Targeted as a place frequented by U.S. servicemen, three were killed and 150 wounded. Ten days later, in retaliation, the United States bombed two cities in Libya, including the home of Libyan leader Moammar Qadaffi. One of his sons was killed in the raid. Then on September 9, Frank Reed, the director of the American University in Beirut, was kidnapped by Hizballah. He would be held for almost four years. Three days after Reed's kidnapping, American University in Beirut's acting comptroller, Joseph Cicippio, was taken. He would not be released for five years. Just one month after that, on October 21, American Edward Tracy was also kidnapped in Beirut and not released for five years.

In 1987 HAMAS – the Islamic Resistance Movement – a Palestinian anti-Israeli group, was founded. It would come to be known for its bombings and suicide attacks against Jews. On January 2, 1987, United Nations negotiator Terry Waite was kidnapped in Lebanon. He would not be released until November 1991. On the 24th of that month, Americans Jesse Turner and Alann Steen were taken and held hostage for four years as well. From 1987 to 1988 the al Muthanna State Establishment and Nuclear Research Center in Iraq began researching radiological weapons, testing three. One hundred bomb casings from this facility are still missing. The Iran-Iraq War was fought throughout this period, from 1980 to 1988. At its conclusion, a bellicose and pugnacious Iraq would ultimately ensure the U.S. became a prime target of Arab terrorism.

1988 also saw the formation of al Qaeda by Usama bin Laden. On February 17 of that year, U.S. Marine Corps Lieutenant Colonel William Higgins was kidnapped and murdered in southern Lebanon by the Iranian Hizballah and Lebanese Party of God. He was serving with the UN Truce Organization at the time. Then on April 14, a car bomb exploded outside of the USO (America's United Service Organization, which provides support and assistance to U.S. troops) in Naples, Italy, killing one sailor. On August 8, an American C-130 Hercules blew up after take-off from Pakistan, killing a U.S. ambassador, the president of Pakistan and 37 others. That same summer Saddam Hussein used chemical weapons to kill large numbers of Kurds in Iraq. Then on December 21, Pan American Flight 103 was blown out of the sky over Lockerbie, Scotland, killing all 259 on board, including U.S. crew members, students and military personnel. The bomb had been planted by the PFLP and Libyan government agents. Eleven others were killed on the ground.

By 1989 the Soviet Union was withdrawing from Afghanistan, beginning the exportation of the jihad to the next battleground: Chechnya. The buildup to the Persian Gulf War, and the war itself, would consume America from 1990 to 1991, and put it at the head of al Qaeda's list of targets. When Iraq initially invaded Kuwait, bin Laden went to the Saudi rulers and offered to put together a force of 30,000 Mujahideen warriors to oust the invader from Muslim lands. When this offer was declined in favor of allowing hundreds of thousands of American troops – and their infidel allies – onto the holy lands of Mecca and Medina, forging a permanent presence there, bin Laden was outraged. Both the United States and Saudi Arabia would forever represent to him the worst of enemies to true Islam.

According to famous Green Beret and CIA operative Billy Waugh, bin Laden gathered his army anyway, turning his burning hatred toward America and his own native country of Saudi Arabia. He sent four thousand would-be terrorist troops to Afghanistan to train at the camps he had set up, and began fomenting unrest among the Saudi citizenry against the ruling family. In response, the Saudis raided his home, and placed him under house arrest. But as a son of one of the most important and wealthy associates to the king and Prince Fahd, they did not seem to know what to do with him. Then in late 1990, Sudan's vice president offered him refuge. The Saudis put pressure on him to accept this offer and eventually, in 1992, he left Saudi Arabia for his new home in Sudan. Many of his Afghan War insurgents accompanied him, and there they formed the beginnings of his new al Qaeda army.[47] The Saudis would eventually strip him of citizenship, preventing him from ever returning to Saudi Arabia. This would constitute the third and last of the signature events that would shape bin Laden in his effort to raise up radical Islam across the world. The first occurred in 1979, with the overthrow of the Shah of Iran. The second was the Mujahideen uprising against the Soviets in Afghanistan. The last was the Iraqi invasion of Kuwait in 1990.

Looking to export both his religious beliefs and military acumen, bin Laden's operatives were first sent to America in 1991. Then in 1992 he made an offer to Hizballah, to join forces in a common effort to kill American troops stationed in Muslim Africa and Asia. Elsewhere, Afghanistan was falling into chaos. By 1992 ethnic civil war, largely as a result of the Muslim extremist Taliban, was tearing the country to pieces. Fifty thousand would be killed before the Taliban would wrest control over the majority of Afghan territory.

On December 20 of 1992, a hotel used by U.S. troops staging for duty in Somalia was bombed, killing 2.

Lead Up to 9-11. With the coming of the new year 1993, America would experience punishment by bin Laden and al Qaeda for its impertinence. In January, an enraged Arab walked calmly down the street outside of CIA headquarters in Langley, Virginia. As with every

---

[47] For an excellent overview of the events of this period, see Billy Waugh, with Tim Keown, *Hunting the Jackal: A Special Forces and CIA Ground Soldier's Fifty-Year Career Hunting America's Enemies*, New York: HarperCollins, 2004, 122 – 125.

morning, employees arriving to work were lined up in their cars outside the gates, awaiting entry through security. He began shooting at the intelligence officers as they sat patiently in their vehicles. Two were killed. The following month, on February 26, a rented van packed with explosives was detonated in the underground parking garage of the World Trade Center North Tower. Though only 6 people – together with an unborn baby – were killed, 1,040 were injured. According to the *Inside Homeland Security* report on terrorist history, this attack included a device designed to release cyanide gas, intended to kill police and emergency response crews. However, the ensuing fire destroyed the poison. It had been the intention of the attack's masterminds – including Ramzi Ahmed Yousef and four others, some from Abu Sayyat – that the explosion would collapse the North Tower into its sister building, bringing both of them down and killing a hoped-for 250,000 people. Again, per *Inside Homeland Security,* Yousef was quoted as saying, "Our calculations were not very accurate this time. However we promise you that next time it will be very precise and the Trade Center will be one of our targets." The Blind Sheik, Omar Abdel Rahman of Egypt, would later receive a life sentence for his role. Bin Laden's own role in this attack was never completely established.

Two months later, on April 14, 1993, terrorists failed at their attempt to assassinate former president George H.W. Bush in Kuwait. The Oslo Accords were signed at the White House in September, supposedly beginning a five year period of transition toward self-determination for the Palestinians. Arab opponents of this peace accord would ensure it was never carried out. Less than one month later, two U.S. helicopters were shot down in the streets of Mogadishu, Somalia, resulting in a catastrophic battle and the deaths of 18 U.S. soldiers. Bin Laden and a group of terrorists he had trained in Sudan were among the leaders of those attacking the U.S. forces. The following year Saudi Arabia permanently revoked bin Laden's citizenship. At the same time other terror groups were coming together. Islamic Jihad and HAMAS ended their conflict with the Palestinian Authority, and

HAMAS entered into a new campaign of suicide bombings. Arafat was given the Nobel Peace Prize.

Many terrorist attacks took place throughout 1993 and 1994, culminating in a failed attempt Christmas Eve by bin Laden associates to crash a jetliner into the Eiffel Tower. Between the end of 1994 and early 1995 four different plots were uncovered in the Philippines. Terrorists working with bin Laden had intended to assassinate the pope; blow 11 different jets out of the skies at once; coordinate the hijacking of several planes in the U.S., flying them into the Pentagon, CIA headquarters, World Trade Towers, and a nuclear facility, as well as several other skyscrapers; and, assassinate President Bill Clinton while in the Philippines.

Then on March 8, 1995, 2 U.S. diplomats were killed and a third wounded when attacked at the U.S. Consulate in Karachi, Pakistan. In November of that year, a Saudi National Guard training base run by the U.S. in Riyadh was attacked by car bomb, killing seven. The following year the Taliban finally seized control over the vast majority of Afghanistan. Under pressure from the U.S., Sudan finally ejected bin Laden, who immediately relocated back to Afghanistan and set up new terrorist training camps. Al Qaeda had grown into an international terrorist network. On June 25 of that year, a truck bomb exploded only 35 yards outside the Khobar Towers, a U.S. Air Force housing facility in Dhahran, Saudi Arabia, killing 19 American servicemen and injuring another 515 people, including 240 U.S. citizens. Two months later, on August 23, Usama bin Laden issued a written declaration of attack against the United States and all Americans, including a demand that the U.S. withdraw its forces from Saudi Arabia. He also called for the overthrow of the Saudi government. In January of the following year, letter bombs sent from Egypt were discovered in several cities in the United States.

Then on February 23, 1997, a Palestinian gunman opened fire on a crowded observation deck atop the Empire State Building, killing numerous tourists before turning the gun on himself. That same month another Arab terrorist had planned to bomb the New York subway. He was stopped with minutes to spare. On November 12, four U.S. government officials and their driver were gunned down in Pakistan by terrorists. Five days later, six terrorists shot 58 foreign tourists to death at the Temple of Hatshepsut in Egypt. On February 23, 1998, Usama bin Laden released his now famous *fatwah*, under the title "World Islamic Front for Jihad Against Jews and Crusaders." This document stated that, "The ruling to kill the Americans and their allies - civilians, and military - is an individual duty for every Muslim who can do it in any country in which it is possible to do it...." In a separate statement he made a connection between the Islamic war against Russia and that of the United States, saying that for everything Russia suffers, America will suffer worse. On June 21, 1998 the U.S. Embassy in Beirut was again attacked, this time by rocket-propelled grenades. Two months later, on August 7, the U.S. embassies at Nairobi, Kenya and Dar Es Salaam, Tanzania were bombed, killing 224 people and injuring more than 5,000. These attacks were carried out by al Qaeda, including bin Laden himself. In retaliation, U.S. cruise missiles hit targets in Afghanistan and Sudan. Bin Laden narrowly escaped from a camp in Khost, Afghanistan before it was struck.

Billy Waugh spent much of the 1990s working undercover in Sudan. There he tracked an Usama bin Laden not yet known to be a genocidal terrorist threat. He also tracked and found the elusive Carlos the Jackal, otherwise known as Ilyas Ramirez Sanchez. According to Waugh, during that time, "Sudan was the center of radical Islam, and its rulers allowed terrorists to build their camps and roam freely."[48] At the time, according to U.S. intelligence – and as corroborated by Waugh – Sudan was full of leaders and operatives from such groups as Abu Nidal, Hizballah, the Egyptian Gama'at al-Islamiyya, the Algerian Islamic Jihad, HAMAS, the Palestinian Islamic Jihad, and Ayatollah Khomeini's "Death to America" program. Along with these

---

[48] Ibid., at 122.

was the Blind Sheikh, Omar Abdel Rahman, who received his U.S. visa while in Khartoum in 1993, allowing him to conduct the first World Trade Center bombing. Bin Laden was there with countless supporters, followers and bodyguards, and by the end of 1993 Carlos the Jackal as well.[49] They had all gone to Sudan under an open-arms policy of embracing Islamist terrorists maintained by that country's vice president, Hassan al-Turabi. Since a coup in Sudan that had thrust the Egyptians out of control, and another that catapulted the Islamist extremists into power, Sudan had been governed by a titular head, president Omar Hassan al-Bashir. But the real power behind the government and the devolution of that country into a terrorist haven was al-Turabi. He and al-Bashir together had violently overthrown the legitimate government at the end of June 1989, creating their own military based dictatorship.

According to a recently declassified DIA report, bin Laden stayed in Khartoum with 700 Arab Afghans. It was from this group that he created the nucleus of the "terrorist fundamentalist political organization 'Al-Kaida [al Qaeda].'" Chief among these was his old friend Emir Khattab. Khattab was from one of the large groups of Chechens, which had existed in Jordan since their exile by the Russian Tsar in 1865. But even for that group of extremist cutthroats, Khattab had a reputation for unbridled brutality. Together they established close ties with numerous other terrorists and terror groups, "all considered founders and principal ideologists of international Islamic terrorism." Among these were: M. al-Masary; Tark al-Fadly, a former field commander in Afghanistan, then based in Yemen; Hassan al-Turabi, the powerful vice president of Sudan; Rashid al-Gannushy of Tunisia; Abdalla Azam from Palestine; Omar Abdal Rachman of Egypt; Kary Kadyr, leader of the Council of Modzakheds in Jellalabad, Afghanistan; as well as leaders of various other Pushtun tribes there. The goals of this group were, at the very least: (1) To overthrow the Saudi regime; (2) To build a "just Islamic state" in Saudi Arabia; and,

---

[49] Ibid. at 123.

(3) Establish a worldwide Islamic state capable of directly challenging the U.S., Russia and China.

According to the DIA report, obtained by Judicial Watch, an American public interest group under a Freedom of Information Act request, the means by which all of this was to be accomplished included "terror, ethnic cleansing, latent penetration, and control over nuclear and biological weapons." They intended to establish their own Islamic regimes in Bosnia, Albania, Chechnya, Dagestan to the east, the entire North Caucasus "from sea to sea," all Central Asian republics, all of Russia, Afghanistan, Pakistan, Turkey, Indonesia, Malaysia, Algeria, Morocco, Egypt, Tunisia, Sudan and all of the countries of the Persian Gulf. By their own doctrine, "Terrorist activities [were] to be conducted against Americans and Westerners, Israelis, Russians (predominantly Cossacks), Serbs, Chinese, Armenians, and disloyal Muslims."

Bin Laden also provided for financial support to be given to a number of groups in order to fund their terrorist reign over his intended victims. Many groups benefited financially from both his own wealth and his ability to raise money for their jihadist cause, including: al Jama'at, al Islamy and al Jkhad of Egypt; Jihad al-Islamy and HAMAS in Palestine; the Armed Islam Group of Algeria; NIF of Sudan; various dissident groups in Saudi Arabia; Arab terrorist groups and training camps in Afghanistan; Taliban and its training camps; al Badr in the Khost area of Afghanistan; the KLA in Bosnia; the Islamic Way; and Wahhabites in Chechnya, Dagestan and nearby regions. Terror cells and training camps were to be established in Russia's Azerbaijan, Tatarstan, Bashkortostan, its Central Asian republics, Chechnya, Ingushetia, Balkaria, Karachi, Adygeya, Tajikistan, as well as both Moscow and St. Petersburg. The express purpose of all camps was to train sappers, spies, communicators, ideologists and propagandists, all in an effort to further the Islamic extremist cause throughout the world.

According to bin Laden, in creating this worldwide Islamic state, "special attention was to be given to the Northern Caucasus and especially Chechnya since they [were] regarded as areas unreachable by strikes from the West," again tying Russia and America together in strategic planning of their Islamic expansion. So, it was in 1995 that bin Laden sent Khattab to Chechnya, along with nine others, to set up training camps for international terrorists there. He established three major camps in the Vedeno and Nojai Urt areas, camps well hidden in the thick mountain forests. They were – according to the Defense Intelligence Agency report – well equipped, with firing ranges and facilities to create mock-ups of target sites, as well as hold training classes for saboteurs and snipers. Groups of terrorists graduated from the camps every two months.

While the camps were being prepared, bin Laden traveled to Afghanistan several times to meet with representatives of many of these terror groups, including Chechen and Dagestani Wahhabites from Gudermes and Grozny. They entered into agreements for the financial funding of the Chechen militants. According to the Defense Intelligence report, "They stressed the necessity of training terrorists drawn from among converted Europeans, Russians, Ukrainians, Cossacks and Ossetians in Khattab's training camps to conduct kidnappings and terrorist acts." U.S. citizens were emphasized as important targets. The kidnapping of Vincent Cochetel, a United Nations High Commission for Refugees' official, in Vladikavkaz in 1998, was one of their accomplishments. Routes for the movement of men and drugs through Central Asia, the Caucasus and into Russia, were also established.

It was also during this time that bin Laden, along with Sudan's al-Turabi, would create the National Islamic Front (NIF), whose campaign of genocide would result in the massacre of hundreds of thousands of Christian African villagers in southern Sudan, and the enslavement, rape and genital mutilation of well more than one hundred thousand women, followed by a similar concentrated decimation of refugees in Darfur in 2004. But al-Turabi – and bin Laden for that matter – did not want to stop merely at Africa. At one point a Sudan newspaper, *Al Rai Al A'm*, quoted Turabi as saying, "We want to Islamize America and Arabize Africa."[50]

In November of 1998, Usama bin Laden was formally indicted by the U.S. Justice Department for the Kenya and Tanzania embassy bombings. Bin Laden would be indicted again on January 12, 1999, along with 11 other al Qaeda members, and added to the FBI's Most Wanted list. Then on October 15, the United Nations Security Council ordered the Taliban to turn bin Laden over. They refused. Exactly two months later, on December 14, a terrorist plot to blow up LAX Airport failed when Ahmed Ressam – a member of an Algerian radical group - was seized by U.S. Customs agents as he attempted to cross the U.S.-Canadian border in Washington state in a car loaded with explosives. Later that month, plots to kill American and Israeli millennium partiers at a Jordanian hotel and other Christian holy sites, was thwarted by intelligence officials.

But it would not be until several months after Ressam's conviction and 27-year sentence on nine counts of terrorism in a U. S. court, that the full import of the millennium plot would become known. At the trial of one of his co-conspirators in July 2001, Ressan told a New York court how he had been trained in 1998 in one of bin Laden's camps in Afghanistan. He detailed how he had been recruited into al Qaeda and made part of a vast international network. According to Ressam, in his second phase of training in the Afghan camps, he underwent a six week program in advanced explosives, after which he had been deployed to Canada with US$12,000 to launch an attack on America. From there, he had recruited additional co-horts to carry out the plot.

January 2000 saw a series of failures for al Qaeda terrorism efforts, though it also established its commitment to kill as many enemies

---

[50] Ibid., at 123.

of Islam – particularly Americans – as possible. In that one month a plot to bomb another Amman, Jordan hotel was thwarted, as was a similar plan to attack a site on Mount Nebo and one on the Jordan River. Another plot to bomb LAX was stymied by U.S. officials. As well, an intended operation against the *USS Sullivans*, whereby it was to be rammed with a small boat loaded with explosives, was stopped. This tactic would later prove successful against a U.S. Navy warship. The next month, U.S. officials received proof of bin Laden's desire to acquire nuclear weapons grade material when al Qaeda defector Jamal Ahmed al-Fadl testified that bin Laden had attempted to purchase uranium for $1.5 million. On July 2, 2000 the Lincoln Memorial, Washington Monument and other national icons in Washington, D.C. were identified by intelligence as terrorist targets. On August 12, four Americans were taken hostage in Uzbekistan. The following month the New Intifada against Israeli occupation began. Then on October 12, catastrophe: U.S. Navy Destroyer *Cole* was attacked by a small boat loaded with explosives at the port city of Aden, Yemen. Seventeen sailors were killed and 39 wounded. Attacking a U.S. Navy ship was an act of war, but our only response was to send the FBI to investigate. Bin Laden is known to have been behind the attack. His father was from Yemen, and having a Burke class destroyer sitting off the coast must have enraged him.

Between the September 13, 1992 signing of the Oslo Accords between Arafat and Yitzak Rabin of Israel, and the year 2000, 256 Israeli civilians and soldiers were killed by terrorists on their own soil.

The turning of the century brought increased commitment of Arab terrorists to bring America to her knees. On December 30, 2000 a bomb was set off across the street from the U.S. Embassy in Manila, Philippines. The following year would see the terrorists redeeming themselves for their earlier failures. On the 11th day of September 2001, American Airlines Flight 11, from Boston to L.A., was hijacked and flown into the North Tower of the World Trade Center. United Flight 175, also originating out of Boston and on its way to Los Angeles, was crashed into the South Tower, just minutes later. American Airlines Flight 77 enroute from Washington, D.C. to Los Angeles was also taken. This one struck the Pentagon. Finally, United Flight 93 from Newark to San Francisco was seized. Efforts by passengers resulted in the plane being flown into the ground, in a remote field of Western Pennsylvania. In all, 2,986 innocent lives were lost that day, and thousands more injured. The cost of these horrors is estimated at $16.5 billion, with more than 200,000 jobs lost due to the impact on the airline industry and the American economy overall. Little more than $300,000 is estimated to have been spent by bin Laden and Ramzi Ahmed Yousef for the 19 hijackers to carry out the plan.

Post 9-11 World. The one-two punch planned by bin Laden for America, did not materialize however. NATO officials stopped a second attack planned for two days later, September 13. Al Qaeda had intended to attack U.S. embassies in Paris, France and Brussels, and a U.S. air base. Just five days from then, anthrax-filled letters were sent from Trenton, New Jersey to five U.S. media offices. Each contained a note that read: "09-11-01, this is next, take penacilin [sic] now, death to America, death to Israel, Allah is great." One person died from exposure to the toxin. On October 7, 2001 U.S. and British warplanes began bombing Taliban and al Qaeda strongholds in Afghanistan. This campaign would continue until March of 2002. The day following the commencement of the Air Force attacks, plots to bomb the United States Embassy in Paris, and NATO headquarters in Brussels, were foiled. That same day, the U.S. Department of Homeland Security was formed.

The very next day, October 9, a second batch of anthrax-laden letters was mailed to two Democratic senators in Washington, D.C. These contained notes that read: "09-11-01. You can not stop us. We have this anthrax. You die now. Are you afraid? Death to America. Death to Israel. Allah is great." Twenty-two people became infected, and four died. The anthrax used was a sophisticated, weaponized form. On October 11, intelligence reported that two nuclear suitcases from the former Soviet Union had reached bin Laden. In November it was reported that, according to bin Laden, nuclear weapons were available in Russia for $10 and $20 million. By November 25, 2001, Mullah Mohammed Omar reportedly said that the nuclear destruction of America was on its way. Early in 2002, a threatened Saddam Hussein offered $25,000 to the families of all terrorist suicide-bombers. On January 23, 2002 *Wall Street Journal* reporter Daniel Pearl was kidnapped in Pakistan. His beheading was videotaped and shown around the world by terrorist affiliated networks. Many more would suffer the same fate in the months and years to come. The rage of the Prophet Muhammed had returned to punish the world once again.

By February 2002 Afghanistan was well on its way to being under control by U.S. forces. On the 14th of that month, Abdul Rahman, Afghanistan's Minister of Civilian Aviation and Tourism was beaten to death at the Kabul airport under bin Laden and Mullha Omar's order; the punishment for his collaboration with Americans. By this time, 942 Palestinians and another 273 Israelis had died in fighting under the new intifada. On September 5, 2002, 32 were killed and another 150 wounded when bombs were set off in Kabul and Kandahar, Afghanistan; areas under the protection of U.S. troops. That same day Afghan President Hamid Karzai narrowly survived an assassination attempt. Members of the Navy's elite counter-terror unit SEAL Team Six saved his life. One innocent bystander was killed in the shootout. Then from October 2 to 24, two Muslim converts – John Allen Muhammed and Lee Boyd Malvo - terrified cities from Washington to Baltimore and beyond, during their Beltway Sniper spree. Over those three weeks, ten people died and another three were wounded, but survived. On October 8, terrorists murdered one U.S. Marine and wounded another in Kuwait. On September 13, 2002, a terrorist cell was uncovered in Lackawanna, New York. It had been planning a number of attacks against America from inside.

On October 12, al Qaeda planted bombs outside two nightclubs in Kuna Beach, Bali. Two hundred two people were killed, and 300 wounded, including Americans and Australians. Six days later al Qaeda detonated another bomb in Manila killing two and injuring 20. Just ten days after that, on October 28, Laurence Foley, the Executive Director for U.S.A.I.D. (U.S. Agency for International Development) in Jordan was assassinated. On November 28, al Qaeda struck again. Three suicide bombers attacked a hotel in Kenya frequented by Israeli tourists. Fifteen people were killed and another 40 injured. Simultaneously, two SA-7 shoulder fired missiles were fired at an Arkia Airlines Boeing 757 outside the Mombasa Airport.

On March 2 of the following year, al Qaeda's military operations chief, Khalid Shaikh Mohammed, was captured in Karachi, Pakistan. Under interrogation, he detailed bin Laden's plan to create a "nuclear hellstorm" in the United States by building and detonating dirty nukes on American soil. Operation Iraqi Freedom was launched that same month. From then, through 2004 and into 2005, hundreds of contractors would die in Iraq. In the first year alone, 177 contract workers from more than 25 countries were killed or missing, many beheaded. More than 1,000 American military servicemen would be killed. With U.S. forces once again present in the Middle East - the land of Muhammed - terrorist forces concentrated there, resulting in a reduction in operations against America on U.S. soil. Still, U.S. government agencies foiled numerous attempts and plans against targets inside the U.S. The American public continued to pay little attention to those reported in the media. Many more would go unreported entirely.

On August 14, 2003 a massive power outage caused complete blackouts across the Eastern United States and Canada. A communiqué from al Qaeda stated that, "It is a message to all investors that the United States is no longer a safe country for their money…." The catastrophe was officially blamed on lightning. Also during 2004, bin Laden was found to have paid between $60 and $100 million to obtain the knowledge of Pakistan's nuclear experts. Former Soviet Union and Chinese nuclear scientists were also found to have been employed by him. Intelligence reports concluded that he paid $75 million for a single purchase of uranium.

On March 11, 2004, bombs exploded on three commuter trains in Spain, killing 201 and injuring more than 1,400. Al Qaeda was to blame. Several months later a new president was installed in that country. In May FBI headquarters issued a report to all of its field offices that bin Laden had publicly acknowledged responsibility for the attacks and was enjoying this "special victory." Soon after, Spain withdrew its troops from Iraq. The FBI report warned that indications from al Qaeda were that it was almost ready to attack the United States again. On August 1, the U.S. came under threat of attacks by suicide bombing at financial buildings in New York, New Jersey and Washington, D.C. Targets included the New York Stock Exchange, Citigroup, Prudential, the International Monetary Fund and World Bank.

On May 29 and 30, 2004 the oil company housing complex in Khobar, Saudi Arabia was attacked, this time killing four Westerners and another 15 non-Muslim Asians. December 6, 2004, the U.S. Consulate in Jeddah, Saudi Arabia was attacked. Five terrorists drove up to the building and assaulted it with small arms fire and grenades, killing five local employees of the Consulate. Saudi Special Forces quickly responded, storming the building and killing all of the terrorists within hours of the takeover. A group called the "Committee in the Arabian Peninsula," and claiming affiliation with al Qaeda broadcast that they were behind the attack. But this was not the first such attack, as the U.S. Consulate there had been assaulted by numerous drive-by shootings over the previous year.

* * * * *

Despite the length of this recitation, even this compilation of terror attacks and threats is but a fraction of all that has been suffered by democratic societies and allies of the United States. A complete depiction of the thousands of deaths and injuries at the hands of

Islamist extremists has been put together by the American College of Homeland Security, from which I have liberally borrowed much of the preceding text. This has been condensed to demonstrate that the threat to the United States, and Americans everywhere, at home and abroad, is not a distant one. Nor is it one that has only raised its ugly head on a few occasions, as so many of us want to believe. Rather, what we are confronting today is merely one small point in time in more than a thousand years of Islamic violence directed at the West. And that cycle of violence is shortening, spiraling ever faster to the point where assaults on us will occur at an accelerating rate.

The question must be asked, exactly what is the state of terrorist presence and preparations in the United States today? One of the things that has proven true about the professionalism of the terrorist groups, is that nothing is done without first establishing all of the logistics, intelligence and resources necessary to launch a successful attack. First they need funding. It is true that the United States has been successful in tying up much of bin Laden's fabled wealth, and his contribution to al Qaeda funds has been significantly reduced. This does not mean, however, that they are under, or even poorly, funded. Since 9-11, record loads of drugs have been moving from Afghanistan through the Panjshir Valley and into the Muslim regions of the former Soviet Union. Though the U.S. and a new, Western-friendly government, have been in control of Afghanistan since the Taliban was ousted in early 2002, opium production in that country has soared.

Prior to the U.S. invasion of Afghanistan in late 2001, only 18 of that country's 34 provinces were involved in the growing and production of opium, amounting to 185 tons per year. Today, with a 2004 bumper crop, that number is up to 28 out of 34 provinces, and has increased to an estimated 4,000 tons annually. This amounts to fully three-fourths of the world's total heroin supply, according to the United Nation's Office on Drugs and Crime (UNODC). This expansion is difficult to stop for several reasons. Between 1994 and 2000, the years of the Taliban's control of much of Afghanistan, opium farming netted the average family merely $750 per year. By year-end 2002, that number was up to $6,500. Efforts by the U.S. and Afghanistan governments to persuade farmers to switch to a different, more legitimate, crop have been unsuccessful, and in many cases the U.S. has not pushed too far, fearing alienation of regional warlords whose cooperation is still desperately needed. And no one has come up with a substitute crop that approaches the revenue for the farmers and local chieftains of opium. As for the Taliban, though it did benefit from some heroin production, it largely controlled poppy growth by simply threatening farmers with their lives.

Drug production, smuggling and sales have resulted in the biggest association between foreign international organized crime and terror groups. Record loads of drugs are now moving from Afghanistan to Russia, creating a framework with al Qaeda on one side of the deal and Russian (i.e., former Soviet) organized crime groups on the other. This has been a natural marriage. For years members of the Taliban and al Qaeda have fought side-by-side against the Russians in both Afghanistan and Chechnya. Through this joint effort, the terror groups have come to develop close relationships with Russian and other Russian-Asian and former Soviet OC (Organized Crime) gangs. Nothing moves in Russia without the blessing of organized crime. And despite otherwise ubiquitous ethnic bigotry and rivalry, the *mafiya*[51] groups have been the most successful at forging business relationships for their mutual benefit. One small example was Abu Maiser who had planned to blow up the New York subway in February 1997. He was stopped just minutes before the planned detonation. He had been living in Brooklyn, the long time heart of the Russian mafiya in America.

As is commonly known, these "Russian" OC groups have long established extensive networks and criminal operations in the United

---

[51] Throughout this text the Russified spelling of "mafiya" will be used to denote former Soviet organized crime groups, vis-à-vis such groups from other nations and regions of the world.

States. On October 10, 1997, prior to 9-11 and our reorientation of government resources, FBI Director Louis Freeh called Russian Organized Crime "the greatest long-term threat to the security of the United States," in testimony before the House Foreign Relations Committee Hearings on International Organized Crime. To make all this work, heroin enters Russia from Afghanistan, via Tajikistan and Kazakhstan, often through Tajikistan's northern border with Uzbekistan. Despite Russia having recently deployed 10,700 border guards in that area, record drug hauls are still being made. Separate seizures netted 345 kilograms (760 lbs.) of heroin on the 18th and 19th of February 2003, and a previous 280-kilogram (617 lbs.) seizure in the same area. More than 600 kg., or 1,322 lbs. of drugs, mostly heroin, were seized in Tajikistan in 2003 alone. In 2002, Russian and Tajik border guards jointly confiscated 6.5 tons of narcotics, 4.9 tons of which were heroin. These numbers only increased in 2004. Once inside Russia, the drugs are partly used for domestic sale and consumption, with most then moved onto Western Europe and the United States. In the eastern part of Russia, ethnically Russian OC groups are working with their Vietnamese and Chinese counterparts for distribution throughout Asia and other countries in which they are active in the drug trade.

None of this is being done without the joint effort, cooperation and agreement of the Taliban and al Qaeda in Afghanistan, and Russian OC groups in other parts of the world. As well, ties and collaboration between Colombian drug cartels and Russian groups has been steadily increasing, broadening even more the market and thus the profits for the terrorists. Many cargo ships owned and managed by Russian and Ukrainian groups are moving cocaine from South America to the U.S. and Europe. In 1999, one such ship was seized when docked in Spain with over 10 tons of cocaine on board. The shipping route for these drugs will sometimes go from South America to Russia, relying on greater Russian corruptibility and criminal latitude, back to Europe and then to the U.S. As the overall relationships between these groups increase, so do the benefits to terror groups, who are integrally involved in much of the Russian drug trade at this point. These same collaborations have seen funds being raised by Islamist terror groups through such criminal enterprises as stock manipulation, credit card fraud, identity and car theft, and even burglaries to finance their operations.

Inextricably interwoven with the drug threat and massive revenues generated from it, is the threat of weapons of mass destruction (WMDs) falling into the hands of al Qaeda and other groups bent on the destruction of America. Known as CBRNs – for Chemical, Biological, Radiological and Nuclear devices – these weapons have been much sought after by bin Laden for years. There has been credible intelligence developed that bin Laden may have obtained up to 20 Russian "suitcase" tactical nuclear bombs. Recent intelligence has established that the Soviet Union maintained both the "suitcase" transportable device, as well as heavier backpack man-portable nuclear weapon systems, along the lines of what our own Special Forces carried for years. The Russian manpack nuke weighed fully 50 kg (110 lbs.), as compared with the U.S. equivalent system of 38 kg. (83.6 lbs.).

During the Yeltsin administration, the Russian government admitted that it had lost at least 100 such tactical nuclear weapons since the collapse of the Soviet Union. It is true that the need for regular, high tech maintenance of these sensitive devices, and the erosion of the timers which allows them to function, makes it very remote that any of them could ever be detonated. The plutonium inside is highly corrosive and turns into a substance called americium as it undergoes a rusting-like process. For this reason, many internal working parts must be made of solid gold, and regularly replaced, if there is to be a chance of the bomb working at all. However, these devices could easily be converted into use as dirty bombs, conventional explosive devices with the ability to dispel high energy radiation across large areas. Reports abound that Chechen mafiya groups working with al Qaeda and other highly placed former officers from the KGB and

Red Army have provided an avenue by which these weapons can be accessed. Reportedly, bin Laden paid for these devices with $30 million and two tons of Afghan heroin – worth $70 million – provided by the Taliban.

Intelligence also has revealed that both Iraq and Sudan were cooperating with bin Laden on CBRN weapons acquisition and development. Bin Laden has also secured the cooperation and efforts of five Muslim Turkmeni nuclear experts who arrived where the weapons he purportedly purchased were stored, hidden in tunnels several hundred meters deep. The leader of this nuclear team had worked on the Iraqi Tammaz reactor before it was bombed. This expert was last believed to be in charge of preparing a nuclear laboratory in a secret base for al Qaeda.

The question is always asked whether the United States has absolute proof that bin Laden has acquired a nuclear weapon or nuclear weapons grade material. The answer to that is: no. And while the information that has been developed may not rise to the level of "actionable intelligence," it is credible and of sufficient legitimacy to warrant more efforts at determining, first, if he or other groups have acquired them, and, second, stopping them from using them. To put this in legal terms, there is more than sufficient evidence to establish probable cause to believe these weapons may have been obtained. In the criminal justice system, a "probable cause" determination is that minimum threshold to believe that someone may have committed a crime. It is also the point at which a suspect begins to see some of his Constitutional rights suspended in furtherance of efforts to gather more evidence. That is exactly where we are with bin Laden and nukes. We have long since passed the probable cause level, and must work steadily toward proving whether he is guilty as charged of this offense; not for his conviction but for our own survival. For those who are in positions to influence U.S. policy and operations, adopting the attitude that "nothing should be done until absolute proof is delivered," condemns America to a disaster far worse than

9-11. For the first time they realize that they were wrong will be when a mushroom cloud blooms over New York City.

But so what of all these errant nuclear devices and radioactive material? How could any of these possibly enter the United States to threaten us, our children and our way of life? To begin addressing this question, each person must first take a realistic look at the inestimable amount of drugs that somehow make it into our country every single day. No one doubts for a minute the success of the drug smugglers and organized crime groups in achieving this. And if they can be brought in, so can anything else. It also must be realized that the United States shares a 1,940-mile long border with Mexico, and we have more than 4,500 miles of border with Canada. Neither of those countries – currently enjoying a type of ad hoc immunity from terrorist attack in lieu of their more attractive neighbor – has taken any great pains to secure these borders, and they are certainly not going to do so for our protection.

It is no secret that from the south, Mexican, Central and South American organized crime groups bring countless illegal immigrants into the U.S. every day. U.S. border, immigration and customs agents detain more than 3,000 daily. Colorado Congressman Tom Tancredo, a vocal proponent of improved border control as an anti-terrorism measure, estimates that between 3 and 5 million people entered the U.S. illegally in 2003 alone. And unlike the days of old when these "illegals" were peasants from Mexico and the Americas to the south, today they include Polish, Russian and Middle Eastern emigrants. And then there were the 25 Chechen illegals reported to have come across that border in July 2004. It has been estimated that already between 7,500 and 10,000 illegal Middle Easterners have crossed into America through Mexico, evidence of an influx of Muslim extremists breaching our own perimeter security. But how much do they want to be here, and how much is that worth to them? The answer can, perhaps, be found in the fact that smugglers are now getting much more money for bringing these illegals across the Mexican border. Whereas the Hispanics continue to pay a mere $1,500 a head for assistance in crossing the border, those from the Middle East are reportedly paying up to $50,000 each. We must all ask ourselves what would be worth them paying that kind of money simply to gain entry into America; for accessing her soft underbelly?

From the north, the situation is little better. Canada, particularly Toronto, is a major operating and jumping off point for Russian organized crime, and has been for years. A May 2004 FBI memo reported that al Qaeda has a terrorist infrastructure in Canada with documented links to the U.S. This has been corroborated by a former head of Canadian Immigration, who has even admitted that Canada has more than 50 known cells of terror groups operating there, including HAMAS and al Qaeda. And anyone from those countries traditionally producing Islamist extremists need only appear on Canada's doorstep and request political asylum. At the very least, each one of them is granted temporary asylum until a hearing is convened to determine their status. Those hearings usually take up to 18 months to be scheduled. During their wait, Canadian banks allow the "refugees" to have money wired to them, according to a Canadian Security Intelligence Service officer, that country's version of the CIA.

A number of the top Russian OC leaders in the United States – *Vory v Zakone* or Thieves within the Code, as they are known in that country – entered America illegally from Canada, often after operating in that country for a period of time. Also, with regard to the international organized crime groups, it is important to note that their historic, favorite method of moving contraband product into the United States was by ship. And while the Transportation Safety Administration now screens the shoes of millions of airline passengers, only 5 percent of the 50,000 shipping containers that arrive in U.S. ports everyday are inspected. Though this number has increased in the past two years, it still remains a mere fraction of the goods being moved across our coastlines into the heart of the country. Each one of these containers is 40 feet long and easily holds the contents of a large, private home.

As we contemplate the realities of this porous access to our nation, we must also acknowledge that as a result of the war in Iraq, there are now thousands of disaffected Hussein-regime Iraqis, with connections to the terror groups' networks, and already working with the elaborate and weapons-rich Russian OC gangs. When the dust has finally settled on a new, and democratically installed government in Iraq, where do we think they are going to go for revenge? The FBI has already been warning state and local agencies to be on the alert for suicide bombers. And all of this must be reconciled with U.S. government officials' belief that a CBRN attack on American soil is 100 percent certain over the next five years. And since, strategically, interdiction is always more critical than response, the question remains, are we – all Americans – doing enough?

But where does this leave our schools, and the threat to our children? It is without doubt that Islamist extremists have determined that assaults on schools are not only fairly easy, but make attractive emotional and symbolic targets. A simultaneous attack on a number of our schools would have incalculable side effects in terms of our lifestyle, labor force, economy and political landscape, not the least of which would be the likelihood of a reinstatement of the draft for military service. What do people think would happen if all of a sudden, not a single parent felt safe sending his children to school? Police forces, already stretched thin, would not be able to guard them. As with our airports after 9-11, the National Guard would have to be called up. But they are already completely committed to service in war zones in Afghanistan and Iraq, and the U.S. economy has already suffered from the exodus from its labor force.

Then, to protect our schools we would have to devise a way to staff millions of trained and armed guards at the front gates of our schools. This would require the reinstatement of the draft, sending shock waves through the economy and the tax base. Moreover, in most families one parent would quit his or her job in order to be available to take the children to school, pick them up after, and in many cases remain there throughout the day to ensure their safety. Grandfathers, armed with shotguns, would be seen patrolling the streets and parking lots outside. The economy, with such an enormous loss of private sector manpower and skills – and the corresponding dip in tax revenues – would come to a screeching halt. The overall impact to American society and our way of life would be devastating.

And again, just as Lt. Col. Grossman points out in his excellent series of books, *On Killing* and *On Combat*, and in his many presentations to groups around the world, the best predictor of future behavior is past performance. Terrorists have assaulted schools in Israel for years. But their lust for children's blood did not end there, as they struck again at Beslan in September 2004. By January 2005 another terrorist assault on yet another school in Russia was barely thwarted by government forces. Added to all this is the fact that intelligence "chatter" from these groups has included plans to attack schools in America for some time. Since then, Chechen leader Basayev has openly admitted more schools will be taken.

Wisely, the U.S. Department of Education has warned all schools across the country to be on the look out for people spying on their buildings and buses. They have provided a long list of indicia of terrorist surveillance and planning. In addition, information on crisis planning resources that all school administrators, security officials and parents should be aware of is available through the Education Department. In an effort to provide school leaders with a single resource to obtain necessary information on critical response planning, U.S. Secretary of Education Rod Paige, together with then-Homeland Defense Secretary Tom Ridge, established a website that contains information on all types of emergencies, including natural disasters, violence in schools and terrorist attacks. Found at www.ready.gov, this site is to be updated regularly for maximum benefit by those professionals charged with the care and safety of our children.

But let us not forget the compelling need to be ready to respond to an attack so horrible as to be unimaginable: an attack on our children. If websites alone were all it took to prevent a terrorist siege of our schools, we would have nothing to worry about. No one believes that is the case, however. We cannot forget the history of terrorists targeting schools. Nor can we forget simple indications that this is already being planned. Remember the Iraqi who was found with Department of Education crisis planning information on his computer, along with the "all hazards plans" of several school districts, including Boyertown, Pennsylvania. There is much America can do to prevent such attacks, but the reality is that, sooner or later, an attempt will be made here in America. There are a great many things that can be done to *prepare our response* to that attack when it comes. But to accomplish this, America must be ready to endure the two things it dislikes most: a change in our lifestyles, and the spending of significant sums of money. Whether we will wait until after there has been a large body count of children to make these changes is all that remains to be seen.

Conclusion

Do not go gentle into that good night,
Old age should burn and rave at close of day;
Rage, rage against the dying of the light.

— *Dylan Thomas*

Since Beslan, Russia has continued to suffer terror attacks in its southern region on an almost unprecedented scale. Islamist extremists are committed to export not only the Chechen War, but Islamic control to the territories surrounding that embattled region. Battles have been bloody and many more have died. On January 16, 2005, Russian Special Forces thwarted a second Beslan-type siege, which would have resulted in hostages and death on that same scale. Russian intelligence obtained information on both the terrorists and the plot, resulting in dozens of raids and searches and leading to the capture of the intended perpetrators. "It was the same plan as Beslan, they were preparing to seize a school," legislator Gadzhi Makachev told Russia's NTV channel.

Russia is not alone. That America continues to be attacked on a regular and constant basis cannot be ignored. That America will yet see terror attacks on her soil of inestimable magnitude is a certainty we must all accept and prepare for. We must be ruthless and proactive, taking the fight to the terrorists overseas, wherever possible. And for us to preserve our nation and our way of life, we must first protect our children. America's schools present all too appealing a target, and as has been demonstrated, the terrorists will strike such targets again and again. The attempt on The *USS Sullivans* assured the attack on the *Cole*. The success of the attack on the *Cole* will likely guarantee a similar attack on another U.S. military vessel. The terrorists will take their time though, as they always do. America, with its sound-bite attention span, has a difficult time understanding that other cultures have far greater patience, and will happily wait for, what to us is, an eternity before acting on a seething motivation.

Americans all over ask, "Why haven't they attacked us again after 9-11, doesn't that mean the threat is over?" They forget that the Islamist terrorists waited almost nine full years between the first and second efforts at bringing down the World Trade Center Towers. And though they have attempted operations in the U.S. since that time – operations that were successfully thwarted by our government and law enforcement agencies – there has been no real apparent effort at another cataclysmic assault. It will come, and they will bide their time in doing it. Likewise, they never attack on those dates and anniversaries that, to a Western mind, seem the most obvious. On those days we are prepared, security is high and everyone is ready. Their history is one of always waiting until we are at our lowest alert level, completely unaware and unsuspecting of another effort to kill thousands. And we must continue to look at their past conduct to accurately anticipate future assaults.

As with The *USS Sullivans* and the *Cole,* efforts to fly aircraft into buildings in earlier years saw the culmination of those plots on 9-11. The same was repeated in Russia days before the Beslan siege, when two commercial jets were brought down by suicide bombers. And the assaults on schools in Israel and Russia are mere harbingers of what is yet to come to the United States. Each time, the terrorists have virtually told us what they were going to do. Each time, they were true to their word. It is time we started listening to them; and preparing.

One of the people we need to be listening to is Billy Waugh. Waugh is a true American hero. Even at age 74 he is strong and muscular, though he walks with decided pain from horrendous combat injuries that would have left most men in a wheelchair for the rest of their lives. He is charismatic, and handsome in a craggy, war torn way. Though he looks far younger, when his eyes sparkle as he tells a story or encounters a friend, he looks half his age. This zest for life and commitment to defending America saw him through many years in the Special Forces, followed by many more working undercover for the CIA. Several years before, at more than 70-years-old, he was still racing about Afghanistan with both of those elite groups, still hunting America's enemies.

At the 2004 gathering of the Special Operations Association – a veteran's group of America's elite military, mostly Special Forces and SEALs – Billy and I were thrown together virtually every morning. In a hall with more than a thousand of America's best-trained commandos, along with law enforcement and security at every entrance, it is a rare opportunity for someone like him to sit, unconcerned about the threats that ordinarily make up his life. By 11:00 o'clock each morning we were both happily drunk, discussing the affairs of the world and his perspective over half a century of battling threats to America. Despite his generally smiling demeanor and positive outlook, he turns deadly serious when the subject of Islamist terrorism comes up. For years he lived in squalor in dusty, fetid Khartoum, hunting the world's worst terrorist up until that time – Carlos the Jackal – and keeping tabs on people like bin Laden, then merely an up-and-coming threat to the U.S. Billy watched bin Laden set up and run terror training camps just outside that capital city, watched everyday as they trained, threw hand grenades, shot automatic weapons, learned to build explosives and even tap telephones. He put together a plan to kill bin Laden, which he could have executed all too easily, but for a tentative American government fearful of what others might think if we undertook such preemptive action. He was forced to sit and watch as bin Laden sent weapons and men into Somalia, training the tribes there to attack the UN and American troops. He was made to sit idly by as al Qaeda took an active role in the deaths of 18 U.S. servicemen in Mogadishu on October 3 and 4, 1993.

According to Waugh, Americans must start recognizing that we are not dealing with a group of people who see anything from our perspective: "Islamic fundamentalists [have] the capacity to believe in something to the point where they would give up their lives for it. We don't have that level of belief for anything in our country, and … part of the shock with suicide bombers and hijackers and people who blow themselves up for a cause is our inability to understand this level of passion and commitment. It seems horribly misguided to us, but it's real and it isn't changing. Our ideas about them have to change to fit reality."[53] It would seem to us that the majority – the hundreds of millions – of peace loving Muslims the world over would condemn the extremists, would come out in opposition of their atrocities. Few do. The religious leaders fail entirely to realize the responsibility for stopping this bloodshed falls squarely on their shoulders.

Billy relates that the level of hatred for America within much of that culture is shocking. It is something we have to respect and work to deal with now. To Billy, back then he could have killed bin Laden, possibly saving the lives of thousands of people, two U.S. embassies, one of the Khobar Towers and the many lives lost there, and the World Trade Center. While he knows he alone could not have prevented the current chapter in terror assaults on America, he is left to wonder if he couldn't have made some greater difference. Where else the War on Terror will take us is not known, but maybe – just maybe – he could have prevented some of the loss we have so far suffered. To Billy Waugh, and men like him, if America is to survive it must change. And in changing it cannot be wringing its hands over an increasing lack of popularity in the world. For it has been us – and not countries like Germany, France and Canada – who have been attacked.

---

[53] Waugh and Keown, *Hunting the Jackal*, 140.

After the Japanese attack on Pearl Harbor on December 7, 1941 Admiral Yamamoto said: "… it seems all we have done is awakened a sleeping giant." America remains that giant, bigger and stronger than ever before. It is far past the time when we need to awaken and destroy those who would destroy us. This is the message that terrorists the world over – and those other nations who suffer at their hands as we have – must all hear. We must become, once again, that giant who rights wrongs throughout the world, lest they kill us in our own homes again and again. For, as President George W. Bush said in the aftermath of 9-11, "If you are not with us, then you are against us."

When viewing the terrorist situation we have inherited, and the history behind its development – including our own complicity – we must begin to realize that the United States has been like an overindulgent parent, too slow to realize the evil of its own progeny, continuing to nurture and even support it long after feeling the sting of its remorseless and conscienceless rage. We have, to a degree, created – or at least helped to create – this monstrosity, and yet have been too slow to recognize that it is something that must now be killed to be stopped. There is no other answer, and the enemy will not permit us one.

We cannot forget the origins of this hatred that is directed at us. From the time of Muhammed through the Crusades and into the post-World War II division of many Islamic lands, the United States has been thrust into an unknowing partnership with the Russians. As Colonel Ryabko pointed out, we have together helped foment the evil, the terror that we now face. The U.S. and the Soviet Union were the two team captains of a divided world after that war, and we drew the resentment of the would-be terrorist community to us. Now Russia has inherited the legacy of retribution of these terrorists, and it is living it every single day. So far, America has managed to avoid such daily attacks on our way of life, but that too will soon end. Bin Laden himself has connected the two countries, and his own plans for attacking the U.S. and Russia as his primary targets have inextricably intertwined us for years to come. The enemy of my enemy is my friend is the doctrine of military and political reality we must now adopt.

So, to an America tucked comfortably into beds at night: sleep well. Close your eyes and go quietly into each gentle night, refusing to acknowledge the danger that lurks outside your doors. But before you do, get down on your knees and pray for protection by those men and women who have already heeded the call, who stand ready to do violence against those who would do you harm. For the day is coming when they, even with their tremendous courage, will no longer be enough. Then, the battle will fall onto the shoulders of each and every one of us.

EPILOGUE

It's Wednesday night in Vladikavkav. Late November, 2004. I think I will not make it home for Thanksgiving, my favorite holiday. The weather has turned quickly from the strange summer-like warmth and sun I have enjoyed since my arrival here, to cold rain and snow, foretelling the winter this part of the mountains has somehow avoided until now. Earlier, as I walked through the school for the final time, measuring distances, photographing the narrowness of hallways, recording their fearsome angles and dark apertures, assessing the obstacles the Russian Special Forces overcame, often with their own blood, the sun had quickly faded and temperature dropped. Far more typical for this time of year in the North Caucasus, I felt that it was the victims' way of telling those of us who had come that it was finally time to go, to leave them in peace.

I have left the Beslan School for the last time. It is to be shortly torn down and a large monument erected in its place. I have already seen the deep pit of early construction a few miles down the road as sullen workers race the approaching winter to prepare its replacement. As I sit in my room in the gothic, Soviet era hotel in Vladikavkaz, I peel threadbare combat boots from weary feet. These same boots have seen me safely throughout Chechnya and Ingushetia on prior occasions, took me racing to the Beslan siege as it was occurring, and carried me twice across the Sudan desert and its war, even to bloody Kosovo and Serbia in years past. As I kick them to the floor I see they are still covered with the dust of the school's debris, set so deep into the fabric sides and treaded soles that seemingly nothing, not even the rain and snow of the fearsome Caucasus Mountains, can cleanse them of the horror that this dust carries with it. I gaze out the window of my bleak little room onto the ancient Terek River below, a giant moving body of water along whose banks the Christian Cossacks battled the Chechens for centuries, and wonder if it can ever be washed away.

After returning from there the first time in September, I was contacted by an old high school friend. She asked, "How do you ever get over something like that?" The answer is, I don't know if anyone ever does, or can. Certainly not the Special Forces men I know who threw themselves into that holocaust, who watched their friends die. Days, even months after, I have seen them break down and cry over the children they could not save, over the men who fell beside them. Each will forever carry with him the guilt of having walked out of that place. My own experiences with this atrocity are far less than most who were there. Less than the brave men of Russia's Spetsnaz, and far less than those held hostage. I was a bystander. Someone who had the luxury of merely picking among the ruins of a shattered building and shattered lives, attempting to make some sense of it all so that America might have a better chance when the horror comes to pay us a visit.

Still, I do not see it ever becoming a distant memory. Perhaps this book was a catharsis, a way of releasing all that I have dragged home with me: thick blood pooled everywhere, bullet and shrapnel spray mingling with blood running down the walls, bodies shredded by bombs and gunfire, others burned beyond recognition. The tiny forms of those who had not yet had their chance in life, terrorized, and then snuffed out for reasons we can never comprehend. Little Aida. The picture of her standing beside that gymnasium window, having long before lost the capacity to know where she was or what she should do, climbing back through it, her bare, spindly legs the last to be seen of her. It is burned into my mind. How do I get over it? How does anyone?

AFTERWARD

Five days after the siege ended, there remained hundreds of children still huddled beneath blankets in area hospitals, unclaimed by parents they would never see again. One little girl in particular is beyond all communication. She sits up in bed all day, covers pulled to just below wide, dark eyes; eyes haunted by all that she has seen. She cannot speak. Like many of the children, she is in such shock she cannot even say her name. Someone recognizes her. It is Aida. Somehow, miraculously, she has survived. Her mother, forced by the terrorists from the gym and into the cafeteria - last seen shot and burned - had not been found.

ABOUT ARCHANGEL

Archangel is a U.S. 501 (c)(3) non-profit, NGO. It exists to provide anti-terrorism consulting, training and related services to United States law enforcement, military and governmental agencies. It also offers these services to other charitable, humanitarian aid groups working in hot zones throughout the world. There is nowhere it will not go. Much of Archangel's work for all of these groups is provided free of charge, or at low cost, in order to provide crucial training and information to those fighting the War on Terror, as well as those attempting to come to the aid of the innocent victims of terrorism throughout the world.

Tax deductible charitable donations can be made to Archangel. These can be arranged through its website at www.antiterrorconsultants.org or by sending a check or money order, along with a self-addressed, stamped envelope to: Archangel, P.O. Box 16850, Golden, CO 80402, or fax request to 303-215-0780. Be sure to note the name of the person making the donation. A receipt with information to receive a deduction for the charitable donation will be returned.

A portion of the proceeds from this book goes to the ongoing work of Archangel.

Beslan Victims Fund

For anyone who would like to donate money to help the victims of the terrorist attack at Beslan, send check or credit card information by mail, fax, or email to info@circon.org. Be sure to mark it as follows: "BESLAN VICTIMS." Donations will be delivered to the victims of the Beslan siege, their families and other agencies providing much needed assistance. Many of the children of the siege are orphaned, or lost both parents and have been taken in by grandparents with little money to support them. Funds will also go to the families of the slain Special Forces soldiers who fought to save the hostages on September 3, 2004.

ABOUT THE AUTHOR

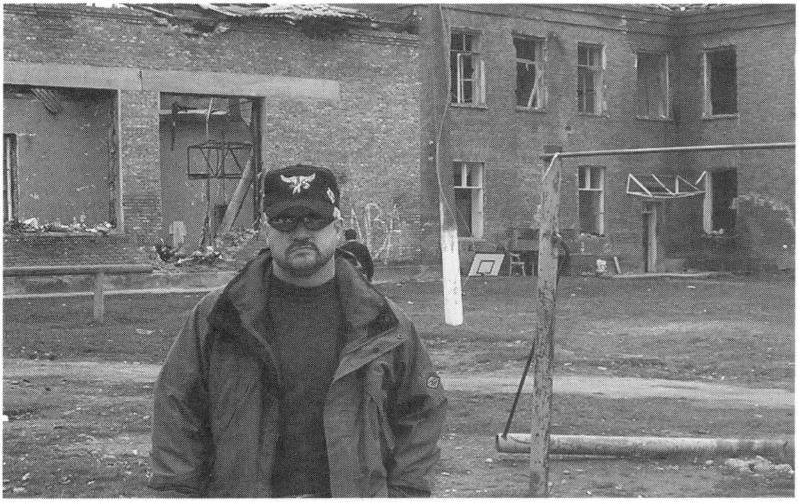

Throughout his life, John Giduck has been a trial lawyer, soldier, business owner, college professor, bullrider, national weightlifting champion, sky diver and scuba diving instructor. He holds a master's degree in Russian Studies and International Affairs from the University of Colorado, with a Certificate in Russian History, Culture and Language from St. Petersburg State University in Russia. He has trained law enforcement departments of all levels across the U.S., and served as a consultant to several federal agencies.

John holds the highest level certification in Homeland Security, and is a member of the Executive Advisory Board of the American College of Homeland Security. He currently devotes his professional time to the Archangel Group, a non-profit NGO providing consulting and training on anti-terrorism to law enforcement and other agencies, and has worked in over 20 countries. As part of that work he is a U.S. Army Special Forces hand-to-hand combat and firearms instructor, and has been inducted into several international martial arts halls of fame.